The Church for the World

The Church for the World

A Theology of Public Witness

Jennifer M. McBride

UNIVERSITY PRESS

OXFORD
UNIVERSITY PRESS

Oxford University Press, Inc., publishes works that further
Oxford University's objective of excellence
in research, scholarship, and education.

Oxford New York
Auckland Cape Town Dar es Salaam Hong Kong Karachi
Kuala Lumpur Madrid Melbourne Mexico City Nairobi
New Delhi Shanghai Taipei Toronto

With offices in
Argentina Austria Brazil Chile Czech Republic France Greece
Guatemala Hungary Italy Japan Poland Portugal Singapore
South Korea Switzerland Thailand Turkey Ukraine Vietnam

Published by Oxford University Press, Inc.
198 Madison Avenue, New York, New York 10016

www.oup.com

Library of Congress Cataloging-in-Publication Data
McBride, Jennifer M., 1977–
The church for the world : a theology of public witness / Jennifer M. McBride.
p. cm.
Includes bibliographical references (p.) and index.
ISBN 978-0-19-975568-4 (alk. paper)
1. Church and the world. 2. Protestant churches—United States.
3. Repentance—Protestant churches—Social aspects—United States.
4. Bonhoeffer, Dietrich, 1906–1945. I. Title.
BR515.M345 2011
261'.1—dc22 2010052074

1 3 5 7 9 8 6 4 2
Printed in the United States of America
on acid-free paper

■ *For my father*
John David McBride
who first taught me to ask hard questions

and

■ *Scott and Marilyn Dimock*
who first offered me a living illustration of
a redemptive public witness
credo ecclesiam

There's the wind and the rain and the mercy of the fallen,
who say they have no claim to know what's right.

—Dar Williams

When theology confesses its own solidarity with all flesh and with the whole world under God's judgment, it receives *hope* in the grace of God... Evangelical theology... is to be pursued in hope, though as human work it is radically questioned by God, found guilty in God's judgment and verdict—and though collapsing long before it reaches its goal, it relies on God who... seeks out, heals, and saves [the theologian] and [her] work. This God is the hope of theology.

—Karl Barth

CONTENTS

PREFACE AND ACKNOWLEDGMENTS

After college my friend Katy traveled to Switzerland where she met with Edith Schaeffer, American evangelical writer and cofounder of L'Abri, a Christian commune in the Alps that was established in the 1950s. No longer involved in the daily activities of the community, Ms. Schaeffer rarely took visitors yet agreed to meet with Katy to discuss her interest in writing. Cutting short her romanticized musings on what the life of a writer might be, Ms. Schaeffer said sternly, "Katy, I write because I have something to say." Upon her return to the States and with crushed sentiments, Katy and I wondered aloud whether either one of us would ever have something to say worth the paper and ink. What I did not realize then is that already, and for at least a decade prior, this project was brewing as I was simultaneously being formed by and subtly resisting (to varying degrees) an understanding of witness that was part and parcel of a North American evangelical faith shaped by parachurch groups and conservative Presbyterian congregations. Although it would not be until I was immersed in an inner-city hospitality house in Washington, D.C., that I would understand my questions and concerns in terms of theology and public life, the following pages addressing public witness give voice and offer a constructive response to the intuitions and unease that laid at the center of my Christian existence from my earliest memories of learning and living the faith.

These years of writing and rethinking dominant assumptions about the church's identity and mission in society have led me to a deeper appreciation of Bonhoeffer's words in *Life Together*: "*Whoever cannot be alone should beware of community... Whoever cannot stand being in community should beware of being alone*."[1] Or as Annie Dillard speaks of the solitude of writing: "Who will teach me to write?...The page, the page, that eternal blankness...which you cover slowly...the page, which you cover woodenly, ruining it, but asserting your freedom and power to act...the page of your death, against which you pit such flawed excellences as you can muster with all life's strength: that page will teach you to write."[2] Such a solitary exercise demands the support of community, and I am grateful for the many people who have engaged the project and walked beside me along the way.

This book began as a doctoral dissertation in the Department of Religious Studies at the University of Virginia. I am thankful that my dissertation director Charles Marsh encouraged my own constructive work and that my committee—Charles Mathewes, Paul Dafydd Jones, Valerie C. Cooper, and Joshua Yates—showed equal concern that my project reach an audience both inside and outside the academy. The method of theological ethnography in part III of this book arises from my involvement with Marsh's Project on

Lived Theology, and I am grateful for the many conversations with the scholars, pastors, and activists involved in the workgroups and institutes that have demonstrated time and time again how important the collaboration of theologians and practitioners is for addressing the many concerns of our contemporary moment.

I had the opportunity to present parts of this work in dissertation form at various events. I am grateful to members of the International Bonhoeffer Society who commented on my work at the 2006 American Academy of Religion in Washington, D.C., and at the Second International Bonhoeffer Colloquium in Berlin, Germany, especially Clifford J. Green, Stephen Plant, Craig J. Slane, Ralf K. Wüstenberg, Barry Harvey, Christiane Tietz, Jens Zimmerman, and Lori Brandt Hale. A section of the dissertation was published in a colloquium volume, *Religion, Religionlessness, and Contemporary Western Culture: Explorations in Dietrich Bonhoeffer's Theology*, eds. Stephen Plant and Ralf K. Wüstenberg (Berlin, Germany: Peter Lang, 2008), and I am grateful for being granted permission to use a revised version here. Thanks to Zach Kinkaid for the opportunity to present my work to a broader audience as part of the Erasing Hate Dialogue Series, which was sponsored by the Matthew's House Project, Baker Publishing Group, and Justice for Children International. I am grateful as well to Bonhoeffer scholars, Peter Frick and James Reimer, who led the 2006 Centenary Bonhoeffer Study Tour through Germany and Poland, and to Theological Horizons and Michael Milton, who provided grants for the trip. Finally, a 2006–2007 Louisville Institute Dissertation Fellowship in the Study of Protestantism and American Culture provided a year of funding. As is true with the International Bonhoeffer Society, the 2007 Louisville Winter Seminar impressed upon me what a gift it is to be a part of a community of scholars who desire that their research serve the church in tangible ways. I am especially grateful for conversations with Jim Lewis, Brantley Gasaway, Seth Dowland, Jennifer Ayres, Josef Sorett, and Laceye Warner.

A 2008–2009 postdoctoral fellowship in Religious Practices and Practical Theology (a joint initiative of Emory University's Candler School of Theology and the Graduate Division of Religion) not only afforded me time and space to restructure this manuscript but also introduced me to a community of interdisciplinary scholars who share an interest in practice and provided helpful guidance in ethnographic writing. Presenting how theology and ethnography are interrelated in my work to a group of religion scholars and anthropologists at the Practical Matters consultation at Emory in March 2009 was quite beneficial as it provided interdisciplinary traction for connecting philosophical theology with ethnography. I also appreciate the opportunity I had to present my work at the Practices doctoral seminar. I am especially grateful for a lengthy conversation with Tom Frank that resulted from my presentation and greatly improved the ethnographic descriptions in part III.

During my postdoc year I taught a spring seminar at Candler, Ecclesial Practice and Public Witness, that drew on the research undergirding this manuscript. The students' mixture of high-level analysis and practical concern for what public witness entails for them as lay or ordained leaders generated exciting and penetrating discussion and helped shape my revisions. I am grateful for the questions and insights of these politically engaged and intellectually honest seminarians: Karl Kroger, Amanda Osenga, Susan Evans, Saul Burleson, and Troy Carter, as well as Christina Repoley and Michelle Ledder, who, along with local activist Heather Bargeron, read a draft of the entire manuscript in spring 2010 and met with me to discuss it in detail. When our initial discussion had to be rescheduled so that we could attend an anti–death penalty protest for the Georgia inmate Troy Davis, which we heard about at the last minute, we were poignantly reminded that being a public witness is more important than simply discussing public witness. Students in a 2010 Candler summer seminar on Dietrich Bonhoeffer and Martin Luther King also engaged portions of this book with passion and insight and provided helpful feedback: Margaret Fulghum, Terri Montague, Drew Zimmer, Brandon Duke, Zeena Regis, Brian Tillman, Tyrel Shields, and Aaron Treadwell. I am grateful as well for the opportunity, while here in Atlanta, to present portions of my work in a series of "clarification meetings" at the Open Door Community and to reflect on and learn about public witness from this "Protestant Catholic Worker" house.

The majority of my revisions have occurred over the past year as I have been directing and teaching in a theology certificate program for incarcerated women at a local state prison. Although this book does not address public witness in regard to the prison system, the Fridays I have spent with the women there for the past year and a half have held me accountable to the kind of engagement and theological honesty I argue for in this book, and my friendships with these women have influenced this text in ways that I am sure I am only partially aware of. I have been struck but not surprised by how readily many of the women have understood Bonhoeffer's theology as well as the arguments I make here, especially concerning the depiction in chapter 3 of Christ standing in solidarity with the real human being. I am grateful for the wise and insightful theologians in my 2009 Bonhoeffer course: Valerie Carter, Teresa Fergason, Amy Walden, Amalia Santos, Cathy Hall, Kathy Dawson, Jerri Bryant, and Vanessa Williams (names used with permission). I am also grateful for the hours of conversation with Kelly Gissendaner (name used with permission), whose comments on the entire manuscript serve as a constructive theology in its own right.

Colleagues at Emory and beyond have reflected with me and helped me think aloud about portions of the book, Luther Smith, Elizabeth Bounds, Andrea White, Gregory C. Ellison, Sarah Azaransky, and Mary Gage Davidson; have read carefully and commented on large portions of the text, Ian McFarland, Jonathan Malesic, Peter Heltzel, Paul Lutter, Timothy P. Jackson, and Joshua Jipp; and have read the entire text, Jürgen Moltmann, Lauren Winner, Eric Gregory, Letitia Campbell, and Mary Button. As an external evaluator, Stephen Haynes read an early draft of the manuscript and provided helpful structural suggestions, and Rachel Muers, also an external evaluator, went above and beyond the call of duty, reading an early and a polished draft and provided numerous specific and insightful suggestions chapter by chapter.

I am grateful for the hospitality of the Eleuthero Community and the Southeast White House, especially Tim Clayton, Cheryl Clayton, Evan Pillsbury, Kelly Ayer, Scott Dimock, Marilyn Dimock, and Sammie Morrison, and for each person who granted me an interview: Loren Ayer, Hilary Barnett, Summer Dye, John Johnson, Kristi Kiger, Iris Lamberson, Jennifer Lowery, Wilma Mpelo, Kathryn Pillsbury, Louis Robertson, Denise Speed, Dave Stankiewicz, Sarrah Stankiewicz, and Mike Wingfield. Moreover, I am thankful for the witnesses of these two communities, which animate my constructive theology and manifest a "living hope" (1 Peter 1:3).

Finally, I am grateful for the support of my family, for my brother and sister-in-law, David McBride and Lucy Jones McBride, for the many playful moments with Archer and Winnie, my nephew and niece, and for my parents, John David McBride and Mary Jane McBride, whose unwavering support extends in many directions. This labor of love is dedicated to my father, the professor, who first taught me to ask hard questions, push existing boundaries, and live courageously into answers, and to Scott Dimock and Marilyn Dimock, who first offered me, while working at the Southeast White House, a living illustration of a redemptive public witness.

Atlanta, Georgia
September 2010

■ The Church for the World

PART ONE
Public Witness in a Pluralistic Society

1 Introduction

Confession and Repentance as Public Witness

On April 21, 2006, several hundred people pack an auditorium at the University of Southern Maine in Portland for a "People's Town Meeting" on the Iraq War. The program is simple. Any individual has the opportunity to speak for three minutes. Halfway through the night, an unknown, evangelical Episcopal priest with no strong ties to a political party and no experience speaking in public gatherings of this type approaches the microphone. Wearing his collar and conscious of his priestly role as an ecclesial representative, he opens by confessing that Christians have been in collusion with military might to the detriment of witnessing to Christ. He says to the crowd,

> As you can see, I am not a politician. I am not a military expert, nor an expert in international affairs. However, as a Christian priest, as a Christian pastor, I felt compelled to come tonight to bear witness to the witness of Christian scriptures relative to these issues. Christian ideas and pieces of the Bible have been used so much in all this—particularly during the build-up to the war in Iraq, in an attempt to justify it—that I simply feel I must speak to give testimony to what the witness of the Christian scriptures is if we read it as a whole and let it speak to us with integrity and do not pick out pieces and do not approach it trying to justify an end upon which we have already decided.
>
> And when I read Christian scriptures—when I read the Bible—with these issues in mind, I see one big thing that comes off the pages boldly. It is this: God will not be mocked. As Martin Luther King Jr. said, "America, you'd better watch out, because God will not be mocked." God perhaps tolerates empires for a season, with all their swagger, all their might, all their... self-justification. Maybe God even allows them in certain ways to accomplish some relatively good things. But that should not be mistaken for God's favor. And that should not be mistaken for God being on our side or fighting for us.
>
> Because, the witness of Christian scriptures is that eventually... God judges... hubris and violence, neglect of the poor and vulnerable, and exploitation of the good creation.... The witness of Christian scriptures is clear that the God who incarnated himself into this world in Jesus Christ knew suffering, was a friend of the poor and broken, confronted empire in his own day, loved justice, and cared for the good creation God made. God will not be mocked but will eventually bring righteous judgment.[1]

Tim Clayton walks away from the microphone feeling like a fish out of water, so nervous that his mouth is parched, aware that what he has said is not perfect. Yet, after he speaks the energy in the room is palpable. The Green Party candidate for governor speaks soon after and says, "I think we ought to give one of Maine's Senate positions to Pastor Tim!" and the crowd responds with a rousing cheer.

In the lobby a diverse group of people gather around Clayton, wanting to talk: a reporter from the *Portland Press Herald* and another from *Lakes Region Weekly*, an independent candidate for the United States Senate and devout Catholic who has devoted his life to social justice work, a woman who says she has lost her faith mostly over her sense that so many Christians in the country support corrupt political acts, and many other people who simply say, "Thank you for what you said."[2]

Why does a crowd standing in an academic hall in one of the country's most unchurched states cheer when Clayton speaks a particularly Christian language communicating God's love in Christ and God's judgment on human sin? Why are his words newsworthy? What is it about Clayton's public witness that draws into conversation a mixture of secular citizens, devout Christians, and those who describe themselves as having lost their faith? Would it be fair to reduce the audience's reception of Clayton's message to a shared political agenda, or does Clayton's witness break through the dualisms partisan politics often creates and offer something unique and new? More generally, given that thoughtful Christians do and will take different views on various policy issues, how can Christian witness concretely attend to specific social and political matters without binding the church to partisan politics, without conferring on politics the power to define what is Christian? Can the church act and speak concretely in the public arena and also offer a faithful witness to Christ?[3] These are the motivating questions of this book.

I highlight Clayton's speech as an example of Christian witness not to promote a particular position on the war but to reflect on why his public witness evokes such a response. Interestingly, Clayton does not articulate directly his political stance (although one may be inferred); rather, his primary concern is the *manner* in which Christians have supported the war and how such support has affected the church's witness to Christ and scripture. He is concerned with the degree and character of theological reflection undergirding Christian endorsement.

At the same time, Clayton's speech exemplifies both the difficulties and possibilities of Christians offering a witness to Christ relative to specific social and political issues. Many people are concerned about Christian social and political presence as evidenced by ongoing public and scholarly conversations. Some secularists find religious persuasion detrimental to a liberal democracy, while some people within various faith traditions worry that dominant Christian views stifle political perspectives derived from non-Christian religious traditions or marginalized streams of Christian thought. This is particularly problematic in regard to white Protestants who often dominate public conversations. Some politically conscious Christians are distraught over the widespread assumption that a Christian politics necessitates loyalty to the political right; other Christians think faith is a private matter that inevitably becomes distorted through politics; and others, both politically conservative and progressive, think faith in Christ compels Christians to speak and act boldly in the public realm. My concern is not whether the church should be involved in public life but *how* the church should be engaged. I want to understand theologically the strength and character of Clayton's public witness and want to construct a theology of public witness that positions the church as a vehicle of concrete redemption in our society.

Within Clayton's witness lie latent themes the following chapters will address. Most notably, Clayton's public witness is rooted in a theology of the cross, not a theology of glory. By "theology of glory" I mean a religious or cultural triumphalism that becomes especially detrimental to a redemptive witness when coupled with sociopolitical power and affluence.[4] A church influenced by a theology of glory will, like Peter, James, and John, want to leave the uncertainties of life in a fallen world, settle onto the mountain of the transfiguration, and from that lofty place witness Christ (Matt. 17:1–13). Such a church desires that the God it serves be revealed not through suffering and the cross but through visible acts of victory and omnipotence. A theology of glory neglects the import of God's trinitarian and christological identity, and, in turn, presents a false depiction of a dominating God based on an incomplete understanding of the nature of God's power and triumph. A privileged and affluent community trying to reflect this God will be formed by that domineering image, becoming—perhaps without even noticing—a self-assured and/or defensive people. A theology of glory may be innocently upheld by Christians who intend to witness to the risen Jesus who is victorious over sin and death, yet if such a witness is not definitively shaped by the crucified Christ, it will be triumphalistic and will not reflect the God whom it aims to exalt. This witness, unfaithful to the full identity and mission of the incarnate God, harms those outside the Christian fellowship and effectively draws people not closer to but farther away from Christ.

In contrast, perhaps what is most striking to the crowd listening in the university auditorium is the disarming nature of Clayton's words inviting conversation not contention. He begins with a nontriumphalistic statement, communicating that he cannot speak authoritatively on matters of war and international affairs, and he does not attempt to prescribe a solution. He does not even articulate directly or in detail a viewpoint that is definitively political. He recognizes the limits of his understanding. Still, he claims a different kind of authority—a responsibility to be a witness to the witness of the Bible. Perhaps, then, what is most striking to the audience is the boldness of his testimony and the concreteness of his theological claims, which are at once a confession of faith and a confession that, regardless of the extent to which the war is or is not warranted, Christians are complicit in the violence, pride, neglect, exploitation, and glorification of power associated with war. Perhaps what is most salient is that Clayton does not exempt himself from the divine judgment of which he speaks nor claim sole ownership of truth. Perhaps it is simply his presence in the conversation. In an e-mail sent that night to Christian friends he previously pastored, he writes, "I know some of you would not be in agreement with as much of what was said as I was... [But] we, as American evangelicals, have simply got to be in these circles and in these rooms and in these moments.... It is at least an education [for us], though in reality it is much more than that."[5] Clayton's ecclesial presence in that concrete moment is indeed much more than an education: Through his confession, concreteness, acceptance of responsibility, and deference to divine judgment, Clayton witnesses to Christ who, in turn, is welcomed into the public conversation.

■ THINKING ALONGSIDE DIETRICH BONHOEFFER

How can that which Clayton achieves in three minutes become a more pervasive and regular part of Christian practice? How may the church participate humbly in our pluralistic society even as it remains faithful to its call to proclaim the ultimate significance of Christ in word and deed? Put another way, how do Christians demonstrate, through their public engagement, the lordship of Christ in a manner that divests the notion of its authoritarian connotations?[6]

This book argues that Protestant churches in the United States may witness to Christ in a nontriumphal manner through an overlapping confession of their own sin and the sin of broader society, which finds public expression in repentant activity. In other words, the church demonstrates Christ's redemptive work and becomes a vehicle of concrete redemption when its mode of being in the world is confession of sin unto repentance. By making confession unto repentance integral to public witness, I am not suggesting that the church's sociopolitical task is to feel bad about itself; rather, I argue that repentance plays a crucial role in the drama of redemption and thus is energized by courage and hope. Through creative, repentant activity in public life, the church participates in God's healing transformation of this world.

Thinking alongside the German pastor-theologian and Nazi resistor Dietrich Bonhoeffer illuminates how such transformation is possible. Bonhoeffer is an appropriate interlocutor for North American conversations about Christian public witness, given the honored place he holds in the imaginations of many U.S. Protestants and the deep admiration many have for him on account of the integrity of his life and thought and his clear devotion to Jesus Christ. Christians familiar with sketches of his life find him a reliable figure to appeal to; he is seen as theologically trustworthy and authoritative especially in relation to memorable passages in popular texts like *Discipleship* and *Life Together*. When taken as a whole, however, Bonhoeffer's work challenges commonly held theological assumptions, ones which I argue need to be disrupted in order for Protestants to offer a humble and faithful witness to Christ in public life. It is his theology as a whole, not simply the seemingly more accessible works, that stimulated and sustained the exemplary "costly discipleship" that so many Christians in the United States readily revere. Fair appropriation of an inspiring figure like Bonhoeffer necessitates that his admirers consider the implications of his thought in its entirety, and a demonstration of these implications is my purpose here.

Bonhoeffer's work as well as his method influences my methodology in three significant ways. First, Bonhoeffer instructs the church to communicate the Word of God concretely in the present moment. In the essay "A Theological Basis for the World Alliance?" Bonhoeffer says:

> The word of the church to the world must therefore encounter the world in all its present reality from the deepest knowledge of the world, if it is to be authoritative. The church must be able to say the Word of God, the word of authority, here and now, in the most concrete way possible, from knowledge of the situation. The church must not therefore preach timeless principles however true, but only commandments which are true today. God is "always" *God* to us "*today*."[7]

This passage underscores the urgency but also raises the question of how the church may communicate the Word of God concretely in its historical moment. My specific concern for our historical moment is how the church may do this without being arrogantly authoritarian, without falling into the trap of polarizing party politics, in short, without distorting its witness to Christ. I respond to this concern by utilizing Bonhoeffer's thought to construct a theological account of a redemptive, public, ecclesial witness.

Second, as in Bonhoeffer's work, the category "church" first and foremost signals a theological concept. Bonhoeffer defines the church, like Martin Luther, as community[8] (or in the Apostle Paul's words, the body of Christ) created and sustained by God and thus grounded in a theology of revelation (1 Cor. 12:12–30).[9] Those seeking to understand the church's contemporary engagement in public life most often turn to sociological accounts, but sociology of religion rarely probes the theologies bolstering Christian public presence; thus it cannot alone answer questions concerning the church's normative identity and mission. Therefore, as Bonhoeffer does in *Sanctorum Communio*, his doctoral dissertation on ecclesiology, I place sociology in the service of theology.[10] Because the church is a theological reality, a redemptive witness necessitates that Christians understand their identity and mission christologically and ecclesiologically.

Sociological investigation has an important function in a theological account of the church, though, for it maintains the concreteness of the empirical, institutional church or local congregation with all its strengths and failings. Bonhoeffer affirms the sociological as well as the theological reality of the church through the terms he employs: *Kirche* (institutional church), *Gemeinde* (translated as both church and community in early editions), *Gemeinshaft* (community) and *Gesellschaft* (society). *Gemeinde* is the word Bonhoeffer uses most often because it connotes the christological and communal identity of the church while also gesturing toward the sociological character of *Gemeinshaft*.[11] Following the lead of the editors of the *Dietrich Bonhoeffer Works* project (the most recent and comprehensive English translation of Bonhoeffer's writings), I will employ the term "church-community" as often as "church" in order to highlight the church as a reality at once revelatory and this-worldly. I intend these terms to encompass a range of ecclesial organization, from congregations within the so-called institutional church to alternative communities that fall outside traditional, denominational establishments.[12] Most fundamentally, along with Bonhoeffer I maintain that Christian life and faith is definitively communal, thus I focus on the public witness of the church-*community* as opposed to the *individual* Christian.[13]

Third, like Bonhoeffer, I wish to develop an ecclesiology in light of our historical moment, in light of "the signs of the times" (Matt. 16:3). My project claims not to construct a public witness for all times and places but to offer a theological account of a redemptive public witness for our pluralistic democracy at the beginning of the twenty-first century. In prison Bonhoeffer reflects on the signs of the times in 1944 and writes that the Western world has "come of age," meaning that it has gained secular autonomy, no longer needing "God" as a foundation for morals, science, politics, and philosophy. Rather than a hindrance to Christian faith, Bonhoeffer says that the "development toward the world's coming of age . . . which has cleared the way by eliminating a false notion of God, frees us to see the God of the Bible, who gains ground and power in the world by being powerless" (July 16, 1944).[14] In other words, Bonhoeffer thinks that this secular landscape enables a fresh perspective and a clearer view of the Christian God than the previous religious terrain, which had amassed false conceptions of God that barred the way to authentic discipleship. Bonhoeffer calls for a "religionless Christianity" (a topic examined in the following chapters) that would respect this historical development while witnessing to the crucified and risen Christ who makes space in the world through weakness.

Our context in the United States is different from what Bonhoeffer perceived to be true for the West. Sociologists now agree that as our society has become increasingly modern, secularization has not taken place in the United States to the extent predicted by early twentieth-century classical, secularization theorists and upheld by second-generation 1960s theoreticians.[15] The majority of U.S. citizens are not growing less religious or spiritual.[16] As a modern culture, we are not losing faith in a transcendent reality nor have we completely abandoned God as a foundation for morals and politics, as seen by the fact that appeals to God often are made in public debate. Therefore, we cannot accurately describe our society as a secular "world come of age,"[17] but as pluralistic, composed of people influenced by and operating within differing religious and secular traditions who must work alongside one another in a common democracy.[18] Within this pluralistic setting, religious and secular forces have not mutually excluded each other; rather, together they shape society in complex and multifaceted ways. Certainly "the separation of church and state" is a dominant metaphor that has shaped, and continues to shape, the imaginations of United States citizens. More debatable are the implications of the phrase and the extent to which faith has been privatized.[19] Undoubtedly, though, the entire modernized world, with the United States as case in point, has not become a mirror image of Bonhoeffer's Western Europe nor of the North American academic enclave as predicted.

Though an epidemic loss of faith has not swept through our society, there exists a lack of clarity and agreement about the purchase particularistic belief makes on believers' public lives in a pluralistic democracy. For Christians, this lack of clarity is not simply pragmatic (into what specific social and political activities should Christian convictions translate, if any?); the confusion is definitively theological. Disharmony about the church's identity and mission in a pluralistic society across and within fundamentalist, evangelical, and mainline Protestant Christianity necessitates that basic, normative, theological questions be given a renewed urgency; for, a church-community's view of its role in public life is rooted, though sometimes only implicitly, in its answer to these most basic and vital questions: (1) What ought Christians be witnessing to through their social and political engagement? (2) More specifically, what claims should Christians be making about the person and work of Christ through their public activity? (3) What claims should Christians be making about their own identity as church and about the relationship of the church to the surrounding world? Making a theological move analogous to Bonhoeffer's above, my theology of public witness will show that, like his world come of age, our pluralistic context actually helps define, clarify, and shape a Christian witness that is simultaneously nontriumphal and faithful to a Christian proclamation of the lordship of Christ. For, both faithfulness to the character of the crucified Christ and the flourishing of our common democratic project demand a humble witness. A humble and faithful public witness would reveal to those inside and outside the visible Christian fellowship the good news of Christ's expansive accomplishment, which is grounded, in the words of Bonhoeffer, in the truth that Christ "exists for others"—for the world—and has affirmed, judged, and reconciled the entire world, both the "religious" and the "secular."[20]

The driving question of this book—how Protestants offer a nontriumphal public witness in a pluralistic society—is at root an inquiry into the relationship between particularity and pluralism. Insofar as this book addresses the relationship between particularistic faith convictions and public engagement in our pluralistic society, it pertains to all professing Christians regardless of class, race, or ethnicity. My focus on confession and repentance as a nontriumphal public witness is aimed, though, mostly at white Protestants who benefit in countless recognized and unrecognized ways from being part of the dominant culture, because this reflects my own social location and the churches and para-church groups in which I was raised. My theology of public witness defines the church as the body called to repentance—as the body called, in the words of Bonhoeffer, to accept guilt or take responsibility for social sin. Bonhoeffer writes, as I do, from a position of social power and privilege and argues from that place that the acknowledgment of guilt is definitive for the church. Although Bonhoeffer does not qualify his statement, it is important to note that the notion of "acknowledging" or "accepting" guilt is problematic and counterproductive if applied to church-communities who are the victims of pervasive sin and injustice, even if by "guilt" one means, as Bonhoeffer does, not an uneasy conscience but the active determination to take responsibility for sin. He uses the potentially problematic term "guilt" as an ethical concept to amplify the Confessing Church's sense of responsibility in relation to the evils of Nazi Germany, and I use it for a similar purpose, to hold Christians who benefit from various degrees of social, economic, and political power accountable for the injustices that plague our society.[21] In our context, "guilt" most often connotes a narrow and individualistic pegging of blame, but Bonhoeffer's use of the term is best understood through the broader category of responsibility. In this way, it resembles an insight of Abraham Joshua Heschel, who (playing on the narrow connotation of the term) contends that "few are guilty, but all are responsible."[22]

Given the centrality of confession and repentance for Christian faith, a nondominant church-community might discern a public vocation in a manner that complements and corresponds to my theology of public witness by actively taking responsibility for a particular social sin or injustice in a spirit of penitence or lament. Yet the manner in which marginalized communities take responsibility for sin may be expressed differently than the repentance of privileged majority groups, and the way in which they define the penitential spirit may vary. For example, Wafik Wahba argues that the penitential spirit is central to the witness of Middle Eastern Christians, who repent in the context of persecution and suffering by taking responsibility through corporate prayer for the healing of the nations, for peace and stability.[23] Similarly, Cheryl Bridges Johns argues that global Pentecostals, the majority of whom live in situations of violence and poverty, place penitence alongside jubilation and have a keen yearning for the in-breaking of the kingdom of God. As with Middle Eastern Christians, Pentecostal worshipping communities become "healing communities" characterized by orthopathos; they join "in God's sorrow as it addresses death and alienation" in the fallen world. Johns says, "In orthopathos repentance is a response to God's passion for humanity. One is moved to grief by experiencing the pathos of God."[24] While focusing on the prophetic, Michael Battle defines the penitential as "practices...that encourage communities to respond appropriately to sin." He argues that "public practices of remorse" and traditions of penitence like the prophetic, which emphasizes the seriousness of sin and the promise of redemption, have always been central to African and African American Christianity. He contends that the penitential spirit may be seen through a "courageous and forgiving spirit more mindful of restorative justice...than retributive justice" as exemplified by Martin Luther King Jr.[25] Of course, the social sin that a minority church-community might need to address may directly concern the sins of that particular church-community. A Black church in an inner-city neighborhood may need to repent for ostracizing adolescent children from its life together instead of entering into the pain and complexity of street culture, for example. Or one minority church may need to repent for harming in word or deed members of another community or its own community, a dynamic identified by womanist critiques of sexism in the Black church.[26] As all of these examples illustrate, repentance is relevant to the political theologies of nondominant communities. The treatment of confession and repentance in this book, however, focuses on and forms in response to my concern about the triumphalistic tendencies of Christians and church-communities in the United States who intentionally and unintentionally maintain and benefit from the status quo.

This study claims that these North American Protestant churches may courageously demonstrate Christ's redemptive work and offer a nontriumphal witness to the lordship of Christ when their mode of being in the world is confession of sin unto repentant action. Still, what follows is not a theology of confession and repentance per se but a theological foundation upon which confession and repentance makes sense as public witness. I construct a theology of public witness through the lens of confession unto repentance because confession and repentance directly correspond to the crucified Christ, whose form, Bonhoeffer argues, the church must take in order to be a faithful witness to the whole of Christ's person and work. For Bonhoeffer, ecclesial witness is threefold, demonstrating Christ's affirmation, judgment, and reconciliation of the world, which corresponds to Christ as the incarnate, crucified, and risen one. The church takes the specific form of the crucified Christ, though, because, as chapter 3 argues, the incarnate God's visible manner of being in the world is centrally characterized by the cross. The crucified Christ in the form of a sinner (Rom. 8:3) is the linchpin that holds together Christ's identity as the incarnate, crucified, and risen one and also Christ's redemptive work of affirmation, judgment, and reconciliation.

■ ADVANCING THE TURN TOWARD ONE'S OWN CONTEXT: GOING BEYOND BONHOEFFER WITH BONHOEFFER

This book stands poised at the juncture of analysis and extension. It is both exegetical and constructive. It is exegetical insofar as it explicates Bonhoeffer's writings, and it is constructive insofar as it furthers the lines of his thinking in order to address the needs of our contemporary moment. Thus, I claim that confession unto repentance is a theme that holds together and illuminates Bonhoeffer's understanding of Christ, the world, and the church, even though Bonhoeffer himself never weaves these three dimensions together explicitly through the theme of repentance. By basing my constructive theology on Bonhoeffer's writings, this book furthers a recent turn in Bonhoeffer scholarship that examines his legacy and thus seeks to understand his theology not only within its historical moment but also by asking how his insights may stimulate biblical and theological reflection on one's own local context.[27] North American theologian Larry Rasmussen and South African theologian John W. de Gruchy inspired this turn and agree that because much of Bonhoeffer's work was born out of the specific situation of resistance to the Nazi totalitarian regime, his writings cannot simply or directly be applied to another context, as if they are a formula for ethical action. Instead, as de Gruchy says, the responsibility lies upon us here and now to go *beyond* Bonhoeffer *with* Bonhoeffer. De Gruchy writes, "All of those engaged in interpreting Bonhoeffer in their own historical contexts are dependent upon, and indebted to, those who painstakingly work with the sources. But the whole point of those efforts, if faithful to Bonhoeffer's legacy, is not simply to obtain accuracy about the sources and their meaning, but to show their significance for contemporary issues facing the church and society."[28] Moreover, while attempting to strike a balance between authorial intent and constructive insight, dynamic engagement with Bonhoeffer's work must fight the temptation merely to restate his ideas as a kind of proof-text, as if the authority of this figure overshadows the need for something genuinely new to grow out of the rich soil of his thought—"in one's own backyard," as Rasmussen says.[29] My study goes beyond Bonhoeffer with Bonhoeffer—in other words, I extend Bonhoeffer's thought within the framework of his theology—by defining a North American ecclesial witness as confession unto repentance and by systematically grounding this witness in the three interrelated dimensions of his thought: (1) christology, (2) his commitment to historical reality or "worldliness," (3) and ecclesiology, which correspond to the three chapters in part II.

Defining Terms with Bonhoeffer and beyond Bonhoeffer: Bonhoeffer's Open Notion of the "Acceptance of Guilt"

Even while faithfulness to Bonhoeffer's theology may lead to reflection on one's own context, accurate interpretation of his writings cannot be abstracted from his historical context or from the unity of his work as a whole.[30] Understanding the unity of Bonhoeffer's theology is vital because much of his writing is either fragmentary or unfinished given the circumstances of his life, imprisonment, and untimely death. With some exceptions, including his dissertation, *Sanctorum Communio*; his habilitation thesis, *Act and Being*; and his book, *Discipleship*, the ten thousand pages of the *Dietrich Bonhoeffer Works* are filled with unsystematic material such as sermons, lectures, letters, essays, and occasional pieces like *Life Together*. Much material has been collected and published after Bonhoeffer's death such as the christology lectures, compiled from student notes, and *Ethics*, compiled from unfinished drafts to which he had hoped to return. Because of the fragmentary and unfinished nature of much of his work, Bonhoeffer often leaves significant terms he employs undefined. Systematically reconstructing a concept may prove fruitful for understanding a particular idea but it also has limits. His use of a particular term often shifts without his clearly signaling the distinctions he is making or perhaps even being aware of the far-reaching implications of his constructive move. Bonhoeffer is a highly creative thinker, and like his two greatest influences, Martin Luther and Karl Barth, he thinks within the tradition while turning traditional terms on their head. He makes these interpretive moves without warning and without walking the reader through his steps of development.

"Acceptance of guilt" and "repentance" are two terms whose meanings are left open to a certain extent. Although Bonhoeffer specifically refers to the "acceptance of guilt" only in *Ethics* and does not provide a clear depiction of what "acceptance" entails, in the section, "Guilt, Justification, and Renewal," he speaks interchangeably about "confessing," "acknowledging," and "taking on" guilt.[31] Concepts such as "bearing," "confessing," and *Stellvertretung* (vicarious representative action) that are integral to his discussion of accepting guilt in *Ethics* undergo a steady development throughout his writings; thus, a framework for understanding the notion is present in most of his major works, even though Bonhoeffer never gives "a detailed, thorough, or conclusive presentation and analysis of the concept."[32] Bonhoeffer also does not provide a precise definition of "guilt." The German term, *Schuld*, refers in Bonhoeffer's writings both to sin and guilt, and is translated in such diverse ways as "culpability," "fault," and "debt" in the English editions of Bonhoeffer's works.[33]

By examining Bonhoeffer's ecclesiology within the framework of the church's public witness, my project illuminates a way to understand and implement Bonhoeffer's open notion of confessing, acknowledging, or accepting guilt. Too often the concept of accepting guilt is linked directly to Bonhoeffer's involvement in the *Abwehr*'s conspiracy against Hitler, and so it is removed from the realm of everyday discipleship. Ordinary Christian life does not require this kind of extremely rare action, which is, as Bonhoeffer writes in his essay "After Ten Years," a "free venture of faith" that depends on a God "who promises forgiveness and consolation to the one who on account of such action becomes a sinner."[34] In her systematic reconstruction of Bonhoeffer's notion of "accepting guilt," Christine Schliesser helpfully expands the notion, yet in doing so, she sets up a dualism that reinforces active acceptance of guilt as a rare deed. Schliesser argues that the primary difficulty in attaining a clear definition is that Bonhoeffer does not distinguish between guilt actively and passively incurred. She defines "actively incurred" as getting one's "hands dirty," as becoming guilty by intentionally breaking divine and/or human law for the sake of the other, with Bonhoeffer's involvement in the conspiracy serving as the prime example.[35] Schliesser then defines guilt nonactively incurred as bearing with others by entering into their "foreign" guilt.[36] Passive acceptance of guilt—what Bonhoeffer calls in *Life Together* "the service [of]...bearing with others"[37]—includes intercession, counseling, and speaking words of forgiveness and so is best understood, Schliesser says, in a pastoral manner and in the context of Christian fellowship. Schliesser argues that guilt passively incurred dominates Bonhoeffer's thought up until *Ethics*, while his later writing is more concerned with the active acceptance of guilt. She concludes that while Bonhoeffer has persuasively shown that passive acceptance of guilt is an inevitable part of Christian life, he has not provided adequate grounding for guilt actively incurred.

Instead of confining the "active" acceptance of guilt to rare deeds, however, in *Ethics*, Bonhoeffer makes acceptance of guilt definitive for the church's identity and mission in the world. Here acceptance of guilt should not be read through the lens of the conspiracy and its intended tyrannicide; rather, by "acceptance" Bonhoeffer means the church's acknowledgment of its complicity in social sin. He defines the church (as shown in chapter 5 in this volume) precisely as the body that actively accepts or, better, confesses and takes responsibility for sin through repentant action. While the words "acknowledge" and "confess" more straightforwardly express his intention for the church, Bonhoeffer utilizes the ambiguous term "acceptance" in order to bind the church's public action to Christ's, whose "acceptance" of guilt is not an acknowledgment of complicity in sin but is nevertheless an active determination to take responsibility for it. A church that accepts guilt first understands that it is always already guilty, that no guilt is entirely "foreign" given both the shared ontological guilt of humanity and also the interconnected nature of all human action. Second, a church that accepts guilt ventures responsible acts in the midst of the world that open the church up to unintentional sin given the unseen consequences of all social and political endeavors.

Repentance Reconsidered

Some of Bonhoeffer's terms are left open not only because of the fragmentary nature of his writings but also because the definitions he offers are so theologically dense, and he uses them in such multifaceted ways, that they need unpacking and untangling. This is true of his use of "repentance" and *metanoia*, its Greek antecedent. *Metanoia* is most commonly translated simply as "repentance," but in scripture, as well as in Bonhoeffer's writings, "repentance" does not have a singular and straightforward meaning.[38] Rather, the concept carries various connotations, including but not limited to "transformation" and "change of mind."[39] These, and other shades of meaning, serve to expand our understanding of the social and political significance of repentance.

The term "repentance" or *metanoia* appears at key moments in Bonhoeffer's thought—but without drawing much attention to itself—and serves as a connecting point between his analysis of Christ, the world, and the church. For example, in *Discipleship*, Bonhoeffer links *metanoia* with the church's conformation to the crucified Christ (a prevalent theme throughout his theology) when he cites Romans 12:2, " 'Do not be conformed to this world, but be transformed into a new form ... by the renewing of your minds' ... The community is called to be ever increasingly transformed into this form. It is, in fact, the form of Christ himself."[40] Then in a famous passage from prison, where Bonhoeffer associates Christ's form, or presence, in the world with his solidarity with it, Bonhoeffer defines *metanoia* as belonging wholly to—"living completely in"—this world.[41] He says, "This is what I call this-worldliness: living fully in the midst of life's tasks, questions, successes and failures, experiences, and perplexities—then one takes seriously no longer one's own sufferings but rather the suffering of God in the world. Then one stays awake with Christ in Gethsemene. And I think this is faith; this is μετάνοια [*metanoia*]. And this is how one becomes a human being, a Christian."[42] In *Ethics*, Bonhoeffer similarly links "repentance" to the church's this-worldly activity when he defines the church's repentance as preparing this "penultimate" world for its redemptive transformation. He says definitively,

"Preparation of the way *means* repentance."[43] As we will see, Bonhoeffer mentions the term "repentance" on other occasions, but only in passing, without providing a clear and conclusive definition.

Although Bonhoeffer presents the notion in theologically distinct and creative ways throughout his writings, only in prison does he state explicitly that the church needs to reconsider the meaning of repentance. Bonhoeffer reflects on the need for a renewed interpretation of repentance and other biblical concepts as he introduces the possibility of a "religionless Christianity," and he suggests that this renewed interpretation be "nonreligious." What Bonhoeffer means by "religionless" or "nonreligious" has been the topic of much debate ever since the 1960s and 1970s "creative misuses" of his prison theology by North American thinkers (such as the "death of God" theologians and theologians of the "secular") who were quick to hail the arrival of a secular age and (mis)read Bonhoeffer's prison letters in that light.[44] Because Bonhoeffer neither provides a technical working definition of religion nor a theory of religion in any of his writings, his reflections on religionless Christianity and a nonreligious interpretation of biblical concepts are, like some of his other terms, inconclusive and vulnerable to misappropriation.[45] In an attempt to correct hasty misuses of Bonhoeffer's letters, scholarship in the last four decades has shown clearly that his prison theology must be read through his early and developing christology. A "nonreligious" interpretation is, at root, a christological interpretation. Indeed, in his prison reflections on religionless Christianity and the need for a nonreligious interpretation of biblical concepts, Bonhoeffer says that "repentance" would find greater meaning if reinterpreted through the lens of the Word become flesh, in other words, through an understanding of the life, death, and resurrection of Jesus. He writes, "At the moment I am thinking about how concepts of repentance, faith, justification, rebirth, and sanctification should be reinterpreted in a 'worldly' way—in the Old Testament sense and in the sense of John 1.14."[46] A couple of months later, in an outline for a book sketched in prison, he writes similarly, "Jesus only 'is there for others.'... Faith is participating in this being of Jesus. (Becoming human [Menschwerdung], cross, and resurrection.)... our relationship to God is a new life in 'being there for others,' through participation in the being of Jesus... God in human form!... 'the human being for others'! therefore the Crucified One.... Hence the interpretation of biblical concepts on this principle. (Creation, fall, reconciliation, repentance, faith, *vita nova*, last things)."[47]

Bonhoeffer suggests in prison that repentance may be understood as conformation to the crucified Christ and participation in the very being of Christ. Yet in prison he is unable to develop further the central role repentance may play in Christ's own mission and identity. My theology of public witness responds to Bonhoeffer's proposal that repentance be reinterpreted christologically, as it offers a foundation upon which repentance may be understood as public witness through an examination of Christ's person and work, the christological value of this world and this life, and the church's cruciform identity and mission in the world.

Thinking within the Movement of Bonhoeffer's Thought

Although Bonhoeffer's fragmentary and unfinished texts hamper tightly constructed definitions of key terms, the open character of his work, "the very *style* of his theological thought" and "its expression in a certain fragmentary *form*" is one of Bonhoeffer's greatest theological contributions.[48] The fragmentary form directly expresses Bonhoeffer's deep conviction that theology cannot speak the dynamic word of God as a closed system. Theology must "subvert the pretensions of a system" and "keep space open" for God's living word to speak concretely in the contemporary moment.[49] Hanfried Müller well describes this dynamic with which my proposal for constructing a theology of public witness is in keeping. Müller says:

> I believe that the right way to follow Bonhoeffer is to take up his development, his path, his intention and the tendency of his work: to follow him rather than to stifle his vigor and vitality with a system. I think that [an] understanding of the whole of Bonhoeffer will come about not by systematizing everything he thought as though it were all on the same level, and thus relativizing it, but rather by taking up the movement of his thought in its entirety as the thing which can lead us further.[50]

The fragmentary form of Bonhoeffer's theology is precisely what enables and sanctions the unfolding of fresh theological insight and the further construction of key terms within "the movement of his thought in its entirety." When Bonhoeffer turns concepts on their head "in 'lightning flashes' of radical theological insight," the text invites, even begs, those who come after him to pick up where he left off and to further his line of thinking to the rhythm of the entirety of his thought.[51]

Thinking within the movement of Bonhoeffer's thought, I define a redemptive public witness as "confession of sin unto repentance." I link confession and repentance through the word "unto" to show that genuine confession of sin cannot be separated from the activity of repentance (which the theological ethnographies in part III depict), nor can concrete repentance occur without an awareness of specific sin. Bonhoeffer directly addresses the necessary unity of confession and repentance when he famously writes in *Discipleship*, "Cheap grace is preaching forgiveness without repentance; it is baptism without the discipline of community; it is the Lord's Supper without confession of sin; it is absolution without personal confession. Cheap grace is grace without discipleship, grace without the cross, grace without the living, incarnate Jesus Christ."[52] Certainly the courage genuinely to confess sin and acknowledge guilt arises out of the promise of Christ's forgiveness, yet, absent responsible repentance, the comfort one finds in the forgiveness of sin amounts to little more than self-justification—what Bonhoeffer calls "cheap grace."[53]

By the phrase "confession unto repentance" I also mean to convey that public witness involves various degrees of speech and act, although I intend the weight of the phrase to fall upon the activity of repentance. Based on Bonhoeffer's theology, I argue that the church witnesses to Christ by taking the form of Christ in the world; therefore, witness is embodied and enacted. When it becomes necessary for church-communities to complement public engagement with speech that is particularly Christian, I suggest this language first be its own confession of sin. By "confession of sin" I do not primarily or necessarily mean a formal statement of confession, like an apology issued by a denomination confessing its racist past. By "confession of sin" I mean more broadly a pattern of speaking characterized by humble acknowledgment of complicity in specific sin and injustice and of the church's inherent interconnectedness in the sin of broader society, as exemplified in Tim Clayton's witness in the opening anecdote. By "repentance" I mean the church's concrete activity in social and political life that arises from its accepting responsibility and acknowledging its complicity in such sin. By granting "repentance" social and political character, I follow Bonhoeffer, who, in those lightning flashes of theological insight, uses the concept to refer to more than the activity of the individual Christian. Most importantly, my phrase "confession unto repentance" describes *an ecclesial mode of being in the world*, encompassing both act and speech, that provides the church with an ethical framework for social and political engagement and a description of a particularly Christian disposition in public life. Through creative and courageous repentant activity, the church participates in God's dynamic and ever-unfolding transformation of this world.

■ JOURNEY TO A REDEMPTIVE PUBLIC WITNESS

Part I: Public Witness in a Pluralistic Society

Before constructing a theology of public witness in part II, it is important to establish why such a theology is needed for the U.S. context by unearthing some unrecognized factors driving Christian conceptions of witness in the United States. In doing so, chapter 2, "Evaluating Public Witness in the United States," considers the notion of witness itself. The chapter first offers Bonhoeffer's prison reflections on religionless Christianity as a frame for evaluating a nontriumphal witness by focusing on a distinction he makes between special favor and this-worldly belonging. He writes, "How do we go about being 'religionless-worldly' Christians, how can we be ἐκ-κλησία, those who are called out, without understanding ourselves religiously as privileged, but instead seeing ourselves as belonging wholly to the world? Christ would then no longer be the object of religion, but something else entirely, truly lord of the world."[54] Chapter 2 argues that Protestants in the United States communicate that they are specially favored when they interpret Christian faith as the possession of right knowledge and/or right morality. This religious stance is the greatest barrier to North American Protestants enacting a redemptive public witness and stems from two tendencies pervasive in the United States: the tendency to identify witness with possession of truth and the tendency to presume that Christians are called in public life to be the standard-bearers of morality. The first tendency arises from lack of sustained reflection on the simultaneous inclusive and exclusive nature of Christ's person and work, and the second logically follows from Bonhoeffer's penetrating critique, written after his second visit to the United States in 1939, that (white) North American theology is essentially ethics uprooted from its christological and ecclesiological grounding and thus disconnected from christological ways of thinking about the identity and mission of the church. The chapter examines Barth's early theology, which provides the most radical critique of "morality" or "religious righteousness" in twentieth-century thought and paves the way for Bonhoeffer's insight. Whereas Barth's devastating critique arguably leaves moral action and reasoning ineffectual, Bonhoeffer provides material for constructing an ecclesial ethic that debunks human righteousness even as it offers a witness to the crucified and risen Christ—an ethic of confession unto repentance developed in part II. This chapter argues that repentance is not a correction or broadening of morality but is the opposite of morality, an alternative mode of being and doing good that expresses that God alone is righteous. Sociological and ethnographic research make evident the tendencies mentioned above and offer descriptions that help assess the tensions and ambiguities inherent in the way most Protestants understand "witness." The chapter ends by reorienting the notion of witness toward conformation to the crucified Christ through an examination of the relationship between presence and proclamation in Bonhoeffer's prison theology.

Part II: A Theology of Public Witness Based on Bonhoeffer's Thought

Part II, (chapters 3, 4, and 5) constructs a theology of public witness through an analysis of the three interrelated dimensions of Bonhoeffer's thought: Christ, the world, and the church. Because the church's public witness faithfully points to Christ by conforming to Christ's manner of being in the world, the primary task of chapter 3, "Christ's Public Presence," is to examine the this-worldly presence of the incarnate God. To do so, I first return to Bonhoeffer's prison reflections surrounding the possibility of a religionless Christianity and a nonreligious interpretation of biblical concepts. There he suggests that repentance be reinterpreted christologically, thus inviting reflection on the possibility of understanding Jesus' public presence in terms of repentance. Implementing Bonhoeffer's fascinating proposal, this chapter argues that the work of the sinless Christ may be understood as repentance, through which the church is then called to participate. Without suggesting that the problem of sin has its origin in God, I argue that God repents in Christ in accordance with the fallen human nature Jesus bears, what Paul calls in Romans 8:3, "the likeness of sinful flesh." I position the unusual and scandalous claim that Christ's public presence may be understood in terms of repentance within a broader theological landscape that characterizes God's revelation through Christ as "hidden." Repentance, as a public expression of God's righteousness in Christ, may be understood as one mode of the unanticipated and startling character of

God's revelation. I then turn to Bonhoeffer's *Ethics*. Whereas his christology lectures center on God hidden in humiliation, *Ethics* emphasizes the this-worldly glory of the incarnation. His early and later thought are interwoven in that in *Ethics* Bonhoeffer argues that it is God's glory to accept guilt. God is visible and present in the world as the humiliated one who takes responsibility for sin in the form of a sinner, and in this way God's belonging to and being for humanity is revealed. Interpreting repentance through the person of Christ directly challenges the common understanding that repentance primarily concerns one's individual standing before God; instead, as participation in Christ, repentance constitutes existence for others. This chapter lays the christological foundation for the book's main argument: The church witnesses to Christ in a nontriumphal manner and demonstrates Christ's being for the world when it takes the form of the humiliated, crucified God by accepting guilt or confessing sin unto repentance.

While chapter 3 examines the person of Christ, chapter 4, "Belonging: Participation in the World's Christological Pattern," focuses on the work of Christ, on Christ's threefold acceptance, judgment, and reconciliation of the world. This chapter argues that the work accomplished on the cross transformed the very structure of reality into what Bonhoeffer calls "Christ-reality" and that the church participates in the world's new ontology centrally by taking the form of the crucified Christ through confession unto repentance. The church-community delves into the ambiguities of existence in solidarity with human sin and completely abandons itself to life's christological structure—to the theological fact that accepting responsibility for sin has transformative power and prepares the way for Christ's concrete redemption. The person and work of Christ lay the foundation for an ecclesial witness that is free to belong wholly to a world already reconciled to God and to enact concrete redemption from that place.

Chapter 5, "The Church's Public Presence: Visibility through Confession and Repentance," builds on the christological foundation laid in chapters 3 and 4 and examines ecclesiology more directly. Because a theology of public witness based on Bonhoeffer's thought must maintain both the concreteness of the empirical, institutional church or local church-community with all its failings *and* the theological claim that the church is Christ's contemporary bodily presence in the world, chapter 5 considers in detail how the church may be at once a sinful body and a body that reveals Christ. It argues that Christ wills to take visible form in a body in order to reveal his continued concrete presence in history, yet the reality of sinful human beings comprising the church necessitates that, in order to be a redemptive public presence, it reciprocally must take Christ's form as the one who accepted guilt and took responsibility for sin. Indeed, as Bonhoeffer argues, taking responsibility for sin is the definitive activity of the church. Through confession unto repentance the church both recognizes the serious and comprehensive nature of its sin and, like Christ, receives God's judgment upon itself out of love for the world. As the body that recognizes its guilt, the church, then, cannot lift itself up as a model of moral righteousness. Instead, by accepting responsibility for sin, the church witnesses to Christ and takes the form of Christ's own reconciling life. The final section of the chapter describes the ecclesial outworking of this form by showing how confession unto repentance may guide the church into specific social and political engagement.

Because the church's exposed sin is incorporated into the logic of witness itself, public engagement based on confession unto repentance resists triumphalism. An ethic of confession unto repentance manifests that God alone is righteous and thereby signals a totally new mode of being and doing good, which disrupts the prevalent presumption among North American Protestants that the church is called to be the standard-bearer of morality in public life. Such a witness has transformative power because it prepares the way for Christ's unfolding redemption as it takes responsibility for sin, suffering, and injustice through repentance.

Part III: Contours of a Repenting Church

Bonhoeffer argues that the theologian must guard against constructing a closed theological system by welcoming lessons learned from an enfleshed church. Part III, "Contours of a Repenting Church," (chapters 6 and 7) offers two ethnographic case studies of church-communities whose work exemplify ecclesial commitments and practices born out of a disposition of confession unto repentance. These theological ethnographies provide detailed pictures of how church-communities conformed to Christ may demonstrate Christ's threefold affirmation, judgment, and reconciliation of the world in a nontriumphalistic manner. Part III demonstrates, through each community's particularity, that confession and repentance may be embodied communally in various ways, yet also discerns, in the conclusion, defining characteristics of a redemptive public witness conformed to Christ.

Chapter 6, "The Eleuthero Community: Confession and Repentance through Unlearning and Learning Anew," examines a church-community (led by our opening exemplar, Tim Clayton) that recognizes that the way North Americans live is unsustainable and damaging to both the environment and the world's vulnerable populations. This community of ecumenical evangelical and mainline Protestants confesses that American Christians have not given the full narrative of scripture its due and have told fractured, false stories leading to disobedient action. Through the priest's teaching and through the life of the community, they are constructing "a holistic biblical narrative... that can handle all of life." As they unlearn and learn anew, the Eleuthero Community demonstrates what repentance as "the renewing of minds" entails (Rom. 12:2). Eleuthero members undergo continuous conversion to the life of Christ and a full vision of scripture, and in response they fashion right relationships with the earth and with a population of Sudanese refugees in Portland, Maine.

Chapter 7, "The Southeast White House: A Local Presence in a Neglected Neighborhood," examines a Washington, D.C., inner-city hospitality house that intentionally has made itself present in "the forgotten quadrant" of the nation's capital. As a local presence it is consciously responding to, and taking responsibility for, society's neglect. This chapter argues that the ministry's very presence in the neighborhood stems from an initial act of repentance as the cofounders turned toward the forgotten quadrant and moved into the neighborhood in order to encounter the neighbor. The chapter argues that the ministry's work may be viewed as an ongoing activity of repentance—a making right—as it fosters relationships and draws other people into its communal life together, connecting people normally divided by race, religion, politics, economics, social standing, geography, and culture.

These theological ethnographies correspond to Bonhoeffer's concern with concreteness—that theology be expressed "in the language of reality"—and are an answer to a common question posed to philosophical theology about its concrete payoff: "But what does this look like on the ground, in real life?"[55] Although my studies of the Eleuthero Community and the Southeast White House are not comprehensive ethnographies nor do they aim, like many ethnographies, to ascertain what these particular communities reveal about society as a whole, I have used ethnographic methods (interviews and participant-observation) to trouble the waters of my systematic thinking, to break open my theology of public witness to the lived realities of redemptive communal practice.

Utilizing both theology and ethnography in my theology of public witness stems from the rationale that philosophical theologians and practitioner-activists need one another to engage more fully the task of cultivating just and redemptive communities. For example, an academic theologian may gain theological insight by reading a church-community in a manner similar to a theological text, and the knowledge gained from the community may be taken as seriously as philosophical or theological works.[56] Just as I chose Bonhoeffer's writings to guide my theology of public witness, discerning him to be an appropriate interlocutor, so too did I chose church-communities that I intuited were on to something, so to speak, based on prior personal engagement with the communities and their leaders and on my analysis of Bonhoeffer's writings. In other words, I chose communities that I thought offered a possible interpretive frame that would help me better understand witness and that could be in mutually productive dialogue with Bonhoeffer.

Interestingly, although I observed commitments and practices that I argue *are born out of a disposition of* confession and repentance, for neither of the communities I chose to study were "confession" and "repentance" prevalent terms used by the majority of the members to describe the community's identity and mission. This fact, combined with Bonhoeffer's open and creative understanding of the meaning of repentance, has paved the way for an expansive and holistic reimagining of what repentance encompasses and entails, with my reading of Bonhoeffer influencing my interpretation of the communities and my reading of the communities influencing my interpretation of Bonhoeffer. Just as Bonhoeffer's theology offers a lens and language in which to analyze and articulate the practices of these lived communities, the communities of faith at times challenged the terms of my constructive theology and reoriented what I was in the process of developing.[57] Thus, while parts II and III of this book may appear to be distinct studies, since they are based on different styles of scholarship (philosophical theology and ethnographic method), both sections bear the fruit of this dynamic interaction.

The interconnection of philosophical theology and ethnography in my theology of public witness has autobiographical roots as well and is the result of something akin to what Latin American liberation theologians call an "action-reflection hermeneutic": Insight is gained through activity in the world, with theological reflection on prior experience influencing subsequent action and thinking. I entered graduate school impassioned and disoriented from two years working in the inner city through the Southeast White House and brought with me concerns and questions about the church's identity and mission that were born from that experience. I readily recognized the need for collaboration between academic theologians and practitioner-activists because I began to wrestle theologically with issues surrounding privilege, poverty, injustice, race, and human flourishing while working at this hospitality house. I became a graduate student in order to speak theologically to the realities I had encountered, and I was determined to maintain my practitioner status and speak out of that formation. So, it was my own practice, my participation as a staff member at the Southeast White House, that led to theological inquiry in the form of becoming a graduate student, which then led me back for ethnographic research. Little did I know in 2001 that I would be returning to the Southeast White House (first in the fall of that year for a seminar paper and then in 2006 for dissertation research) for answers that I had left that setting to find.

Although my experience working in this inner-city hospitality house has radically informed subsequent theological questioning and thinking, theological reflection has been indispensible and has guided the ethnographic research comprising this theology of public witness. I have set out first and foremost to articulate a theology—to articulate the manner in which Protestants should be engaged in social and political life through a study of Bonhoeffer's christology, theology of this-worldliness, and ecclesiology—because I agree with that 1939 observation Bonhoeffer made, namely, that white North American Protestants lack sustained and substantive theological thinking about the identity and mission of the church. This lack too often results in a public witness gone awry.

The church will remain confused about the public role of Christian faith in a pluralistic democracy if it cannot first answer the most basic and important questions of its faith: Who is Christ? What does Christ's life and work proclaim to the world? What is the church's identity? What is the church's role within society? In order to answer these questions, I intend to offer both a faithful reading of Bonhoeffer's theology and to participate faithfully in Bonhoeffer's legacy, which includes engagement with actual church-communities. Bonhoeffer's legacy compels the contemporary theologian to move beyond him, proceed down paths his undeveloped insights point, and risk speaking out of her particular historical context.

2 Evaluating Public Witness in the United States

Before constructing, in part II, a theological foundation upon which confession and repentance make sense as public witness, it is important to establish why a theology of public witness is needed for the U.S. context. This chapter first identifies some underlying and unrecognized factors driving common understandings of witness and then examines the manner in which various subgroups of Christians are present in public life. In order to be as clear and concrete as possible, I provide descriptions and some specific examples of a faltering public witness in the United States garnered from various sociological studies, particularly those concerned with Christian social and political engagement in a pluralistic democracy. North American Protestantism is vast, and so any constructive critique must try to avoid broad brush strokes that blur important details and distinctions among various Christians. While avoiding oversimplifications, a burden of this chapter is to depict *tendencies* shaping Christian witness in the United States that are difficult to quantify but manifest themselves in patterns or trajectories that can be examined theologically. The chapter ends by reorienting the notion of witness toward conformation to Christ, specifically through an examination of the relationship between presence and proclamation in Bonhoeffer's prison theology—between the church's mode of being in the world and the efficacy of its language.

CALLED FORTH BUT NOT SPECIALLY FAVORED: BONHOEFFER'S PRISON REFLECTIONS AS A FRAME FOR EVALUATING PUBLIC WITNESS

The task of constructing a theology of public witness for our pluralistic society resembles Bonhoeffer's interest in prison in formulating a "religionless Christianity" and a "nonreligious interpretation" of biblical concepts for his "world come of age." Although the term "witness" does not appear often in his prison writings, the crux of Bonhoeffer's reflections concerning the possibility of a religionless Christianity and the need for a renewed interpretation of biblical concepts like repentance revolves around witness, specifically around how the church—and, at times, individual Christians—should demonstrate and articulate the reconciliation and redemption accomplished through Christ in an era increasingly a-religious.

In his first letter introducing the idea of a religionless Christianity, Bonhoeffer asks a question that provides a helpful frame for thinking about public witness in the United States. His inquiry, although arising out of his own historical context of a world come of age, parallels the driving concern for our pluralistic context, namely, how the church may witness to the lordship of Christ in a nontriumphal manner. Bonhoeffer asks, "How do we go about being 'religionless-worldly' Christians, how can we be ἐκ-κλησία, those who are called out, without understanding ourselves religiously as privileged, but instead seeing ourselves as belonging wholly to the world? Christ would then no longer be the object of religion, but something else entirely, truly lord of the world."[1]

A number of Protestants might agree that Christ is not an "object of religion." "Christianity is not a religion; it's a relationship [with Jesus]" is a common mantra in evangelical circles.[2] Yet Bonhoeffer's inquiry exposes a mindset that is present even among Christians who downplay the label "religious" or who assume that they are not susceptible to the faults of "religion" as they define them. Although Bonhoeffer critiques "religion" in diverse ways throughout his writings, here he describes being religious as viewing one's self or group as specially favored. While other manifestations of his critique of religion in a world come of age identify mindsets and postures that are also present among Protestants in our pluralistic society (from relegating God to the boundaries of life, since modern human beings can rely on vast developments in knowledge and technology for everyday existence; to primarily addressing inward, private, subjective problems; to otherworldly and escapist; to self-centered and mainly concerned with the church's self-preservation),[3] none of them directly addresses, as well as his above inquiry does, what is at the heart of a faltering public witness in the United States. This is because Bonhoeffer's primary concern in a world come of age is that religion pushes God out of public life, but in our context, religion rushes into the public square and asserts power and influence there as much as it evades it. This chapter argues that, given our pluralistic landscape, North American Protestants weaken their witness to the depth and breadth of Christ's redemption and thus impair their mission of communicating in word and deed the good news of Christian faith if they convey, through their witness, that they are religiously privileged.

Bonhoeffer affirms that the church has been chosen for a specific mission or vocation—is called forth to witness to Christ's lordship and to the expansive power of Christ's redemptive work. Still, by suggesting that the church hinders its mission if it presumes that it is specially favored, he names the difficult but vital task of offering a public witness that is simultaneously bold and humble. While some North American theologians involved in contemporary conversations about ecclesial witness worry that Christians have relinquished their boldness and lost a sense of the church's distinct identity and mission as a result of trying to adhere to the unspoken rules of democratic liberalism,[4] I am more concerned that a significant and visible portion of Protestants already consider themselves distinct in a manner that obscures a faithful witness to the crucified Christ—namely, by interpreting their distinctive "chosen" status through the lens of a theology of glory, not a theology or ethic of the cross. For Bonhoeffer, the cross demonstrates that God through Christ has chosen to "belong wholly to this world," to be in solidarity with humanity in sin and redemption. In order to be Christ's witness in and for the world, the church conforms itself to the incarnate, crucified, and risen Christ by also belonging wholly to this world. It does this, I argue, by taking responsibility for its present complicity in social sin through repentant activity that makes concrete Christ's work of cosmic reconciliation and redemption. Thus, the church's election is not for itself as if salvation's reach ends there, but like Christ, the church exists for others. It exists to participate in the healing of this world.

In contrast, the church that too quickly bypasses the cross by settling into a theology of glory—the church whose manner of dwelling within the world is not decisively shaped by the crucified Christ—cannot help but take a triumphant posture before the world. Certainly many Christians rightly attribute the church's (eschatological) victory over sin and death to the grace of God and the work of Christ and do not intend to convey an arrogant confidence in their religious beliefs and in their status before God. Still, whether mindful of this or not, *Protestants in the United States risk understanding themselves as—and often communicate to others that they think they are—specially favored when they interpret Christian faith as the possession of right knowledge and/or right morality.* Christians intend to be witnessing to Christ, but their proclamation becomes self-referential, offering little more than an invitation to become like us—to think like us and act like us. This religious stance is the greatest barrier to North American Protestants enacting a redemptive public witness and stems from two tendencies pervasive in the United States: the tendency to identify *witness to* with *possession of* truth, which arises from lack of sustained reflection on the simultaneous inclusive and exclusive nature of Christ's person and work, and the tendency to presume that Christians are called in public life to be the standard-bearers of morality.

■ THE TENDENCY TO CONFLATE WITNESS WITH POSSESSION OF RIGHT KNOWLEDGE

The Distinction between Witness and Truth

Many North American Protestants lack a theologically rich description of witness as a concept distinct from the possession of truth. Christians misunderstand the exclusive nature of the faith when they do not appropriately distinguish between the *person* of Christ as truth—"*I am* the way, *the truth* and the life" Jesus says in John's Gospel (14:6)—and the church's second-order knowledge, interpretations, and beliefs *about* the truth. This distinction is central and foundational for Bonhoeffer's christology. In his 1933 lectures he says that Christ as person is judgment upon the human logos. He is "counter Logos" in that he appears in history, not in the form of an idea that can be assimilated into or classified within the order of human knowledge, but as the Word become flesh.[5] Because Christ is person, not idea, truth simply cannot be possessed, for no person can ever rightly possess another. "You believed that you knew the truth, you possessed it... and in that way you have made yourself God," Bonhoeffer writes a year before delivering the christology lectures, "You have robbed God of [God's] truth, and from God's perspective it became a lie."[6] When Christians assume they are called and specially favored to be a purveyor of truth, they exert a self-referential and triumphalistic *religious* exclusivity that trades the particular and dynamic life, history, and person of Christ for static, epistemic self-certainty. The latter then functions, often in vain, as the platform on which Christians try to convince others of the validity of their faith.

Instead of a *religious* exclusivity that inadvertently makes an idol of its own beliefs, a nontriumphal proclamation of the lordship of Christ arises from *christological* exclusivity, what the Barthian scholar George Hunsinger aptly calls "exclusivism without triumphalism and inclusivism without compromise."[7] Public witness based on a "nonreligious" exclusivist christology is *inclusive* as it appeals to the expansive accomplishment of Christ, who, according to the witness of Colossians, has reconciled "all things" to God, thus affirming the integrity of a realm outside the Christian religion. It is *without compromise* because it maintains that the ultimate significance of Christ is a nonnegotiable foundation for Christian faith, discipleship, and witness. Indeed, Colossians 1:13–20 attests to both; Christ is the world's source and center, and the new ontological whole comprising the entire world: "He himself is before all things, and in him all things hold together" (v. 17). Such radical inclusiveness is possible, as chapter 4 argues more fully, precisely because the entire world has been reconciled to God through Christ: "For in him all the fullness of God was pleased to dwell, and through him God was pleased to reconcile to himself all things, whether on earth or in heaven, by making peace through the blood of his cross" (1:19–20).[8] Finally, public witness based on an exclusivist christology is *nontriumphalistic* because it recognizes and respects that Christ—the embodied Word of God—alone has the status of truth, while the church has the status of witness to (but not possessor of) truth. Witness is the church's very raison d'être; its purpose, in the words of Bonhoeffer, is to manifest Christ by taking Christ's form in the world or, as Barth says, by being a secondary form of God's "own reconciling life."[9]

Sharing Bonhoeffer's christological distinction between person and idea—and sharing leadership in the church struggle—Barth juxtaposes human (including religious) ideology with Christ's utter exclusivity as "the One Word of God" in the first formulation of the Confessing Church's "Barmen Declaration," the 1934 confession of faith that rejected the authority of the Nazified German Christian church. He later develops this distinction between truth and witness with great precision in *Church Dogmatics* IV/3, "The Glory of the Mediator," and does so in a way that helps clarify why understanding the simultaneous inclusive and exclusive nature of Christ's person and work is so vital for a faithful witness. Barth writes, "Jesus Christ as attested to us in Holy Scripture is the one Word of God whom we must hear and whom we must trust and obey in life and in death."[10] Although the "concrete content of this Word" or revelation is the particular history of Christ's reconciling love, the normative, superior, and singular character of this Word is "hard and offensive," he says, not only for those "who are without" faith but initially and constantly "for those who have already come to faith in

Jesus Christ."[11] The one Word of God is an offense even (or *especially*) for the church because it demands that by virtue of their calling Christians must "submit themselves first with all their Christian views and concepts, dogma and institutions, customs, traditions and innovations, to the relativization and criticism that comes through Jesus Christ as the one and only light of life."[12] Since the person of Christ is the exclusive truth and the "total and complete declaration," all other words are subordinate, incomplete, nonnormative, and thus constantly open to reproach.[13] Even the church's true beliefs about Christ "can hardly have, or arrogantly claim, equal truth for themselves. Even as true words of God, they must still distinguish themselves from this one Word, keeping their distance and conceding and accepting the fact that it alone is truth."[14] In short, the utter exclusivity of truth in Christ cannot serve as a foundation for the "exaltation and self-glorification of the Christian in relation to other [human beings]."[15] It is quite the opposite. The normative, superior, and singular Word of God enjoins the church to a humility that is cognizant of the finitude and fallenness of its own words and knowledge and that, in turn, is continually open to constructive criticism about its theological, social, and political claims.

Barth complements his depiction of God's one Word with the Johannine metaphor of light in order to describe how the exclusive and exhaustive Word "that speaks for Himself" and "does not need the help of any other" nevertheless radiates radical inclusiveness by inspiring "true words" in manifold places through the "free shining of His light."[16] Reiterating the sheer exclusivity of truth in Christ, he writes, "Jesus Christ is *the* light of life. To underline the 'the' is to say that He is the one and only light of life. Positively, this means that He is the light of life in all its fullness, in perfect adequacy; and negatively, it means that there is no other light of life outside or alongside His, outside or alongside the light which He is."[17] This metaphor of light helps us imagine how Christ's fullness or perfect adequacy actually illuminates inclusiveness. "As Jesus Christ lives, He also shines out," and human beings "reached by his light, participate in His revelation."[18] The brilliance of Christ's lordship is such that it lifts into prominence other entities, which serve as reflectors of Christ's truth and glory, and it is precisely this brilliancy that disallows triumphalist Christianity. As "the source of light whose shining gives light without," Christ kindles lights across a great canopy that envelops not only the biblical prophets and apostles (the direct witness) and the church (the indirect witness) but also the broadest reaches of the world.[19]

Barth groups these multiple witnesses into two spheres, the inner sphere of the Bible and church and the outer sphere of the world."[20] As the direct witness, the Bible is the authoritative, permanent, and standard address to the church-community (although not the Word of God itself) when it is understood as a holistic narrative or an "abiding whole... in light of [Jesus Christ] its center."[21] The church depends on scripture's witness for its own and so "the church's word can be true only to the extent that it receives its shape in the school of the prophets and apostles, allowing itself to be continually tested, awakened, directed and corrected by their word."[22] Although the church must derive its witness from the Bible, this fact does not ensure that the church's words will be true or its interpretations correct. The "goodness and authority" of the church's indirect witness is "to be measured," not by whether it can point to disparate verses in scripture to legitimate its own claims, but by how effectively the community looks through the biblical witness to Christ in order to take the "form of His life," the one Word through which God speaks.[23]

Bonhoeffer and Barth both emphasize conformation to Christ and share an understanding that the church's true words must, like Christ, be an incarnate interconnection of word and deed; thus true words have the character of narrative more than abstract, principled proposition.[24] Barth calls biblical and ecclesial true words "parables of the kingdom" and he calls true words spoken from the outer sphere "secular parables."[25] His terminology serves as an analogy (but not a perfect fit) for our pluralistic context since he defines the spheres in such a way that neglects the presence and integrity of religions other than Christianity.[26] Thus, in order to do justice to our pluralistic context, we must read Barth's "secular parables" more broadly as any voice other than Christian. Although he does not explicitly locate religions other than Christianity onto the map of the inner and outer spheres, his christology makes room for the validity of particular theological points within other religious schemes. All human words, whether spoken inside or outside the visible Christian fellowship, are measured by the same criteria—by whether or not they demonstrate the reconciliation of God with human beings and human beings with each other and conform to the eschatological vision of the restoration of creation in the kingdom of God. The criteria for truth spoken outside the church is whether or not it may be christologically redescribed, as the apostle Paul does on Mars Hill, for example, when he quotes the Greek poet Epimenides of Knossos, who writes of Zeus, "For 'In him we live and move and have our being' " (Acts 17:28). As "secular" parables, true words spoken outside the church may appear disconnected from Christ; yet, as reflections of the one and only Word of God, they participate in what has been accomplished through his person and work.

While the biblical witness is the standard and permanent authoritative address to the church-community, secular parables are occasional, irregular, and context dependent.[27] They do not replace scripture but serve as a "commentary" on it for specific times and places. Barth says that secular parables will not "disturb or disrupt" the Bible's "general line but rather illuminate it in a new way at some particular point... If it is a true word... it will not lead [the church] away from Scripture but more deeply into it." For this reason, secular words "are not to be overlooked, let alone rejected." With great attention and openness, the church must cultivate a "readiness to hear, and to test, whether what is heard is perhaps a true word which Christianity cannot ignore as such." Certainly, the church-community will need carefully to discern the messages it receives from others. Still, "the more seriously and joyfully" the church recognizes the expansive lordship of Christ, "the more

[it] shall be able to receive true words from the secular sphere" as gifts "given by its Lord."[28]

Respect for Christ's inclusive lordship enables humble dispossession. The church-community that refuses to equate Christian faith with a static possession of right knowledge is empowered to respond to criticism as a body eager to confess and repent of faulty thinking and actions. Barth says, "When Christianity is called to repentance, it is a criterion that, no matter where the summons may come from or in what language, angry or offensive perhaps, it may be couched, it has to do with a true word addressed to it on the commission of its Lord."[29] In Bonhoeffer's language, repentance is the church's "religionless" response to the world's valid complaints against it. Through confession and repentance, the church communicates not that it is specially favored but that it humbly recognizes Christ alone as ultimate truth.

Evidence of the Conflation of Witness and Truth

The sociologist Robert Wuthnow argues in *America and the Challenges of Religious Diversity* that among the most serious questions U.S. citizens face today is how to navigate contemporary challenges of religious and cultural diversity.[30] A significant portion of his study examines how Christians understand themselves in the context of American diversity, specifically in the context of religious pluralism. While my project is not concerned with how Christians make sense of their identity and mission in relation to other religions, per se, Wuthnow's research validates my concern that sustained theological reflection on the exclusive and inclusive nature of Christianity is rare, if not completely lacking, within most Protestant churches in the United States.

Based on his "Religion and Diversity Survey," Wuthnow places the Christians he interviewed in one of two categories—as either "inclusive" or "exclusive"—and demonstrates that each group understands Christianity through one lens at the peril of the other.[31] "Inclusive" Christians tend to compromise basic tenets of orthodox faith, such as a central conviction of the ultimate significance of Christ, even as they take their Christian identity seriously, while "exclusive" Christians tend to fuel triumphalism as they settle into a rigid self-certainty based on a narrow conception of salvation, which makes sense of the world by erecting sharp distinctions between Christians and non-Christians in various realms of human life such as the religious, social, and political. Both groups miss the paradoxical nature of Christian exclusivity that includes within it the definitive inclusiveness that Bonhoeffer states above: Christ as Lord *of the world*—a lordship that is demonstrated through the expansive, *inclusive* work of cosmic reconciliation and redemption inaugurated by the cross. Moreover, instead of grasping the paradoxical unity of exclusivity and inclusivity, Wuthnow reports that many U.S. Protestants adhere often unreflectively to disparate and mutually invalidating claims; they permit a great deal of "mental bargaining" in order to maintain their beliefs, be committed

Christians, and live amid American diversity. Even for laypeople whose beliefs resist Wuthnow's categories—for Christians who are well aware of tensions in their faith, are willing to do the hard work of rethinking dominant assumptions, and desire a theological framework that overcomes a significant measure of unproductive ambiguity and bargaining, there are few resources for deeper theological reflection on the inclusive and exclusive nature of Christian faith.[32] My theology of public witness seeks to be such a resource.

While it would be presumptuous and naïve to maintain that every Protestant in the United States fits neatly into one of Wuthnow's categories, or that the two categories provide an exhaustive account that considers every possible denominational, subcultural, socioeconomic, or personal nuance, Wuthnow's research offers descriptions and a basic sense of some prevalent characteristics among Protestants today. These descriptions, in turn, are helpful for assessing the tensions inherent in the way various Protestants understand "witness." While many might agree that the notion is familiar and even central to Christian scripture and tradition, it has been emptied of theological depth and richness by the subcultures that most often appropriate the word. Fundamentalist and conservative evangelicals (two groups that constitute Wuthnow's "exclusive Christians") have flattened the notion by investing it with a narrow, technical meaning: "witnessing" has come to mean the task of verbal evangelism through which individuals are "led," in the words of these conservative subcultures, "to accept Jesus as Lord and Savior." In the New Testament, however, witness (Greek, *martyria*) encompasses a matrix of meaning, including but not limited to everything from John the Baptist prophetically preparing the way for Jesus, to God's self-revelation in Jesus, to the disciples' eyewitness accounts about Jesus (with the common thread being the orientation of the witness: most often the disciples and church-communities in the New Testament testify to the person and work of Jesus or to truths about God's kingdom revealed through Jesus).[33]

Both the exclusive and inclusive Christians Wuthnow studied tend to assume the technical meaning conferred on it by the conservative subcultures, although it is important to note that this use of "witness" does not exhaust the way North American Protestants understand the concept. One may hear, for example, Christians in progressive faith-based circles speak of witness in prophetic terms; they offer a "prophetic witness," meaning they take a stand on a peace or justice issue, though the particular issue and the stand they take are not clearly prescribed. They, too, tend to dilute the term of its theological (and in this case, christological) potency, for their ethical stand may be only loosely, if at all, articulated in relation to bearing witness to the person and work of Christ. The problem this poses for a nontriumphal public witness (the problem of reducing christology to ethics) will be explored in the following section, but first I examine the commonly held assumption that being a witness primarily means proclaiming the lordship of Christ through a verbal evangelism intent on "saving souls."[34] Because worries about triumphalism are directed most often at conservative Christians who have invested the notion with this specific meaning, and because inclusive as much as exclusive Christians tend to assume this meaning, I evaluate witness with this common appropriation in view.

Inclusive Christians' Tension and Compromise

According to Wuthnow's study, inclusive Christians exhibit ambiguity about the distinctive nature of Christian faith and thus show a great deal of ambivalence about the missionary impulse in Christianity. They do not "shy entirely away from the idea of being a witness," in that they are open to talking about Christianity to people who express interest in learning about their faith and tradition, yet they tend to offer a witness that reflects a general sense of God's love and acceptance, not one that reflects a God who is known in a particular way through the person and work of Christ.[35] Wuthnow writes:

> Inclusive Christianity is an intriguing amalgam of explicit theology and implicit cognitive strategies that have emerged in response to religious diversity. The explicit theology resembles what people hear in sermons in their churches and runs parallel to the ways in which many clergy have been trained: that the essence of Christianity is love and acceptance, that God is ultimately unknowable but is sufficiently loving and gracious to draw all people into the divine presence without respect to religious traditions, and that Jesus is an example of how to know and serve God.[36]

In other words, inclusive Christians tend toward the compromising inclusivity, mentioned above, that undercuts a specific witness to the one Word of God.

Inclusive Christians take their Christian identity seriously in the sense that they are skeptical of "spiritual shoppers" who draw haphazardly from a number of religions without committing themselves to one tradition; yet, they maintain openness to other religions by describing their commitment to Christianity in terms of preference and practicality.[37] One's cultural background influences what tradition one finds oneself within, and maintaining commitment to that one tradition allows an individual to benefit from accumulated experience and wisdom. Inclusive Christians find religiously varied expressions of spirituality equal in value and often describe their attraction to Jesus and the Bible as a matter of taste. Theology, doctrine, and tradition function as an organized structure where one may express this spirituality, but the claims about God underlying the theology, doctrine, and practice are not taken so seriously as to pose unsettling questions that the inclusive Christian must attend to in order to make sense of her life and faith. Jesus is central to the faith of inclusive Christians, who often mix orthodox claims (like Jesus is divine and God is triune) with explanations that compromise theological orthodoxy (like Christianity is "my way" of understanding God, and Jesus is a great spiritual leader). They regard the Bible as God's word, but tend to approach it not as an authoritative narrative conveying God's will but as a collection of spiritual truths and practical wisdom that makes more sense to them than other scriptures. Wuthnow rightly argues that this focus on "spirituality" reveals a definitively individualistic orientation toward Christian faith, and although inclusive Christians differ from "spiritual shoppers" by indicating the need to contend with sin, like "spiritual shoppers," faith is still valued primarily as a vehicle for self-actualization, with human subjectivity (as opposed to divine objectivity) directing one's relationship with God. Attention to individual spiritual expression often eclipses a robust account of divine judgment and the cost of Christian discipleship.[38]

Ambivalence over the distinctive nature of Christianity diminishes any perceived need for a particular witness and in turn affects the inclusive Christian's view of the role of church. Among those interviewed there was little to no sense that Christian life and faith requires the *ecclesia*. Although inclusive Christians offer reasons for being involved in church that are compatible with Christian teachings, Wuthnow shows that they are seldom justified theologically. Most speak in broad humanistic terms about feeling energized by fellowship or in practical terms about congregations providing a place to serve, but few, if any, mention the significance of the church as the body of Christ, for example. None of the inclusive Christians interviewed articulate that the church qua church is itself a witness given its particular identity and vocation in the world.

Exclusive Christians' Tension and Triumphalism

"Witness" is a more pronounced category for exclusive Christians who believe in the unique truth of Christianity. However, exclusive Christians also display the common misunderstanding that "witness" refers more to a task than an ecclesial identity and that the purpose of witnessing is to convert or convince the listener by promoting a system of belief or attempting to provide biblical or existential "evidence" for Christianity's truth. As previously mentioned, inclusive Christians often define "witness" in the same way, which is why many hesitate to do it. While the New Testament encourages church-communities to be ready to give "an accounting for the hope that is in you" (1 Peter 3:15), the witness of exclusive Christians does not rest on an inclusive hope in the expansive power of Christ's cosmic accomplishment. Rather, they aim to convert or convince because the stakes are high: "When they stop to think about people who follow religions other than Christianity, a substantial number of Americans say they have absolutely no doubt that only Christians will go to heaven," writes Wuthnow.[39] Similar to inclusive Christians, exclusive Christians in the United States tend to have an individualistic and subjective orientation toward Christian faith and thus lack a robust ecclesiology: Salvation is defined solely in terms of the individual's chosen beliefs, which in turn affect her eternal destiny. Inclusive and exclusive Christians differ, however, in that while the former have a broad yet theologically indiscriminate understanding of salvation, the latter have a Christ-centered and narrow conception of salvation. Exclusive Christians are not misguided in believing that Christianity makes exclusive claims about the person and work of Christ and about the historical uniqueness of Jesus. Rather, such Christians functionally deny Christ's expansive lordship when they reduce christology to epistemological claims that privilege human belief *about* Christ over divine accomplishment *through* Christ, thus neglecting the cosmological and ontological effects of Christ's person and work (which will be examined in chapter 4).

Like inclusive Christians, most exclusive Christians presume human subjectivity directs one's relation to God. The Reformed doctrine that maintains that faith is a divine gift that the individual is incapable of mustering on her own is not at play for many exclusive Christians; rather, most assert that individuals gain salvation by choosing Christ or by "making a decision for Christ."[40] The emphasis on "choosing" or "receiving" Christ resembles the decisions made by the first disciples in response to Jesus' command, "Follow me" (Matt. 4:19; Mark 2:14; Luke 5:27), yet exclusive Christians tend to understand this decision not in terms of discipleship based on the life and teachings of Christ but in terms of correct belief. As Wuthnow says, "Exclusive Christians are more likely to believe in the existence of a single set of right answers, which a person questions or tampers with at his or her peril."[41] They tend to deny that the Bible requires any significant interpretation—or *theology*—to be understood. Instead many Christians with an exclusivist worldview assert that they have complete confidence in the Bible's plain speech and commonsense application. Neglecting, for example, the universalistic impulses in Pauline apocalyptic thought (see chapter 4), exclusive Christians readily conclude that the Bible "provides proof" that only Christians will be saved.[42] Wuthnow says, "When asked why they think it is necessary to believe in Jesus to be saved, the most typical response of Christians with an exclusivist worldview is to refer to the Bible, not to elaborate or explain why the Bible says what it does, but simply to assert that the Bible is their source as if saying anything more would somehow diminish the flat fact of the Bible's absolute veracity."[43] Moreover, instead of being costly, "making a decision for Christ" leads to a prosperous life, personal fulfillment, and happiness. Wuthnow says, "Jesus becomes so attractive to the exclusive Christian that he or she finds it difficult to understand why anyone who has heard about Jesus—and most people have, they presume—would not immediately become a Christian."[44] Wuthnow argues that although Christians with an exclusivist worldview have absorbed liberalism's norms of freedom to worship, civility, and noncoercion, exclusive Christians display "a kind of arrogance, arrogance that is by no means restricted to exclusive Christians but that takes special form among them. This is the arrogance of believing that they are simply happier, less confused, more sure of truth, and better able to lead good lives than anyone else."[45]

Wuthnow's research also shows that many exclusive Christians exemplify a significant degree of ambiguity and tension about their exclusivist claims. Christians with an exclusivist worldview think that their faith demands they "witness to" or try to convert others, but most do not try fervently to do so. Underscoring that the way the exclusive Christian functions in the world does not correspond to the utter gravity of their soteriological claims, Wuthnow asks provocatively, "But how is it possible to believe that only Christians are saved, to look across the room at one's coworker...and murmur to oneself, "Such a shame, she's going to hell?" Wuthnow observes that exclusive Christians do not seem "sufficiently troubled by this fact to do much about it."[46] While some Christians remain undisturbed by this inconsistency, others articulate the tension between the weight of the claim and their hesitancy to "witness" or try to convert friends and family. For example, one woman who adamantly believes that "Jesus is the only way" (by which she means that people must "make a decision for Christ" to go to "heaven")[47] and that she should be telling all her friends this "so they won't go to hell" also is troubled by the attitude that "we are right and they are simply wrong." Wuthnow concludes that tensions like this result for many "in a tattered view of the world, the pieces of which are held together only by the loosest of logic, if that, and more commonly by retreating into a safe community of like-minded believers where people do not ask vexing questions."[48]

Triumphal Witness and the Zeal for Evangelism: Exclusive Christians on College Campuses

While Wuthnow's research features Christians who display a significant amount of tension over being a witness, Paul Bramadat's careful and compassionate ethnographic study of a university fellowship group provides a closer look at exclusive Christians who enact their zeal for evangelism. In *The Church on the World's Turf*, Bramadat, an "outsider" to evangelical Christianity, examines an InterVarsity Christian Fellowship (IVCF) chapter at the secular McMaster University in Southern Ontario. Bramadat provides the first and only book-length ethnography of any evangelical campus group, which serves, he argues, as a case study into the nature of evangelicalism in North America. The nondenominational IVCF chapter at McMaster comprises students mostly raised in conservative evangelical families whose denominational affiliations range from Baptist to Mennonite to Pentecostal to Presbyterian. The primary mission of this middle- to upper-middle-class, mostly white, student-led group is to witness to the lordship of Christ. In conjunction with a range of vital Christian practices—deepening one's own spiritual life through Bible study, fellowship, and prayer; loving the neighbor; exploring the "relevance of Christian faith to every issue of private life and public concern"; and affirming "vocations as full-time service to God"—the first official IVCF goal is "to witness to the Lord Jesus Christ as God incarnate and to seek to lead others to a personal faith in Him as Saviour and Lord; EVANGELISM IS A PRIME OBJECTIVE."[49] The purpose of witnessing—by which they mean verbal evangelism—is to foster conversion, normally through an emotional appeal to faith rather than an emphasis on the intellectual or theological foundations of the tradition.

Bramadat describes the students' soteriology in a manner similar to Wuthnow: "Almost all of the IVCF participants I met are fairly certain that non-Christians are going to suffer in hell for eternity and that Christians will receive the ultimate heavenly reward for what many members refer to as their 'obedience' to God."[50] Witnessing or "leading others to Christ" is a prime objective and is stressed at all IVCF meetings because it is the means by which nonbelievers find entrance into a salvific "personal relationship with Jesus Christ."[51] Mirroring Wuthnow's description of exclusive Christians, the IVCF students at McMaster focus on the individualistic and subjective quality of faith, asserting that everyone has equal access to salvation but must choose it (as they themselves have done). Students are trained in "friendship evangelism," the practice of sharing the good news of Christ's life, death, and resurrection in the context of relationships with non-Christians, and Bramadat describes this form of witnessing as "non-confrontational and, from what I have observed (and experienced myself as one of the 'friends'), quite sensitive to non-Christian convictions."[52] Students learn communication techniques focused on maintaining a dialogue, interpersonal skills like not interrupting when someone else is talking, and positive body language. Over the course of three years, Bramadat says that only in one instance did an IVCF student (a new member who had not been "enculturated in IVCF witnessing conventions") use an aggressive, patronizing, or condemning tone with him.[53]

Although the practice of "friendship evangelism" is intent on being respectful, Bramadat argues that the students' understanding of witness cannot help but relegate the non-Christian to the category of "other."[54] He says, "By requiring the believer to distinguish quite formally between self and others and to position himself or herself in the *role of disseminator of truth*, witnessing contributes significantly to IVCF students' distinct self-understandings, as well as to the definition of others. Witnesses by definition adopt a position of superiority... Consequently, witnessing requires adopting (to various degrees) a paternalistic approach to one's others."[55] Although witnessing often occurs for IVCF students in the context of friendship, the practice also entails a significant measure of calculation and maneuvering that, while not definitively manipulative, undermines the naturalness and equality of the friendship. Students are trained to recognize and take advantage of apt situations that may be transformed into "witnessing opportunities."[56] Rhetorical patterns among the IVCF members reinforce their sense of distinction and cultivate a dualistic understanding of the world. One is either "saved" or "unsaved," either an evangelical Christian or a "non-Christian." Exemplifying the type of arrogance Wuthnow describes, IVCF students refer to unbelievers compassionately yet paternalistically as "lost" or "sick." Bramadat writes, "The more one uses and hears this rhetoric, the more thoroughly it becomes integrated into one's imagination... This highly specialized rhetoric helps evangelicals construe their experience of the world in a manner which emphasizes the essential antagonism between their values and the practices of those in a fallen world."[57]

Given that students are trained in witnessing techniques and encouraged to think strategically about witnessing opportunities, a further weakness in the exclusive Christian's conception of witness is the methodological approach to salvation. In her study of the dominant cultural forces that contemporary Protestant sermons reinforce, Marsha G. Witten finds that pastors who preach about conversion tend to "codify" it. Witten argues that these pastors lay out procedures for "getting saved... like instructions in a recipe; they are prosaic, methodological, and direct... The steps enumerated are presented as the most straightforward, time- and labor-saving path towards the given end... Comply with the instructions, the language suggests, and conversion will follow."[58] Such systematizing makes conversion efficient for the individual and suggests that one has significant control over one's salvation. While Bramadat does not discuss IVCF students' understanding of conversion, the logic behind their witness complements Witten's description. The students and pastors studied both approach salvation with an attitude of productive efficiency. The witness of the exclusive Christian, in a certain sense, markets Christ and commodifies salvation through emotional appeals to personal fulfillment. Embedded within the exclusive Christian's logic and practice of witness is the implication that Christ can be bought and sold.

The inclusive and exclusive Christians that Wuthnow and Bramadat describe share the assumption that being a witness fundamentally entails converting and convincing others of one's own beliefs. This understanding of witness is solidified by an individualistic orientation toward Christian faith that both groups maintain and by the presumption that human subjectivity directs and defines one's relationship with God. Bonhoeffer's theology of revelation, in contrast, begins with divine objectivity in Christ and positions the church's witness not as a means but as an end in itself that participates in God's already accomplished reconciliation with the world as it takes the form of the crucified Christ. This account of witness challenges both the inclusive Christian's tendency to compromise a witness to the ultimate significance of Christ and the exclusive Christian's narrow conception of salvation and triumphalist presumption that she is, as Bramadat says, "the disseminator of truth."[59] Defining discipleship primarily by the task of guiding others to a belief that "Jesus is Lord" ironically does not do justice to the expansive lordship of Christ, because it neglects Christ's cosmological and ontological accomplishment (the very reason for Christian hope) that certainly cannot be constrained by subjective human belief.[60]

While many people are inclined to raise their finite and fallen theological, social, and political claims to the status of truth, the temptation is especially great for Christians who rightly discern that Christian identity and mission necessitates bearing witness to Christ. The exclusivist worldview of the conservative Christian described by Wuthnow and Bramadat conflates "witness" and "truth," relegating witness to a self-referential proclamation that declares that other people's eternal destinies depend on whether or not they "think like us" or "choose what we have chosen." Such a proclamation will drown out the profoundly better good news to which the church is called to witness in word and deed: Christ's person and work reveal that God is for human beings and God's being-for-others constitutes God's very essence; thus, Christ's loving lordship is of inconceivable consequence, immeasurably more than we think or imagine (Eph. 3:20).[61] The simultaneous inclusive and exclusive character of Christ's person and work challenges North American Christians to re-examine the content of the *evangelium* and the notion of witness itself.

■ ASSESSING THE PRESUMPTION THAT CHRISTIANS ARE STANDARD-BEARERS OF MORALITY

Thus far I have discussed "witness" but have not evaluated public witness per se. While the aim of the previous section was to challenge the way many Protestants understand the notion by examining the tendency to conflate witness with truth, this section considers a second tendency that may be recognized more prominently in the public arena: Protestant Christians in the United States emanate a belief that they are specially favored when their "witness" in the public square functions as the promotion of various moral standards. The "religious" character of Protestant faith is manifested publicly most often through a presumption that Christians are the standard-bearers of "right and wrong." While exclusivist Christians like fundamentalists and many evangelicals are more notorious for utilizing morality rhetoric, exclusive and inclusive Christians (ranging from fundamentalists to evangelicals to mainline Protestants) are all prone to ethical instead of christological ways of thinking that reduce the church's public witness to truth claims about morality or to ethical activity itself. Not only does focus on morality exude religious favor, which in our context furthers the unproductive polarization pervasive in social and political debates, it is also christologically shallow and an impediment to discipleship.

Beyond Morality: Bonhoeffer's Challenge to North American Christians

The presumption that Christ calls Christians to be standard-bearers of morality in public life follows logically from Bonhoeffer's penetrating critique, written after his second visit to the United States in 1939, that (white) North American theology is essentially ethics uprooted from christological ways of thinking about the identity and mission of the church.[62] Bonhoeffer's observations mostly stem from his stay as a Sloane Fellow at Union Theological Seminary in New York City during the 1930/1931 academic year and from his visits to the many churches that extended speaking invitations to him. According to Eberhard Bethge's biography, Bonhoeffer was frustrated that Union favored ethics courses analyzing contemporary American society over scriptural exegesis and dogmatics. His professor, Reinhold Niebuhr, criticized Bonhoeffer's seeming lack of concern for the political and the ethical, to which Bethge responds, "Privately Bonhoeffer was already concerned about the implications of the ethical concreteness of revelation, but he defiantly insisted that the correct premises had to come first and must remain independent of any premature interest in their ethical effects."[63] In other words, ecclesial ethics must arise from an understanding of the person and work of Christ, which in turn has implications for the identity and mission of the church as the body of Christ. Insisting the correct theological premises come first guards the church against placing political commitments before theological truth, against disguising political loyalties in theological garb.

Bonhoeffer also was disturbed by the sermons he heard preached in North American churches, with the exception of Black churches and in particular Harlem's Abyssinian Baptist Church, where Bonhoeffer became an active congregant. In his 1939 essay "Protestantism without Reformation" Bonhoeffer writes, "One may also say that nowhere is revival preaching still so vigorous and so widespread as among the negroes, that here the Gospel of Jesus Christ, the savior of the sinner, is really preached and accepted with great welcome and visible emotion."[64] In contrast, white American Christianity is characterized by "the neglect of christology."[65] The white church where Bonhoeffer heard Christ preached as the savior of the sinner in 1939 was the fundamentalist Broadway Presbyterian Church, but Bonhoeffer quickly learned that fundamentalist pastors were not proclaiming a Christ who turned the church's attention to the social needs of urban workers and to the activities Bonhoeffer came to admire in the Union seminarians who were influenced by the Social Gospel.[66] Bethge writes that Bonhoeffer's "stay in America reinforced his basic interest in the concrete reality of the word of God. His problem now was how this concreteness was to be developed."[67] Constructing a North American ecclesial ethic based on Bonhoeffer's thought that is at once christologically grounded and socio-politically concerned is the task of part II. There I argue that the church demonstrates and proclaims Christ to the world, not through an ethics that promotes the church's pious devotion and good works, but through an alternative, alien ethic conformed to the crucified Christ, who accepted divine judgment by taking responsibility for sin. As chapter 5 argues, Bonhoeffer disrupts the deep-seated presumption that Christians are called to be the standard-bearers of morality by defining the church as the body called "to live beyond the knowledge of good and evil" by exclusively accepting guilt and taking responsibility for sin. For now, I turn to the end of Bonhoeffer's 1939 essay for a summary of his rebuke of "the whole of contemporary American [white] Christianity," a critique that is just as relevant today:

> American theology and the American church as a whole have never been able to understand the meaning of "criticism" by the Word of God and all that signifies. Right to the last they do not understand that God's "criticism" touches even religion, the Christianity of the churches, and the sanctification of Christians, and that God has founded his church beyond religion and beyond ethics... In American theology, Christianity is still essentially religion and ethics. But because of this, the person and work of Jesus Christ must, for theology, sink into the background and in the long run remain misunderstood.[68]

Bonhoeffer observed that U.S. Protestants have little to no awareness that acceptance of God's criticism—God's present judgment on the Christian and the church—is essential for faithful discipleship and a redemptive public witness.

Barth's Radical Critique of Morality

Bonhoeffer learned to critique "religion" and "ethics" as that which evades divine judgment from Barth, whose early writings he first encountered in 1924 and for whom he became somewhat of an apologist, although a critical one, at Union. In a passage from a 1928 Barcelona lecture, delivered a few years after discovering Barth's *krisis* theology and a few years before arriving at Union, Bonhoeffer elaborates on religion and morality with words that sound, as Stephen Haynes says, as if they could have come directly from Barth's *Epistle to the Romans* or from his essays in *Word of God and Word of Man*.[69] Bonhoeffer says,

> Every knowledge, every moral claim before God, violates [God's] claim of exclusive honor, encroaches upon [God's] honor and majesty... Human knowledge of God remains precisely that: human, limited, relative, anthropomorphic knowledge. The human desire to believe remains precisely that: human desire accompanied by ultimately human goals and motives. The human religious path to God leads to the idol of our own hearts, which we have created in our own image. It is not knowledge or morality or religion that leads us to God—even religion is merely a piece of our own bodily nature, as Luther once put it—there is absolutely no path leading from human beings to God, for such a path is ultimately based on human capabilities... If human beings and God are to come together, there is but one way, namely the way from God to human beings. Here all human claims are at an end; God alone has the honor...
>
> Religion and morality contain the germ of hubris... the germ of pride, of arrogance. People think they have discovered deep within themselves something that does after all resemble the divine, or even is divine, something elevating us to the level of the divine, something giving us the right to make claims. In this sense, religion and morality can become the most dangerous enemy of God's coming to human beings, the most dangerous enemy of the Christian message of good news. Thus, the Christian message is basically amoral and irreligious, paradoxical as that may sound.[70]

In his collection of speeches, *The Word of God and the Word of Man*, Barth critiques morality's "religious" character and argues that focus on morality hinders the church from recognizing what Bonhoeffer later posits from prison: The church is not specially favored but rather belongs wholly to this world. Barth unmasks morality as the "religious righteousness" to which Christians adhere for a self-imparted or illusory sense of exoneration from present complicity in the sin and injustice that saturates us and our world. Barth says,

> We tear ourselves loose from the general unrighteousness and build ourselves a pleasant home in the suburbs apart—seemingly apart! But what has really happened?... Is it not our very morality which prevents our discerning that at a hundred other points we are... *blind and impenitent* towards the deep real needs of existence?... There seems to be no surer means of rescuing us from the alarm cry of conscience than religion and Christianity.[71]

Instead of the church immersing its conscience more deeply in the choppy waters of sinful reality and human suffering, Christians "take flight" to morality, where there is "a wonderful sense" of comfort, safety, and security from unrighteousness. Instead of belonging wholly to this world, the religiously righteous church denies that "the whole burden of sin and the whole curse of death still press heavily upon us" by virtue of the simple fact that the church exists in this fallen world.[72] Barth depicts religious righteousness as cowardliness that refuses to admit present complicity in specific sin and seeks false comfort in devotion to moral principles instead. He also exposes the sinister side of some religiously righteous Christians who so fear the breakdown of moral order that they turn their desires toward domination.[73] Acting as if it were "in possession of a gold mine and in the so-called 'religious values,'" religion positions itself as a "competitive power *over against* other powers in life, as an alleged superior world *over against* the world."[74] This religious lust for domination "permits itself simply everything," including God, whom it tries to tame, possess, manage, and put to use in an unwieldy world.[75] However, "religion's blind and vicious habit of asserting eternally that it possesses something, feasts upon it, and distributes it, must somehow cease," Barth says, if we are ever to have a humble, transformative Christian witness.[76]

Christians are "fixed firmly, very firmly, in human righteousness," because we presume that the Bible functions as our "source-book for godly living" when in actuality "it offers us not at all what we first seek in it."[77] Certainly, Christians may point to passages of instruction and illustrations of virtue, "but large parts of the Bible are almost useless" as a "moral curriculum," says Barth. Indeed, the Bible is often an "embarrassment in the school" of moral instruction. We may want scripture to present us with a blueprint plan that would eliminate the ambiguities of human life but, instead, it too often unsettles our certainties about right and wrong. Barth says, "At certain points the Bible amazes us by its remarkable indifference to our conception of good and evil. Abraham, for instance, as the highest proof of his faith desires to sacrifice his son to God; Jacob wins the birthright by a refined deception of his blind father; Elijah slays the four hundred and fifty priests of Baal by the brook Kishon. Are these exactly praiseworthy examples?"[78] Moreover, while the Bible gives a framework for considering the complex issues we struggle with in such areas as economics, marriage, education, technology, and international politics, it does not offer tidy solutions to particular human dilemmas. Instead, we find in the Bible "a strange new world" more attentive to the "doings of God" than the doings of humanity. Scripture's "chief considerations are . . . the establishment and growth of a new world," Barth says, characterized by God's righteousness, by "*God's* sovereignty, *God's* glory, *God's* incomprehensible love."[79]

Barth's first major work, his 1919 commentary on the *Epistle to the Romans*, was described as a bomb that dropped on the playground of modern theologians because in it he depicts this strange new world in which God is utterly distinct from human beings.[80] Nineteenth-century German liberal Protestant theology had made religious experience and human ethics the object of reflection and hence had attempted to "speak of God simply by speaking of man [*sic*] in a loud voice."[81] However, Barth says that proper theological thinking must begin with God's self-revelation and radical in-breaking, and only from this earth-shattering and decentered perspective may it speak accurately about human beings. He reads in Paul's letter to the Romans the radical statement that God alone is righteous: "There is no one who is righteous, not even one" (Rom. 3:9–18), and Barth's explosive discovery, which echoes Luther's Reformation insight four centuries earlier, has just as much revolutionary potential for North American Protestant churches today.

The claim itself that God alone is righteous would be one to which most, if not all, Protestants in the United States would intellectually assent given the foundational belief in divine grace, but Barth's unrelenting critique of morality situates Christians' present activity within this statement in such a way that binds the church to the rest of the world in radical solidarity. Religious Christians in the United States mistakenly confuse the New Testament lesson that in Christ human beings "become the righteousness of God" (2 Cor. 5:21) with the idea that faith in Christ fosters, enables, or ensures *human*, *religious* righteousness or right morality. Yet, Barth says that faith is never identical with morality; for, a faith that distinguishes Christians from other human beings is nothing but unbelief. Like the rest of humanity, the Christian lives "to the end of his days under the annihilating effect of the fall... There is no escaping the problem of life."[82] The Christian that "boasts that he possesses something" that enables human righteousness, "even if that something be" a decision of faith, the reception of grace, or a recognition of his own brokenness "still retains confidence in human self-justification" instead of recognizing, as Job does, that he is but "dust and ashes."[83] Barth says:

> Just as surely as the recognition of the sovereignty of God overthrows all confidence in human righteousness, it sets erect no other ground of confidence. [Human beings] are not deprived of one security, in order that they may immediately discover for themselves another... There is therefore no alternative for us but to remain under the indictment [that "there is no one righteous"]; and only he who remains here without any attempt to escape... is able to praise God in [God's] faithfulness.[84]

Further exemplifying the "infinite qualitative distinction" between God's righteousness and human righteousness, Barth cites Job, "Though I be righteous my own mouth shall condemn me; though I be perfect he shall prove me perverse" (9:11–21).[85] When Christians grant that their faith makes them moral, they "secretly identify" themselves with God and make the wholly otherness of God's righteousness "ordinary" and "harmless."[86] "If God is to us no longer what we are not," God's righteousness loses its "essential, sharp... ultimate significance" as divine power and initiation that breaks into our world of sin and suffering in order to make all things new.[87]

Repentance as an Alternative to Religious Righteousness

Barth's early theology provides the most devastating critique of "morality" or "religious righteousness" in twentieth-century thought. Although it includes a challenge to religious arrogance or self-righteousness, his critique is more radical and severe than that. His notion of divine crisis undermines confidence in *any* human activity—including Christian activity—and asserts instead the necessity that God's grave and loving judgment break into all past, present, and future action in order to make right and redeem. Barth's relentless critique of religious righteousness arguably leaves moral action and reasoning ineffectual, and thus begs for a constructive proposal for an ecclesial ethic that discredits human righteousness even as it offers a witness to Christ.[88] Arguably, the primary ethical category for Barth is witness; still, a witness faithful to the person and work of Christ necessitates a particular ethic—that of the cross.[89]

While Barth's unwavering critique of morality may seem to denounce all forms of ethics, his all-embracing contrast between *God's* righteousness and *human* righteousness provides a way to evaluate the church's public activity. His contrast implies more than a distinction between two fundamentally different agents, God who is capable of righteousness and we human beings who are not. It also suggests two diametrically opposing models of righteousness or contrasting ethical modes—one religious and one religionless, one an ethic of religious righteousness and the other an ethic of the cross, what I have defined more concretely as an *ethic of confession and repentance.*

Through my critical and creative engagement and extension of Bonhoeffer's theology in part II—specifically through an examination of the crucified Christ—I will define God's righteousness in Christ as repentance. Like Bonhoeffer, Barth also defines divine righteousness through the cross, as God's faithfulness and forgiveness in Christ, but he neither discusses if the church may enact God's righteousness nor depicts what it may mean for the church actively to "become the righteousness of God," as the Apostle Paul says.[90] Barth and Bonhoeffer both deem repentance the recognition that "in us dwells no good thing" and "that there is none good save God," with Barth's discussion of Job's tumultuous encounter with God falling under the heading "the goodness of God leads to repentance" (Rom. 2:4).[91] More importantly, each theologian evokes repentance as an alternative to (rather than correction of) religious exclusivity and arrogance. Barth says that repentance is "not the last and noble and most refined achievement of the righteousness of [human beings] in the service of God... What is pleasing to God comes into being when all human righteousness is gone, irretrievably gone... when [human beings] have abandoned all ethical and religious illusions."[92] Or as he says in *Church Dogmatics* IV/2, "Where, then, is the witness?—we might ask. The answer is that the witness of the disciple consists in the fact that he refrains from attesting his piety as such."[93] Barth's evaluation of crisis in his early theology, however, does not lead the church beyond the recognition that

God alone is good and toward a constructive ecclesial ethic based on God's righteousness in Christ.

Through my reading of Bonhoeffer I claim that the church actively demonstrates and animates God's righteousness in Christ in its particular context when it takes the form of Christ and, like Jesus himself, not only repudiates at all times and in all places any claim to goodness—"Why do you call me good?" Jesus says to the rich young man; "No one is good except God alone" (Mark 10:18)—but also actively accepts responsibility for the world's sin and suffering.[94] An ethic of confession and repentance is ironic in that it is an *ethic* manifesting *that God alone is righteous* and thereby signals a totally new mode of being and doing good, which disrupts religious sensibilities and prevalent presumptions in the United States about the character of Christian ethics.

Given both Bonhoeffer and Barth's theologies we may understand, then, the singular and normative character of God's righteousness using a method similar to our discussion about truth and witness: No one is righteous but God; yet, the church witnesses to Christ when it casts aside its moral certainty and takes the form of Christ's righteousness, the alien form revealed through the cross, characterized (as shown in chapter 5) by living beyond the knowledge of good and evil by taking responsibility for sin through repentance. Now, with this critique of morality in mind, it is important to gain a clear and concrete understanding of the extent to which American Protestants reduce Christianity to ethics and the manner in which various Christians do so.

The Reduction of Christianity to Ethics

The burden of this section is to convey how extensively Protestant imaginations are dominated by what Barth calls "religious righteousness" or "morality" and how pervasively Christianity is reduced to ethics in public discourse. To repeat, Protestant Christianity is vast and multifaceted; my intention is to provide neither an exhaustive account of how all Christians understand morality within the various subsets of Protestantism nor an exhaustive description of the subcategories themselves. Such a task would be a demanding project in and of itself. Instead, what follows are examples and descriptions gathered from sociological studies that examine Christian social and political engagement in a pluralistic democracy. These examples and descriptions, ranging across a spectrum of Protestantism, show how pervasively Christians make sense of their public engagement through the category of morality as opposed to Bonhoeffer's understanding of ethics as conformation to the incarnate, crucified, and risen Christ.[95]

For over a quarter of a century, public perception of Christian social and political engagement has centered on the "Religious" or "Christian Right," an extension and amalgamation of the Moral Majority (formally established in 1979 by the fundamentalist pastor Jerry Falwell) and the Christian Coalition (founded in 1989 by the Pentecostal pastor Pat Robertson).[96] Falwell's objective was to transform fundamentalist Christians who cared only about "saving souls" into "conservative Christians or evangelicals" who would reclaim the dual mission of individual evangelism and cultural influence that was lost after the 1925 Scopes Trial.[97] As "Bible-believing" fundamentalist, Pentecostal, charismatic, and evangelical Protestants, the Christian Right viewed themselves as morally elite citizens whose mission in the last decades of the twentieth century was to combat the immoral "godless elite" who advocated gender equality, gay rights, abortion rights, and teaching evolution in public schools.[98] In the name of "Christian values" and for the sake of saving America's moral order and experiment in democracy, the Christian Right sought political dominance, as illustrated in the triumphant words of a Christian Coalition activist: "We think the Lord is going to give us this nation back one precinct at a time."[99] With seven million strong in the 1980s, the Moral Majority became the most visible Christian lobby and fund-raising organization for the conservative Christian agenda.[100] In a 1997 interview celebrating Focus on the Family's twentieth anniversary, James Dobson summarizes the Religious Right's sense of mission in society: "As Christians, I believe we are obligated to defend the principles of morality and righteousness in this representative form of government."[101]

In "The Return of Jeremiad and the Specter of Secularization," Joshua Yates describes how the Religious Right continued to mobilize into the twenty-first century around a chronic fear of a secular coup d'état, even though any threat of totalizing secularization had been discredited empirically since the 1970s. Yates argues that "the mere specter of secularization" was enough to promote a "religious resurgence" expressed through "a specifically religious version" of the political jeremiad.[102] The "jeremiad" takes its name from the Bible's Lamentations of Jeremiah and was introduced into American history by Puritan preachers who warned their congregants to prepare for judgment day, "to *remember* the Covenant, *repent* from sin, and *return* to God," says Yates.[103] Over time the jeremiad altered its specifically ecclesial orientation and became a literary device used in public discourse throughout the last three centuries to bemoan various social and political ills. With the rise of the Religious Right, Yates says, "the Puritan brand of the jeremiad returned" but now as a political force battling "an encroaching godlessness," a threat so great because it undermines the nation's alleged Christian founding and stability.[104] By the 1990s the Puritan jeremiad had become institutionalized through the founding of numerous evangelistic para-church ministries, special interest organizations devoted to fighting abortion and promoting the traditional family, a burgeoning private school and homeschool movement, and a number of national and international media corporations.[105]

Arguably the peak of the Religious Right's influence has passed, symbolized by the death of Jerry Falwell in 2007. Still, public voices within the movement remain, even in what some describe as a post–Religious Right era, and the movement's impact on religious and political attitudes lingers on. There are numerous critiques of the Religious Right, but for our purposes it is enough to highlight that by institutionalizing the jeremiad and establishing their own organizations and empires as a competitive power, the Christian Right counters Bonhoeffer's appeal to belong wholly to this world.[106] Instead, the movement quite explicitly communicates that Christians are specially favored and exemplifies Barth's description of religiously righteous Christians who so fear the breakdown of moral order that they turn their desires toward domination. The Religious Right, using Barth's words, "takes [its] place as a competitive power *over against* other powers in life, as an alleged superior world *over against* the world."[107] It assumes a transcendent voice authorizing itself to "*remind*... fellow citizens about their covenantal heritage, call for national *repentance*, and *return* their country back to God."[108] As an outward directive, their call for moral repentance casts guilt on the nation instead of the church, thus, stripping repentance of its "religionless" character and reinforcing the message that Christians are specially positioned as judges over society. Broader society, in turn, recognizes this antagonism for what it is and resists Christian domination. The Religious Right's public persona has neither witnessed to the good news of divine-human reconciliation nor demonstrated reconciliation among human beings. Rather, it has bolstered the divide.

In *Christian America? What Evangelicals Really Want*, sociologist Christian Smith studies the way "ordinary evangelicals" view their role in public life in order to correct both the media's overly simplistic association of conservative evangelicals with the Religious Right and also the common misperception that politically visible evangelical leaders speak on behalf of most evangelicals. Evangelicals are actually the most internally diverse category of Protestant Christians in the United States whose commonality lies, Smith says, in their dedication to biblical authority, personal evangelism, and influencing culture through "Christian morality and values."[109] Smith argues that ordinary evangelicals should be distinguished from the dominant image of being "contentiously exclusivist" or "intolerant of diversity" based on intentionality. The average evangelical desires to influence the world not by gaining "control over the reign of politics" like the Religious Right but through "strategic relationships or personal influence."[110] Bramadat's study of the InterVarsity group reinforces this point. Although IVCF students care about shaping cultural trends, the connection between "witnessing" and public life is indirect; the average evangelical seeks to shape culture mostly by fostering individual conversion.[111] While strategies of political activists are "alarmist, pretentious, and exclusive," ordinary evangelicals (who have absorbed both uncritically and critically a good amount of liberalism's respect for individual autonomy and difference) emphasize "love, respect, mutual dialogue, aversion to confrontation, [and] tolerance for diversity of views."[112] Smith's study serves the important purpose of shattering stereotypes that demonize and homogenize well-meaning and diverse evangelical Christians.

Even so, the distance that many evangelicals keep from the Religious Right often has less to do with disagreement on the issues and more to do with ordinary evangelicals subordinating the political to the "spiritual." Unlike the theologies of

Bonhoeffer and Barth that emphasize the coming of the kingdom of God and the restoration of this world, the average American evangelical, according to Smith's study, does not see an organic theological connection between sociopolitical transformation and discipleship. Smith says that ordinary evangelicals believe that "the world's problems are ultimately rooted in spiritual problems residing in individual human hearts; that solving these problems involves an inner spiritual transformation that cannot be forced but only comes through voluntary personal religious conversion; and that the most effective strategy for real change, therefore, is personal evangelism."[113] At the same time, Smith says, evangelicals hold a "countervailing conviction" that there is value to Christian participation in politics. In fact, evangelicals are the most politically oriented of any North American Protestant group in that they believe Jesus calls them to be a public witness, to be "salt and light" to the world (Matt. 5:13–16).[114] This translates politically into the nondescript task of speaking "the truth" or being a "moral presence."[115] Although many evangelicals "disavow [the Religious Right's] aspirations towards cultural dominance," a kinship exists as evangelicals advocate for "'better morality'" in society, with the issues espoused by the Religious Right often animating their moral vision and swaying their vote.[116] The political practice of voting serves the priority of the spiritual when evangelicals elect to office other conservative Christians whose hearts (they reason) have already undergone the inner, spiritual transformation necessary for guiding society toward moral ends. Furthermore, although the political intensions of religious spokespersons and ordinary evangelicals are "worlds apart," Smith admits that when ordinary evangelicals "deploy their own cultural language to express their [moral] concerns," they, too, sound "exclusive and imperious to outsiders."[117]

Exasperated by the Religious Right's direct and indirect influence over many evangelicals, progressive evangelicals have been gaining a more unified political voice over the last decade most prominently through the ongoing leadership of Jim Wallis and his magazine *Sojourners*. In his study of the rise of contemporary progressive evangelicalism, Brantley Gasaway describes how a loose network of progressive evangelicals has existed since the early 1970s—as long as the first rumblings of the Christian Right—and cites the 1973 "Chicago Declaration of Evangelical Social Concern" as a document defining the hope expressed for a new era of Christian social engagement:

> We confess that we have not acknowledged the complete claims of God on our lives. We acknowledge that God requires love. But we have not demonstrated the love of God to those suffering social abuses. We acknowledge that God requires justice. But we have not proclaimed or demonstrated his justice to an unjust American society... We affirm that God abounds in mercy and that he forgives all who repent and turn from their sins. So we call our fellow evangelical Christians to demonstrate repentance in a Christian discipleship that confronts the social and political injustice of our nation.[118]

The leaders calling for a Christian repentance that would issue in the transformation of unjust social structures and the creation of a more egalitarian society included Ron Sider (professor at Eastern University and, among other works, author of the 1977 book *Rich Christians in an Age of Hunger*), John Alexander (editor of *The Other Side*, which ceased publication in 2004 due to financial difficulties), and Jim Wallis, who along with other students at Trinity Evangelical Seminary began publishing in 1971 the *Post-American*, which changed its name to *Sojourners* four years later. Over the past thirty years, the closest manifestation of a unified contemporary progressive evangelical movement has been the work of Wallis and *Sojourners*.[119]

In line with the Chicago Declaration's emphasis on repentance and social responsibility, in 1981 Wallis authored *The Call to Conversion*, a clear, detailed, and theologically sophisticated appeal for ecclesial conversion, especially in regard to poverty and war. Written by a pastor-activist who had been engaged in communal struggles against specific injustices, Wallis calls the book "a manifesto of Christian discipleship."[120] Because the book serves as a theological basis for Wallis's work, his publishers at HarperCollins suggested he revise and republish it, which he did in 2005 after the huge success of *God's Politics*, a book that I argue veers from the definitive theological grammar of repentance in the 1973 Declaration and his 1981 "manifesto" and succumbs to the dominant discourse centered on morality.

In the 2005 New York Times best seller *God's Politics: Why the Right Gets It Wrong and the Left Doesn't Get It*, Wallis claims to offer "a new vision for faith and politics in America" that cannot be reduced to a Religious Left (the Religious Right's opposition), because the vision is neither ideologically predictable nor partisan.[121] Critiquing both the Religious Right and the secular Left he says, "The religious and political Right gets the public meaning of religion mostly wrong—preferring to focus only on sexual and cultural issues while ignoring the weightier matters of justice. And the secular Left doesn't seem to get the meaning and promise of faith and politics at all."[122] Although Wallis wants "to transcend old divisions," he defines his movement in opposition to the Religious Right, which "has hijacked the language of faith to prop up its political agenda—an agenda not all people of faith support," an agenda Wallis counters with a similar morality rhetoric.[123] Instead of speaking a genuinely alternative language of christological conformation that would direct and reshape the church's identity and mission in society, Wallis veers from the Chicago Declaration's central call to repentance and instead offers a "new moral politics," one that advocates "consistent moral ground" and a "return to the moral center."[124] Wallis has not discarded the Christian call to repentance; in fact, a handful of times in *God's Politics* he promotes "humility," "self-reflection," "self-criticism," and "accountability" over against "triumphalism" and "self-righteousness."[125] Still, our theological critique of morality shows that repentance is not a correction or broadening of morality but the opposite of morality, an expression that God alone is righteous. In *God's Politics*, Wallis does not challenge the rhetoric of morality; rather he plays right into the dominant discourse. He critiques the 2004 election's single-issue "moral values voter" and asks, "Where is the real debate in the moral values conversation?... It's time to spark a public conversation in this country over what the 'moral values' in politics should be—and how broadly and deeply they should be defined."[126]

By broadening morality to include progressive social issues, Wallis offers not a theology (not a christology or ecclesiology) that fundamentally disrupts Christian (mis)understandings of public witness; rather, he simply adds a "fourth [political] option." The first option is to be conservative across the board "from cultural, moral, and family concerns to economic, environmental, and foreign policy issues." The second option is to be liberal in all areas; the third is to be libertarian; and the fourth is to be "conservative on issues of family values, sexual integrity and personal responsibility, while being very progressive, populist or even radical on issues like poverty and racial justice."[127] While Wallis's Jesus in *God's Politics* is not a "*selective* moralist," he is still a moral systematician who provides the Christian with "moral response[s]" to all contemporary social and political issues, including war and peace, the environment, poverty, and economics.[128] Wallis's public discourse on theology and politics rests on scriptural mandates and, with several thousand references from the prophets and from Jesus legitimating his priority of poverty and justice issues, he would win any proof-texting match with the Religious Right.[129] Still, the method of validating a specific political position with a loose tie to a general biblical mandate fosters shrill moralism whether in the form of a liberal prophetic stance against the powers or a conservative Christian utilization of the powers.[130]

Wallis's commendable intent in *God's Politics* is to call Christians to a prophetic faith that cares about all matters of justice, proposes solutions, and offers mediations between the false dichotomies that the current political landscape fosters, such as the debate about whether poverty is an individual *or* a social responsibility, and he uses the prophets as exemplars of social vision: "The biblical prophets were never just complaining; they were imagining a newer world," he says.[131] In recent years, *Sojourners*' Web-based advocacy network has helped shape the vision of a better world and has brought needed clarity and voice to various issues that should concern people of faith. Moreover, Wallis's dependence on morality discourse (which may have begun as a rhetorical strategy against the Religious Right) is less severe in his subsequent book, *The Great Awakening: Reviving Faith and Politics in a Post–Religious Right America*, where he now primarily emphasizes the "moral" dimension of an issue as a corrective to special interests and power politics.[132] Although his 2008 text has a structure more similar to *God's Politics* than *Call to Conversion*, in a sense it shares more with the latter in that he draws on a deeper well of theological, biblical, and historical sources, defining the "moral center" in terms of the common good, for example. A progressive evangelical public witness inspired by Wallis has much to offer; nevertheless, my concern is that when Wallis relies on the rhetoric of "morality," as he continues to do in media sound bites, for example, he only weakens the prophetic, iconoclastic energy of the church's witness and risks positioning progressive evangelicals as one more side in the battle over morality.[133]

Mainline Protestants may at first seem to fall outside the scope of our analysis, since mainline clergy rarely use morality as a political clarion call in a manner similar to either Falwell or Wallis.[134] We may be tempted to view morality discourse only as a product of American "conservative" fundamentalist and evangelical Christianity, but Barth pins his critique of ethical religion on modern liberal Protestant theology, which many mainline churches inherited through the education of their pastors. As we saw, for Barth, ethical religion is a futile attempt to interpret God on the basis of human experience, to confine God to our own human constructs instead of remaining faithful to divine revelation—to the picture of Christ revealed in scripture. In other words, the moral religion of the fundamentalist or evangelical Christian actually manifests modern liberal theology's influence over all of North American Protestantism. In this regard "conservative" and "liberal" Christians in the United States have more in common than they recognize, as Bonhoeffer suggests in his critique of North American "Protestantism without Reformation."

Mainline denominations (the six largest being the United Methodist Church, the Evangelical Lutheran Church in America, the Presbyterian Church USA, the Episcopal Church, the American Baptist Churches in the USA, and the United Church of Christ) are commonly regarded as "liberal" due to their modern liberal theological heritage, their open hermeneutic to scripture that lends itself to more diverse theological perspectives within denominations and congregations than is often afforded to conservative churches, and their receptiveness to social-structural concerns like the plight of "the poor."[135] For most of the twentieth century and into the twenty-first, many of these denominations have had a presence on Capitol Hill through denominational advocacy offices that partner both with nonprofits and special interest groups to promote socially liberal policies concerning the environment, international economics, First Amendment rights, and social welfare.[136] However, the perception that mainline Christians are definitively politically liberal is misleading. If a mainline congregation even knows it has an advocacy office, the average local congregant often thinks the denomination's progressive Capitol Hill counterpart does not represent her political convictions. Mainline Christians vote Republican as much as Democrat, although they are often moderate, pro-choice Republicans.[137]

Robert Wuthnow and John H. Evans's volume, *The Quiet Hand of God: Faith-Based Activism and the Public Role of Mainline Protestantism* describes mainline Christian presence in public life after 1970 and shows that "mainline congregations' public presence is of a different sort" than the Protestant subgroups just discussed.[138] Their distinct presence is not primarily a function of being more liberal; rather, mainline Christians often have a "quiet" presence in politics due to the fact that these "historically old-line Protestants" blend into mainstream culture.[139] While many conservative Christians "have adopted a kind of oppositional identity to mainstream American culture" and have maintained this identity as a persecuted people even as they have become a dominant power and presence (giving them "a sense of being special, of having certain rights that need to be protected, and of needing to be vocal about their views in American politics"), mainline congregants have acted primarily as stewards of civil society, thus shaping and upholding the status quo.[140] Wuthnow writes that although mainline Protestants are just as diverse as other Americans, the image of these Christians predominantly being wealthy "WASPs" (white Anglo-Saxon Protestants) is not altogether inaccurate; for, the historically mainline denominations exhibit American privilege and power in their membership. Mainline Christians hold great influence in the broader community, with most members comprising the more privileged sector of society. Their individual and denominational resources are considerable, given their financial capital and social, educational, and professional networks, and many mainline Christians are themselves influential community leaders.[141] Like evangelicals, mainline congregants are also deeply engaged in public life. Yet, while evangelicals are the most likely Christian group to take a uniform side in partisan politics, mainline Protestants engage in more local civic activity than any other Christian demographic. Still, "mainline civic distinctiveness is less a product of any internal features of mainline religion and more a product of the position traditionally held by mainline congregations within communities' civic hierarchies."[142] In other words, the sociopolitical activity of most mainline Christians is less a result of their trying to enact a particular Christian witness as church-community and more a result of their being responsible individual citizens who already fully participate (and have a socially and politically efficacious voice) in "the workplace, in higher education, in discussions of scientific and technological development, and in activities of community organizations."[143] Many mainline congregations lack intentional theological reflection about the church's identity and mission as *church-community* in society.

Local mainline congregations manifest a religion of ethics when, absent sustained theological reflection, the church body functions primarily as a pool of volunteers. Given congregants' civic mindedness, many mainline churches operate as highly organized entities that can readily "mobilize volunteers" for community soup kitchens, homeless shelters, and day care centers.[144] Both religious and secular Americans expect these churches to be "springs of volunteerism, community resources, and civic skills" for nonprofits and community organizations, and thus expect Christians to be active in society in "fairly innocuous" ways.[145] Mainline Christians often cite the scriptural mandate in Matthew 25:40 to care for "the least of these" as the spiritual impetus behind their social activity, but sustained theological reflection is needed for mainline Christians to go beyond society's expectation to bandage wounds.[146] In *Congregations in America*, Mark Chaves shows that like other Christian congregations, mainline Protestants mostly engage "in activities that address the immediate, short term needs of the recipients for food, clothing, and shelter" while "rarely bring[ing] the needy into the life of the congregation" in such a way that radically transforms the church's identity and mission or the surrounding society.[147]

Furthermore, while mainline churches have a reputation for social commitment, social ministries normally fall on a handful of highly motivated individuals who on their own initiative commit themselves to certain issues. Even the most active congregations spend less than 3% of their total budget on outreach work.[148] This is not to devalue the important social service done by mainline and other congregants; as Chaves says, "A very small amount of actively involved [congregants] still add up to a substantial amount of activity" in the nation as a whole.[149] The greater point, though, is that the public engagement of mainline Christians rarely gets beyond ethical religion and its innocuous volunteerism, which introduces a minority of Christians in a local body to the sufferings of the world without penetrating the comfortable lifestyle and self-interest of the church as a whole. The average clergyperson reports that the top priority of the church is the congregants' spiritual well-being, which includes the creation of a "family-like atmosphere" or "fellowship activities" that meet "the spiritual and social needs of their own members"—the implication being that the spiritual needs of Christians can somehow be divorced from the church's participation in God's healing movement in the world.[150] Thus, the average mainline congregation qua congregation rarely enacts a particularly Christian, transformative public witness that communicates Christ's being for others. Although the mainline churches' "quiet" presence does not generate the clamor of religious exclusivity in the public sphere that we hear from some fundamentalist and evangelical Christians, both "conservative" and "liberal" Protestants in the United States suffer from lack of theological reflection on what it means to be a church that defines its identity and mission in terms other than those delineated by ethical religion.

■ THE PRIMACY OF FORM FOR CHRISTIAN WITNESS

Bonhoeffer's prison theology provides a helpful lens through which we may reorient witness away from the triumphalist and compromising tendencies above. He suggests that while witness entails both word and deed, of primary importance is the character of the church's public engagement—its form or mode of being in the world—which correlates more with the church's *action or incarnate presence* in the world than with its public speech. Bonhoeffer argues that the church witnesses to Christ by taking the form of Christ in the world.[151] The church conforms to the crucified Christ, I argue, through repentant activity, with the language of confession of sin serving to complement public engagement when speech becomes necessary. In other words, public witness is demonstrated first through action, with speech that is intelligible in a pluralistic society arising out of this action.

In his first letter introducing the idea of a religionless Christianity, Bonhoeffer reflects on Christian language in a world come of age and worries that Christian speech has become unintelligible to society at large. "What keeps gnawing at me is the question, what is Christianity, or who is Christ actually for us today?" He continues:

> The age when we could tell people that with words—whether with theological or with pious words—is past... What does a church, a congregation, a sermon, a liturgy, a Christian life, mean in a religionless world? How do we talk about God—without religion, that is, without the temporally conditioned presuppositions of metaphysics, the inner life, and so on? How do we speak (or perhaps we no longer even "speak" the way we used to) in a "worldly" way about "God"?[152]

Similarly, in a sermon he wrote in prison for his godson, "Thoughts on the Day of Baptism of Dietrich Wilhelm Rüdiger Bethge," Bonhoeffer worries that Christian language has become profoundly impoverished and is bound to lose its transformative power unless the church alters its "form"—the shape it takes—in the world.[153]

Given that Bonhoeffer spoke more about a nonreligious interpretation of biblical concepts than about "religionless Christianity" itself, on first reading, it is difficult to know whether Bonhoeffer's prison theology is more concerned with the form the church takes in the world or with the language of the church's proclamation.[154] He uses the phrases "religionless Christianity" and "a nonreligious interpretation" in an overlapping manner, even though the former connotes Christian practice while the latter suggests that Bonhoeffer's chief concern is the efficacy of language. Early studies of Bonhoeffer's prison theology tended to separate practice and proclamation: the English-speaking world became fascinated by the idea of practicing Christianity without "religion" while German scholars analyzed the question of hermeneutics in Bonhoeffer's letters, and argued that, like Rudolf Bultmann (whom he was reading at the time), Bonhoeffer was interested in reconceptualizing Christian faith (or demythologizing the Bible) in order to make Christianity acceptable to modern culture's sophistication and rationality.[155] In doing so, both sets of scholars missed Bonhoeffer's principle interest in the church faithfully bearing witness to Christ. The nonreligious interpretation Bonhoeffer sought was not a language fashionable for the contemporary moment.[156] Reflecting years before prison on form and speech, Bonhoeffer wrote, "Certain forms and traditions will indeed have to be given up so that we may perhaps attain to more felicitous and freer forms... But a radical cure, such as deleting the words cross, sin, grace, etc. from our vocabulary will accomplish nothing."[157] For Bonhoeffer, concern over form contextualizes and concretizes the hermeneutical task. The church's mode of being in the world is the prime concern for witness because the manner in which the church is present and active in public life determines whether the church's proclamation is intelligible to, and liberating for, humanity.

Still, while form is primary, Bonhoeffer is concerned with *both* words and deeds, with both a renewed verbal proclamation of the gospel based on fresh christological interpretations of biblical concepts and a practice of faith derived from the church's renewed presence within the world. In "Thoughts on the Day of the Baptism," Bonhoeffer says:

> But we too are being thrown back all the way to the beginnings of our understanding. What reconciliation and redemption mean, rebirth and Holy Spirit, love of one's enemies,

> cross and resurrection, what it means to live in Christ and follow Christ, all that is so difficult and remote that we hardly dare speak of it anymore. In these words and actions handed down to us, we sense something totally new and revolutionary, but we cannot yet grasp it or express it. This is our own fault.[158]

Although Bonhoeffer wants to restore Christian language and meaning, in this same baptismal sermon, he suggests that given the failures of religion in a world come of age, Christian witness cannot be repaired through verbal proclamations of faith but only through *Beten und Tun des Gerechten*, that is, through "prayer and the doing of justice" among human beings.[159] The church that refused to take the form of the crucified Christ during the horror of the Nazi reign in turn forfeited its capacity to proclaim the revolutionary and redemptive character of its faith.

The phrase *Beten und Tun des Gerechten* may be connected with a concept Bonhoeffer mentions twice in letters dating from the same period: *Arkandisziplin* (the discipline of the secret).[160] While reflecting on religionless Christianity, Bonhoeffer suggests that this ancient practice of concealing liturgical practices from public view takes on renewed importance for modern Christians. In classical Christianity, the arcane discipline protected the mysteries of Christian faith from being misunderstood and profaned by the unbaptized who did not have the hermeneutical benefit of being initiated properly into the tradition. In his intriguing argument for the concealment of Christian identity in contemporary public life, Jonathan Malesic contends that although Bonhoeffer's use of *Arkandisziplin* drew from the ancient concept as understood by church fathers like Cyril of Jerusalem, Bonhoeffer expands the notion to include protecting the profaning of Christian identity and language *from Christians themselves*, who corrupt and compromise the faith by using it, or allowing it to be used, for partisan politics and social privilege. Earlier scholars studying Bonhoeffer's notion of *Arkandisziplin* agree that Bonhoeffer exhorts the church to care for its own terms and to guard its language against exploitation, although they do not take the argument as far as Malesic does and claim that Christians should conceal their *identity* in public. Following Eberhard Bethge's early interpretation, these scholars tend to describe "prayer and righteous action" as counterpoints or two sides of a dialectic. Prayer (outside public scrutiny) represents the "discipline of the secret," they argue, while righteous action, or doing justice, refers to the church's proper public engagement.[161]

By deeming confession unto repentance a nontriumphal witness, my theology of public witness offers a new appropriation of Bonhoeffer's phrase *Beten und Tun des Gerechten* for the North American context—one that does not rest on the kind of radical Christian silence that Bonhoeffer suggests Christians have cornered themselves into in a world come of age. In my theology of public witness, confession of sin correlates to prayer (to the liturgical practice that makes space for a church-community to hear God's judgment and be convicted of its complicity in a specific social sin) while repentant action in public life correlates to doing justice. Although Malesic has shown convincingly that Bonhoeffer places greater importance on the notion of the secret discipline than may be inferred from his two brief references in prison, when taken as a whole Bonhoeffer's theology demonstrates that the church need not be silent in the public square and can even speak a particularly Christian language *if* that language arises from its conformation to the crucified Christ. Because the loudest voice and the most conspicuous Christian presence in the public square since the late 1970s has been triumphalistic expressions of the Religious Right, a particularly Christian language of confession of sin and a distinctive public identity based on repentant action would be a welcomed corrective. Apropos of words written for a baptism, I suggest there is something "totally new and revolutionary" in a public witness based on the traditional words and acts of confession and repentance. As shown in part III in the ethnographic study of the Eleuthero community, verbal confession arising from acts of repentance fits Bonhoeffer's description of a "new language" simultaneously traditional and radical that "shocks people," is "liberating and redeeming," and proclaims God's "peace with humankind" and the coming of God's kingdom.[162]

Bonhoeffer also writes about the relation between Christian conformation and proclamation in the 1932 essay "The Nature of the Church." He says, "The first confession [of faith] the Christian congregation makes before the world is its action. It interprets itself."[163] While there is no reason to assume Bonhoeffer has repentance in mind, confession unto repentance is indeed an action that confesses faith in Christ or "interprets itself," for confession of faith in the lordship of Christ is inextricably connected to confession of sin. Put more simply, confession of Christ's lordship happens again and again when the church confesses its present complicity in sin. As part II will show, true recognition of sin leads to acts of repentance that prepare the way for the kingdom of God, for those spaces within which peace, justice, healing, and reconciliation reign through the lordship of Christ. Christians enacting repentance in public life by taking responsibility for sin and suffering consequently gain the capacity to proclaim the word of reconciliation and redemption with transformative efficacy. Of primary importance is that the church's presence in public life be conformed to Christ's mode of being in the world. Part I has suggested that confession unto repentance serves as the ecclesial mode of being in the world that faithfully reflects Christ in a pluralistic society. Part II now grounds this claim theologically.

PART TWO

A Theology of Public Witness Based on Bonhoeffer's Thought

3 Christ's Public Presence

The Foundation and Form for Ecclesial Witness

A theology of public witness based on Bonhoeffer's thought begins with Jesus Christ. Even though his 1933 lectures, originally published in English as *Christ the Center*, represent his only explicit study of christology, the whole of Bonhoeffer's thought from his dissertation, *Sanctorum Communio*, to his *Letters and Papers from Prison* may be understood as a christology motivated by his interrelated interests in ecclesiology, this-worldly discipleship, and Christian ethics.[1] Specifically, a theology of witness based on his writings begins with christology because the church must know to what—or more accurately as Bonhoeffer would say, to *whom*—it witnesses. Certainly, in order to have theological significance witness need not point directly or only to Jesus, for witness is always already happening in the life of God. The Spirit witnesses to the love of the Creator and Redeemer; Jesus witnesses to the Father, and so on.[2] Similarly, human beings may witness other human beings in a theological sense by *seeing* them, by recognizing them as "occasions" of gratitude and joy or as exemplary models of faith and courage.[3] Bonhoeffer's christocentricism is helpful for this project, though, given the driving question of how to witness to the lordship of Christ in a nontriumphal manner. While the absence of a developed pneumatology or a thoroughly systematized Trinitarian theology in Bonhoeffer's thought is noteworthy, his rigorous christocentricism is an asset in that it probes theological questions and instigates insights that might otherwise be neglected.[4] Furthermore, a theology of witness begins with christology because, as argued in the previous chapter, public witness must be understood as the concrete *form* the church takes in the world. Witness to Christ is conformation to Christ. This chapter lays the christological foundation for the book's main argument: The church witnesses to Christ when it takes the form of the humiliated, crucified God, the form I define as acceptance of guilt, or confession of sin, unto repentance.

Because the church's public witness faithfully points to Christ by conforming to Christ's manner of being in the world, the primary task of this chapter is to examine the incarnate God's this-worldly presence. To do so, I first return to Bonhoeffer's prison writings penned during the horror of the Nazi regime, when the dwindling resistance of the Confessing Church caused his thinking about a redemptive witness to be a matter of utmost urgency. There, in his reflections surrounding the possibility of a religionless Christianity and a nonreligious interpretation of biblical concepts, he suggests that repentance be reinterpreted christologically, thus inviting reflection on the possibility of understanding Jesus' public presence in terms of repentance. Next, I place my initial reflections about a christological reinterpretation within a larger conversation about the unanticipated or "hidden" character of God's revelation. I examine a dominant notion in Bonhoeffer's 1933 christology lectures—Christ as hidden in humiliation—and ask in what manner is Christ hidden in the world and in what manner humiliated? Finally, I turn to Bonhoeffer's *Ethics*. Whereas his early christology lectures center on the hidden character of God's revelation in Christ, his later writing, *Ethics*, intended to be his magnum opus, emphasizes the glory of the incarnation in the midst of reality. His early and later thought are interwoven in that *Ethics* shows that it is God's glory to accept guilt. In this way, God is visible and present in the world as the humiliated one who takes sin upon Godself. In doing so, God's belonging to and being for humanity is revealed.

While the term "christology" often points to an examination of the metaphysics of the incarnation or the mode of hypostatic union, my study of Bonhoeffer's christology will not be preoccupied with these dogmatic issues. Bonhoeffer himself shows that these kinds of inquiries seek after the wrong question. In his 1933 lectures he says that the proper christological question is not "How are you possible?" but "Who is this God-human?"[5] Just as Martin Luther emphasized the humanity of Christ in a manner distinct from most theologians before him by risking radical theological claims that result from steadfastly maintaining Christ's humanity and divinity "without division," so Bonhoeffer bypasses metaphysics and takes the Chalcedonian formula as a given, not a problem to be solved, in order to get to the heart of Christian faith and witness. In the incarnation God involves Godself in the world and in sinful flesh to such a degree that God really embraces powerlessness. Of ultimate significance for my study of Christ's public presence is that the manner in which God makes Godself present is thoroughly human. Christ embraces the condition of human guilt in solidarity with real human beings in order to redeem.[6]

The church's public witness, when conformed to the crucified Christ, centers on the christological fact that Christ not only dies for humanity's sin but publicly lives with our sin. Thus, in order to understand what it means to be conformed to the crucified Christ, the church must not only look to the cross but also to Christ's this-worldly existence. The crucifixion discloses what was always already happening in the life of Christ, who, as we will see, took the likeness of sinful flesh, was baptized with sinners in response to the call to repent, refused to be called good, and instead accepted responsibility for sin. The cross, then, is not as much the pivotal moment for Christian witness as the remarkable disclosure and logical culmination of what Christ's public existence already reveals: God in Christ draws human guilt into divine life, where it is then overcome.[7] The radicality of Bonhoeffer's christology, in turn, drives his ecclesiology. Bonhoeffer's christology compels the church to acknowledge that if this is what God does—if *God* takes responsibility for sin, suffering, and injustice—then the church, as the body of Christ, must do the same. The church witnesses to the incarnate, crucified, and risen Christ and participates in the redemptive powerlessness of God in the world, when it takes responsibility for sin through concrete acts of repentance.

■ REINTERPRETING REPENTANCE CHRISTOLOGICALLY

In prison correspondence dating from April 30, 1944, through August 1944 to his closest friend, Eberhard Bethge, Bonhoeffer asks how the church demonstrates Christ's loving lordship over the world in a changing historical situation. As we have seen, he introduces the correlated phrases "religionless Christianity" and a "nonreligious interpretation" of biblical concepts as a possible practice and proclamation that would convey Christ's presence in and for the world. Although he was not able to develop a model of religionless Christianity and a nonreligious interpretation of biblical concepts because of the limitations of his imprisonment and his resulting execution, it is clear from his first letter addressing these ideas that Bonhoeffer thinks the church's witness necessitates faithful adherence to Christ's contemporaneity and concrete presence in the world. He says, "What keeps gnawing at me is the question, what is Christianity, or who is Christ actually for us today?"[8] He continues by asking how "a church, a congregation, a sermon, a liturgy, a Christian life" can be enacted in such a way that communicates Christ's being for the world, and he asks a week later how "the concepts of repentance, faith, justification, rebirth, and sanctification" find greater meaning when understood in a "'worldly' way—...in the sense of John 1:14," in other words, christologically, in light of the incarnate God.[9] In prison, Bonhoeffer does not develop a proposal examining the role repentance plays in Christ's own identity and mission, but the ingredients for a christological reinterpretation may be found in his prior writings. Guided by the prison reflections into an examination of these texts, this chapter offers a "nonreligious" christological interpretation of repentance, which serves as a foundation for public witness.

Theology That Sparks Reformations

The triumphalistic tendencies of Christian public presence today require a renewed shift in our thinking about repentance, one that will reform the church's public witness and shape its redemptive activity in a pluralistic society. Repositioning and reinterpreting repentance as central and nonnegotiable for Christian life and thought has proven, historically, to be a catalyst for needed reformations. The document that sparked the entire Protestant Reformation begins with Martin Luther's redescription of "repentance." Similarly, Karl Barth, the great twentieth-century theologian, challenged and changed the course of modern theology by making *krisis*—the divine judgment and promise that makes human repentance and new life possible—a corrective to the prominence liberal theology gave to human goodness, experience, and reason.

Bonhoeffer stands within the tradition of these two thinkers whose radical theological insights fostered new foundations for understanding the astounding message of scripture; for, his expansive use of such terms as "repentance" and "acceptance of guilt" find precedence in Luther and support in Barth.[10] Luther opens his Ninety-Five Theses, officially titled "Disputation on the Power and Efficiency of Indulgences," with a radically fresh understanding of repentance that hearkens back to the New Testament.[11] His first thesis reads, "When our Lord and Master Jesus Christ, said, 'Repent' [Matt. 4:17], he willed the entire life of believers to be one of repentance."[12] Luther's thesis at once denigrates the then-prevalent practice of penance and elevates repentance to the status of faith itself. As we will see, Bonhoeffer makes the same move in his prison theology when he equates repentance with discipleship. Repentance is "allowing oneself to be pulled into walking the path that Jesus walks," he says.[13] By defining repentance as discipleship, Luther and Bonhoeffer each insist that, in Luther's words, "inner repentance is worthless" unless it manifests in "various outward" forms.[14] Likewise, Bonhoeffer and Luther both view confession of sin or "daily contrition and repentance" to be the continual outworking of one's baptism and the definitive activity of the Christian.[15] They both insist that the guilt Christians confess be all-encompassing, although Bonhoeffer takes this idea a step farther than Luther. Luther says that Christians are to "acknowledge the guilt of all sins, even the ones we are not aware," while Bonhoeffer says explicitly that, as the contemporary manifestation of Christ, the church-community accepts the guilt of the whole world.[16] Before the world, the church proclaims *mea culpa, mea culpa, mea maxima culpa.*[17] Bonhoeffer's description of accepting guilt or bearing sin is rooted in Luther's theology, and, like Luther, Bonhoeffer derives the concept from christology.[18]

Bonhoeffer's suggestion in prison that "repentance" may be interpreted nonreligiously and may be christologically redescribed finds support in Karl Barth's theology. Behind Bonhoeffer's fascinating proposal is the implication that the work of the sinless Christ may be understood as divine repentance, through which the church is then called to participate. By deeming Christ's work "divine repentance" I am not suggesting that the problem of sin has its origin in God. I mean that God repents in Christ in accordance with the fallen human nature Jesus willingly bears. In *Church Dogmatics* IV/1 Barth connects repentance with the work of Christ and describes repentance, like Bonhoeffer, as taking responsibility for sin out of love for human beings: "The Son of God in his unity with the Israelite Jesus... accepts personal responsibility [for sin].... In the one Israelite Jesus, [God]... willed to confess himself a sinner, and to be regarded and dealt with as such. What is all our human repentance... compared with *this perfect repentance*?"[19] Neither Bonhoeffer nor Barth explicitly defines or describes the notion of christological repentance, yet each connects repentance with the Son of God taking responsibility for sin "in the form of a sinner."[20]

Barth discusses participation in the Christ event as it pertains to human repentance more fully in *Church Dogmatics* IV/2 §66.4, "The Awakening to Conversion." Here Barth refers to repentance, or the *metanoia* Jesus and John the Baptist preach, as "conversion."[21] "We have substituted the word conversion for what Luther called penitence because," Barth says, "the latter term almost inevitably evokes associations... with a momentary event (whether once-for-all or repeated)."[22] Instead of isolated occurrences, Barth defines repentance or "conversion" as continuous movement. To be a Christian means to be always "engaged" and "caught up in the movement of conversion," to be a people "who constantly stand in need of reawakening."[23] Like Luther and Bonhoeffer, Barth places repentance within the context of daily discipleship. He says, "In explanation of the term *metanoia* we may take as our starting-point the fact that literally it speaks first of a change of mind, of a shift in judgment, of a new...standpoint. But we must be careful not to leave it at that....We often overlook the continuation."[24] Christians are in need of continuous conversion not only because they continue to sin but also because the shift in judgment concerning Christ, the world, and the church is so distinct from human presuppositions and religious sensibilities that this change of mind must be continuously revisited, deepened, revised, renewed, in short, continuously formed within them. Barth's analysis of conversion supports Bonhoeffer's reflection in prison that *metanoia* is continuous transformation fueled by "living unreservedly" in life's complexities and by taking seriously not one's own sufferings, "but those of God in the world."[25]

Corresponding to Bonhoeffer's words from prison, Barth argues that repentance is not for oneself but for others. Barth says that the church's "conversion and renewal is not...an end in itself, as it has often been interpreted and represented in a far too egocentric Christianity....When we convert and are renewed in the totality of our being, we cross the threshold of our private existence and move out into the open....In and with our private responsibility we also accept a public responsibility." Thus, for Bonhoeffer and for Barth, repentance is socially and politically significant. Each theologian argues that the reason why the church's repentance is not a private end in itself is precisely because repentance participates in the transformative power of the Christ event. Barth says:

> What are we with our little conversion, our little repentance and revising, our little ending and beginning, our changed lives?...*It is in His conversion that we are engaged.* It is in His birth, from above, the mystery and miracle of Christmas, that we are born again. It is in his baptism in Jordan that we are baptized with the Holy Ghost and with fire. It is in His death on the cross that we are dead as old men, and in His resurrection in the garden of Joseph of Arimathea that we are risen as new men....*It is because this is the case...that the awakening to repentance is the power of the Gospel*, and that it has the force and depth and teleology which are proper to it, and claims man in totality....It remains for us to know that in the whole capacity of our Christian existence, we are borne by the great movement which He has fulfilled.[26]

Therefore, as witness to and participation in Christ, repentance certainly includes but is much more than human repudiation of sin. After praising all its merits, Barth critiques the "striking over-emphasis on *mortificatio*" in Calvin's doctrine of repentance and argues instead that vivification, God's Yes to life, "is the meaning and intention" of mortification, God's No to sin.[27] Thus, Barth argues that the impetus behind repentance is not divine retribution but God's kingdom of divine-human and intrahuman flourishing. Because it is in *Christ's* repentance that the church is engaged, the church's repentance reveals and releases divine power and redemption in the world. The witness is transformative for both the church and the world.

While the above discussion by no means exhausts the support Bonhoeffer's theology, and the implications of his theology, find in Luther and Barth, they demonstrate that Bonhoeffer stands in a tradition of two highly influential thinkers who sparked needed reformations in the church and academy. As with Bonhoeffer, Luther and Barth not only risked radical theological (especially christological) claims, but, by doing so, fundamentally reshaped the boundaries of theology. In his christology lectures, Bonhoeffer calls Christ the "boundary" and the "rediscovered center."[28] In the spirit of this paradox, we may say that Bonhoeffer's theology stands within a tradition that ventures beyond the frontiers of theological thinking and from there rediscovers its center in the staggering person and work of Christ.

Repentance Rooted in the Gospel Drama

Not only does repentance take on multiple meanings throughout Christian history and within various theological traditions, it also is understood in manifold ways throughout the canon. Thus, "one cannot start with the presumption that all biblical sub-corpora will be equally concerned with the notion at hand or that they will handle the notion in the same way."[29] There is no single biblical or Christian concept of repentance. The scriptural grounding for my use of repentance in this theology of public witness centers on the Synoptic dictum "Repent, for the kingdom of God is at hand" (Matt. 3:2, 4:17, Mark 1:15), because through this phrase, John the Baptist and Jesus associate repentance with social and political existence, specifically with God's in-breaking kingdom. Furthermore, as we will see in chapter 4, Bonhoeffer connects ecclesial mission with repentance through the Baptist's same call to "prepare the way for the Lord" (Matt. 3:3).

Arguably, the maxim "Repent, for the kingdom of God is at hand" is a crucial theme in the New Testament and must, therefore, be integrally interwoven into Christian understandings of discipleship and witness.[30] The significance of John the Baptist's formula for discipleship is not immediately evident, though; for, beyond the Synoptic Gospels, Acts, and Revelation, there is no explicit demand in the New Testament to repent. The Greek verb *metanoeō*, commonly translated as "repent," only occurs once in the remainder of the New Testament (2 Cor. 12:21) and the noun *metanoia*, or repentance, occurs a mere eight times in the letters.[31] The Apostle Paul never calls the churches specifically to repentance, although he and the authors of Hebrews, James, and Peter share an understanding of initial conversion as coming to faith by turning from sin and evil to God. Thus, without speaking directly of the notion, the letters imply that repentance is a one-time fundamental transformation from death to life.[32] Church-communities whose theologies derive mostly from the epistles, or who read back from the epistles to the baptism scene, could falsely conclude that ongoing ecclesial repentance is not central to the life and witness of the church-community.

John the Baptist's dictum is vital, however, for understanding the New Testament because the gospel is primarily concerned with the coming of the kingdom of God that is defined by, and inaugurated through, the person and work of Christ. The Baptist's words definitively connect repentance to the kingdom come and coming. "The Synoptics suggest that sinners are not compelled to repent simply because sin demands repentance; instead, sinners are compelled to repent because *a new period in history has begun*."[33] Given that during the first century *metanoia* literally meant "change of mind"—specifically, "a fundamental change in thinking that leads to a fundamental change in behavior and/or way of living"—John the Baptist's preaching of repentance should be viewed as a call to align one's thought and action in accordance with this new era about to unfold through the person and work of Christ.[34] Similarly, in Luke-Acts, the preaching of repentance "often has to do with a change in thinking regarding Jesus' identity" that results in "a change in the way people think about and live in relationship with others."[35] Maintaining an accurate understanding of Jesus, though, is a task more difficult for Christians than one might expect. Mark's Gospel highlights how difficult it is to understand Jesus' identity and mission and those closest to him have just as hard a time as anyone else, with the disciples often associating the messiah with power and privilege instead of suffering and the cross (Mark 3:21, 6:14–16, 8:14–21, 8:27–28).[36]

Because the call to repent is a call for Christians to change their social and political thought in accordance with the kingdom of God that is defined and inaugurated by the person and work of Christ, the Synoptic accounts direct the reader further into the narrative of Jesus' life, death, and resurrection for an understanding of what repentance means and entails. John's Gospel (which does not record John the Baptist's preaching and takes an indirect approach to repentance by introducing the reader to a number of penitential characters without using the term *metanoia*) does the same, namely, positions repentance within an unfolding drama centered on Christ. In other words, although the Gospel of John does not prescribe repentance as a duty like the Synoptics, through the narrative it urges its readers to inhabit repentance, thereby suggesting with the other Gospels that repentance should be understood as "an ongoing way of being in Christ"—as being caught up in the drama of redemption.[37]

Repentance as Discipleship: Being Caught Up into the Way of Jesus Christ

Just as the Gospel accounts encourage ongoing repentance as readers follow Jesus deeper into the narrative, so, too, does Bonhoeffer equate repentance with discipleship. Repentance is not simply an act of turning that places Christians on the "right road"; it is the right road itself.[38] Repentance is following along the path blazed by

Jesus Christ. In a letter written on July 16, 1944, Bonhoeffer says that "the starting point" for understanding God's way in the world (and thus the church's form or witness) is the suffering Christ "who gains ground and power in the world by being powerless." In the same letter he says that the Christian must "live a 'secular' life" by which he means living publically, living wholly in the midst of the world and thus in solidarity with the world's sufferings. "It is not a religious act that makes someone a Christian," Bonhoeffer says, "but rather sharing in God's sufferings in the worldly life."[39] Curiously, he names participation in God's sufferings *metanoia*. With little explanation accompanying his comment, Bonhoeffer deepens the common understanding of repentance from an act of the sinful human being turning toward God to a pattern integral to the life of discipleship itself. *Metanoia* is "not in the first place thinking about one's own needs, problems, sins, and fears," he writes, "but *allowing oneself to be caught up into the way of Jesus Christ*, into the messianic event, thus fulfilling Isaiah 53 [...and] the words of John the Baptist, 'Behold the Lamb of God, who takes away the sin of the world' (John 1:29)."[40] Bonhoeffer makes this fascinating link between repentance and Christ's presence in the world while citing Isaiah's Suffering Servant and John the Baptist's recognition of the Lamb of God, but his insight in prison remains on the level of intuition. He asks, "But what is this life like? this life of participating in God's powerlessness in the world? I'll write about this next time, I hope."[41]

The genuineness and openness of Bonhoeffer's question concerning what a life of participation in the redemptive powerlessness of God in the world—what a life of *metanoia*—amounts to is intriguing given that Bonhoeffer had referred on occasion to his experience first in the church struggle and then in the military resistance as a kind of penitence. In a January 1938 circular letter, "To the Young Brothers of the Church in Pomerania," written to the Finkenwalde seminarians and the pastors of the Confessing Church, Bonhoeffer says, "But just as in our personal life there is only one way, the way of repentance, of patience under God's word, in which God restores us to our lost communion, so too it is in the church struggle. Without penitence, i.e., unless the church struggle itself becomes our penitence, we shall never receive back the gift we have lost, the church struggle as gospel."[42] Then, in the wake of the Confessing Church's failure to enact costly discipleship, Bonhoeffer defines the political conspiracy "in a most unpolitical way, namely, as an act of repentance."[43] After a 1942 meeting with Bonhoeffer and the conspirator Hans Shoenfeld, George Bell, Bishop of Chichester, reports, "[Bonhoeffer] was obviously distressed in his mind as to the lengths to which he had been driven by force of circumstances in the plot for the elimination of Hitler. The Christian conscience, he said, was not quite at ease with Schoenfeld's ideas. 'There must be punishment by God.... We do not want to escape repentance. Our action must be understood as an act of repentance.'"[44] Although Bonhoeffer never systematically examines how repentance participates in the redemptive powerlessness of Christ in the world, he lives out possible answers within his historical context.[45] More relevant to this project, his previous *theology* contains resources for thinking about repentance as a disposition and activity in our participatory democracy.

As far as we know, Bonhoeffer does not return in subsequent letters to the question of what participation in the powerlessness of God in the world entails. Still, just as his correspondence with Bethge elicits creative and constructive thinking from both men, the text invites contemporary readers to derive from it further insight about the character of God's presence in the world. What associations can be made between Bonhoeffer's prison reflections on repentance and the scriptural texts he cites in that July 16 letter—between Isaiah's Suffering Servant and Bonhoeffer's claim that God's suffering in public life "wins [God] power and space in the world"?[46] Could the narrative of Jesus' baptism by John illuminate how human repentance participates in God's public presence?

Jesus Numbered with the Transgressors through Repentance

When read through the lens of Isaiah's Suffering Servant, participation in the powerlessness of God in public life entails being "numbered with the transgressors" (53:12). While God's suffering in the world includes more than the crucifixion (Bonhoeffer cites Christ's "hour of grieving" in Gethsemane as one example), divine suffering culminates in the fulfillment of Isaiah's prophecy when Christ in the form of a servant "[bears] the sin of many" (53:12).[47] "He was pierced for our transgressions, he was crushed for our iniquities . . . and the Lord has laid upon him the iniquity of us all . . . the Lord makes his life a guilt offering," writes the Hebrew prophet (53:5–6, 10). As we will soon see in an examination of *Ethics*, Bonhoeffer interprets Christ's sin-bearing not passively as mere assent to divine justice but more radically as an active acceptance of guilt, a determination to be numbered with sinners and present to humanity as such.

Isaiah's Suffering Servant, who places himself in solidarity with sinners as "a lamb led to the slaughter" (53:7), is the one whom John the Baptist defines as the presence of the kingdom of God: "Behold, the Lamb of God who takes away the sin of the world!" (John 1:29). The opening act of the story of Jesus' public ministry begins at the Desert of Judea with John the Baptist preaching, "Repent, for the kingdom of God is near. . . . 'Prepare the way for the Lord, make straight paths for him,'" and then moves onto the banks of the Jordan in which people confessing their sins were being baptized (Matt. 3:1–6). When Jesus comes to the Jordan River he not only fulfills John's prophecy of the kingdom drawing near but also, by being baptized, appropriates the practice of confession and repentance to his own work as redeemer. Being baptized by John—the one who was not worthy even to untie the thongs of Jesus' sandals—was not an arbitrary act of humility for the sinless Christ. The public ministry of the incarnate God is inaugurated precisely through baptism—through the act of human beings confessing sin in response to the call to repent. Barth makes this same observation when he says, "[Christ's] first public appearance is that of a penitent in unreserved solidarity with other penitents who confess themselves to be such in the baptism of John."[48] Like the masses whom John baptized, Jesus' baptism signals repentance.

By being baptized with sinners, Jesus inverts the ministry of John the Baptist, who asserts that he must decrease so that Jesus may increase (John 3:30). Matthew's Gospel records John trying to deter Jesus from being baptized by him: "I need to be baptized by you and do you come to me?" asks John, to which Jesus replies, "It is proper for us to do this to fulfill all righteousness" (Matt. 3:14–15). By being baptized, Jesus enacts divine righteousness and reverses John's intentions. In the incarnation God becomes a servant so that humanity may be exalted, consequently manifesting that there is nothing human beings may do for God—such as repent—that God has not already done for us. Stimulated by Bonhoeffer's comments in prison, I suggest that because the event of Jesus' baptism introduces repentance as an activity defining God's righteousness, defining the incarnate God's work of redemption, the category of repentance offers a fresh perspective on Christ's cross. The Lamb of God, the sinless Suffering Servant, is the one who is to accept responsibility for sin on the cross in order to repent, in order to change the ontological structure of the world and turn the course of history toward reconciliation and redemption. The cross is an act of divine repentance and divine righteousness in that through the crucifixion God takes responsibility for sin and makes right for eternity all that is not.

By viewing the first act of Christ's public ministry as a response to John the Baptist's call to repent, we have begun to interpret the concept of repentance on the basis of participation in the life of the incarnate, crucified, and risen God. If Jesus' public activity may be understood as repentance then it follows that human repentance may imitate God's presence in public life and participate in Christ's redemptive work. Of course, such an interpretation directly challenges common understandings. In that July 16 letter equating *metanoia* with discipleship, Bonhoeffer says that the primary impetus energizing repentance is not, as Christians often assume, preoccupation with individual sin and need but "allowing oneself to be caught up into the way of Jesus Christ."[49] In his outline for a book sketched in prison, he defines this way and thus repentance itself as existence for others.

Bonhoeffer's definition echoes the Synoptic Gospels and Acts, where repentance is exclusively concerned with human relations with one another. As the New Testament scholar Guy Dale Nave argues, "At no time before, during, or immediately after the writing of the New Testament documents" were *metanoēo* or *metanoia* ever used to convey an individual's "returning to God.... Nowhere in the Synoptics or Acts does *metanoēo* or *metanoia* explicitly or implicitly suggest [this]."[50] The impetus behind repentance, in other words, is public concern for social flourishing rather than private concern for one's status before God. As a faithful response to God's coming kingdom, repentance is more public than private. As public witness concerned with social flourishing, repentance manifests Christ's lordship, then, not by the church showing the world how it turns to God in pious devotion, be it through "moral" behavior or right belief; rather, the church witnesses to Christ through the manner in which it relates to other human beings and to society at large.

To say that repentance is primarily concerned with social flourishing is not to deny its relation to transcendence. Emphasizing God's human form as God's mode of being for others, Bonhoeffer says, "Jesus' 'being-for-others' is the experience of transcendence!... Our relationship to God is no 'religious' relationship to some highest, most powerful, best being imaginable—that is not genuine transcendence—but our relation to God is a new life in 'existence for others.'"[51] For Bonhoeffer, Christ's "existence for others" first and foremost means that the incarnate God makes Godself present in the world by belonging wholly to humanity, by being thoroughly human; (only secondarily, by virtue of fallen creation, does Christ's determination to belong to humanity lead to crucifixion).[52] Appealing again to discipleship as christological conformation or "participation," he writes, "Faith is participation in this being of Jesus. (Becoming human [Menschwerdung], cross, and resurrection)... Our relation to God is a new life in 'being there for others,' through participation in the being of Jesus... God in human form!... 'the human being for others'!, therefore the Crucified One."[53] If repentance is "not in the first place thinking of one's own needs, problems, sin and fears" but "being caught up in the way"—or being—of God in human form then repentance is best understood as existence for others, an expression of profound solidarity with the whole of humanity. A church that participates in the being of the baptized, crucified, and risen Christ is a community that is "numbered with the transgressors" and present in public life as such.

■ CHRIST AS HIDDEN IN HUMILIATION: THE 1933 CHRISTOLOGY LECTURES

The unusual, and even scandalous, claim that Christ's public presence may be understood in terms of repentance finds a home within the paradoxes of Christian faith, especially when positioned within a broader theological landscape that characterizes God's revelation through Christ as hidden. In other words, repentance, as an act of God's righteousness in Christ, may be understood as one mode of the hidden God. This section examines the notion of God hidden in humiliation, a concept implicitly grounding Bonhoeffer's theological point of departure in prison, which he developed explicitly in his early christology lectures. The section describes in what way Christ is "hidden" in the world and in what way "humiliated" in order to gain greater clarity about God's public presence and its redemptive character.

God's Hiddenness in Luther's Theology of the Cross

Although Bonhoeffer does not explicitly refer to his christology as Martin Luther's theology of the cross, Luther's influence is pervasive and profound. Like Luther, Bonhoeffer accentuates the humanity of Christ to such an extent that God's presence in the world is tied, indeed bound, to the human Jesus. "Anywhere you can say, 'Here is God,' you must also say 'Here is Christ the man,'" writes Luther.[54] Bonhoeffer inherited from Luther a christology that accounts for Christ's contemporary bodily presence in the world, that discusses the *person* of Christ in "a modern sense" as "a protagonist with a history," that communicates that God is *pro nobis* (for us), and that defines discipleship neither merely as a life motivated by Christ nor simply an imitation of Christ but as taking Christ's very form (*sacramentum*) in the world.[55] God's presence in the world, as displayed most poignantly through the crucifixion, is not evident but hidden—hidden in the cross that Luther depicts, following the Apostle Paul, as foolish, offensive, unexpected, and scandalous (1 Cor. 1:18–31).

Central to Luther's theology of the cross is God's hiddenness. Luther's first mention of the hidden God occurs in the *Lectures on the Psalms* (the *Dictata* of 1513–1516), where he refers to the incomprehensibility of God and says that God hides Godself in faith, in light inaccessible, in the incarnation, in the church, in the Virgin Mary, and in the eucharist.[56] In this text and in the Heidelberg Disputation, Luther refers to God's hiddenness not outside revelation but paradoxically *within* revelation.[57] God's incomprehensibility refers not to a God shrouded in anonymity but to a God who may be intimately known as the crucified one "hidden in suffering."[58] The "hidden" character of revelation indicates that the manner of God's visibility is unexpected and offensive to human, religious sensibilities.

Luther contrasts his theology of the cross with a "theology of glory" that erroneously seeks the power of God in the world through visible acts of omnipotence and triumph, as exemplified in John's Gospel when Philip asks Jesus to "show us the Father and that will be enough for us" (14:8). In Thesis Twenty of the Heidelberg Disputation, Luther says, "Christ forthwith set aside [Philip's] flighty thought about seeking God elsewhere and led him to himself, saying, 'Philip, he who has seen me has seen the Father' [John 14:9]. For this reason true theology and recognition of God are in the crucified Christ."[59] Luther's theology of the cross witnesses to the hidden God who chooses to reveal Godself not through characteristics typically associated with divinity but through humiliation and weakness.

The Hidden God in Bonhoeffer's Prison Theology

Although Bonhoeffer does not explicitly say so, his prison insights about God's presence in the world are grounded, like his christology lectures, in the hidden God.[60] Recall that Bonhoeffer says that a "world come of age" ironically is beneficial for Christian faith in that human beings who no longer depend on an abstract and general idea of "God" for morals, politics, science, and so forth, also no longer seek God's presence in a false manner through visible acts of omnipotence. A "world come of age," then, opens up a way of seeing God hidden in the cross, "the God of the Bible, who gains ground and power in the world by being powerless."[61] In his July 16, 1944, letter, Bonhoeffer depicts the hidden nature of Christ's lordship, and once again he inserts the idea of repentance into his discussion by briefly defining it as "*ultimate* honesty." He suggests that the church witnesses to God through "repentance, through *ultimate* honesty" about the perplexing fact of God's hidden presence. This passage, to which I keep referring, is now worth quoting in full. Bonhoeffer writes,

> And we cannot be honest unless we recognize that we have to live in the world—"*etsi deus non daretur*" [as if there were no God]. And this is precisely what we do recognize—before God! God [Godself] compels us to recognize it. Thus our coming of age leads us to a truer recognition of our situation before God. God would have us know that we must live as those who manage their lives without God. The same God who is with us is the God who forsakes us (Mark 15:34!). The same God who makes us to live in the world without the working hypothesis of God is the God before whom we stand continually. Before God, and with God, we live without God. God consents to be pushed out of the world and onto the cross; God is weak and powerless in the world and in precisely this way, and only so, is at our side and helps us. Matt 8:17 makes it quite clear that Christ helps us not by virtue of his omnipotence but rather by virtue of his weakness and suffering!
>
> ... Human religiosity directs people in need to the power of God in the world.... The Bible directs people towards the powerlessness and suffering of God; only the suffering God can help. To this extent, one may say that the previously described development towards the world's coming of age, which has cleared the way by eliminating a false notion of God, frees us to see the God of the Bible, who gains ground and power in the world by being powerless. This will probably be the starting point for our "worldly interpretation."[62]

Bonhoeffer qualifies God's omnipotence by focusing on God in human form, but this does not mean that he ignores transcendence. The sign of God's transcendence is God's immanence, God's hidden nearness with and for humanity. "God is beyond in the midst of our lives," he writes.[63]

Given the manner in which Christ is present in the world, Bonhoeffer attributes some positive import to a world come of age, which has shed its naïve, untested faith. Lacking God as a hypothesis for human knowledge and unsolved problems, a world come of age not only operates without God as a premise but also without a *false notion* of God to which many religious individuals are prone to appeal—the *deus ex machina*. Religious individuals often assume that, as with the divine figure in ancient plays, the biblical God mechanically swoops down onto a scene of human drama, intervening at the point where human beings become lazy and their powers fail. A world come of age has no patience for this religious fantasy, and Bonhoeffer grants this a positive development in history. Instead of the distant *deus ex machina* who at the most fitting moment suddenly appears and delivers human beings from consequences of their own careless making, Bonhoeffer understands the biblical God to be always already intimately present, hidden in humiliation, suffering with and for others amid the reality of sin and injustice.

A world come of age challenges disciples to take responsibility for others *etsi deus non daretur*, "even if there were no God" to descend on the scene of human complacency and selfishness. In doing so, the world's adulthood brings to "an unexpected light" that, indeed, humanity must live without a God who shelters human beings from our fallen condition, without a God who serves as a barricade against sin and suffering unfolding within human life, and thus without a God who releases human beings from responsibility for this life.[64] The church's repentance first involves "intellectual honesty," which arises from a tried faith that understands "that the God who is with us is the God who forsakes" our religious need for an ostentatiously powerful God.[65] Christians must admit that, because they worship a God who refuses to stop all suffering but instead enters into it, they cannot provide tightly wrapped, systematic answers to the greatest human questions about evil and suffering. Indeed, they must confess that it may be "that Christian answers are just as uncompelling" or compelling as other explanations.[66] Instead of providing easy answers, Christ calls the church-community, whose faith has been tested and has "come forth as gold" (Job 23:10) amid the ambiguities and unsolved problems of life, to take responsibility for others by inhabiting this world in an intentional manner that makes space for the hidden God who wins power in the world through weakness.

Although Bonhoeffer's primary intent in the July 16 letter is to describe God's presence specifically in a "world come of age," his implicit appeal to the *deus absconditus* positions his theological "starting point" (of God winning power through weakness) much earlier than prison. Bonhoeffer reflects on the hidden God as early as his 1933 christology lectures. These lectures summarize his previous christological understanding and also pave the way for his thinking thereafter.

The Hidden God and the Christological Incognito

Bonhoeffer's christology, explicitly laid out for the first and last time in the 1933 lectures, is rooted in the notion of God hidden in the humiliation of sinful flesh. Bonhoeffer says, "This God-[human], Jesus Christ, is present and contemporary in the form which is in 'the likeness of sinful flesh,' i.e., in hidden form, in the form of a stumbling block. That is the central problem of christology."[67] God is not hidden as a human being. The scandal lies not in the incarnation, which is the revelation itself, but in the humiliation where Christ as wholly God and wholly human takes on what Romans 8:3 calls the *homoioma sarkos*, "the likeness of sinful flesh."[68] Bonhoeffer carefully distinguishes between Christ's humanity and humiliation such that the doctrine of the offense, the *scandalon*, applies only to the humiliation bound up in sin, not to the finitude itself. To make this distinction, Lutheran orthodoxy speaks of Christ passing through two states. The incarnation is not confined to the first state, the *status exinanitionis*, the humiliation characteristic of his life from the manger to the cross, but also refers to the *status exaltationis*, the exaltation, which glorifies the incarnation eternally within the life of the Trinity. As opposed to a Reformed theological perspective, Bonhoeffer's Lutheran heritage claims that the incarnation as such is not the humiliation.[69] The finite bears the infinite (*finitum capax infiniti*) with the incarnate divine logos freely choosing to undergo humiliation.

Bonhoeffer applauds Lutheran theology for narrowing the *scandalon* only to the humiliation of sinful flesh and not to human flesh per se; however, he finds a discussion about the succession of states too focused on the nature of the incarnation and not on the person of Christ. His concern centers on the whole Christ, the incarnate one who is *at once* humiliated and exalted. The opening of John's Gospel makes clear that the incarnate one is the glorified God: "The Word was made flesh and we beheld his glory" (1:14); thus Bonhoeffer says, "God's becoming human is God's message about the glorification of God, who honors [Godself] by being in human form."[70] The exaltation of God in human flesh, in turn, becomes the glorification of the human being who will participate for eternity in the life of the triune God. Although Christ is hidden in humiliation, Bonhoeffer stresses that his embodiment in human flesh is the image of the invisible God (Col. 1:15). The incarnation is the true revelation in which God freely binds and freely exalts Godself. Still, to say that human beings behold the glory of God in the incarnation is not to claim that it is recognizable as such. "The ultimate mystery of the Trinity," according to Bonhoeffer, is that God glorifies Godself in humanity.[71] The exaltation and the humiliation cannot be separated in the earthly life of the incarnate one, and thus the glorification of God in sinful flesh sounds "improbable and strange."[72] Bonhoeffer says, "The revelation of the incarnation in Jesus Christ is not visibly a glorification of God" because Christ's mode of existence in the fallen world is "incognito, as a beggar among beggars, as an outcast among outcasts, as despairing among the despairing, as dying among the dying."[73] The exalted, incarnate one also bears the likeness of sinful flesh. He is the humiliated, crucified one.

Bonhoeffer's reference to the "incognito" arises from Søren Kierkegaard's pseudonymous *Philosophical Fragments*,[74] although Kierkegaard's most helpful discussion of the christological incognito occurs in *Training in Christianity*, a text Bonhoeffer certainly admired, for he suggests that his fiancée, Maria von Wedemeyer, read it to inaugurate her budding interest in theology.[75] In the chapter "The Offence," §2 "*The form of a servant means unrecognizableness (an incognito)*," Kierkegaard defines an incognito as "something less than it is" and argues that God as an individual human being "is the greatest possible, the infinitely qualitative remove from being God, and therefore, the profoundest incognito."[76] By becoming less than he is, by taking the human form of a servant, Kierkegaard says that Christ in "free determination... bound himself once and for all" to human beings. God's free determination to bind Godself to humanity through the incarnation is "an almightily maintained incognito," and God wills and maintains his servant status to such an intense degree that "in a sense, the assumed incognito has power over Him." Kierkegaard says:

> Only thus is there in the deepest sense real seriousness in the assertion that He became "very man," and hence also He experiences the extremest suffering of feeling Himself forsaken of God, so that at no moment was He beyond suffering, but actually in it... It is a strange sort of dialectic: that He who almightily... binds Himself, and does it so almightily that He actually feels Himself bound, suffers under the consequences of the fact that He lovingly and freely determined to become an individual man—to such a degree was it seriously true that He became a real man.[77]

Kierkegaard emphasizes that Christ was truly human, the "real *Mensch*" as Bonhoeffer develops in his *Ethics*, who experienced human life in all its depth and fullness. The irony of the incarnation, however, is that by willing to come near in the revelation of the human Christ, God establishes new depths for divine-human intimacy but also makes direct communication with human beings an impossibility. God imparts Godself in Christ, the image of the invisible God, and yet, as Kierkegaard explains, the revelation of God in human form cannot help but be hidden and indirect. Kierkegaard argues that the fact that *God* becomes truly human makes it impossible for God to communicate directly as God, in other words, to speak in a manner that makes obvious that it is God communicating. Even though God comes near to humanity to be known by humanity, the communication God makes as a human being is always indirect. Kierkegaard says, "When one says directly, 'I am God, the Father and I are one' that is direct communication. But when the one who says it is an individual man, quite like other men, then this communication is not just perfectly direct; for it is not just perfectly clear and direct that an individual man should be God—although what he says is perfectly direct."[78] God's communication is characterized by a "contradiction," God in the form of a servant, God in human form, and it is this contradiction that makes the revelation hidden.

Kierkegaard takes the significance of the incognito a step further. Not only are the incognito and its indirect communication consequences of God taking human form, there is also positive intent behind divine hiddenness. Kierkegaard argues that Christ wills to conceal his divine identity in public (as seen in the Gospels, for example, in his preferred title, the "Son of Man"), for he wills to take the form of a servant and does not consider "equality with God something to be grasped" (Phil. 2:6). Echoing the opening section in *Works of Love*, "Love's Hidden Life and Its Recognizability by Its Fruit," Kierkegaard suggests in *Training in Christianity* that a work of love is always hidden. He says, "A man who chooses then an incognito... has in mind perhaps the Socratic maxim, that in order to will the Good truly, one must avoid the appearances of doing it."[79] Christ avoids receiving credit for the redemption his life and work accomplishes; he "strives with might and main to maintain the incognito," and in doing so manifests the christological righteousness mentioned in the previous chapter, that new mode of being and doing good which communicates that God alone is righteous. Like Luther before him and Bonhoeffer after him, Kierkegaard asserts that Christ's hidden character in the world is central to God's identity and righteousness and thus central to a proper understanding of Christ's redemptive presence in public life.

The Sinless Christ Hidden in the "Likeness of Sinful Flesh" (Rom. 8:3)

Just as Kierkegaard deems God in human form a "contradiction," so too may we characterize divine repentance, understood as a public expression of Christ's righteousness, as a contradiction. The paradox lies, of course, in the claim that the sinless Christ repents of sin, or as it has been articulated more traditionally in reference to the cross, that Jesus bears sin and in doing so is both sinless and sin-full. Christ exists "as sinner among sinners"—even as the *peccator pessimus*, Luther's term for "the worst sinner"—and yet as "sinless among sinners."[80] Adopting the "almost unbearably severe" language of 2 Corinthians 5:21 (as Barth calls it), Bonhoeffer says that Christ "*is really made sin* for us."[81] "He is himself thief, murderer, adulterer, as we are, because he bears our sin," contends Luther.[82]

The paradox that the crucified Christ is both sinless and sin-full in his bearing is one to which Protestantism has become accustomed. Because of this, Bonhoeffer cautions his listeners from resolving the contradiction too quickly by balancing the two claims in such a way that abstracts God from full immersion in the fallen world, thus leaving the Christian imagination with a comfortable vision of a sinless Christ acting in a vacuum, floating through the world unaffected by the ethical complexities and systemic forces of this-worldly existence. What's at stake is the degree of Christ's solidarity with fallen humanity and thus its redemptive efficacy: "Did Jesus, as the God-human who is humiliated, enter wholly into human sin? Was he a human being like us, with our sinfulness? If he was not, then did he really become human at all? Can he help us human beings at all? And if he was as we are, in the same peril in which we are, how can he help us escape that peril?" asks Bonhoeffer.[83] What is also at stake—for this project—is how appropriate it is to speak of Christ's life and death as acts of confession and repentance and thus to speak of the church's repentance as participation in the Christ event. Applying the term *repentance* to Christ's work of redemption amplifies Bonhoeffer's questions above; specifically it raises the question of the precise relation between Jesus and sin. While this will be touched on to a certain extent below, it is important to remember that Bonhoeffer defines repentance not egocentrically in terms of individual sin and need but in terms of existence for others; thus our inquiries about a penitent Jesus would do well to focus not on the probability of whether or not Jesus the individual sinned but on how christological repentance serves as a mode of existence for others. Certainly in the christology lectures Bonhoeffer affirms that the sinlessness of the incarnate God is a central doctrine on which all christological and soteriological thinking rests: Jesus is sinless in that he obeys the will of God to the end; he is not controlled by death-dealing powers and principalities intent on destroying and oppressing human beings, rather he continuously submits to the will of a loving, redeeming, and reconciling God. The Pauline texts used to support a doctrine of a sinless Christ (Phil. 2:5–8; Rom. 5:18–19; Rom. 15:2–3; 2 Cor. 8:9) all rest on Christ's obedience; still, for Paul, obedience is not so much an ethical category—Jesus is not an exemplar of morality—as it is a matter of faith. Obedience means faithfulness to a God whose will is free to be scandalous.[84] Even as Bonhoeffer (following Paul) affirms the sinlessness of Christ through the notion of obedience, he guards against distancing Jesus from sin too hastily precisely because such a move detracts from the profundity of the incarnation and from Jesus' solidarity with real human beings.

Bonhoeffer intensifies the paradox of the sinless Christ's intimate encounter with the condition of sin through his analysis of Romans 8:3, Paul's claim that in the incarnation God took "the likeness of sinful flesh" in order to "deal with sin." While the term "likeness" may seem at first to distance Christ from humanity's fallen condition, in his lectures (as well as in *Ethics*) Bonhoeffer makes clear that Christ not only *appears* to take sinful flesh, God's self-humiliation expresses itself in that Christ *takes* sinful flesh—the very flesh of fallen humanity, the intrinsically damaged state of human nature "as it is."[85] This interpretation of the *homoioma sarkos* is in line with the majority of contemporary scholarship; as Ivor J. Davidson says, "A fair consensus—in modern discussion at least—has it that what Paul is *not* doing [in using the term 'likeness'] is signaling a distinction in the essential nature of the flesh in which the Son appears. The concrete form in which the divine purpose is effected is a 'true likeness' (cf. Phil 2:7) to the *sarx* that is prey to the dominion God intends to destroy."[86] Jesus' flesh was our fallen flesh, Bonhoeffer says, with its tendency to sin and self-will, and to this extent he differed not at all. He was tempted in the same manner, only the stakes were higher. He lived continuously within struggle, tension, and conflict, because the forces that are contradictory to God's will were also embedded in his flesh. As a result of bearing sinful flesh and living within a fallen world, "he was not the perfect good," Bonhoeffer argues, meaning that he did things that "looked like sin": "He became angry, he was harsh to his mother, he escaped from his enemies, he broke the Law of his people, he stirred up revolt against the rulers and religious men of his country." Of central importance to this theology of public witness is the fact that, in his public life, Jesus is clearly identified as a sinner. "Beyond recognition he stepped into [humanity's] sinful way of existence," Bonhoeffer says, and in doing so "robs sin of its power."[87]

Although Bonhoeffer cautions against preoccupation with technical examinations of the metaphysics of the incarnation since such inquiries often divert one from the primary task of relating to the person of Christ, one further clarifying note about a way to distinguish between "fallenness" and "sinfulness" may be helpful for understanding the work of the sinless Christ as divine repentance, and thus the person of Christ as a penitent. In his article examining Christ's human nature, Ian McFarland argues that while "in all other human beings the nature and the hypostasis are inseparable (so that if the former is fallen the latter is sinful)," it is appropriate to distinguish Christ's fallen nature from his sinless person since "fallenness is a property of nature and sin of hypostasis."[88] In other words, while Christ in his hypostasis does not sin (hence the traditional claim that Christ is sinless), he was fully immersed in humanity's fallen condition by inhabiting the human nature Paul refers to as sinful flesh. Christ's bodily encounter with fallen existence—and in this sense, his intimate involvement with sin—is a result of God freely choosing to be visible to the world through sinful flesh. *It is this astounding reality that allows us to understand the work of Christ through the category of repentance.* Just as Paul makes a connection in Romans 8:3 between Christ's sinful flesh and his salvific solidarity on the cross, so, too, may we view Christ's assumption of humanity's damaged condition as an integral component of divine repentance, of God actively accepting responsibility for sin.[89]

Although Bonhoeffer affirms the sinlessness of Christ doctrinally, he argues that because Christ bears sinful flesh and his acts occur within the fallen world, they are most accurately described not as "sinless" but "ambiguous." The observable acts of Jesus are not evidence for his sinlessness; it is not an existential given that Jesus was without sin. Even that is hidden and thus becomes a matter of faith. Faith in the hidden God confesses that bearing sin is good, that living by perceived folly is wisdom, and that weakness is the expression of divine strength. Or as Bonhoeffer says, faith in the person of Christ acknowledges that "the one who struggles is perfected, the unrighteous one is righteous, the one who is rejected is the holy one."[90] Because it is *he* who does these ambiguous acts, who saves the world and condemns himself, "on this basis, of *the One* who he is, we must dare to make and to endure all the most scandalous assertions about this God-human who has been humiliated."[91]

Christology, then, must strictly center on the question, "Who is this human being who is said to be God?"[92] Bonhoeffer answers:

> If Jesus Christ is to be described as God, we may not speak of his divine being, nor of his omnipotence, nor his omniscience; but we must speak of this weak [human being] among sinners, of his manger and his cross. If we are to deal with the deity of Jesus, we must speak of his weakness. In christology, one looks at the whole historical [human being] Jesus and says of him, that he is God. One does not look first at a human nature and then beyond it to a divine nature, but one has to do with the one [human being] Jesus Christ, who is wholly God.[93]

The only faithful question and the only one with which christology is rightly concerned is this question of "Who?" because it upholds God in the form of human person. According to Bonhoeffer, the Chalcedonian formula of 451, which established the doctrine of the incarnate God, decisively put an end to all other questions meant to distract one from following the way of Jesus Christ. It affirms Jesus Christ in two natures, "without confusion," "without change," "without distinction," and "without separation."[94] This definition safeguards the mystery of *how* one Christ in two natures is possible and condemns similar questions, like "How can i deal with you?" similar questions, like "How can I deal with you?" in such a way that bypasses the costly demands the call of discipleship makes—demands that include being immersed with Christ in the messiness of sinful existence.[95] The logic of the incarnation bars human beings from dividing the divine from the human nature and then appealing to characteristically divine powers to endorse human behavior based on the assumption that Christians can recruit a dominating or religiously righteous God onto the side of particular human judgments and religious prejudices. The one who asks in faith, "Who is this Christ?" questions her capacity to fully comprehend a God whose freedom over the world expresses itself in the improbability of sinful flesh.[96] The church that consistently asks this question with ultimate honesty opens itself up to God's transcendence that breaks into, unsettles, and reforms the church's limited understanding. The question of "Who?" describes relation: Who is Jesus Christ in relation to the world, to the church, in relation to me as individual? This continual inquiry invigorates an ever-progressing, dynamic relationship with the person of Christ. And only when the church-community intimately knows Christ as person, not as religious idea, can it recognize his actions—the ambiguous behavior expressed in sinful flesh—as redeeming love for a world under sin and death.

The Incognito of the Resurrected Jesus

Christ's divine presence is hidden not only in a life that culminates on the cross but also in the resurrection in that Jesus does not allow himself to be known publicly as victor. Even belief in the resurrection does not negate the stumbling block or simplify the ambiguity. Bonhoeffer says, "We have seen the exalted one, only as the crucified; the sinless one, only as the guilt-laden; the risen one, only as the humiliated."[97] Thus, the followers of Christ within the Gospel narratives experience Eastertide not as a victory celebration but as a time characterized by chaos, fear, doubt, and confusion as much as joy and amazement (Matt. 26; Mark 16; Luke 24; John 20). The incognito remains with the risen Christ, as portrayed in the Gospel account of the walk to Emmaus in which "Jesus himself came up and walked along with [two disciples], but they were kept from recognizing him" (Luke 24:15). Only when Jesus broke bread and gave it to them—only in this eucharistic gesture toward the cross—were their eyes opened before he disappeared once again. Twice Luke's Gospel makes clear that they recognized him only and precisely through the broken bread.

The incognito of the resurrected Jesus is made even more explicit through Christ's absence in the empty tomb. The two individuals walking to Emmaus recount, "Some of our women...went to the tomb early this morning but didn't find his body. They came and told us that they had seen a vision of angels, who said he was alive. Then some of our companions went to the tomb and found it just as the women had said, but him they did not see" (Luke 24:22–24). Bonhoeffer calls the historical fact of the empty tomb "one of the most decisive elements in christology":

> What does the story of the empty grave mean before the report of the resurrection? If the grave is really empty, then it is the visible authentication of the resurrection. If it is not empty, then Christ was not resurrected. It seems as though our "resurrection faith" is bound up with the story of the empty grave... This is the final stumbling block, which we have to accept as believers in Christ. Either way, there is a stumbling block. The impossible possibility that the grave was empty is the stumbling block of faith. The affirmation of the empty grave is also a stumbling block. Who is going to prove to us that the disciples did not find Jesus's body?... To the very end, even through the empty grave, Jesus remains incognito, in the form of a stumbling block. Jesus does not emerge from his incognito, not even as the Risen One. He will not lay it aside until he comes again... visibly as the Eternal, the God who became human, in divine power and glory.[98]

What distinguishes the nonreligious from the religious Christian as well as the believer from the unbeliever, then, is not a lifting of the incognito but the capacity to acknowledge and make peace with the ambiguity of the church's confession. The proclamation of Easter faith is indeed Christ's victory over the powers of sin and death which establishes Christ's lordship over the world, yet Christians confess the lordship of a hidden God. Witness to Christ, then, does not entail trying to undo God's manner of being in the world through cheap attempts to make the hidden God's work and will comprehensible—such as simplistic moral judgments that discount the complexity of sociopolitical life or trite explanations and pious clichés that disregard the personal pain and turmoil endured by human beings. Instead, as Luther says in Thesis Twenty-One of the Heidelberg Disputation, witness to Christ "calls the thing what it actually is."[99] Disciples of Jesus are able to encounter the reality of evil, sin, and suffering with ultimate honesty that does not attempt to cover for the hidden God. The incognito of the crucified and risen Christ offers the church a nontriumphal theological place to stand in the midst of personal and sociopolitical complexity and enables the church to encounter humanity's doubt, suspicion, and protest against the hidden God with empathy instead of judgment.[100] The church witnesses to Christ fully aware of the christological "contradiction": God's revelation in human form seen "through a glass darkly" (1 Cor. 13:12).

Christ's Contemporary Hiddenness

While God's hidden character could be misinterpreted as clandestine, God's lacking forthrightness, or divine disinterest in truly being known, as we saw in Kierkegaard's description of the incognito, God in hidden form is the result of unfathomable nearness and intimacy. The church's witness, then, entails making Christ's nearness and contemporaneity concrete.[101] Because Christ is person, he is present and contemporary in space and time, Bonhoeffer says, here and now.[102] His being Christ here and now is a belonging to or a being *for*—for me, for us, in other words, for others. Christ's being-for is the divine essence in that "God's being is a being-in-relation. God is one who is always on the way toward the other in communion."[103] Thus, Christ *pro nobis* is an ontological assertion. Bonhoeffer says that Jesus is for humanity in that "he stands in their place... goes to the cross, carries the sins and dies," yet the place of Christ refers to more than the historical cross.[104] It also refers to the ontological structure of human beings in the contemporary moment. Bonhoeffer says in the christology lectures, "Where does [Christ] stand? For me, he stands in my place, where I should be standing. He stands there because I cannot, that is, he stands at the boundary of my existence and nevertheless in my place.... This boundary lies between my old self and my new self, that is, in the center between myself and me. As the limit, Christ is at the same time the center that I have regained."[105] Bonhoeffer's theology focuses on the inherent social implications of Christian faith, yet here he begins his discussion of Christ's contemporaneity with a declaration of utmost intimacy: Christ for me, the individual, here and now. Although Bonhoeffer critiques "religion" for missing Christ in the midst of the world by being too individualistic, inward, and private, he never invalidates personal faith or the reality of "Christ... in me" (Gal. 2:20).

Because "it is the nature of the person of Christ to be center, both spatially and temporally," Christ's presence is not restricted to the individual. Rather, as mediator he penetrates into the center of existence as a whole, into the center of history and nature, of time and space. Bonhoeffer says:

> History lives between promise and fulfillment. It carries the promise within itself, to become full of God.... But history relates itself to this promise much as the individual [human] relates to the law: it cannot fulfill it.... [The] promise is not to be proved by anything; it is only to be proclaimed. This means that the Messiah, Christ, is at one and the same time the destroyer and fulfiller of all messianic expectations of history. He is the destroyer insofar as the visible Messiah does not appear and the fulfillment takes place in secret. He is the fulfiller insofar as God really enters history and he who is expected is really there.[106]

Christ will not be the visible and demonstrative center of history until the kingdom comes in full. Even then, the significance of history remains tied to an event "that takes place in the deepest desolation of human life, on the cross. History finds its meaning in the humiliated Christ," he says.[107]

Christ's Contemporary Humiliation

Bonhoeffer discusses Jesus' humiliation not only in terms of sinful flesh and the cross but also in reference to Christ's contemporary bodily presence. In doing so, he incorporates into his description of humiliation some of the places Luther locates God's hiddenness in *Lectures on the Psalms*, such as the eucharist and the church. God in God's freedom not only suffers the cross but also wills to remain present and public through contemporary humiliation. The humiliated incognito simultaneously displays God's *radical freedom* over the world and God's willingness *to sustain vulnerability* within the world.

In his christology lectures, Bonhoeffer argues that Christ is consistently present in history as the exalted and humiliated one through the structures of Word, sacrament, and community. First, he says that Christ simultaneously maintains freedom over the world and sustains vulnerability within the world as Word, which includes both scripture and the church's proclamation. God maintains radical freedom over the world in that the divine logos is judgment upon all human words. He is the "counter Logos," the Word become flesh, and as human person Christ is neither subject to proof nor human possession.[108] Christ the counter Logos is not an ossified, static idea or principle but is the Word "in the form of living address" that is every time unique and new. Bonhoeffer argues, though, that although God maintains freedom over the world as the dynamic, living address that disrupts human thinking, Christ also sustains vulnerability in the world through the church's proclamation.[109] While a conscientious church may wish to avoid humiliating Christ through the inadequacy or erroneous nature of its proclamation, speaking the Word of God in the concrete moment is a matter of obedience and thus must be risked. Bonhoeffer says, "I could not preach if I did not know that I am speaking *God's Word*, and I could not preach if it were *I* who is supposed to be speaking God's Word."[110] Aware of the impossible command to utter the Word of God, Bonhoeffer opens his christology lectures with the reflection that Christian speech—and we may add, public witness—must begin in silence. The community only speaks rightly out of a proper humility that recognizes that Christian faith cannot be proved, guaranteed, or assured through successful debate. It can only be lived and confessed.[111] While witness in the concrete moment may necessitate articulating the reasons for the church's faith and hope, public proclamation "is not the same as loudly shrieking out propaganda"; for witness takes the form of a person, not an idea.[112]

As living address, the divine Logos is not "timeless" truth but truth spoken into the historic, concrete moment (whether through the words of scripture or the proclaimer) that requires the "response" and "responsibility" of community.[113] The divine Logos, in other words, is relational truth. By requiring response and responsibility, however, the radical freedom of the living Word makes itself again dependent, this time on the hearing community that may distort, misinterpret, or misrepresent the gospel message, whether innocently or otherwise. Bonhoeffer says, "Christ goes through the ages, questioned anew, misunderstood anew, and again and again put to death."[114] Although Christ is the divine Logos, the counter-idea, that cannot rightly be possessed, God sustains vulnerability in the world by freely binding Godself to human words, human response, and human responsibility. Furthermore, the Word of God is humiliated not only in the inadequacy of human speech and thought but also in its vulnerability to human critique. For example, Christ as Word freely binds himself to scripture that is authoritative and yet also is exposed to historical criticism. Bonhoeffer says, "One must be ready to accept the concealment within history and therefore let historical criticism run its course.... Through the Bible in its fragility, God comes to meet us as the Risen One. Thus as long as we live on earth, we must go ahead and use historical criticism, inadequate though it is. For us, the historicity of Jesus has both aspects, that of history and that of faith. The two are linked together by our saying that this is the way the historical Jesus humbled himself."[115] The believing community recognizes the significance of historical criticism as furthering faith in the humiliated Christ.

Second, Bonhoeffer says that Christ is exalted and humiliated in the form of the eucharist. In the sacrament, Christ "is present to us in the sphere of our body's tangible nature. Here he is by our side as a creature, in our midst."[116] In the eucharist, the transcendent God binds Godself to the natural elements of the created and fallen earth in order to be in solidarity with us who as creatures also belong to, and are united with, creation. God wills to bind Godself to nature in the eucharist, for in doing so Christ becomes the new, restored creation. Bonhoeffer says:

> In the sacrament [Christ] breaks through fallen creation at a defined point. He is the new creature. He is the restored creation of our spiritual and bodily existence.... As new creature he is in bread and wine. Thus bread and wine are a new creation. They are really nourishment for a new being. As elements of the restored creation, they are not for themselves, but for [human beings]. This being-for-[human beings] is what makes them a new creation.[117]

It is precisely by belonging wholly to creation that Christ is the new creation intended by God. In turn, as new creation, he provides nourishment for us, strengthening us to be the same God-intended being-for others. Again, Bonhoeffer cautions against drawing oneself into the question of *how* exactly Christ is present here in the sacrament. Of significance is that this sacrament is the full presence of the exalted and humiliated Word of God because it is the proclamation of the good news that God is for humanity, indeed, for all of creation. For Bonhoeffer, the eucharist is not a symbol that interprets the Word of God but is itself the divine Logos, here and now, concealed in humiliation. Christ, the "brother and Lord," the "creature and creator," is present with and for us "in no other way" than as a humble creature.[118]

The form of Christ in the eucharistic sacrament helps clarify why Christ's existence as the humiliated one is intrinsic to his *pro nobis* structure and hence beneficial for us. The eucharist displays Christ's contemporary bodily presence in and for the world. Connecting the elements to Christ in a very literal manner, Bonhoeffer says, "John the Evangelist reports that from the crucified body of Jesus Christ there issued water and blood, the elements of both sacraments (John 19:34–35)."[119] Through the eucharist God gives Christ's body as nourishment; in doing so, God affirms that embodiment is the primary and necessary space through which we are intimately connected to the world, each other, and our own fragility.[120] We are our bodies, such that if we scorn our mortality and construct impenetrable defenses against our vulnerability to pain, poverty, and powerlessness, we acquire instead a heart of stone, incapable of communion, interdependence, and solidarity with others' suffering and joy. God gives Godself a body that Ezekiel describes as a "heart of flesh" in order to counter the fallen human's "heart of stone" (Ez. 36:26). God's movement toward humanity penetrates the flesh, strikes the stone, and releases the baptismal water whose current carries us deeper into communal life with others (Ex. 17:1–7). The significance of Christ's bodily presence, then, is not only that God draws near to humanity by becoming human, but that human flesh—indeed God's flesh—is the particular locus through which reconciliation and healing take place and through which human beings palpably receive and communicate with others.

Christ's humiliation and exaltation in speech and sacrament are specific instances of his primary contemporary form—the church itself. For Bonhoeffer, the church is "itself revelation" because it is Christ's concrete, contemporary presence in the world.[121] As a secondary form of revelation, the church simultaneously humiliates and exalts the incarnate God to whom it witnesses. Bonhoeffer says, "This Christ existing as the church is the whole person, the one who is exalted and the one who is humiliated. His being...church...has the form of a stumbling block."[122] How this stumbling block is both sinful and a revelation of God is the subject of chapter 5. There I argue more fully that the church that hides God in the humiliation of sin makes Christ visible through repentance. The christology lectures gesture toward this when Bonhoeffer says that the church as divine revelation "remains human in repentance"; they conclude with a vision of a church that "humbly confesses its sin, allows itself to be forgiven and confesses its Lord."[123]

■ ECCE HOMO, BEHOLD, THE ACCEPTER OF GUILT: BONHOEFFER'S *ETHICS*

Whereas in the 1933 lectures Bonhoeffer speaks about the hidden God, in *Ethics* he develops the corresponding notion of Christ's visibility on the cross. Such visibility is, of course, another way of speaking of God hidden in humiliation. The strength of emphasizing Christ's visibility is that it offers a positive account of Christ's public presence to which the church may be conformed.

Earlier I argued that repentance and the confession of sin integral to it are activities of divine righteousness and offer a fresh understanding of Christ's cross. In *Ethics*, Bonhoeffer makes this connection more explicit through the interrelated concepts "acceptance of guilt," "repentance," and "responsibility." Recall that Barth says that Christ "accepts personal responsibility" for sin, and he names this Christ's "perfect repentance."[124] As with Barth, we may understand Bonhoeffer's use of acceptance of guilt and responsibility through the category of repentance: Repentance means taking responsibility for sin. Bonhoeffer writes:

> In an incomprehensible reversal of all righteous and pious thought, God...*declares [Godself] as guilty towards the world*, and thereby extinguishes the [world's] guilt...God

> treads the way of humble reconciliation and thereby sets the world free. God wills to be guilty of our guilt; God takes on the punishment and suffering that guilt has brought on us. *God takes responsibility for godlessness*... Now there is no more godlessness, hate, or sin that God has not taken upon [Godself], suffered, and atoned. Now there is no longer any reality, any world, that is not reconciled with God and at peace. God has done this in the beloved son, Jesus Christ. Ecce homo![125]

God's declaration of guilt is an act of strength and intentionality, for Christ's sin-bearing on the cross is not passive assent to divine justice but a radical assumption of guilt. Christ glorifies God by accepting responsibility for sin, in turn letting divine judgment fall on God's very self. "Jesus Christ *is*... God's judgment on himself," Bonhoeffer says in his christology lectures.[126] By becoming "the one whom God has judged," Christ accepts and assumes guilt, deeming himself responsible for the world's sin and suffering.[127]

By stating that God "declares" Godself guilty, Bonhoeffer stretches christological language beyond the church's familiar and potentially domesticated understanding of the righteous and sinless Christ atoning for sin by risking statements that sound irreverent, even blasphemous (of which Jesus himself was accused): *God* as guilty toward the world, *God* as responsible for godlessness. Moreover, by framing this discussion with the term *Ecce Homo*, Bonhoeffer echoes Nietzsche's work by the same name.[128] In *Ecce Homo*, Nietzsche writes, "A god come to earth ought to... take upon oneself... *guilt*—only that would be godlike."[129] The faith of Bonhoeffer shares some insights with the atheism of Nietzsche, who out of profound hostility toward Christianity tries to overturn traditional forms of religious thought and morality. Certainly for Bonhoeffer, Christ's acceptance of guilt is a dynamic act, an objective determination that the guilty verdict falls on him instead of others, rather than an expression of a subjective emotion or a burdened conscience.[130] As in the christology lectures, in *Ethics* Christ remains for Bonhoeffer "guilty yet sinless."[131] Still, by emphasizing Christ's acceptance of guilt, Bonhoeffer expands his understanding of God's work on the cross beyond the doctrine of substitutionary atonement and toward Nietzsche's scandalous statement above: that God's declaration of guilt reveals God's identity. In a fallen world, it is the definitive expression of God's goodness and love.[132] Undoubtedly, as Bonhoeffer shows in *Discipleship*, there is scriptural precedent for understanding salvation as substitution, which necessitates a *righteous* God. God's righteousness is exchanged for humanity's unrighteousness: "God made him who had no sin to be sin for us, so that in him we may become the righteousness of God (2 Cor. 5:21); "Jesus Christ... gave himself for us to redeem us from all wickedness and to purify for himself a people that are his very own, eager to do what is good" (Titus 2:14).[133] Indeed, Christ's cross entails an exchange setting fallen humanity free, but our freedom is for responsible action and for the other, not freedom from the cross itself. Christian freedom necessitates conforming to the goodness and righteousness of Jesus, "who entered into community with the guilt of other human beings."[134] God's declaration of guilt is even more offensive and religiously incomprehensible than the wrongful punishment of a morally perfect God, whose followers, in turn, can claim similar persecution in their own lives. A God who accepts responsibility for sin and calls followers into conformation is decisively free from religious manipulation and control.

Christ, then, does not seek to glorify God by displaying human standards of "ethical perfection."[135] In *Ethics*, Bonhoeffer roots his critique of morality or religious righteousness in the incarnate God. He says, "In an incomprehensible reversal of all righteous and pious thought," Jesus concerns himself with being neither "a private saint" nor "a religious enthusiast." Recall from the critique of morality in chapter 2 that divine and human righteousness stand in opposition to one another. By taking sin upon himself, Jesus counters a human ethic of religious righteousness. Bonhoeffer says:

> Jesus does not want to be considered the only perfect one at the expense of human beings, nor, as the only guiltless one, to look down on humanity perishing under its guilt. He does not want some idea of a new human being to triumph over the wreckage of a defeated humanity.... Because he loves them, he does not acquit himself of the guilt in which human beings live. A love that abandons human beings to their guilt would not be a love for real human beings... it is God's love that lets Jesus become guilty.[136]

God does not love who human beings ought to be; rather, God's love places Christ in solidarity with real human beings and establishes an ethic suitable for sinful humanity, an ethic of christological conformation rooted in repentance and the confession of sin. Jesus does not establish new, abstract, ethical ideals for his disciples to follow nor endorse religious righteousness as a witness to God's intentions for the rest of the world. In *Ethics*, for example, Bonhoeffer interprets the Sermon on the Mount not as impossible ideals to which persons must attain but as accomplishable and responsible acts for human beings who recognize sin.[137] The poor in spirit, the mourners with hearts of flesh, the meek, the merciful, those who desire to make right that which is not, the peacemakers: these are real human beings who participate in the redemptive powerlessness of God in the world, following after the form of Christ who at no time "acquit himself of the guilt in which human beings live."[138]

In *Prayerbook of the Bible*, Bonhoeffer says even more explicitly that Christ confesses sin, this time in solidarity with contemporary human beings. In his study of the Psalms, he argues that human beings do not naturally know how to pray rightly and that prayer must be learned through the Psalter and the Lord's Prayer, which is the "crown and unity" of the Psalms.[139] Bonhoeffer says that Jesus not only teaches Christians how to pray, but also wants to pray with us, indeed must pray with us: "Only in and with Jesus Christ" can Christians "truly pray."[140] The prayers Christ prays alongside the church include those of repentance, the seven penitential Psalms (Ps. 6, 32, 38, 51, 102, 130, 143) as well as those that deepen the recognition of sin (Ps. 14, 15, 25, 31, 39, 40, 41, etc.).[141] Bonhoeffer addresses the question of how the

Son of God prays these penitential Psalms along with the sinful church: "How can the sinless one ask for forgiveness?" He answers:

> In the same way that the sinless one can bear the sins of the world and be made sin for us (2 Cor. 5:21). Jesus prays for the forgiveness of sins, yet not for his own but ours, which he has taken upon himself and for which he suffers. He puts himself completely in our place; he wants to be a human being before God as we are. So Jesus prays even the most human of all prayers with us, and precisely in this, shows himself to be the true Son of God.[142]

Christ continuously enters into human guilt by praying the Psalter's confession of sin with the church.

Christ can pray the Psalter in genuine solidarity with human beings in the contemporary moment because he has already entered history and experienced reality in the form of a sinner. Because the incarnate God in fallen flesh does not exempt himself from guilt, Bonhoeffer refers to Jesus Christ as the "Real One" and, in doing so, alludes to and christologically redescribes the depiction of the human being as *ens realissimum* (the most real being) by Nietzsche and the nineteenth-century German philosopher Ludwig Feuerbach.[143] To be placed, to find oneself already within reality, is to be human. Bonhoeffer says, "Jesus Christ does not encounter reality as one who is foreign to it. Instead, it is he who alone bore and experienced in his own body the essence of the real, and who spoke out of the knowledge of the real like no other human being on earth."[144] Jesus enters fully into historical reality, and in a fallen world this entails accepting guilt and suffering. Bonhoeffer says that the whole of Jesus' life may be summed up by this one word in the Apostles Creed—"suffered."[145] In *Discipleship* he says that Christ drank the cup of suffering "to the dregs" on the god-forsaken cross, and again in prison he affirms that to be truly human, human beings must "drink the earthly cup to the dregs."[146] Christ as the quintessential human being drinks incarnate life to the full, including the waste and residue of sin, and thereby overcomes suffering through suffering. This is also why Luther deems the community of the cross capable of "calling the thing what it actually is," capable of attending to reality instead of escaping into ideals. Only by courageously and fully entering into the painful, messy, ambiguous character of existence does life have redemptive efficacy, as revealed in Christ, who "bore our flesh... bore the cross... bore all our sins and attained reconciliation by his bearing."[147] *Ecce homo*—"behold what a human being!"—not the *homo religiosus* but simply and fully the real human being who is "not ashamed to be crucified for us as an evildoer."[148]

In becoming the quintessential human being who belongs wholly to the world by drinking the earthly cup to the dregs, Christ affirms human life and points toward the *telos* of a redeemed humanity. A new emphasis in Bonhoeffer scholarship on the theme of Christian humanism has led some scholars to the insight that Bonhoeffer reverses the theological formulations of patristic thinkers like Athanasius and Augustine, who assert that "God became human so that human beings might become divine." Bonhoeffer highlights that God became human so that human beings might become more fully human—"truly human" as the Chalcedonian statement defines Christ.[149] Christ is the human being par excellence, whose life and death reveal that participation in divine glory and divine righteousness entails belonging wholly to the world. In a fallen world, this necessitates the willingness to repent and take responsibility for the sin entrapping and injuring ourselves and others.

Jesus is not only the remarkable and responsible human being par excellence, but also the person of Christ is the very being of a new humanity.[150] Bonhoeffer signals a participatory ontology through the biblical phrase "in Christ."[151] Christ has a particular identity—the incarnate God who is the image of the invisible God—but he is simultaneously the representative of humanity, which he bears in his body out of obedience to the Father and out of love for the world. The Apostle Paul parallels Christ with scripture's first human being, who is also both a particular individual and a communal representative whose bodily disobedience had ontological repercussions for us all. In order to show the same expansive influence of Christ's ontology, Paul calls Christ the second or final Adam (1 Cor. 15:45).[152] Echoing the christology lectures' focus on Romans 8:3 and taking it to its christological conclusion, in *Discipleship* Bonhoeffer says that through the incarnation, Jesus Christ becomes not simply an individual person but "human 'form,' sinful flesh, human 'nature,' all that he bore, therefore, suffers and dies with him.... Jesus thus brings humanity not only into death with him, but also into the resurrection."[153] Because Christ as representative has brought all of humanity with him into the resurrection, "it is no longer possible to conceive and understand humanity other than in Jesus Christ."[154] Indeed, Christ has fulfilled "all that human beings were supposed to live, do, and suffer;" however, this does not negate the life of the contemporary church through which Christ is bodily present.[155] The church takes the form of Christ, the real human being who accepts responsibility for sin, by being the new humanity who likewise lives for others through repentance.

I have argued that God's glory is to accept guilt, that God's righteousness is expressed through divine repentance—and that *this* is the manner through which God is hidden in humiliation and visible in public life. God wills to be present to humanity in sinful flesh, as a penitent numbered with the transgressors, as a criminal on the cross. Bonhoeffer emphasizes the astounding character of Christ's presence when he says that on Golgotha Jesus dies "the public death of the sinner."[156] He says, "The wondrous theme of the Bible that frightens so many people is that the only visible sign of God in the world is the cross."[157] Christ's work is indeed public: on the banks of the Jordan, on the road leading to Jerusalem, in the courtyard before the Sanhedrin and then before Pilate, and on Golgotha. In those spaces he is baptized with sinners, rides a donkey, is condemned for blasphemy, and hangs under a mocking sign. Although his ministry leads him into the middle of the public spheres of life, Jesus never lays claim to the public square. His visibility in the middle is always characterized by the cross, and it is only from this middle that new life comes forth.[158]

In the midst of public life, Jesus takes the form of a sinner. For, the work accomplished by Christ is that of repentance. Although this may sound shocking, perhaps downright strange, this scandalous claim is fully compatible with an orthodox christology, including an affirmation of Jesus' sinlessness. God's repentance in Christ is a result not of divine sin but of divine love—a love that wills to take responsibility for the sin that humanity has generated collectively through time. Understanding repentance in this way is the hermeneutical key for thinking about Christ's presence in the church and the church's presence in our society today. The triumphalistic tendencies of Christian witness has necessitated this renewed reflection on repentance, and a christological reinterpretation has shifted the primary focus from one's individual standing before God to existence for others, to ecclesial concern for social flourishing. Since Jesus' person and work is characterized by repentance so, too, must be the public activity of church-communities called to be the redemptive presence of Christ in our pluralistic democracy. As the church takes the form of the penitent Jesus in public life, it shares in the redemptive power of the Christ event, the very foundation for Christian witness. Ecce homo!—behold, the penitent, the accepter of guilt, the glory of the human being who is exalted through humility.

4 Belonging

Participation in the World's Christological Pattern

The previous chapter examined Christ's public presence as the primary source for the church's public witness. The church offers a nontriumphal witness in a pluralistic society not by viewing itself as religiously or morally favored but by taking the form of the crucified Christ, who belonged wholly to this world through a divine righteousness expressed through repentance. While the previous chapter focused on the *person* of Christ, this chapter examines the *work* of Christ—Christ's threefold acceptance, judgment, and reconciliation of the world—and argues that his cosmic accomplishment transformed the very structure of reality such that the grain of the universe is now patterned after the life, death, and resurrection of Jesus. The church participates in the world's new ontology centrally through repentance; for, when the church-community delves into the ambiguities of public life while acknowledging its solidarity with sinful humanity, it faithfully abandons itself to life's christological structure: to the theological fact that accepting responsibility for sin has transformative power and prepares the way for Christ's concrete redemption. Ecclesial repentance, then, witnesses to both the person and work of Christ; it simultaneously mirrors Jesus' public presence and participates in the world's christological pattern. Together the person and work of Christ lay the foundation for a public witness that is free to belong wholly to a world already reconciled to God and to proclaim good news and enact concrete redemption from that place.

Many Protestant Christians in the United States may be suspicious of, or resistant to, an argument grounded in Bonhoeffer's theology that the church faithfully witnesses to Christ through this-worldly belonging. Bonhoeffer's most popular work in the United States is a book he wrote while directing the Confessing Church's Finkenwalde seminary, published in English as *The Cost of Discipleship*, that when read without attention to his totalitarian context may be misinterpreted as a call for the church in a democratic society strictly to separate itself from the sinful world. Moreover, there is biblical precedent for a negative understanding of the terms "world" and "flesh" in Pauline and Johannine texts, which also appear to counter a call to this-worldly belonging. This chapter first will examine *Nachfolge* (*Discipleship*) in light of its historical context. I argue that although *Discipleship* paints an incomplete picture of Bonhoeffer's theology if read in isolation from his other writings, when situated historically, theologically, and biblically the book does not contradict this-worldly belonging but may be used to support the radical character of a faithful public witness found throughout his works. I will then return to the examination of *Ethics* begun in the last chapter in order to develop more fully Bonhoeffer's understanding of

Christ's relationship to this world. The world's new ontology—the threefold christological pattern—is interwoven such that Christ's affirmation includes divine judgment and divine judgment enables the world's reconciliation and redemption. The church demonstrates the dynamic interrelation of the world's new ontology when it takes the form of the crucified Christ (the center of the threefold christological pattern) and accepts God's judgment through a repentance that prepares the way for Christ's redemption. Because the world has been reconciled to God through Christ, though not demonstratively redeemed, the church is called to witness to this already accomplished reconciliation by being a concrete redemptive presence through responsible acts of repentance.[1]

■ CONTEXTUALIZING BONHOEFFER'S *DISCIPLESHIP*

Reading *The Cost of Discipleship* in the United States

Bonhoeffer is readily appealed to as a theological authority among a wide array of North American Protestants yet he is often misunderstood. Scholarship of the 1960s notoriously misused Bonhoeffer's fragmentary *Letters and Papers from Prison* to support conclusions that counter his theology as a whole, and *The Cost of Discipleship* is vulnerable to misappropriation to a similar extent. Along with *Life Together*, *The Cost of Discipleship* is generally considered the most accessible of Bonhoeffer's writings, able to be plucked from the religion shelf of most large-scale bookstores and digested by many North American readers. In 1995, Touchstone expanded its readership by publishing the first paperback English translation since 1964, and in 1997 the prominent evangelical magazine, *Christianity Today*, placed *The Cost of Discipleship* on their list of the top fifteen "best devotional books of all time."[2] However, readers of the definitive *Dietrich Bonhoeffer Works* 2003 edition may gain a different understanding of the book's message and intent than attained through the popular 1995 English version as a result of a structure more faithful to the original, a more accurate translation, and an afterword explaining the historical context.[3] A reading lacking access or attention to historical nuance and detail paints a picture of the world that is antithetical to the majority of Bonhoeffer's writings.

Bonhoeffer's theology typically is marked by "this-worldliness"—the church immersed within the messiness and ambiguity of concrete, historical reality. The description of the "world" in *The Cost of Discipleship*, however, is governed by metaphors of warfare that position the church at times on the offense invading the world and at times on the defense awaiting divine deliverance from this world. The popular 1995 Simon and Schuster Touchstone edition reads as follows:

> ...The church *invades* the life of the world and *conquers territory* for Christ....The member of the Body of Christ has been *delivered* from the world and called out of it.
>
> ...Thus while it is true that the Body of Christ *makes a deep invasion* into the sphere of secular life, yet at the same time the *great gulf* between the two is always clear at other points, and must become increasingly so.

> ...The Ecclesia Christi, the disciple community, *has been torn from the clutches of the world*....The object of their calling in Jesus Christ, and of their election before the foundation of the world, was that they should be holy and without blemish...[God] is holy both in his *perfect separation from the sinful world* and in the establishment of his sanctuary in the midst of that world....God makes a covenant with his people and separates them from the world.
>
> ...The communion of saints is *barred off from the world with an unbreakable seal*, awaiting its ultimate *deliverance*....The sanctification of the church means its *separation from all that is unholy, from sin*;...The church must claim a definite sphere in the world for itself, and so define clearly the frontier between itself and the world....The sanctification of the world is really a *defensive war* for the place which has been given to the Body of Christ on earth. The *separation of the church and the world* from one another is the *crusade* which the Church fights for the sanctuary of God on earth.
>
> ...*For the church, the world and all its vices belong to the past.* It has *broken off all contact* with those that do such things, and it is its duty always to shun them (1 Cor. 5:9). For "what communion hath light with darkness?" (2 Cor. 6:14).[4]

Many of the phrases italicized above are translated differently in the new edition and sound less severe; for example, in *Dietrich Bonhoeffer Works* (DBWE) volume 4, the first passage reads, "The church-community has, therefore, a very real impact on the life of the world. It gains space for Christ....All who belong to the body of Christ have been freed from and called out of the world." The second reads, "The body of Christ is thus deeply involved in all areas of life in this world. And yet there are certain points where the complete separation remains visible, and must become even more visible. However, whether in the world or separated from it, Christians in either case seek to obey the same word: 'Do not be conformed to this world, but be transformed into a new form,'" and the third begins not with a violent image of "being torn from the clutches" of the world but with the Pauline claim that the church "is no longer subject to the rule of this world."[5]

These differences are significant; still, the oppositional language in *The Cost of Discipleship* cannot be explained simply by an imprecise translation. Bonhoeffer's entire discussion of the church and the world in *Nachfolge* seems to rest on a theological framework he decisively rejects in *Ethics*: the church and the world are not two separate and warring realms, he will argue, but are one reality reconciled in Christ.[6] Although, as I show below, more is at play than a simple two realms paradigm, in *Discipleship*, Bonhoeffer does slip into dualistic thinking that untethers God's righteousness from Christ's cross. Divine holiness is defined not in the paradoxical and scandalous manner examined in the previous chapter but as "being completely set apart from the sinful world." The church then must also separate itself from the world, he argues, especially in the chapters "The Visible Church-Community" and "The Saints." Bonhoeffer writes that the visible church is to be "holy and blameless" and lives "in a new space of [its] own" which is "God's realm of holiness in the world."[7] The chapters preceding these examine the Sermon on the Mount and rightly speak of the central, definitive role the sermon plays in following after the incarnate and crucified Christ; still, in part 2 of *Discipleship*, Bonhoeffer casts Jesus' teachings not in terms he will use in *Ethics*, namely that these practices place the church in solidarity with real human beings, but in terms of separation and distinction, of a "better righteousness" that "towers over" the "unbeliever."[8] The world from which the disciples remove themselves is "the world [that] crucified Christ," which is "not in need of reform but [is] ripe to be demolished."[9]

Whereas my study of Bonhoeffer's work before and after *Discipleship* (the 1933 christology lectures, *Ethics*, and *Letter and Papers from Prison*) has defined God's righteousness in Christ as repentance and has described Christ as belonging wholly to this world in fallen flesh and on the cross, in *Discipleship* Bonhoeffer writes that *metanoia*, the transformation to which the church is called, consists of taking "the form of Christ" who is "not of this world." The church, which is not to be "conformed to this world" but is to be "transformed into a new form... by the renewing of minds" (Rom. 12:2), looks to its Lord "in heaven," he writes.[10]

Certainly Bonhoeffer tries to guard the reader from a self-righteousness born from the message of separation and distinction. For example, he says that Christians "do not possess any special right or power of their own."[11] He attempts to shield the disciples from a spiritual pride that could stem from understanding one's identity as distinct from the world by introducing a delicate balance between the visible and hidden aspects of discipleship. He writes, "'Let your light shine before the people...' ([Matt.] 5:16), but: pay attention to the hiddenness! Chapters 5 and 6 [of Matthew's Gospel] collide hard against each other. What is visible should be hidden at the same time; at the same time both visible and not to be seen."[12] Bonhoeffer tries to resolve the inconsistency by asserting that the disciples are to hide their "extraordinariness" from themselves.[13] However, in doing so, he merely introduces a complicated psychological mind-game into the life of discipleship. How can human beings practically hide their "extraordinariness" and "righteousness" from themselves, not letting the left hand know what the right hand is doing (Matt. 6:3), without lapsing into false humility or spiritual pride? Bonhoeffer rightly concludes that such a balance can be found in the cross which is at once visible and hidden, but in this text he does not show the reader what he makes clear in the christology lectures, namely that the cross hides God in the form of a sinner, in the humiliation of sinful flesh. Only by taking the form of the crucified Christ, who belonged wholly to the world by taking responsibility for sin as a penitent, can the church stand unified in genuine humility as a body whose redemptive work is at once hidden and visible before the world: Because the church's work centrally includes the confession of sin, its "goodness" is hidden; still, the church's witness is visible in the world through responsible acts of repentance. As this brief analysis of his discussion of the visible and hidden aspects of discipleship exemplifies, some ideas in *Nachfolge* are simultaneously challenged and enhanced when positioned within Bonhoeffer's thought as a whole.[14]

The potential for a United States audience to miss, in an isolated reading of *Discipleship*, the centrality of the concept of this-worldliness in Bonhoeffer's theology may be further exemplified through his statement that the essence of the cross "is not suffering alone; it is suffering and being rejected" for the cause of Christ.[15] Bonhoeffer adds rejection to suffering in order to emphasize that Christ's suffering was stripped of dignity and honor. For some Christians in the United States, however, feeling rejected by the world is a badge of Christian honor. Read out of context, Bonhoeffer's emphasis on rejection may serve to reinforce a victim mentality present within some segments of North American Christianity that promotes a belief that in our democratic society Christian identity alone necessarily positions Christians as rejected, even persecuted, by the surrounding "secular" culture. A victim mentality leads to such trivialized expressions of faith as campaigns to "save Christmas," rather than to humble recognition that sometimes it is a self-assured attitude toward the unbelieving world or an ambition to dominate public life that non-Christians understandably find repellent.[16] Certainly, one may find statements in *Discipleship* that discourage an antagonistic stance against the world. For example, Bonhoeffer says, "Christians are in the world and they need the world; they are fleshy; for the sake of their fleshy nature, Christ came into the world."[17] Still, for a North American audience that tends to view itself as religiously favored and to ground witness in an assumption that Christians are called to be the disseminators of truth and the standard-bearers of morality, Bonhoeffer's language of Christian distinction and worldly separation overpowers his few direct affirmations encouraging positive this-worldly engagement. An ahistorical reading of *The Cost of Discipleship* does little more than communicate the popular formula that Christians are *in* the world but *not of* the world—a pithy saying that nevertheless risks neglecting the central christological point that Christ and the church exist *for* the world.[18] As we have seen, radical this-worldly belonging based on Christ's public presence positions the church in profound solidarity with humanity's sin and guilt, with Christ's definitive *pro nobis* character unsettling a static, simple distinction between being *in* and *of* the world.

Discipleship in Historical Context

While *The Cost of Discipleship* is vulnerable to misappropriation in a participatory democracy, when read in light of his historical context one may see that the language of separation became an impetus for this-worldly engagement in the form of resistance to totalitarianism for Bonhoeffer's contemporary readership. In other words, Bonhoeffer's message of separation from the world is subordinate to his message of responsible engagement within the world. Bonhoeffer intends *Discipleship* to be read as God's word for his concrete moment, for he opens the preface by asking, "What does [Jesus] want from us *today*?"[19] Because he had already developed many of the ideas while serving as the director of the Finkenwalde seminary, his primary audience is the young pastors-in-training entering the Confessing

Church's resistance to Nazi ideology and rule, a resistance defined institutionally by its refusal to incorporate into the Reich church government.[20] The question concerning God's will in the concrete moment is thus an inquiry into how Confessing Church members are to remain defiant toward Nazi totalitarianism as faithful followers of Christ, especially since sustained and radical resistance to the Nazi regime was rare even within the Confessing Church.[21] The "world" to which Bonhoeffer refers is primarily this context of totalitarianism and the seductive powers of security and concession tempting Confessing Christians and holding sway over the national church.

The lure of safety proved to be a powerful force among Confessing Church seminarians. By the fall of 1935, just months after the seminary Bonhoeffer directed relocated from Zingst to Finkenwalde, the Nazis had enacted a Law for the Protection of the German Protestant Church with a regulation that abolished the legal status of the Confessing Church's polity, institutions, and seminaries or those of any other religious group claiming independence from the authority of the Reich church. Nazi ordinances had branded Finkenwalde seminarians "illegals," and throughout 1936 a number of pastoral candidates succumbed to what some described as an almost unbearable pressure of "becoming legal."[22] Those candidates who gained security under the state-sanctioned church commission in essence abandoned the call to radically separate themselves from the "world" and did not heed the message of the Barmen and Dahlem Confessions that proclaimed the exclusive lordship of Christ. More clearly than the previous English translations, the revised edition of *Discipleship* accentuates through translation and footnotes Bonhoeffer's pointed references denouncing the Reich church.[23] When discussing the Sermon on the Mount, he says, "Jesus also knows those others, the representatives and preachers of the national religion, those powerful, respected people, who stand firmly on the earth inseparably rooted in the national way of life, the spirit of the times, the popular piety. But Jesus does not speak to them; he speaks only to his disciples when he says, blessed—for yours is the kingdom of heaven" (Matt. 5:10).[24] In language that severely rebukes the national church, Bonhoeffer admonishes the Confessing Church to remain within its call. Again referencing the Sermon on the Mount, he speaks about the salt that is meant to sustain the world but "loses its taste," "stops being salt," and can "never again be salty" (Matt. 5:13). He says, "It ceases to be effective. Then it really is no longer good for anything except to be thrown away.... Everything, even the most spoiled stuff, can be saved by salt. Only salt which has lost its saltiness is hopelessly spoiled.... That is the threatening judgment which hangs over the disciples' community.... The community that has stopped being what it is will be hopelessly lost. The call of Jesus means being the salt of the earth or being destroyed."[25]

A further regulation that directly affected the Finkenwalde seminarians was issued in March 1937, approximately six months before the Gestapo closed the seminary. The 13th ordinance of the Law for the Protection of the German

Protestant Church now sought to eradicate from public life those church-communities that illegally tried to remain independent from the national church's authority.[26] The Nazis used tactics of intimidation and terror to squelch church autonomy, and the year 1937 was marked by interrogations, harassment, arrests, and the imprisonment of many Confessing Church members. In words likely addressed directly to the Finkenwalde seminarians and to other Confessing Church congregants who were enduring and overcoming the pressure to join the Reich church, Bonhoeffer says in the chapter, "The Saints,"

> The church-community has to muster the courage to separate itself from the sinner. "Have nothing to do with that person" (2 Thess. 3:14); "part company with them" (Rom. 16:17); "do not even eat with such a one" (Lord's Supper?) (1 Cor. 5:11);... The church-community which separates itself from the sinners is called to confront them with the word of admonition. "Do not regard them as enemies, but admonish them as believers" (2 Thess. 3:15).[27]

Within historical context, one hears Bonhoeffer's message of separation as a radical call to live courageously in the midst of the world: "Where will the call of discipleship lead to those who follow it? What decisions and painful separations will it entail?... Only Jesus Christ who bids us follow him knows where the path will lead. But we know that it will be a path of mercy beyond measure. Discipleship is joy," he writes.[28]

Bonhoeffer's theology of separation from the world of Nazi totalitarianism is further addressed in the short chapter, "Discipleship and the Individual." Here Bonhoeffer says more clearly that the disciple's separation from the world is a call to engage the world through Christ, the mediator. Discipleship causes a break not from the world itself but from immediate or direct access to the world. Like Abraham who renounces natural, ethical, and religious immediacy when obeying God's command to sacrifice his son Isaac, so disciples are to reject any engagement with the world that is not mediated through Christ.[29] Although a mediated relationship with the natural, ethical, and religious causes a separation, Christ the mediator leads the church back into the world that God loves. Bonhoeffer says,

> There is no gratitude for nation, family, history, and nature without a *deep repentance* that honors Christ alone above these gifts. There is no genuine tie to the given realities of the created world; there are no genuine responsibilities in the world without recognition of the break, which already separates us from the world. There is no genuine love for the world except the love with which God has loved the world in Jesus Christ. "Do not love the world" (1 John 2:15). But "God so loved the world that he gave his only Son..." (John 3:16).[30]

As in *Letters and Papers from Prison*, in this passage Bonhoeffer connects discipleship with repentance. Here he shows that a paradox lies within repentance: Christians turn away from the world in order that they may turn toward Christ the mediator, who then leads them back into the midst of this-worldly reality.

As the above passage exemplifies, an examination of *Discipleship* illustrates the complex theological significance of the term "world." The Greek word *kosmos*, often translated simply as "world" in the New Testament, has both negative and positive connotations given its broad range of meaning in scripture from "universe" or "cosmic space" to "the sum of all created being" to "fallen creation" to "the earth" or "the abode of humanity" or simply "humanity" to "the theatre of history," "the theatre of salvation history" or "the locus of revelation in Christ."[31] These multiple meanings make it difficult to summarize succinctly the church's multivariant relationship to "the world." Even in light of the historical context of *Discipleship*, in which "world" mostly refers to the allure of the Nazi regime, Bonhoeffer later recognizes in prison that his emphasis in that book on separation from the sinful world is theologically dangerous. A resounding No to the world unaccompanied by a more pronounced Yes silences the affirmation Christians are called to proclaim through their Christ-shaped worldly engagement. The No proclaimed upon the world is not untruthful or inaccurate, rather it is misleading as an isolated proclamation. Any reading of reality that does not position Christ's No within Christ's all-encompassing Yes leads to an overly positive evaluation of the church and overly negative estimation of this-worldly life. Recall his July 21, 1944, letter, written the day after his colleagues' failed attempt at tyrannicide, in which he tells Bethge, "I thought I... could learn to have faith by trying to live something like a saintly life. I suppose I wrote *Discipleship* at the end of this path. Today I clearly see the dangers of that book, though I still stand by it. Later on I discovered, and am still discovering to this day, that one learns to have faith by living in the full this-worldliness of life... This is μετάνοια [*metanoia*]. And this is how one becomes a human being, a Christian."[32] Bonhoeffer later recognizes the dangers of his portrayal of holiness and his dualistic rendering of the church and world. At the same time, he does not dismiss the entire work. Certain christological affirmations unifying his theology are present in the text and traces of his characteristic this-worldliness can be detected.[33] For example, in his discussion of the relationship between faith and obedience in *Discipleship*, Bonhoeffer makes a point, similar to the one above, about learning to have faith. He argues that because "only the believers obey, and only the obedient believe," faith demands a *situation* in which obedience is called for, in which Jesus' followers may learn to believe.[34] He writes, "A call to discipleship thus immediately creates a new situation. Staying in the old situation and following Christ mutually exclude each other.... If they want to learn to believe in God, they have to follow the Son of God incarnate and walk with him."[35] The main difference between this passage and the one above is that here Bonhoeffer does not name this experience of being situated or placed as "living completely in this world"—as "this-worldliness."[36]

Some pastors who trained at the seminary were deeply troubled by discussions, which arose immediately after the publication of Bonhoeffer's letters from prison, that criticized *Discipleship* for presenting too narrow a picture of the church's relation to the world and that wondered whether the writings from Finkenwalde represent a period less true to Bonhoeffer's overall thinking. [37] These pastors had endured the consequences of concretely living according to Bonhoeffer's biblical and theological teachings—they had followed Christ into a new situation in which they would learn to believe—and engagement with the theology in *Discipleship* strengthened them to resist the Reich church. In a letter sent in 1985 to the editors of the German edition of *Nachfolge*, a former student Heinz Fleischhack shared that he was "repeatedly concerned" while reading the correspondence compiled in *Letters and Papers from Prison* until he read that Bonhoeffer "[stood] by what [he] wrote" in *Discipleship*.[38] Hearing Bonhoeffer's lectures at Finkenwalde inspired him and other seminarians toward this-worldly discipleship and courageous resistance, for they understood the message of separation as a call to break free from Reich church governance and the Nazi regime.[39]

When attentive to historical context, one sees how Bonhoeffer's theology of separation from the world is a call to costly discipleship within the world. Still, Bonhoeffer's historical context does not resolve the complexity inherent within any theological depiction of "the world." Some of Bonhoeffer's theological claims in *Discipleship* deserve further examination. Specifically, the claim that the form of Christ is "not of this world" appears directly to oppose christological belonging as developed in the previous chapter. Instead of dismissing Bonhoeffer's statement as inconsistent with the rest of his theology, in the following section I supplement *Discipleship* with Paul's apocalyptic thought in order to show that Bonhoeffer's claim holds legitimacy in an important sense; for, Christ does not belong wholly to the world if by "world" one means the destructive cosmic power Paul names "the flesh." Without contradiction and in accordance with the thrust of Bonhoeffer's theology, certain strands of Paul's apocalyptic thinking also teach that the church belongs to the world as the body conformed to the crucified Christ and governed by the power of "the Spirit."

▪ POSITIONING *DISCIPLESHIP* WITHIN PAULINE APOCALYPTIC THOUGHT

Bonhoeffer divides *Nachfolge* into two parts, first a study of discipleship in the Synoptic Gospels with particular attention to the Sermon on the Mount and then an analysis of the New Testament letters where Paul establishes a new set of terminology about discipleship rooted in the sacrament of baptism and the gift of the Spirit.[40] Bonhoeffer's language of separation from the world sounds particularly stark and dualistic when he engages Paul's letters in part 2 and speaks in Pauline fashion of invasion and battle.[41] The manner in which he calls the church to distinguish itself from "the world" resembles Paul's apocalyptic perspective, where a war has been waged between two cosmic powers, "the Spirit" and "the flesh." However, instead of a direct examination of the powers, Bonhoeffer writes of an antagonism between two separate spatial realms, "the church" and "the world," and in doing so, he risks obstructing his intended message. For, *Discipleship* is concerned not with the church's relationship to the world broadly construed but addresses the Confessing Church's relationship to the national church, which has fallen prey to the seductive forces of Nazi totalitarianism—in other words, to the destructive and oppressive power of "the flesh" expressed in Nazi rule.[42] Reappraisals of apocalyptic impulses in Paul by such scholars as J. Louis Martyn, J. Christiaan Beker, and, most recently, Douglas A. Campbell, are particularly helpful for resolving the rhetorical and conceptual discrepancy between *Discipleship* and Bonhoeffer's other writings.[43] These scholars show that although Paul introduces a dualism between the forces of "the Spirit" and "the flesh," Paul's thinking leads not to a dualistic rendering of the church and the world (as *Discipleship* articulates) but to a positive construal of this-worldly reality which has been unified in Christ.[44] As we will soon see, in *Ethics* Bonhoeffer bases the church's radical this-worldly belonging precisely on the world's cosmic reconciliation and ontological unity, perspectives that are central to Paul's apocalyptic thought.[45]

Notably, though, Bonhoeffer scholarship has been slow to see and hesitant to name Pauline apocalyptic logic at work in Bonhoeffer's writings, with the exception of Philip G. Ziegler, who, also drawing on the studies of Martyn and Beker, reexamines the relationship between Paul's apocalyptic perspective and Bonhoeffer's theology. Ziegler focuses on *Ethics*, arguing that "draft upon draft of that manuscript, Bonhoeffer is working out a theological ethic whose intent is to conform to the contours of Paul's apocalyptic gospel," wherein the advent and event of Christ has ontological consequences (reality is remade) as well as the epistemological and ethical consequences discussed in chapter 2 (patterns of thinking are disrupted and there is a radical reversal of what constitutes righteousness or "morality").[46] Moreover, Ziegler suggests that these Pauline apocalyptic thought forms are present not only in the 1940s, when *Ethics* was drafted, but also in the 1930s, the period enveloping Bonhoeffer's teaching at Finkenwalde and the writing of *Discipleship*. There are seeds of the Pauline apocalyptic, buried and suffocating under the church/world conceptual frame he rightly comes to reject, that can nevertheless be detected in *Discipleship*'s discussion of baptism, its language of invasion, and its heightened emphasis on the Spirit and the community of the cross it forms, as exemplified most directly in this passage opening his analysis of Paul's letters in part 2: "The name of Jesus Christ is spoken over the baptismal candidates... Having been rescued from the rule of this world, they now have become Christ's own. Baptism thus implies a *break*. Christ invades the realm of Satan... Past and present are thus torn asunder. The old has passed away, everything has become new.... In baptism we die together with our old world... It is the death in the power and community of the cross of Christ."[47] Although *Discipleship* de-emphasizes the cosmic impulse of Paul's apocalyptic gospel in favor of a focus on justification of the sinner and the forgiveness of sin, there are nevertheless hints of Pauline apocalyptic thought forms in this text that unite Bonhoeffer's later writing with the Finkenwalde period, thought forms that burst open once he dismantles his dualistic church/world conception.

A Sketch of Paul's Apocalyptic Thought

The difficulty in understanding Paul's apocalyptic thinking is that it is often distorted into what Beker calls "its Pauline opposite" either by contemporary apocalyptic sectarians who ignore the christological core of Paul's theology or by the mainline establishment who, embarrassed by negative connotations that have come to be associated with the apocalyptic, dilute Paul's message of the in-breaking of God's future and God's promises into our present.[48] Apocalyptic thinking has come to be associated with the sectarian imagination that is bent on doomsday end-time predictions and motivated by self-centered ideologies, rather than the cosmic vision of Paul's theology that beckons hope in the final triumph of God over the powers of sin and death for the sake of the whole world, a vision that Beker argues propels Christians toward the "larger concerns of our interdependent and pluralistic world."[49] Christians attentive to the cosmic implications of Paul's apocalyptic thought find themselves in radical solidarity with humanity (indeed, with the "whole created universe" (Rom. 8:18–25)) who, like the church, long for the concrete realization of God's promises in time—who yearn for healing to triumph over suffering, liberation over bondage, human flourishing over devastation, in short, who long for death to be "swallowed up by life" (2 Cor. 5:4). Beker argues that this all-embracing apocalyptic hope rooted in the Christ event defies the sectarian's egocentric understanding of salvation and the this-worldly neglect that accompanies it. Paul's apocalyptic gospel invites active participation in God's redemptive work in the world through a cruciform existence.[50]

Central to Paul's theology of the cross and resurrection is his apocalyptic landscape in which two opposing eras, the old age characterized by evil and sin and the new age characterized by grace and redemption, are dynamically interrelated. Because the term "apocalypse" or "apocalyptic" has become familiar to North Americans through pop-theology and novels like the *Left Behind* series, the word often connotes otherworldliness, with the old age or cosmos referring to this world and the new age referring to an afterlife "in heaven." However, Paul's apocalyptic categories are not static polarizations "up there" and "down here."[51] They are not isolated from one another nor do they follow after one another. Rather, Paul imagines the new creation (understood spatially and temporally) as dynamically invading the old age, and Christ's invasion into the old cosmos instigates a temporary cosmic dualism between the powers Paul names "the Spirit" and "the flesh." Indeed, it is the coming of Christ into the world that unleashes this cosmic conflict between the two ages and the powers that define them. As the new creation, Christ penetrates the old cosmos in order to liberate humanity and creation from our enslavement to suprahuman powers.[52]

While Paul focuses the trope of cosmic warfare primarily on the cross, where deliverance from the power of sin and death already has been accomplished and the reconciliation of God and the world has been sealed for eternity, he also speaks of the old cosmos as "this present evil age" (Gal. 1:4). In doing so, Paul affirms that even with the advent of Christ, the old age, in a significant *existential* sense, is still present as an active agent. Like the mortally wounded villain who causes as much destruction as possible before dying, the old age, which has been defeated, "does not give up without a struggle."[53] The death-dealing powers of the old cosmos are quite evident and pervasive even at this juncture of the passing of the enslaving age and the dawn of the new creation.[54] At the same time, the invasion of the new creation does inaugurate radical newness, and so it is no longer fitting to refer without nuance or irony to our contemporary time as the "present evil age." Paul sees the power of the old cosmos, "the flesh," as an "*alien occupying* power," not a description of the world's ontology.[55] Martyn says, "The great turning of the ages in Christ's death/resurrection is *the fact*."[56] Christ's in-breaking is "an event of cosmic, apocalyptic proportions" that has changed "the very world in which human beings live."[57]

In an *ontological* sense, then, the old cosmos has died, as described in Galatians 6:14–15, a passage that Martyn argues contains the concepts at the core of Paul's apocalyptic thinking. These include the in-breaking event of the cross, "*May I never boast except in the cross of our Lord Jesus Christ by which the cosmos has been crucified to me and I to the cosmos*," the defeat of dualisms, "*For neither is circumcision anything nor is un-circumcision*," and the world's new unity in Christ, "*What is something is the new creation*."[58] Martyn argues that the cosmos that has been crucified with Christ is the fallen age founded on pairs of opposites or antimonies, those that Galatians 4:3 and 4:8–9 refer to as the "elements" or "principles" of the cosmos that "in one form or another . . . all people had formally considered permanently dependable" for structuring human life in the world, and Paul's letter presupposes the widespread tradition that recognizes these elements as pairs of religious opposites.[59] In Galatians 3:27, the sacrament of baptism indicates the washing away of religious dualisms, which are replaced by unity in Christ.[60] The next verse names a few of the enslaving opposites from which Christ has liberated the cosmos: Jew and Greek, slave and free, male and female, and Martyn adds the dualisms of the sacred and the profane and of morality and immorality.[61] Martyn's study of Paul's apocalyptic perspective is a particularly helpful link to Bonhoeffer's theological critique of religion and morality, which counters "religion" with costly discipleship based on the crucified Christ. Like Bonhoeffer, Martyn does not define the term "religion" explicitly, except to say that "religion is the human enterprise that Paul sharply distinguishes from God's apocalyptic act in Christ."[62] Indeed, Martyn roots Paul's entire apocalyptic thinking in this opposition between Christ's cross and the destructive consequences of "religion." Speaking in an ontological sense, he says, "The advent of Christ is the end of religion."[63] All religious dualisms that could position the church as specially favored over other human beings have been terminated by Christ. This news is "an astonishing—indeed, a frightening—announcement," because it exposes just how evil these comfortable dualisms are, dualisms by which the majority of human beings—including Christians—still sinfully abide.[64] As exemplified all too clearly through the Nazi regime, the dualisms founding the fallen cosmos animate "forces of oppression and dehumanization."[65] Church-communities who accept these live by "the flesh" and obscure the liberation accomplished by Christ.

Paul describes "the flesh" not only as an assertive actor struggling against God's liberating Spirit but also as human perception distorted by the religious dualisms founding the old cosmos. In other words, the powers of the flesh and the Spirit refer to *patterns of thinking* (Rom. 12:2), the former characterized by dualisms that position human beings against one another and the latter characterized by a new vision of solidarity: "From now on we regard no one according to the flesh" (2 Cor. 5:16), writes Paul, because we have been given the eyes to see the world already reconciled to Christ—"Open your eyes, the new has come!" (2 Cor. 5:17).[66] The church that lives by the power of the Spirit is called no longer to abide by the structure of the old cosmos; it no longer makes sense of the world through divisive categories. Rather, the church proclaims and demonstrates the enclosure of humanity in Christ. Martyn's translation of 2 Corinthians 5:17 well describes Christ's all-encompassing liberation and the power of the church, given by the Spirit, to recognize the world as the realm of Christ: "Therefore if anyone is in the realm of Christ"—if anyone is empowered by the Spirit to see reality through Christ's reconciling work—"there is a new creation"; there is redemption. "The old age has passed away. Open your eyes, the new has come! All of this is from God who causes the new to break in by reconciling the world to himself through Christ, and by trusting his powerful word of reconciliation to the ambassador who stands at the turn of the ages."[67] That Christ has reconciled the world to God means that he is lovingly lord over it. Christ judges religious thinking that resists the all-encompassing unity that he, the agent of reconciliation and the lord of the world, has accomplished.

Therefore, while Christians tend to assume that "living according to the flesh" means "being of this world," Paul's apocalyptic thought depicts "the flesh" in a manner startling to our religious sensibilities. Certain strands of Paul's theology affirm that the church *should* belong wholly to this world and be in solidarity with a humanity reconciled to Christ as it resists the divisive power of "the flesh." The church is to be "in the world but not of the world," then, only (or at least primarily) in the sense that it is called to reject a pattern of thinking and a pattern of action that conforms to the structure of the old cosmos. In *Discipleship*, Bonhoeffer's claim that Christ's form is not of this world holds validity, then, in this particular sense. The form of Christ does not belong to the passing evil age but to the present age reconciled to God. The church that takes Christ's form rejects the pattern of dualistic thinking Paul calls "the flesh" in favor of repentance, the pattern of thinking defined by the practice of accepting responsibility for sin and suffering in solidarity with the whole of humanity, especially with those that come out on the losing side of divisive dualisms, the humiliated and marginalized whom dominant society despises and rejects: "Do not be conformed to the pattern of this world," Paul writes, "but be transformed *by the renewing of your minds*" (Rom. 12:2).[68]

Paul's apocalyptic logic prohibits the church from viewing itself as religiously privileged and specifically contradicts special favor based on morality. If the church turns Paul's theology into a message about religious righteousness or even confines the gospel to the forgiveness of individual sin, "the profound radicality of Paul's apocalyptic picture is seriously domesticated," because Paul is "far from reducing" Christian life and witness "to a matter of morals vis-à-vis an ethical code."[69] Paul's central concern is with cosmic powers that have a life of their own beyond the activity of individual human beings. In the apocalyptic struggle between "the Spirit" and "the flesh," Martyn says, "vices and virtues attributable to individuals have lost both their individual nature and their character as vices and virtues." Passages such as Galatians 5:16–25 are often misinterpreted as a straightforward inventory of moral and immoral acts, but the significance of such a list is that it describes actions "that are without exception effected by two warring powers," one of which is intent on creating human community and the other on devastating it.[70] Paul redefines the traditional catalog of vices as consequences or "effects" that arise from the cosmic power of "the flesh," which destroy community, and he redefines the traditional catalog of virtues as "the fruit borne" by the Spirit that builds and sustains community (Gal. 5:22–26).[71] Christ's death on the cross "for our sin," then, refers to something even greater than the forgiveness of individual wrongdoing. As Martyn explains, "God would not have to carry out an invasion in order merely to forgive erring human beings." The "root trouble lies deeper" than individual sin "and is more sinister."[72] The power of the cross is distorted by Christians who define a life of faith in terms of morality, or salvation merely in terms of the forgiveness of an individual's sins; for, the cross is "the watershed event for the whole cosmos, affecting everything after it."[73]

The church distorts its witness and lives according to "the flesh" not only when it presumes special favor based on its understanding of morality but also when it presumes special favor based on its faith in Christ, in other words, when it operates within a religious dualism we may call "faith and unbelief." Christ's own unifying faith and obedience has defeated this religious dualism.[74] With particular attention to Galatians 2:16, New Testament scholars such as Martyn and Richard B. Hays argue that when Paul opposes saving faith with law observance, he is not referring to the human being's faith *in* Christ but to the faith *of Christ* himself.[75] The argument revolves around the translation of Paul's genitive construction, *pistis Chritsou Iêsou*. Martyn translates Galatians 2:16 as follows: "As Jewish Christians, we ourselves know that a person is not rectified by observance of the Law, but rather by [*pistis Chritsou Iêsou*] the faith of Jesus Christ. Thus, even we have placed our trust in Christ Jesus, in order that the source of our rectification might be the faith of Christ and not observance of the Law; for not a single person will be rectified by observance of the Law."[76] Martyn argues that this verse is one of the most densely packed theological statements in Paul's letters and its meaning is crucial for grasping the radical nature of Paul's thinking. The astonishingly good news the church proclaims to the world is this: Through Christ's saving faith "God has set things right without laying down a prior condition of any sort. God's rectifying act, that is to say, is no more God's response to human faith in Christ than it is God's response to human observance of the Law. God's rectification is not God's response at all. It is the *first* move; it is God's initiative, carried out by him in God's faithful death," writes Martyn.[77] The good news is so good precisely because it lacks condition; it is a message absent all contingency. "See that in the literal crucifixion of Jesus of Nazareth God invades without a single if. Not *if* you repent. Not *if* you learn. Not even *if* you believe. The absence of the little word if, the uncontingent, prevenient, invading nature of God's grace shows God to be the powerful and victorious Advocate who is intent on the liberation of the entire race of human beings."[78] Because faith is not a human possibility, Paul does not lay before the world the option of accepting or rejecting faith. Instead, Paul spreads the good news of the faith and obedience of Christ. The church witnesses to the cosmic reconciliation accomplished by Christ's faith and obedience.

Christ's salvific faith, however, does not preclude the vital importance of the *church's faith in* Christ. God gives the church God's Spirit, and through this power, the church responds to the faith of Christ with faith in Christ. God's liberating event establishes the church as a body with a particular identity and mission in the world. The church is the communal presence of Christ on earth, and its mission is to participate in Christ's ontological liberation through concrete acts of redemption.[79] Through the power of the Spirit, the church enacts God's redemptive power by communally taking Christ's form in the world, the form Paul's letters and Bonhoeffer's christology define as that of the *crucified* Christ (Gal. 4:19; Phil. 2:5–11, 3:10). In Galatians 4:19, Paul implies that conformation to Christ's death is not instantaneous with faith in Christ; rather, formation is a process fashioned over time through tangible obedience, such as responsible acts of repentance in the midst of the world. The church shares deeply in the struggle between the powers of "the Spirit" and "the flesh" as it habituates itself to Christ's form through repentant activity. Repentance, as this analysis of Paul's apocalyptic thought argues, is not a religious condition that must be met by the human being before God reconciles, but is the responsibility laid upon the church by virtue of its faith to participate in God's unfolding redemption.[80]

■ PARTICIPATING IN THE WORLD'S CHRISTOLOGICAL PATTERN

This-Worldly Reality as "Christ-Reality"

Just as Paul's apocalyptic thinking defines the cross as the event transforming the world's ontology, in *Ethics*, Bonhoeffer bases the church's radical this-worldly belonging on the world's cosmic reconciliation and ontological unity in Christ. Bonhoeffer writes, "The central message of the New Testament is that in Christ God has loved the world and reconciled it with himself. This message presupposes the world needs reconciliation with God but cannot achieve it by itself.... It is the task and essence of the church-community to proclaim precisely to the world its reconciliation with God, and to disclose to it the reality of the love of God."[81] Bonhoeffer claims that the world *is* reconciled *at present* to God, even given the existential reality of sin and evil, of injustice, broken community, and dehumanization; for, the world's present is defined by the decisive work of Jesus Christ in the past. He says, "*In Jesus Christ the reality of God has entered into the reality of the world*.... The irreconcilable opposition of ought and is finds reconciliation in Christ, that is, in ultimate reality."[82] In other words, the ultimate reality of God—God's free and loving determination to belong wholly to the fallen world through Christ—leads God straight into the reality of sin and death, uniting what is with what should be: a world reconciled to God.

In *Ethics*, Bonhoeffer challenges the intentional and unintentional dualistic thinking that Paul renounces in his epistle to the Galatians. He is specifically concerned with the dualistic thinking in his own tradition that materializes in what he calls the "pseudo-Lutheran" teaching of two realms. Mirroring Paul's apocalyptic thought, Bonhoeffer claims that two realms thinking denies the dynamic participation of all things in Christ (of which Colossians speaks) by presupposing that the church and the world are static entities without overlap or nuance "standing side by side and battling over the borderline":

> For in him all things on heaven and on earth were created, things visible and invisible, whether thrones or dominions or rulers or powers—all things have been created through him and for him. He himself is before all things, and in him all things hold together.... For in him all the fullness of God was pleased to dwell, and through him God was pleased to reconcile to himself all things, whether on earth or in heaven, by making peace through the blood of his cross (Col. 1:16–20).[83]

Bonhoeffer argues that the antagonism that pits Christ and the world "as two realms bumping up and repelling each other" denies the reconciliation accomplished in Christ, in the words of Colossians, that "in him all things hold together." Dualistic thinking operates as if segments of the world are autonomous, as if there are parts of reality that have not been taken up and borne by God. He writes, "Giving up on reality as a whole, either we place ourselves in one of two realms, wanting Christ without the world or the world without Christ—and in both cases we deceive ourselves."[84] An accurate interpretation of reality arises, then, only from an understanding of the person of Christ who is at once ultimate divine reality and concrete human reality, who is at once fully God and the real human being. "The place where the questions about the reality of God and the reality of the world are answered at the same time is characterized solely by one name: Jesus Christ. God and the world are enclosed in this name. In Christ all things exist (Col. 1:17). From now on we cannot speak rightly of either God or the world without speaking of Jesus Christ."[85] By defining this-worldly reality strictly in terms of Christ, Bonhoeffer is not collapsing the triune God and humanity. Nor is he suggesting God's kingdom of peace and justice, redemption and restoration, has fully come. His concern is that the church recognizes that the world's ontology is now constituted by the pattern of the incarnate, crucified, and risen Christ, which envelops both the present reality of sin and the unfolding of redemption. Indeed, it is the decisive, reconciling work of Jesus Christ in the past that enables redemption to be realized in the present and that legitimates hope in the future fulfillment of God's promises in time.

Because "God and the world are enclosed" in the name of Jesus and in him "all things exist," Bonhoeffer argues that this-worldly reality now has the structure of Christ's very life.[86] As a result of the incarnation, in which Jesus in fallen flesh reconciles the whole world to himself by entering fully into sin and death, there is now an "ontological coherence" between the reality of the world and the reality of God, previously kept distinct by God's creating ex nihilo.[87] Such ontological coherence results in a "Christo-universal" vision, a christocentric understanding of all reality rooted in the *theologia crucis*.[88] Because Jesus says, "I am . . . life" (John 14:6), life "can never again be separated from this 'I,' from this person," writes Bonhoeffer.[89] The life of the crucified Christ embraces the world as it is, suffering "the reality of the world at its worst," and so Bonhoeffer designates the one realm containing both God and world "Christ-reality."[90] As Paul's apocalyptic thinking shows, the world's identity, then, can no longer be narrowed to its fallen structure but envelops the whole of its christological constitution. As the body with eyes to see that "the new has come," the church bases its witness on Christ-reality, on the reality that the world is accepted, judged, and reconciled by the lived love of the humiliated Christ, with even the darkest corners of the world "being drawn ceaselessly into the event of Christ."[91] Christ-reality is thus definitive of the world's ontology but is not static. Even as humanity is accepted, judged, and reconciled, it must also be continually drawn by God into the life, death, and resurrection of Jesus. The church participates in this dynamic movement of God in the world, and thereby witnesses to a God on the move intent to liberate and save (1 Tim. 2:1–6; John 12:32), by aligning itself with reality's definitive christological pattern.

The incarnation, crucifixion, and resurrection of Jesus Christ constitute the threefold christological pattern of this-worldly reality, for they correspond to God's acceptance, judgment, and reconciliation of this world. Bonhoeffer writes in *Ethics*, "In becoming human we recognize God's love towards God's creation, in the crucifixion God's judgment on all flesh, and in the resurrection God's purpose for a new world."[92] God's belonging wholly to humanity rests in the unity of the incarnation, crucifixion, and resurrection such that making any of the three absolute distorts the picture of the world portrayed by the life of Christ. Isolating a theology of affirmation based on the incarnation will lead to uncritical support of the status quo; a narrow theology of the crucifixion will leave the world judged and condemned; and a *theologia gloria* confined to the resurrection will foster a triumphal idealism disconnected from the church's culpability in present realities of sin and injustice.

The church participates in and witnesses to the threefold christological pattern of the world in the same way that it witnesses to the public presence of the person of Christ: by taking the form of the incarnate, crucified, and risen God through repentance. I have argued thus far that the church offers a nontriumphal witness to Christ's lordship by taking the form specifically of the crucified Christ, since God's visible manner of being in the world is characterized by the cross, and Christ in the form of a sinner is the linchpin that holds together the incarnation (Christ in fallen flesh), the crucifixion (Christ taking responsibility for sin), and the resurrection (Christ bearing the marks of the cross and refusing to be known publically as victor). In *Ethics*, Bonhoeffer defines conformation to Christ in a manner that reinforces how central humility and repentance are to an accurate picture of the whole of Christ as the incarnate, crucified, and risen one. By being conformed to the *incarnate* one who has shown us "what being really human means," the church witnesses to the fact that:

> The human being should and may be human. All super-humanity [Übermenschentum], all effort to outgrow one's nature as human, all struggle to be heroic or a demigod, all fall away from a person here because they are untrue. The real human being is the object neither of contempt nor deification, but the object of the love of God.... The real human being is allowed to be in freedom the creature of the Creator. To be conformed to the one who became human means that we may be the human beings that we really are.[93]

Simultaneously, by taking the form of the *crucified* Christ, the church witnesses to the reality that as fallen creatures, human beings are both beloved by God and stand as sinful before God and each other. "To be conformed to the crucified—that means to be a human being judged by God," writes Bonhoeffer. Through their conformation to the crucified Christ, Christians "demonstrate in their lives that before God nothing can stand except in judgment and in grace." Similarly, to be conformed to the *risen* one "means to be a new human being before God" who lives "in the world like anyone else. [New human beings] often differ very little from other people. They are not concerned to promote themselves... Transfigured into the form of the risen one, they bear here only the sign of the cross and judgment. In bearing them willingly, they show themselves as those who have received the Holy Spirit and are united with Jesus Christ"—the judged penitent who lives for others—"in incomparable love and community."[94] Christological belonging based on the incarnation, crucifixion, and resurrection thus leads to truthful recognition of who we are as human beings and this in turn leads to human flourishing. By being conformed at once to the incarnate, crucified, and risen Christ through humility and repentance, the church aligns itself with the christological current of existence that carries humanity toward its ultimate healing.

Christ's Acceptance Includes God's Judgment and God's Judgment Is the World's Redemption

As the christological structure of reality, the incarnation, crucifixion, and resurrection are not to be thought of chronologically or linearly. Instead, as an interwoven pattern, the Christ event declares the simultaneous divine "affirmation and protest," Christ's Yes and No continuously proclaimed upon the whole world, including the church.[95] Given this interwoven christological pattern of transformation, divine affirmation of humanity includes divine judgment upon it. The world stands affirmed in Christ's incarnation, but one would have to be utterly blind to the present, palpable power of sin and injustice if the claim of the world's acceptance by God did not at first cause one to stammer in dispute or disbelief. Bonhoeffer writes of God's Yes in *Ethics* as he learns from the Abwehr details about Nazi atrocities, and such flagrant evil then and now makes a theological claim of this-worldly acceptance and reconciliation seem outrageous and perhaps even reprehensible. For Bonhoeffer, though, Christ's affirmation of humanity is a rejection of the Nazi desire for a superhumanity and thus an affirmation that God is on the side of the oppressed, marginalized, and dehumanized. Christ's affirmation of the world is not God's "confirmation of the existing world" nor God's blessing on the status quo.[96] Rather, Christ's affirmative Yes at once includes the severity of crisis, Christ's judging No, and thus does not arise from the sinful world itself. God expresses divine acceptance through the revelation of the incarnate Christ, who has come toward humanity from beyond humanity, who, as Barth says, journeys "into the far country" of this fallen world.[97] Still, the way of Christ into the far country is "not a distant and strange life unrelated to us," says Bonhoeffer, because it is the life of the incarnate God, not the superhuman but the real human being in fallen flesh, who has freely chosen to affirm and save humanity by belonging wholly to this fallen world. Christ's this-worldly belonging both contradicts and affirms the human such that "no one who knows Christ can hear the Yes without the No and the No without the Yes."[98] Christ's being for others contradicts a world in which human beings diminish and destroy each other in various degrees and innumerable ways, and Christ's being for humanity affirms the world precisely by coming near and entering into such earthly life. Christ's acceptance of the world is demonstrated by the fact that he works within the conditions of its fallen structure, patiently serving it, instead of displaying characteristics of "human love" that desires to dominate and control.[99] In other words, God respects the integrity of the world by allowing the world to remain world, yet, in order for humanity to flourish fully in life's strength, God "reckons with the world as world" by exposing sin through christological judgment.[100]

As judgment, the cross suffered by the incarnate God exposes human life that strays from its God-intended "origin, essence, and goal" into death, destruction, and diminution.[101] Bonhoeffer writes,

> Jesus Christ, the crucified—that means that God speaks final judgment on the fallen creation.... [In the cross of Christ] human beings cannot boast of their being human... Here human glory has come to its final end in the image of the beaten, bleeding, spat-upon face of the crucified. Yet the crucifixion of Jesus does not mean... the annihilation of creation.... God... makes an end of death and calls a new creation into

> life. . . . The resurrection has already broken into the midst of the old world as the ultimate sign of its end and its future, and at the same time as living reality. . . . Jesus has risen as human; so he has given human beings the gift of resurrection.[102]

The cross both protests against sin and contradicts its triumph by becoming this "hidden Yes to a new life . . . [which] is not present other than [as] hidden under the mark of death, of the No."[103] Christ's judging No proclaimed upon the world contains the hidden Yes because Christ comes into the world not to condemn but to save (John 3:17). Bonhoeffer writes, "The secret . . . of this judgment, this suffering and this dying, is the love of God for the world, for human beings. What happened to and in Christ has happened to all of us. Only as judged by God can human beings live before God. . . . In the figure of the crucified, human beings recognize and find themselves. . . . Only in the cross of Christ, and that means as judged, does humanity take its true form."[104]

The church witnesses to God's judgment on the sin that distorts and degrades God's creatures by taking humanity's "true form" as judged (the form the incarnate God first took for us) through repentance.[105] The church plays a central role in exposing sin in the world by acknowledging it in itself—in its own communal life and in its relationship with other human beings and society at large. Receiving God's judgment on behalf of itself and the world through repentant activity in public life is the way in which the church, like Christ, respects the world's integrity, respects its worth as creation and respects its future fulfillment made known through the promises of God. Respecting the world's integrity requires great faith that "Christ gives up nothing that has been won but holds . . . in his hands" even the world fallen "under the control of Satan" (1 John 5:19). Bonhoeffer reminds his readers that in an eschatological sense "even the devil, unwillingly, must serve Christ" and that it is precisely this " 'evil world' " here and now that is reconciled, for "there is no part of the world, no matter how lost, no matter how godless, that has not been accepted by God in Jesus Christ."[106] Faith in Christ no longer allows one "to speak of the world as if it were lost, as if it were separated from God. It is nothing but unbelief to give the world . . . less than Christ," he says.[107] Anything less than the church's belief in the world's reconciliation and its future redemption is a "fanatic belief in death" by those who have yet to comprehend fully that "the power of death has been broken; the miracle of the resurrection and new life shines right into the world of death."[108] The church-community that deems the world lost denies the person and work of Christ and the christological structure of reality, for it does not take seriously the profound implications on all of life of the incarnation, crucifixion, and resurrection.

As the church accepts God's judgment upon itself, it witnesses to the fact that the fallen world needs judgment proclaimed upon all that distorts the beauty and fullness of life. Indeed, humanity's redemptive flourishing depends on the affirmation of this divine judgment. Like Paul's apocalyptic thought, Bonhoeffer's theology holds that we live at the juncture of the passing of the evil age and the dawn of the new creation. Although Christ-reality deems human beings accepted, judged, and reconciled, human history is still full of sin, and we live "stretched between" the No that is judgment on death and destruction and the hidden Yes of redemption.[109] "Humanity still lives, of course, in the old, but is already beyond the old. Humanity still lives, of course, in a world of death, but is already beyond death. Humanity still lives, of course, in a world of sin, but we are already beyond sin. The night is not yet over, but day is already dawning," he writes.[110] Humanity finds itself *beyond* sin and death only *in* God's judgment on the very sin, diminution, and destruction in which we continue at present.

Because God's judgment in Christ is the world's redemption and because humanity only finds itself beyond sin by accepting God's judgment upon its own past and present sin, the cross may be understood as both the ontological structure of, and the ethical model for, transformation. In other words, the cross creates a new ontological structure of reality that enables, in turn, a christocentric model of transformation. While an ecclesial ethic of the cross and an ecclesial witness to Christ's lordship will involve "dying, suffering, poverty, renunciation, surrender, humility, self-deprecation, and self-denial," Bonhoeffer boldly claims in *Discipleship* that participation in the form of the crucified Christ is joy; for, given the christological structure of this-worldly reality, "these very forms . . . already contain the Yes to new life."[111] Because "God *uses* judgment, not as an end in itself, but as a refining fire for salvific purposes . . . in the service of the word of promise," repentance as that ecclesial ethic—as the church's acceptance of God's judgment upon itself and the entire world—is an active response to God's promise to renew, restore, and redeem; "for no matter how many promises God has made, they are Yes in Christ" (2 Cor. 1:20).[112] As the acceptance of divine judgment, repentance participates in the unfolding of redemption. Thus, it is an activity energized by hope for the world and humanity, animated by joyful expectation as much as lament, and oriented toward future transformation as much as past and present sin.[113] Ecclesial repentance is the Yes to earthly life that clears space for "what is created, to becoming [and] growth, to flower and fruit, to health, to happiness, to ability, to achievement, to value, to success, to greatness, to honor, in short, the Yes to the flourishing of life's strength," writes Bonhoeffer.[114]

Because Christ simultaneously proclaims Yes and No, because affirmation of the world includes judgment and God's judgment leads to reconciliation and redemption, the church's new life in Christ does not construct dualisms, siphoning out what God rejects from what God accepts and reconciles. Instead, life in Christ perceives in every aspect of reality the Yes already contained in the No and the No already contained in the Yes. All things whether deemed Christian or worldly are brought before God's judgment, and through that merciful judgment all things are being transformed into good. All things are worthy through the love of Christ; all things, in every new moment, must be judged; all things gain fullness through the form of the crucified and risen Christ. Bonhoeffer writes,

> Both the flourishing of life's strength and self-denial, growth and death, health and suffering, happiness and renunciation, achievement and humility, honor and self-deprecation belong inextricably together in a living unity full of contradictions. Any attempt to isolate one from another, to play one off against the other, or to appeal to one against the other is an unholy destruction of the unity of life.[115]

The unity of life is filled with paradoxes born from the interwoven pattern of the being of the incarnate, crucified, and risen God. The unity of life is precisely that which is found in the humiliated and glorified Christ. The pattern of Christ's life defines and establishes life anew.

■ THE CHURCH'S THIS-WORLDLY BELONGING

The Ultimate and the Penultimate

In order to describe more clearly the unity of life—the relationship between this world (upon which Christ proclaims his simultaneous Yes and No) and the new earth remade (the eternal kingdom come in full, the Yes which no longer will necessitate the No)—Bonhoeffer refers in *Ethics* to *die Letztes und die vorletzten Dinge*, literally "the last and the things before the last."[116] In order to convey both the qualitative and temporal sense in which Bonhoeffer uses these categories, the English editions translate the phrase as the "ultimate and the penultimate," such that the "ultimate" refers to what is most important and also to what is final.[117]

As is true with a number of concepts Bonhoeffer employs, the "ultimate" and the "penultimate" do not have a fixed meaning throughout his writings. Bonhoeffer first mentions the penultimate in an August 26, 1928, sermon in Barcelona, where he broadly defines the "penultimate" as this world and everything that happens in it.[118] Bonhoeffer's last use of these categories occurs in a letter to Bethge on December 5, 1943. He writes that Christians live in the penultimate but place their faith in the ultimate, and he tells Bethge that in *Discipleship* he only hints at this dynamic but plans on developing it further, for the consequences of understanding this are "far-reaching" for ministry, biblical interpretation, and Christian ethics.[119] Presumably, Bonhoeffer intends to go back to his discussion of the ultimate and penultimate in *Ethics* since he conveys a week later how important it is for him to finish this manuscript.[120] Indeed, this discussion is essential to the book, for he tentatively suggests as a title for his unfinished *Ethics*, "Preparing the Way and Arrival" (a phrase he uses in this manuscript to describe Christian discipleship in the penultimate) and he defines "preparing the way" as "repentance."[121] The church's life in the penultimate—its discipleship and public witness—centers on repentance.

Before Bonhoeffer describes the church's role within the penultimate as preparing the way for Christ through repentance, he first eliminates two patterns of thinking about the ultimate and penultimate that position them in fundamental disunity. The "radical solution" corresponds to Bonhoeffer's discussion of dualisms and imagines the ultimate or eternal as a complete break with the penultimate. In this model, the penultimate world opposes Christ who is, in turn, "the destroyer and enemy of everything penultimate" and the "sign that the world is ripe to be consigned to the fire."[122] Such a model upholds the aforementioned fanatic belief in death: "What will happen to the world as a result is no longer important; the Christian has no responsibility for that. The world must burn in any case. Let the whole order of the world break down under the word of Christ," concludes such a Christian.[123] The God of this extreme solution is a wasteful creator who is willing to cast aside creation gone awry in unbelief and disobedience. For the "radical" Christian, God's judgment is not something that finds all of life (including the Christian's life) lacking and incomplete; rather, divine judgment makes a strict division between those who are for and those who are against Christ. Elsewhere in *Ethics*, Bonhoeffer addresses Jesus' claim "whoever is not for me is against me" (Matthew 12:30) and harmonizes it with the seemingly contradictory statement of Mark 9:40, "whoever is not against us is for us." Bonhoeffer explains that Christ's claim, "whoever is not against us is for us," is Christ opening up participation in the work of reconciliation and redemption to all who struggle for "justice, truth, humanity and freedom," regardless of whether or not they do so under the banner of the church, while Christ's caution of "whoever is not for me is against me" addresses the church tempted toward lukewarm devotion.[124] The gospel's simultaneous inclusive and exclusive claims belong together because "the more exclusively [Christians] recognize and confess Christ as our Lord, the more will be disclosed to us the breadth of Christ's lordship" within and over the penultimate.[125]

Bonhoeffer describes the second pattern of thinking that misunderstands the relationship between the ultimate and penultimate as compromise. He writes,

> Here the ultimate word is divorced in principle from all that is penultimate. The penultimate retains its inherent rights, but it is not threatened or endangered by the ultimate.... Penultimate things must be done in responsibility for this world that God created.... The ultimate stays completely beyond daily life and in the end serves only as the eternal justification of all that exists, as a metaphysical cleansing of the indictment that burdens all of existence.[126]

Because Bonhoeffer begins his theological analysis of the ultimate and the penultimate in *Ethics* with a remark about "the justification of the sinner by grace alone," some scholars assume Bonhoeffer's opening remark provides the lens for understanding these concepts, and so they define the ultimate as "the last word of justification."[127] Yet, interpretations of Bonhoeffer that place the ultimate/penultimate discussion in terms of law and gospel risk subsuming Bonhoeffer's thought under the position he is countering here. Interpretations that define the ultimate too narrowly as the individual sinner's justification overlook the crucial point that Bonhoeffer's intent is to find a way to speak about the unity of life. He develops this vocabulary in order to describe the ontological unity of this-worldly Christ-reality that at once envelops both the ultimate and the penultimate.[128]

Bonhoeffer's description of the position of compromise is specific, yet he gives no indication of who he has in mind beyond the Western cultural Christianity that he criticizes in a previous chapter, "Heritage and Decay."[129] Although there is no evidence that Bonhoeffer was directing his criticism particularly at Reinhold Niebuhr, Niebuhr's discussion of the "impossible ideal" of agape corresponds systematically to Bonhoeffer's description of compromise. Indeed, in his essay "Protestantism without Reformation," Bonhoeffer criticizes Niebuhr's theology as part of the general problem of Anglo-American theology:

> *Reinhold Niebuhr*...one of the most significant and most creative of contemporary American theologians, whose main works must be known for a survey of the theological situation,...the sharpest critic of contemporary American Protestantism and the present order, has for years been making a deep impression by his strong emphasis on the cross as the midpoint and end of history, coupled with a strongly active political theology....But even here a doctrine of the person and redemptive work of Jesus Christ is still missing.[130]

Niebuhr defines the ultimate as agape, as God's sacrificial love made manifest on the cross, and he describes agape as hovering over history instead of breaking into this penultimate world with transformative power. Niebuhr's Christian realism contends that human beings cannot live according to an ethic of the cross (such as Christ's teaching in the Sermon on the Mount) and also act responsibly in history. While the cross serves as the last or ultimate word of forgiveness, this pattern of thinking grants the cross little transformative power in history. As Bonhoeffer says, it "serves only as the eternal justification" or "metaphysical cleansing" of any and all sinful activity deemed necessary for living responsibly in this world. In a solution of compromise, as exemplified by Niebuhr, Christ's ultimate word is "divorced" from present, concrete reality and thus loses its this-worldly power to judge and redeem.

The Penultimate Means Repentance

Having rejected the radical solution as well as the solution of compromise, Bonhoeffer reconstructs the relationship between the penultimate and the ultimate by defining the penultimate precisely as the space in which the church prepares the way for Christ's transformation through repentance, that is, through an ethic of the cross characterized by responsible action in the world. In *Ethics*, Bonhoeffer specifically turns to the words of John the Baptist as recorded in Luke's Gospel for guidance on how the disciples prepare the world for its coming transformation: " 'Prepare the way of the Lord, make his paths straight. Every valley shall be filled, and every mountain and hill shall be made low, and the crooked shall be made straight, and the rough ways made smooth, and all flesh shall see the salvation of God' " (Luke 3:4–6). Luke's Gospel then records John the Baptist exhorting the crowd of followers toward specific acts of repentance, the fruit of sin's genuine confession, which establishes the broad expanse for God's smooth passage and the clear view for all of humanity to see God's goodness. Repentance is not merely inward but is outwardly costly; it is responsible action—"visible, creative activity on the greatest scale."[131] Whole valleys are lifted: the depth of human poverty, misery, and bondage hinders the experience of reconciliation and the realization of redemption and thus disciples labor to end these realities. "It is hard for those thrust into extreme disgrace, desolation, poverty and helplessness to believe in God's justice and goodness," writes Bonhoeffer; "the hungry person needs bread, the homeless person needs shelter, the one deprived of rights needs justice, the lonely person needs community."[132] If disciples leave these needs unmet all the while proclaiming God's coming in Christ, the guilt falls on us who in our wealth and power have withheld from others or who, even with our financial charity, have remained safe and secure on top of our mountains which we refuse to make low. The penultimate must be cared for and preserved for the sake of the ultimate, for God's transformative word of peace, justice, reconciliation, and redemption. Bonhoeffer writes, "Those who proclaim the word yet do not do everything possible so that this word may be heard are not true to the word's claim for free passage, for a smooth road."[133] The word of God demands that its way be prepared, that paths within the world be made straight for Christ's coming concrete transformation.

The task of the church, then, is to prepare the way for Christ in the world. Still, there is circularity to this preparation, for (as depicted in the previous chapter) Christ has already made his own way by being hidden in the humiliation of sin and guilt in his life and death. The church participates in this path-clearing preparation by taking the form of the penitent Christ, confessing its sin and accepting the guilt that falls upon the world with which it is intimately connected. The church's confession of sin recognizes the permeable nature of the church and world that together constitute one Christ-reality. The shared sphere of sin and redemption (and the shared sin itself) places the church not in opposition to but in partnership with the broader world.

The permeability of the visible church and broader society does not negate the church-community's distinctiveness. The church-community is visible in that it has a specific language and vocation of proclaiming and demonstrating humanity's acceptance, judgment, and reconciliation through the liturgy of confession and the act of accepting responsibility for sin through repentance. The church is also the body that recognizes the penultimate's dependence upon the ultimate, and so its impetus for repentance is Christ's coming transformation, not faith in an autonomous human capacity to restore social and political structures ourselves. Repentant activity is visible and laborious but it consists of deeds desperately depending on divine grace, done in humble recognition of human limits. Bonhoeffer says,

> Preparing the way for Christ cannot *simply* be a matter of creating certain desired and constructive conditions, such as creating a program of social reform. Preparing the way

> is indeed a matter of concrete intervention in the visible world, as concrete as hunger and nourishment. Nevertheless, everything depends on this action being a spiritual reality, since what is finally at stake is not the reform of worldly conditions but the coming of Christ.... This means that visible deeds... must be deeds of humility before the coming Lord, which means deeds of repentance. Preparation of the way means repentance (Matt. 3:1).[134]

By placing the coming of Christ as a higher goal than reforming worldly conditions, Bonhoeffer is not shifting his focus off historical reality; rather, he is highlighting the distinctiveness that the church brings to public life. The coming of Christ's kingdom will result in concrete restoration, peace, and justice. Bonhoeffer stresses, though, that preparation through repentance is a theological response that places sinners in harmony with Christ's judgment on past and present sin and that humbly recognizes that in order to move beyond the old, we humans must participate in the event that already happened in Christ. Repentant activity includes but requires more than attempts at various social reforms, for the repenting church knows that it is Christ who ultimately must create life out of human labor. Thus, confession of human inadequacy occurs even within repentant activity. Such a confession is no excuse for meager effort. New life continues to blossom within earthly life through the work of human beings who accept responsibility for the world.

Therefore, the church-community's confession of sin unto repentance is confession on top of confession, for in the last analysis, human beings cannot initiate Christ's coming. Christ makes his own way. The chief confession of sin is the "recognition that we ourselves can never prepare the way and therefore the demand that we prepare the way leads us to repentance in every respect," says Bonhoeffer.[135] Repentance is paradoxically, then, both a call to utter humility and "a commission of immeasurable responsibility."[136] Humility is learned when the church refuses self-made preparation—methods and schemes which seek to stronghold, manipulate, or force an unbelieving world toward the beliefs the church itself holds. Through self-made preparation, the church tries to blaze its own trail instead of following after the crucified Christ who is himself the way. In contrast, preparing the way through visible repentant activity leaves the resulting redemption in Christ's hands, and thus is characterized by an extravagant love for the world that believes all things, bears all things, hopes all things, and endures all things (1 Cor. 13:7).[137] The church-community courageously *bares* all by confessing its own sin and the overlapping world's sin and *bears* all in responsibility out of a profound trust and hope that all will be redeemed. Because the church-community trusts Christ will indeed come, it prepares the way with joyful expectation and has eyes to see instances of redemption occurring even in our present. These glimpses of eternity are "revealed only in the depths of the earth," in other words, only through intimate worldly engagement, and thus responsibility entails attending in utmost seriousness to this penultimate world.[138]

Repentance as Profound This-Worldliness and the Hope for Concrete Redemption

Foundational to this theology of public witness is the claim that the church witnesses to Christ in a nontriumphal manner when it rejects a notion of special favor and instead belongs wholly to this world. Repentance is the central way that the church belongs wholly to the world, not only because through repentance the church confesses its solidarity with the rest of humanity in sin and redemption, but also because repentance is the primary way in which the church lives in the penultimate and participates in the world's new ontology. As Bonhoeffer contends above, "The penultimate means repentance." Repentance, in turn, is an expression of what he calls in prison "profound this-worldliness," that is, this-worldly belonging that aligns itself with the life, death, and resurrection of Jesus.[139] As we have seen, repentance aligns with Christ's life as the church-community immerses itself in the complexities of public life while acknowledging its solidarity with fallen humanity; it aligns with Christ's death as the church accepts responsibility for sin; and it aligns with Christ's resurrection as its activity prepares the way for and leads to concrete redemption.

As the paramount expression of this-worldly belonging, repentance is also an integral component of what Bonhoeffer calls in prison "the polyphony of life"—the multidimensional character of discipleship that beckons Christians to make "room in ourselves, to some extent, for God and the whole world."[140] Because repentance that is based on the life, death, and resurrection of Jesus is discipleship and discipleship calls Christians to embrace the polyphony of life, repentance fosters a profound commitment to—and love for—this-worldly existence. In contrast to this radically open posture, focus on repentance and confession of sin too often leads Christians to close themselves off, to turn inward and insulate themselves and their own from a contaminating fallen world. Concerned that many people operate out of one-track minds and thus are unable to open themselves up to both the world and God (are unable, in other words, to inhabit the tensions and paradoxes inherent in Christian faith), Bonhoeffer speaks in musical metaphor about these tensions, stating that "life becomes whole only when a person is standing in this polyphony."[141] Embracing life's polyphonic character allows human beings to be "wholly present" to the "beauty and the troubles here on earth" all the while being "particularly aware of the fragmentary and incomplete nature" of our small yet significant lives.[142] As fragments, our lives are a matter of completion for God—"they are fragments that must be fragments"—and so human beings need not "bemoan the fragmentariness of our life but rather rejoice in it," he says, trusting that with them God is designing the "mosaic" of a new world and a new humanity.[143] The fragmentary building blocks of lives lived in genuine this-worldliness lay the foundation for God's total restoration of the world when they are "deeply rooted in the soil" of past and present historical reality through a discipleship that loves God "with our whole heart, not to the detriment of earthly love or to diminish it, but as a sort of cantus firmus to which the other voices of life resound in counterpoint."[144] Commitment to genuine this-worldliness that harmonizes love for historical reality with total love of God "makes life harder" because it opens human beings up to profound loss (for, the more one loves, the more one has to lose), "but it also makes [life] richer and more vigorous" because it makes belief in, and commitment to, the redemption of this world all the more poignant. "It is only when one loves life and the earth so much that without them everything seems to be over that one may believe in the resurrection and the new world," he says.[145]

In prison, Bonhoeffer laments that instead of loving life and the earth with such passion, Christians devalue the penultimate. He contends that Christian diminishment of this world results from reading "the New Testament far too little in light of the Old" and from taking "our thoughts and feelings too quickly and too directly from the New."[146] Ignoring the Old Testament while reading the New too readily leads Christians living in our Western individualistic culture to a religious, otherworldly, and inwardly focused understanding of faith, in which salvation becomes "redemption from cares, distress, fears and longings, from sin and death, in a better world beyond the grave. But is this really the essential character of the proclamation of Christ in the gospels and by Paul?" asks Bonhoeffer.[147] In order to address this, Bonhoeffer distinguishes between a faithful "Christian hope of resurrection," which stems from the Old Testament concern "for God's blessing which includes in itself all earthly good," and a religious "mythological hope" that bypasses the earth's good while evading its tasks and difficulties.[148] Religious hope draws an affluent church not into a "profound this-worldliness" but into "a shallow and banal this-worldliness" in which Christians direct their spiritual energies toward an ephemeral world-beyond while prospering under various manifestations of privilege and comfort.[149]

Bonhoeffer's theology of this-worldliness is most evident in the later writings of *Ethics* and *Letters and Papers from Prison*, although it also appears in his 1932 address, "Thy Kingdom Come: The Prayer of the Church for the Kingdom of God on Earth," delivered during the liturgical calendar's last "week of repentance." In "Thy Kingdom Come," Bonhoeffer exhorts the church to cast off its otherworldliness, "that devious trick of being religious, yes even 'Christian,' at the expense of the earth." Christians become religious when they "disdain the earth" by appealing to "eternal victories [that seem] so easily achieved" because they require little to no commitment to present historical reality. An otherworldly preoccupation exposes the church-community to be nothing more than "weaklings" who try to assert strength by deeming the world the enemy and then "build[ing] for ourselves a strong fortress in which we dwell safe and secure with God."[150] Bonhoeffer calls otherworldly preoccupation "secularism"—"pious, Christian secularism"—because it renounces Christ's lordship over this world. He says,

> We are weak; we cannot bear having the earth so near, the earth that bears us. We cannot stand it because the earth is stronger than we and because we want to be better than the evil earth. . . . Christ does not will or intend this weakness; instead he makes us strong. He does not lead us in religious flight from this world to other worlds beyond; rather, he gives us back to the earth as its loyal children.[151]

Instead of world-denying religious flight, repentance as discipleship leads the church unreservedly into the messiness and complexity of historical existence, engagement which alone ushers forth concrete redemption.

Whereas christological repentance and resurrection hope are concerned with the concrete redemption of this world, religious hope manifests itself in an individualistic and otherworldly notion of salvation. Bonhoeffer echoes Barth's observation in *The Word of God and the Word of Man* that the Bible witnesses to a salvation that encompasses so much more than individuals going to heaven. Scripture witnesses to the establishment of *a new world*. Barth writes,

> Can one read . . . even as much as two chapters from the Bible and still with good conscience say, God's word went forth to humanity, his mandate guided history from Abraham to Christ, the Holy Spirit descended in tongues of fire upon the apostles at Pentecost, a Saul became a Paul and traveled over land and sea—all in order that here and there specimens of [human beings] like you and me might be "converted," find inner "peace," and by a redeeming death go some day to "heaven." Is *that* all? Is *that* all of God and [God's] new world? . . . [Do] not these things stand in rather strange relation to so small a result—if that is really the only result they have? Is not God—greater than that?[152]

While God is concerned with the individual human person, Bonhoeffer, like Barth, proposes that faithful Christian discipleship has more important concerns than attending to the question of, and turning the gospel into a message about, individual salvation. He says,

> I know it sounds outrageous to say that, but, after all, isn't it fundamentally biblical? Does the question of saving one's soul even come up in the Old Testament? Isn't God's righteousness and kingdom on earth the center of everything? And isn't Rom. 3:24ff. the culmination of the view that God alone is righteous, rather than an individualistic doctrine of salvation? What matters is not the beyond but this world, how it is created and preserved, is given laws, reconciled, and renewed. What is beyond this world is meant, in the gospel, to be there *for* this world—not in the anthropocentric sense of liberal, mystical, pietistic, ethical theology, but in the biblical sense of the creation and the incarnation, crucifixion, and resurrection of Jesus Christ.[153]

In contrast to religious preoccupation with individual soul-saving, Christian hope maintains that what lies beyond this world is meant *for* this world. Christian affirmation of the world and love for this life is energized by "the constant knowledge of [Christ's] death and resurrection," and the church expresses this knowledge incarnationally as it immerses itself within the Yes and the No that Christ proclaims upon the world. Ecclesial witness arising out of the Yes is "the power of living…granted to us by Easter" that strengthens the church-community to be a people deeply enmeshed within the grime and grit of existence.[154] Constant knowledge of the resurrection fosters courage within the church to turn toward human diminution and to encounter it through responsible, repentant action.

Sharing Bonhoeffer's hermeneutical method of reading New Testament redemption through the lens of Hebrew Scripture, Archbishop of Canterbury Rowan Williams asserts in his sermon, "Building Up Ruins," that redemption is not a generalized and abstract future utopia but commitment to past and present historical reality. His sermon begins with Isaiah's prophecy that "they will build up the ancient ruins; they shall raise up the former devastations" in order to frame the Christian truth that restoration of sin is concrete and specific, beginning here and now (61:4). Israel's hope in scripture was for a return to the land given them, to "the ruins of the past" because "it is on that ground or nowhere that restoration begins."[155] Without the redemption of a specific past in which the new "stands on the same earth as the old," a new age would devalue the reality of past defeat, injury, and injustice—the details to which God's love, forgiveness, and restoration attends. Williams explains,

> Israel cannot deny her memory, her past, without denying her God, without suggesting that God is not faithful.…For Israel, to think of redemption and of the coming reign of God is, inevitably and necessarily, to think of her own particular memory of victory and defeat, her own story now brought to conclusion—not to think of bland universal prosperity, but of the binding up of her own particular wounds and the recreation of her city.[156]

In this sermon as well as in his book *Resurrection*, Williams links Jewish understandings of redemption to the witness of the risen Christ.[157] The resurrected Jesus appears to the disciples in all the particular places where he met them previously "to repair the devastation" of sin such that new life is recapitulation, a gathering together—not a cancellation—of the old: "Risen life…is built from the bricks and mortar, messy and unlovely, of our past.…*Our* earth, *our* dull and stained lives, these are the living stones of God's new Jerusalem.…He builds…on the devastations of our history, builds the everlasting city where the marriage of earth and heaven are celebrated," writes Williams.[158]

In prison, Bonhoeffer also ponders the significance of the past and asserts that "gratitude and repentance are what keep our past always present to us."[159] Confession of sin through repentance is itself an affirmation of worldly living in that confession serves as memory that has been preserved for the unfolding of redemption. Bonhoeffer cites Ecclesiastes 3:15, "God will call the past to account," to show that "God seeks what is past" for the good of those who have injured others and have been injured by others.[160] In *Ethics*, Bonhoeffer states in reference to the expansive nature of Christ's redemptive efficacy that "nothing is completely lost.

It is only stripped of evil and remade."[161] Reflecting in prison on the redemption of past and present earthly realities led Bonhoeffer, like Williams, to Irenaeus' doctrine of recapitulation. He writes,

> For the last week or so these lines have kept running through my head:
>
> Let pass dear brothers every pain;
> What you have missed I'll bring again.
>
> What does this "I'll bring again" mean? It means that nothing is lost, that everything is taken up in Christ, although it is transformed, made transparent, clear and free from all selfish desire. Christ restores all this as God originally intended it to be, without the distortion resulting from our sins. The doctrine derived from Eph. 1:10—that of the restoration of all things, *recapitulation* (Irenaeus)—is a magnificent conception, full of comfort. This is how the promise "God seeks what has been driven away" is fulfilled. And no one has expressed this so simply and artlessly as Paul Gerhardt in these words that he puts into the mouth of the Christ-child. . . . Doesn't this passage, in its ecstatic longing combined with pure devotion, suggest the "bringing again" of all earthly desire?. . . a new creation through the Holy Spirit. . . . "*I* will bring again"—that is, we cannot and should not take it back ourselves, but allow Christ to give it back to us.[162]

The doctrine of recapitulation frees the church-community to immerse itself within an earthly love that risks the heartbreak, suffering, and humiliation associated with belonging wholly to the world; for such love is grounded in a hope that all of life will be restored to its intended flourishing.

With confidence that nothing is lost because everything is remade, the church-community delves into the most difficult places of human existence in a solidarity of guilt and with a complete abandon to life's christological structure. Belonging wholly to this world by accepting responsibility for sin has transformative power and prepares the way for the fullness of Christ's coming redemption of this world, which already has been affirmed, judged, and reconciled. The church-community that receives and accepts Christ's No by taking humanity's true form as judged through repentance addresses the world in which it stands with a mighty Yes. Bonhoeffer writes,

> The key to everything is the "in him". . . . It is certain that we can claim nothing for ourselves and may yet pray for everything; it is certain that our joy is hidden in suffering, and our life in death; it is certain that in all this we are in a fellowship that sustains us. In Jesus God has said Yes and Amen to it all, and that Yes and Amen is the firm ground on which we stand. . . . The truth is that if this earth was good enough for the man Jesus Christ, if such a man as Jesus lived, then, and only then, has life meaning for us.[163]

Christ has said "Yes and Amen" to this penultimate world; to real human beings; to the church-community taking its true form as judged; to repenting and preparing the way; to sharing the sufferings of God in the world through a protest against death, destruction, and diminution; to the cross as the ontological structure of and ethical model for transformation; to the cross as genuine worldliness; to the unity of life; and to the flourishing of life's strength. And that Yes—that melodious, utterly redemptive Yes—is the firm foundation upon which the church-community enacts its public witness. Christ's Yes is the foundation on which the church affirms the world and the courage by which the church honestly faces itself and bares itself before the world in "gratitude and repentance."[164]

5 The Church's Public Presence

Visibility through Confession and Repentance

Building on the christological foundation laid in the previous two chapters, I now attend to ecclesiology more directly. The analyses of Christ's public presence and the christological pattern of the world's new ontology have paved the way for my central ecclesiological claim: North American Protestant churches offer a nontriumphal witness to Christ and become vehicles of redemption in our pluralistic society when they take the form of the crucified Christ through confession unto repentance.

The interconnection of christology and ecclesiology is central to the New Testament witness. Paul explicitly relates the two through the claim that the church is the body of Christ (1 Cor. 12), and Bonhoeffer interprets this quite literally, defining the church as the continued physical presence of Christ in the world. Bonhoeffer's ecclesiology, summed up in his axiom "Christ existing as community," establishes the church as a "reality of revelation" in which the lordship of Christ is evidenced and proclaimed.[1] Yet, this revelation is also a body broken by its own persistence in sin. A theology of public witness based on Bonhoeffer's thought must address how the church may be at once a sinful body and a revelation of Christ. It must maintain both the concreteness of the empirical, institutional church or local church-community with all its failings and the theological claim that the church is Christ's contemporary manifestation in the world. Grappling with the reality of the church means asking how the church, with sin dividing its own members and injuring those outside the Christian fellowship, can hold the power of renewal and life, thus accurately revealing the divine? The paradox is that the broken, sinful body is a vehicle of transformative power in the world as the community that, taking the form of Christ, confesses sin unto repentance. Christ wills to take visible form in a body in order to reveal his continued concrete presence in history, yet the reality of sinful human beings comprising the church necessitates that it reciprocally takes Christ's form, the form of the penitent in fallen flesh who accepts responsibility for sin.

THE CHURCH AT ONCE WORLDLY AND REVELATORY

The Visible Church as the Presence of the Hidden God

Bonhoeffer christologically makes sense of how the church can be a community of sinners while still being Christ's presence in the midst of the world through the notion of hiddenness. In his 1933 christology lectures he continues with the motif, "Christ existing as community," that he introduces and develops in his first two works, *Sanctorum Communio* and *Act and Being*. Both of these books are devoted to exploring the nature of "Christ existing as community," the former through an examination of human sociality and the latter through philosophical theology.[2] Nevertheless, it is the 1933 lectures that best articulate how the church may be both a sinful body and a revelation of Christ.[3] Recall that the christology lectures describe Christ as simultaneously revealed and hidden, at once exalted and humiliated. The lectures read,

> The Word wishes to have the form of a created body. . . . The church *is* the body of Christ. . . . When applied to the church, the concept of body is not only a concept of function, which refers only to the members of this body. It is a comprehensive and central concept of the mode of existence of the one who is present in his exaltation and humiliation. This Christ existing as the church is the whole person, the one who is exalted and humiliated.[4]

Put simply, Christ is at once glorified and humiliated through the church.

Recall, too, that Christ is present *pro nobis* in space and time in the Word, the sacrament, and also in the church-community, but always as hidden in humiliation. Bonhoeffer says, "His being as church, as with Word and sacrament, has the form of a stumbling block," since Christ is associating and even identifying himself with this sinful body. The church is the very presence of Christ—"is itself revelation"[5]—and although it represents a new humanity, like Jesus, it dwells "in the world of the old Adam, 'in the likeness of sinful flesh,' under the age of sin."[6] The church remains within the world of the old humanity in respect to its sin and represents the new humanity when it takes the form of Christ, who accepts responsibility for this sin. The nontriumphal character of the repenting community stems from both witnessing to a God hidden in humiliation and also from its own humiliating sin. "It is with the humiliated one that the church goes its own way of humiliation," says Bonhoeffer.[7] The church and its members must undergo "the shame of the cross," "the public death of the sinner" before each other and the rest of the world in order to participate in the form of Christ; for, only his form gives value and utility to the church's brokenness and opens up space in public life for a righting of injustice, for redemption and healing.[8]

The Church as Collective Person

As public witness, the church's confession unto repentance primarily consists of communal, rather than individual, acceptance of guilt. The social and political character of confession and repentance arises from the nature of the church as God's continued revelation in Christ existing as *community*. Bonhoeffer's dissertation, *Sanctorum Communio*, which first introduces the maxim, focuses on the church as a collective person in order to understand its inherent sociality and its relationship to God's revelation in Christ. Bonhoeffer's concept of person includes corporate as well as individual existence and hence mirrors Hegel's *Geist* in which individuals participate in an overarching collective spirit.[9] In fact, Bonhoeffer's

"Christ existing as community" is a christological redescription of Hegel's phrase, "*Gott als Gemeinde existierend*."[10] Bonhoeffer's maxim also echoes the familiar Pauline imagery of the church as the body of Christ in 1 Corinthians 12, in which Christ is both the head and the whole collective person: "the foundation, cornerstone, pioneer, and master builder" as well as "a real presence" unifying the individual members within Christ's very body, which has already taken historical form in the person of Jesus.[11]

Because God creates and sustains the collective person in history from outside history, "only the concept of revelation can lead to the Christian concept of church," or "Christ existing as community."[12] The church as a "reality of revelation" is neither mere human-religious community nor the kingdom of God come to earth; rather, it is, according to *Sanctorum Communio*, "simultaneously a historical community and one established by God."[13] Bonhoeffer writes, "The relationship of Jesus Christ to the Christian church is thus to be understood in a dual sense. (1) The church is already completed in Christ; time is suspended. (2) The church is to be built within time upon Christ as the firm foundation. Christ is the historical principle of the church."[14] Assessing the church's historical and revelatory character, Bonhoeffer writes, "Our problem has been how to discern to what extent the reality of God's revelation in Jesus Christ simultaneously establishes the church as a reality of revelation."[15] In other words, the text explores in what manner and how concretely we may interpret the visible church as a revelation of the "self-communication of God's love for humanity."[16] What is necessary is a witness that communicates that the church is for, not against, the world.

While the strengths of *Sanctorum Communio* are manifold (including that it introduces and establishes humanity's social existence as a central theological category),[17] Bonhoeffer's description of the church as collective person in the dissertation does not address adequately how the church can be at once the revelation of the new humanity in time *and* a congregation of sinful, and continually sinning, human beings. North American Christians must restrain ourselves here from a hermeneutical quick fix, from bumper-sticker theology that is tempted to interject at this point that Christians "aren't perfect just forgiven," thereby implying that a verbal proclamation that God forgives sin and an abstract belief in the Holy Spirit's sanctifying activity is a suitable, faithful witness or the revelation itself. While some theologians involved in conversations about public witness want to ground witness in the church's identity as forgiven sinners,[18] it is unclear how this self-understanding—how the knowledge of the forgiveness of *my* sin—makes evident and intelligible God's love for all of humanity and demonstrates Christ's transformative, concrete redemption of the world to those who are not a part of a Christian tradition. This is especially a problem given the quietism and apathy that too readily arise from Christians accustomed to assured forgiveness and lavishing in a significant degree of comfort and privilege. Many North American Protestants are so familiar with the message that we are a forgiven and redeemed people that this good news no longer awakens us to the ways that we remain complicit in sin—especially the myriad social/structural evils of our political, social, and economic systems—to the ways we harm those outside the visible Christian fellowship and injure and oppress people on society's margins whom we fail to recognize as brothers and sisters. Under these circumstances, the church stands before the world not as forgiven sinners but as a body needing to confess and repent for things done and left undone. Bonhoeffer's serious inquiry into how the revelation of Christ establishes the church, not only as an eschatologically redeemed new humanity, but as *a redeeming presence participating in Christ's transformative activity in the midst of the world* is absolutely vital to the church's public witness and mission. For the Christian who looks both back into history and also out into her present moment and recognizes the church's own consistent failings, a concern of utmost urgency is the degree to which the broken, sinning church-body can be the redeeming presence of Christ within the world. As Clifford Green summarizes, *Sanctorum Communio* defines "revelation as the restoration of human sociality in the new humanity of the Christian community;" yet, we must honestly ask how Bonhoeffer's theological description (which is indeed committed to concreteness) relates to and makes sense of the church's actual witness.[19]

In *Sanctorum Communio*, Bonhoeffer's description of Christ's real *presence* in the church (which is made manifest through human togetherness, through being with and for each other) is not congruent with the reality of the church's *present* sinful deeds (the ego's self-assertion over others inside and outside the church that taints this same body). *Sanctorum Communio* makes the bold claim that "the church is the presence of Christ in the same way that Christ is the presence of God," but then Bonhoeffer quickly clarifies that the church is never actually a " 'pure' " manifestation of God; it is only the body of Christ as an "invisible eschatological entity."[20] The church is indeed an eschatological reality, but Bonhoeffer's appeal here to an invisible otherworldly age (even one that proleptically has redemptive import now) abandons a degree of historical concreteness that already concerns his early theology.[21] Bonhoeffer does not explain the simultaneous relationship of identity and difference between Christ and "Christ existing as community" beyond scripture's implication that although the church is the body of Christ, complete identification between the two should not be made.[22]

Sanctorum Communio's imprecision about the nature of identity between Christ and the church is rooted in the fact that it is more ecclesiology—a sociology of the church—than christology, which alone can account for the theological continuity between sin and redemption, humiliation and exaltation, hiddenness and visibility in a concrete, worldly manner. From this ecclesiological starting point, Bonhoeffer has no choice but to split apart the church's visible and hidden aspects. His dissertation suffers from the absence of the foundational insight his later christology lectures articulate, that "Christ existing as the church is the whole person," at once exalted and humiliated, at once visible and hidden in worldly concreteness.[23] The 1933 lectures account for the continuity of the incarnate Christ who is hidden in "the likeness of sinful flesh" and glorified through his free determination to belong wholly to the world as one numbered with the transgressors. Just as the cross is the most visible and direct expression in a fallen world of Christ's being for others, which defines the new humanity, so the church as a fallen body manifests the new humanity primarily by belonging wholly to the world through confessing its own sin and accepting responsibility for the sin of broader society with which it is intimately related. In the christology lectures, the hidden nature of the church does not refer to a perfected, eschatological reality but actually points to what is visible and concrete now—the humiliating sin. The hidden nature of the church refers to the revelation itself.

Hence, Bonhoeffer begins to accomplish in these lectures what he sets out to do in the first dissertation—explain how the church is *concretely* a revelation of Christ in the world. In *Sanctorum Communio*, Bonhoeffer grants the church's sin and disunity objective, theological significance in the context of the Last Supper; however, this brief passage begs for a more detailed explanation of how the church as a broken community of sinners is also a revelation of Christ in the contemporary moment. Bonhoeffer says,

> The revealed community-of-love had to be broken up one more time by its founder's own action, though not before Jesus had tied them tightly together with a close bond at the very last hour.... Jesus says: just as I break this bread, so my body will be broken tomorrow, and as all of you eat and are filled from *one* loaf, so too will all of you be saved and united in me alone.... When Jesus is arrested and the disciples forsake him... the disciple community seems to be broken up. This has a meaning that is theologically significant and is not simply to be dismissed as the weakness or disloyalty of the disciples. It is an event with objective meaning; it had to happen this way, "so that everything would be fulfilled," one would like to add.[24]

Bonhoeffer touches on the reality of sin in the first disciple-community, implying that its brokenness mirrors Christ's crucified body, but he does not explain its theological import or objective meaning for the church's identity beyond the role the disciples played in fulfilling prophecy. An honest evaluation of Christian witness in the United States must go further and admit that the church's vast, visible failures *are* a stumbling block for many people who might otherwise be drawn into the community of faith. The church as revelation *is* hidden in humiliation. By definitively claiming that the church is such in the christology lectures, Bonhoeffer is making no excuse for this sin. The church's humiliating sinfulness is revelation only insofar as it (like the life and death of Christ) reveals the *theologia crucis*—the incarnate God whose glory is in suffering with and for others by taking responsibility for sin through repentance. Only a theology of the cross can account for the church as the visible presence of Christ in the same way that Christ is the visible presence of the triune God. Only christology establishes the continuity of the church as worldly and revelatory, and it does so by recognizing the church as a redemptive revelation or witness that is at once hidden as a stumbling block in the humiliation of its sin and visible in its confession and repentance. *Sanctorum*

Communio's basic flaw (which weakens other discussions within the work as well) is that it fails to establish continuities between God and the church-community and within the basic social relation itself.[25] It is this problem of continuity that Bonhoeffer seeks to work out in *Act and Being*.

In his habilitation thesis, *Act and Being*, Bonhoeffer develops the axiom, "Christ existing as community," into a christological claim that the revelation of Christ is the very being of community itself.[26] God reveals Godself through and in cruciform community.[27] Bonhoeffer's new social ontology (Christ existing as community) is "the solution to the problem of act and being in the interpretation of revelation" because it accounts for continuities between God's revelation and human community while also preserving the difference between God and humanity.[28] Revelation would exclude being or the possibility of coherence between God and humanity if God's in-breaking self-witness were only act or a series of acts on a wholly other world. Conversely, revelation would exclude act or the possibility of difference, thus conflating God and humanity, if revelation were pure being. In order to establish the church as God's act and being, Bonhoeffer develops Barth's maxim, "God's being is in God's act" beyond the trinitarian self-relation of Father, Son, and Spirit (God's primary objectivity in which the triune persons are the original acts of God's being) to God's being in Christ (God's secondary objectivity). Then, through christology, he inverts Barth's early focus on the wholly other God and anticipates Barth's later theology that asserts God's freedom as *for*, not from, humanity.[29] Bonhoeffer writes, "The community of faith is God's final revelation as 'Christ existing as community' . . . God's freedom has woven itself into this person-like community of faith, and it is precisely this which manifests what God's freedom is: that God binds Godself to human beings."[30] Taking his cue from Martin Heidegger's philosophical insight that being is always being-there-in-the-world such that it is impossible to shed one's concreteness and arrive at a pure, metaphysical understanding of being itself, Bonhoeffer shows that God's being in Christ (and human participation in Christ's being) is the relational activity of being free for others "there" in the midst of the world.[31] And God in Christ is "there" in the world, I have maintained, as one numbered with the transgressors. The church is the revelation of Christ—indeed, is Christ's very body—as a community of penitent sinners.

In *Act and Being*, Bonhoeffer establishes continuity not only by explaining how the revelation of "Christ existing as community" is both act and being, but also by developing how persons within the community are a "synthesis of act and being [both as] . . . *individual person and humanity*."[32] In doing so, he argues that there is an intrinsic interrelation between individual and communal existence. Bonhoeffer says that "the notion of the individual pure and simple is an unworkable abstraction. Human beings are woven into sociality" and are always either "a part of a community in 'Adam' or in 'Christ.'"[33] Furthermore, persons are both individual and humanity "never in separation but always in unity . . . At no time are human beings one of these alone."[34] Utilizing the concept of collective person,

Sanctorum Communio describes the paradoxical community of isolation, which *Act and Being* evaluates within the framework of simultaneous difference and identity: "The reality of sin . . . places the individual in a state of utmost solitude, a state of radical separation from God and other human beings . . . But the reality of sin places the individual at the same time, both subjectively and objectively, into the deepest, most intimate bond with humanity, precisely because everyone has become guilty."[35] Because each person is guilty, "each individual is Adam; everyone is entirely responsible."[36] Bonhoeffer is not uncovering here the mystery of how Christianity may uphold both the doctrine of original sin and the culpability of the individual; rather, given this teaching, he is highlighting the inherent interconnectedness of individual and social reality. He says in *Act and Being*,

> I am I and humanity in one. In my fall from God, humanity fell. . . . The interrelation of individual and humanity is not to be thought of in terms of causality—rather it is the knowledge given the individual in God's judgment. I myself am Adam—am I and humanity in one. In me, humanity falls. As I am Adam so is every individual but in all individuals the one person Adam is active.[37]

In his 1932 lectures, *Creation and Fall*, Bonhoeffer offers a theological interpretation of Genesis and further describes the nature of collective guilt.[38] He writes, "The guilt of the act becomes boundless because no [one] commits it for [oneself] but each [person] is guilty of the deed of the other. Adam falls because of Eve, Eve because of Adam. Not in such a way, however, that the other person immediately takes my burden away but so that he burdens me infinitely with his guilt."[39] Sin can never be isolated to an individual act or an individual person because all sin feeds off of previous sin, whether structural or personal, whether done to others or done by others to oneself.

Bonhoeffer's interpretation of the fall in the Garden of Eden corresponds to the Torah's witness to human solidarity in sin as depicted through the priestly stream of penitential theology, which articulates the corporate inter- and intragenerational character of sin. Mediated through a priest, God's people express sorrow and take collective responsibility for sin committed in their midst (intragenerational) and by past generations (intergenerational). A defining character of priestly theology is the belief that human beings are profoundly interconnected in sin and redemption such that culpability and responsibility are necessarily collective.[40] The priestly stream's corporate understanding of sin in turn depicts repentance as a definitive expression of what being *a people* chosen by God entails. Repentance is "a regular component of covenantal faithfulness" and "a regular rhythm of life in a fallen world" for the believing community.[41]

Similarly, Bonhoeffer argues that human beings' inherent interconnectedness, over generations and within a specific time, operates in a positive manner within the community of Christ, where one another's sin and burdens are collectively borne. He writes in *Sanctorum Communio*,

> The church-community is structured such that where one of its members is, there too is the church-community in its power, which means the power of Christ and the Holy Spirit. It is conceived of as a single life to such an extent that none of its members could be imagined apart from it.... Christians can and ought to act like Christ: they ought to bear the burdens and sufferings of the neighbor.... It must come to the point that the weaknesses, needs, and sins of my neighbor afflict me as if they were my own, in the same way as Christ was afflicted by our sin.[42]

In *Act and Being*, Bonhoeffer continues this line of thought, "In the community of faith [the]... humanity in which I stand and which I am also myself—quite independently of me prays for me, forgives sin in sermon and sacrament. There, wherever I am, it is always the whole humanity, precisely because I am its member."[43] Whether approached negatively through an examination of the nature of guilt or positively through the church's activity of bearing sin and suffering, Bonhoeffer argues that human existence, and thus human flourishing and redemption, is inherently communal.

The Church as Vicarious Representative for the World

The inherent interrelatedness of individual and social existence provides the necessary precondition for vicarious representation (*Stellvertretung*), the concept Bonhoeffer introduces in his early work that is central to his later ecclesiology in which "the church exists for others."[44] In *Ethics*, under the heading "the structure of responsible life," Bonhoeffer says that all responsible activity is based on vicarious representation. "We are required to act on behalf of others," he says, be it through human beings' various roles as parents, politicians, lawyers, doctors, and so on, or in the specifically Christian manner of taking responsibility for sin.[45] Bonhoeffer develops his understanding of vicarious representation throughout his works alongside the notion of accepting guilt and he emphasizes the christological foundation of both concepts.[46] The incarnate, crucified, and risen God is "the responsible human being par excellence," and given that the pattern of the world's ontology is now based on the life of Christ, "all human life is in its essence vicarious representation."[47]

Bonhoeffer discusses the church's vicarious redemptive action within most of his early works, however, only in the context of *Christians* who intercede for, forgive, and actively love one another, while *Temptation* (1932) and *Ethics* each speak of the church, like Christ, as a vicarious representative *for the world.*[48] The language Bonhoeffer uses in *Sanctorum Communio* is not the intrinsically broad-reaching being-for-others found in his later thought; rather, it is "being-with-each-other" which entails "being-for-each-other" *within* the church-community itself.[49] This is not to say that he intends vicarious representation to be enacted exclusively in and for the church; there are passages within *Sanctorum Communio* that resemble the all-embracing expanse of his later work. He says, for example, that Christ's vicarious action is "the love of God" through which "humanity has been brought once and for all... into community with God."[50] Still, Bonhoeffer's early theology clearly distinguishes between "being in Adam" or "being in Christ" in a manner that overdetermines ecclesiology and that seems strictly to separate each collective person.

In *Act and Being*, Bonhoeffer says that human beings are either in Adam—"turned inward into one's self, *cor curvum in se*, [having] torn themselves loose from community with God and, therefore, also from that of other human beings, and now they stand alone, that is, in untruth"—*or* they are in the church which is "turned outward towards Christ. The person [in the church-community] now lives in contemplation of Christ. This is the gift of faith, that one no longer looks upon oneself, but solely upon the salvation that has come to one from without. One finds oneself in Christ, because already one is in Christ."[51] By defining the collective persons of Adam and Christ in this way, Bonhoeffer challenges Heideggerian notions of potentiality (the autonomous human capacity to achieve authentic living), arguing that being in Christ is a reality already concretely established in Christ's historical person rather than a possibility depending on human effort for its realization. While he is correct to assert ontological transformation as divine gift and the concrete reality of revelation, Bonhoeffer's claim in *Act and Being* that human beings are always either a part "of a community in 'Adam' or in 'Christ'" is much too rigid to square with his later understanding that all reality is Christ-reality: All of humanity is accepted, judged, and reconciled to Christ such that the church is simply the body in which Christ-reality is acknowledged, demonstrated, and proclaimed.[52] Christ, after all, is not wholly other than Adam but is, as the Apostle Paul describes, the second Adam dwelling in sinful flesh: "For if the many died through one man's trespass, much more surely have the grace of God and the free gift in the grace of the one man, Jesus Christ, abounded for the many.... Therefore, just as one man's trespass led to condemnation for all, so one man's act of righteousness leads to justification and life for all" (Rom. 5:15, 18). Or, as he writes more precisely to the church in Corinth, "for as all die in Adam, so all will be made alive in Christ" (1 Cor. 15:22). Affirming the universal thrust of these Pauline statements and the interrelated ontology of humanity, Bonhoeffer boldly claims in *Ethics*, "The church-community is separated from the world *only by this*: it believes in the reality of being accepted by God—a reality that belongs to the whole world."[53]

The church's distinctiveness, then, belongs to its identity as witness and vicarious representative of the world. The church community is "the place where the witness is given to the foundation of all reality in Jesus Christ." The community is the "narrow space" proclaiming and demonstrating Christ's love, judgment, and reconciliation with all of humanity as well as the space that vicariously envelops the entire world.[54] Bonhoeffer says,

> It is intrinsic to God's revelation in Jesus Christ that it occupied space in the world. It would, however, be fundamentally wrong simply to explain this space empirically. When God in Jesus Christ claims space in the world—even space in a stable because

> "there was no room in the inn"—God embraces the whole reality of the world in this narrow space.[55]

The spatial metaphors describing the church in the New Testament (temple, building, house, body, etc.) are necessary for understanding the church as the entity that makes Christ visible but are not meant to distinguish the church as collective person from a collective person called "the world."[56] The danger of adhering too strictly to spatial images is that they become the foundation for the dualistic thinking discussed in the previous chapter, even though it is true that the church's worship, institutional order, communal life, and discipleship take particular shape in the world. Bonhoeffer's theology in *Ethics* supplements the argument in *Act and Being* by reestablishing being-in-Christ with Christ-reality, within which the whole world dwells; for in Christ, humanity lives and moves and has its being (Acts 17:28). In light of his later theology, we may revise Bonhoeffer's argument in *Act and Being* and say, "The church is the solution to the problem of act and being in the interpretation of revelation" when its acts harmonize with the world's new ontology, in other words, when it witnesses to life's christological structure through responsible repentance.

Not only is Bonhoeffer's discussion of act and being helpful for understanding how the church may be at once worldly and revelatory, it also helps clarify the relationship between the justification of the sinner through forgiveness and the continual activity of confession unto repentance, particularly for Protestant communities who tend to emphasize forgiveness at the expense of righting wrongs by doing penance. As responsible action in the world, works of repentance (or penance) do not deny Christ's justifying activity (as Protestants may worry) but actually reveals it, if it is understood as a making right (*Tun des Gerechten*)[57] by participating in Christ's redemptive form, rather than a punishment for sin or an attempt to gain salvation through works. Recall that in scripture repentance is directly connected to a God who keeps promises, not to a retributive God intent to punish for punishment's sake.[58] Bonhoeffer's insight that the church is "Christ existing as community" places justification (being) and continuous repentance (act) inextricably together and bypasses the point at which the traditional debate over faith and works reaches an impasse. Bonhoeffer says, "The church and the individual, convicted in their guilt, are justified by the one who takes on and forgives all human guilt, namely Jesus Christ. This justification of the church and the individual consists in their becoming participants in the form of Christ."[59] Because "Christ existing as community" is both act and being, being justified and doing acts of justice through repentance must occur simultaneously for the church to be a secondary form or witness that points to and participates in the being and activity of Christ. Since all of humanity has been accepted, judged, and reconciled to Christ, what is at stake in the church's participation in Christ's form through responsible repentance is not its otherworldly salvation but its this-worldly, revelatory witness. Justification by faith does not "[free] us from the toils of sin" inherent in living in this world; rather, it frees the church to serve others in the same manner that Christ serves the world—by taking responsibility for sin.

■ CONFESSION UNTO REPENTANCE AS THE CHURCH'S DEFINITIVE ACTIVITY

The Exclusive Acceptance of Guilt

Just as Christ is the vicarious representative of the world, so too is the church, as the physical manifestation of Christ in the world, a vicarious representative for all of humanity. The church carries on the work of Christ by receiving God's judgment on behalf of itself and the entire world with which it is intimately related. The church-community accepts God's judgment "as the company of those who recognize their sin and gratefully submit to the love of God" through confession unto repentance.[60] In *Act and Being*'s aforementioned passage, Bonhoeffer says that the knowledge given in God's judgment to those judged is that they themselves are Adam and thus are entirely responsible. In *Ethics* he says,

> Confession of guilt happens without a sidelong glance at others who are also guilty. This confession is strictly exclusive in that it takes all guilt upon itself. When one calculates and weighs things, an unfruitful self-righteous morality takes the place of confessing guilt face-to-face with the figure of Christ. Christ conquers us never more strongly than by completely and unconditionally taking on our guilt and declaring it Christ's own, letting us go free. Looking on this grace of Christ frees us completely from looking on the guilt of others and brings Christians to fall on their knees before Christ with the confession: *mea culpa, mea culpa, mea maxima culpa*. With this confession the whole guilt of the world falls on the church, on Christians, and because here it is confessed and not denied, the possibility of forgiveness [along with repentance and redemption] is opened.[61]

By claiming that it is culpable, indeed *mea maxima culpa*—that it is responsible for all—the church is the secondary form of Christ's reconciling life and thus "a sign of the living presence of God."[62] Because "the church-community's relation to the world is completely determined by God's relation" to it, the church's confession unto repentance arises out of the same divine affirmation and love for the world.[63]

Just as Christ simultaneously represents God to humanity and humanity to God, so the church-community simultaneously represents "Christ before human beings [and] human beings before Christ."[64] It vicariously represents Christ to the world by taking the crucified Christ's form of penitent sinner, and it vicariously represents the world to Christ in the exact same manner, namely by being "the people whose knowledge of [humanity's] falling away…is kept fresh" through repentance.[65] As Bonhoeffer says in *Discipleship*, "The community of Jesus Christ vicariously represents the world before God by following Christ under the cross."[66] By taking Christ's form, the church both acknowledges its own need to be judged and also participates in Christ's redemption as the body continuing the work of Christ's vicarious representation in historical concreteness.[67] Divine judgment of the world, embodied in the crucified Christ, begins "with the household of God" (1 Peter 4:17) and so the church is, after Christ, "a kind of first fruits" (James 1:18; 1 Cor. 15:20) for all of humanity.[68] In this extraordinary manner, the church continues the vicarious work of Christ with one defining difference: it not only accepts responsibility for the sin of the world but also confesses its own disobedient activity. In turn, Christians "cannot lift themselves above other people or establish themselves as models because they recognize themselves as the greatest of all sinners."[69]

Acceptance of guilt is the only exclusive claim about itself that the church has over the world. The crucified God's acceptance of guilt is a "christological fact" and as "Christ existing as community," it is the defining factor for the church as well.[70] Bonhoeffer says, "This does not mean that the church, alongside other things it is and does, is also the place where genuine guilt is acknowledged.... It is tautological to say that the church is the place where guilt is acknowledged. If it were otherwise, the church would no longer be church."[71] In *Creation and Fall*, Bonhoeffer claims that Christians live from the middle of history, from Christ, and thus taking his form through confession unto repentance allows the contemporary church to be responsible without necessarily being personally culpable from the beginning. "Because the origin of the confession of guilt is the form of Christ and not our individual transgressions, therefore, it is complete and unconditional," he says in *Ethics*.[72] The sin that the church confesses as the body taking the form of Christ is not "the occasional mistake or going astray"; rather it is the corporate and complexly intertwined actions that found and shape our local communities, nation, and global world. Bonhoeffer says,

> The church confesses its timidity... its dangerous concessions.... Through this it has often withheld the compassion it owes to the despised and rejected. The church was mute when it should have cried out.... It has witnessed oppression, hatred, and murder without raising its voice for the victims and without finding ways of rushing to help them.... The church confesses that it misused the name of Christ... by not resisting strongly enough the misuse of that name for evil ends. The church has looked on while injustice and violence have been done, under the cover of the name of Christ.... The church confesses that it has looked on silently as the poor were exploited and robbed, while the strong were enriched.... The church confesses that it has coveted security, tranquility, peace, property, and honor to which it has no claim, and therefore has not bridled human covetousness, but promoted it.[73]

While this confession refers to Bonhoeffer's historical context of totalitarianism and the deportation and oppression of the Jews, his litany may serve as a confession for Protestant church-communities in the United States today: *The church has withheld the compassion it owes to the despised and rejected; the church has not resisted strongly enough the misuse of the name of Christ for political ends; the church has coveted security, tranquility, prosperity to which it has no claim.*[74] This litany is particularly helpful because it directs one's thoughts to the social/structural sins that so often seem too overwhelming to confront, but that are nevertheless those for which the church must accept responsibility.

The Power of Public Confession

Confessing sin, though, is not simply an acknowledgment of what the church has failed to do. Bonhoeffer grants confession innovative power. Through a reading of *Ethics* I have argued that the church's acceptance of responsibility has transformative power because it participates in the threefold christological pattern of the world's new ontology and so prepares the way for Christ's concrete redemption.[75] In *Life Together*, Bonhoeffer also speaks of the power of confession and more directly deems confession itself a force that breaks through sin. There he examines confession of sin within Christian community and so speaks only of Christians' mutual confession and forgiveness; still, his insights may be placed in the service of a theology of public witness. The discussion in *Ethics* of accepting guilt and the discussion in *Life Together* of confessing sin are linked by a phrase appearing in both, "the public death of the sinner."[76] In each text, the public death of the sinner refers to Christ, whose form grants confession its power. In *Ethics*, Bonhoeffer says, "The justification of the church consists in... becoming participants in the form of Christ... Only as drawn into the shame of the cross, the public death of the sinner [*des öffentlichen Sündertodes*], is the church—and the individual in it—received into the community of glory."[77] And in *Life Together* he writes, "We cannot find the cross of Jesus if we are afraid of going to the place where Jesus can be found, to the public death of the sinner [*zum öffentlichen Sterben des Sünders*]."[78] Although "public" confession in *Life Together* is simply confession before another Christian while the "public" confession in *Ethics* is the church's witness through responsible action in society, in each instance the power of confession rests in its public nature. The power is the presence of other human beings. Redemption is made possible because sin is named and exposed.

In *Life Together*, Bonhoeffer identifies four breakthroughs that occur in public confession: breakthroughs to community, the cross, assurance, and new life. First, he says that genuine community is established through the honesty and vulnerability inherent in confessing sin: "Those who remain alone with their evil are left utterly alone.... We can admit our sins and in this fact find community for the first time," he says.[79] The healing judgment of the cross is unleashed, though, only by confessing *actual, specific, concrete* sins, because a general or vague acknowledgment of one's sinfulness leads merely to self-justification. The public confession of sin is a breakthrough in that it frees Christians from deceptive self-forgiveness that evades God's judgment and thus bypasses the assurance and energizing power of God's forgiveness.[80] Bonhoeffer says, "When I go to another believer to confess, I go to God.... God gives us this assurance [that we are not dealing with ourselves but with the living God] through one another."[81] Because one encounters God through "public" confession, "an acknowledgment of my sins to another believer frees me from the grip of self-deception, so the promise of forgiveness becomes fully certain to me only when it is spoken by another believer as God's command and in God's name."[82] The breakthrough to new life then occurs since "confession is conversion…Confession is following after…Confession is the renewal of the joy of baptism."[83]

Because public confession cultivates community, unleashes the power of the cross in concreteness, and energizes continuous renewal, public acceptance of guilt grants the church the power to address those overwhelming social/structural sins. Although Bonhoeffer's discussion of breakthrough in *Life Together* is within the context of mutual confession among Christians, we may say in a similar manner for a theology of public witness that taking responsibility for concrete sin in public life also frees the church from the deception of self-forgiveness, from the church excusing itself from responsibility for complex structural sin. Just as acknowledging specific sin leads the individual Christian to the promise of God's forgiveness, confronting a specific social sin through confession brings the church-community face to face with Christ's promise of concrete redemption. In order to show the importance of specificity, Bonhoeffer cites Jesus' pointed question, "What do you want me to do for you?" directed at Bartimaeus shouting, "Jesus, Son of God, have mercy!" (Mark 10:46–52). A church-community that accepts responsibility for sin, suffering, and injustice immerses itself in a specific situation, shouts with Bartimaeus, and stands ready with an answer. Bonhoeffer says, "Before confession we must have a clear answer" to the question, "What do you want me to do?" The church's concrete repentance is the "answer to [Christ's] promise of life."[84] Through specific confession and repentance, church-communities encounter and confront the sin and injustice that was previously too overwhelming to attend to, and in turn they encounter and confront God's promise of redemption.

Bonhoeffer's admonition that the church exclusively and completely bears guilt may seem naively and imprudently to excuse others, who are perhaps just as responsible for specific injustices. The exclusive acceptance of guilt could become just another religious endeavor—a heroically pious, empty exercise that never becomes embodied in healing activity because it avoids an honest and laborious evaluation of the situation at hand. In *Life Together* Bonhoeffer warns the Christian community against making confession "into a work of piety," an expression of religious righteousness or a religious spectacle, thus reducing it to "prattle."[85] The church avoids this in public life by recognizing human interdependence, and in doing so, does not arrogantly work alone but humbly acknowledges its need to partner in responsible activity with other human beings outside the visible Christian fellowship. Instead of isolating itself from broader society, the church's exclusive and genuine claim of guilt establishes its identity and mission before the world and clarifies the proper impetus behind faithful Christian activity in public life.

■ BEYOND THE KNOWLEDGE OF GOOD AND EVIL

The Ecclesial Impossibility of Being Both a Confessor and Judge of Guilt

By highlighting the church's exclusive claim of guilt, Bonhoeffer seeks to correct the Protestant tendency (examined in chapter 2) to define the church's identity and mission in terms of morality and challenges the common misperception among Christians that God's gift of faith to the church includes within it a revelatory understanding of good and evil. In *Discipleship* he writes, "Did [the disciples] receive special powers, measuring standards, or talents, which enabled them to assume a special authority towards others?"[86] In *Ethics* he continues this line of thought and asks, "Should a few super-righteous people... try to prove that not the church but all others are guilty? Would a few churchmen... presuming to be called on as judges of the world, proceed to weigh the mass of guilt... and distribute it accordingly?"[87] Emphasizing that the church exists for others and that Christ's form is central to church identity, he continues, "*Free confession of guilt is not something that one can take or leave; it is the form of Jesus Christ breaking through in the church.* The church can let this happen to itself, or it will cease to be the church of Christ."[88]

Contrary to religious thinking, God's gift of faith to Christians is not the knowledge of good and evil; rather, such knowledge actually exemplifies a falling away from God, as the Genesis story describes. In *Creation and Fall*, Bonhoeffer reflects on the position of the tree of knowledge and the tree of life, which are each planted in the middle of the garden. As humanity's limit, the tree of knowledge is not on the edge but in the middle of existence because God intends it not to be a temptation that one strays into but a grace that establishes human beings' freedom to live truthfully and humbly as creatures before God and before each other while flourishing within God's goodness.[89] Bonhoeffer says that in their delight, worship, and reverence toward God, Adam and Eve "live beyond good and evil" in a unity that does not know one from the other.[90] However, by eating the fruit of knowledge, human beings begin to dwell within disunity, shattering the relational union of Creator-creature by constructing for themselves a new identity as judge over good and evil. Such judgment—then and now—only leads to human death, destruction, and diminution. "The tree of knowledge is the tree of death" because "the human no longer knows his limit and middle," writes Bonhoeffer.[91] By living out of their own new middle, human beings break their limit as creatures and position themselves as equal before God and as superior over other human beings.

In order for humanity to return to the origin of human flourishing, God positions the cross of Christ as the new tree of life, the redeeming middle.[92] Christ's cross is the ontological event and ethical model that, as previously shown, has transformed reality into one Christ-reality, thus reuniting what the fall has divided. After the fall, human beings do not enact the will of God as creatures who live beyond good and evil; rather, as described in Paul's apocalyptic thought, humanity thinks within dualisms, specifically within the division *tob* and *ra*, the Hebrew words for good and evil, whose meanings, Bonhoeffer notes, extend beyond our understanding of these terms to something more like "full of pleasure" and "full of pain." Christ-reality reunites *tob* and *ra* such that suffering is no longer evil's possession alone but also belongs to the polyphony of life, to the joy of belonging wholly to the world. Conversely, the sign of the perfect good in this world now consists in Christ's work on the cross.[93]

Bonhoeffer begins the *Ethics* section "Guilt, Justification, and Renewal" by emphasizing again that an ecclesial ethic must be rooted in Christ's form, which, as I have argued, is characterized by an exclusive acceptance of guilt. The religious community that does not claim exclusive guilt but rather operates out of the knowledge of good and evil lives in the state of disunion intrinsic to this knowledge, with God, each other, and the rest of humanity, precisely because it sets itself up as judge.[94] As judge, the community stands in opposition to the form of Christ, which alone brings worldly transformation: The "counterimage" to the form of Christ is the human being as judge.[95] Judging is reprehensible, then, "not because it springs from dark motives" but because it contradicts the crucified Christ.[96] Bonhoeffer says,

> While we distinguish between pious and godless, good and evil, noble and base, God loves real people without distinction. God has no patience with our dividing the world and humanity according to our standards and imposing ourselves as judges over them.... God stands beside the real human being and the real world against all their accusers. So God becomes accused along with human beings and the world.[97]

After the judges have accused others and thus accused God, the weight of their judgment collapses in on themselves: "Do not judge or you too will be judged" begins Matthew 7.[98] Every judgment by the Christian is a fall from the crucified Christ, who has established the church and given it its mission. The church, then, cannot simultaneously be both a confessor and a judge of guilt; for, genuine confession of sin and acceptance of guilt constitutes obedient conformation to Christ and communion with God while judging others constitutes disobedient disunity. "The deed... called Christ" judges not others but oneself and thus invites reconciliation among human beings.[99]

Being for God as Being against God

A fair reading of the judgment pervasive within North American Christianity is, like Bonhoeffer says above, not that it stems from negative intentions, but rather that it is rooted in a desire for all human beings to uphold what various church-communities interpret as God's standards for righteous living. (Of course, inherent within such a seemingly admirable aim is the "human love" of which Bonhoeffer speaks in *Life Together* that ignores limits by attempting to shape and control others).[100] No Christian who takes seriously a Reformed faith centered on the doctrine of grace would intellectually assent to the idea that goodness or righteousness is a possibility she holds outside of Christ and the work of the Holy Spirit. Still, Bonhoeffer's interpretation of the Fall in Genesis revolves around an insight apropos for our context in the United States—the serpent's temptation is "thoroughly religious... With the first religious question in the world, evil has come upon the scene."[101] The evil lurking within the serpent's question is the religious enthusiasm that deceives the church into establishing its own " 'will to be for God.' " Bonhoeffer says, "Disobedience towards God is wrapped up in the reality of [their] 'being for God.' Only because the question is asked in a way that Adam [and Eve] can understand it as a new possibility of 'being for God' can it lead to [them] 'being against God.' "[102] Paradoxically, the church-community faithfully witnesses to Christ and serves God not by attempting to "be for God" but by belonging wholly to humanity. The church conformed to Christ is "for God" by being for human beings. Any attempt to be for God that is not christologically shaped remains under the control of the ego.

Although Bonhoeffer's later thoughts on religionless Christianity and a world come of age challenges his understanding here that human beings' sin in the world is primarily religious, his words in this lecture certainly characterize a great deal of American Christianity, which operates instinctively out of a moral framework of good and evil. Because the church's sinful desire to be like God consists in its "attempt to want to be 'for God,' to ordain a new way of 'being for God' in a special way of being religious," its attempt to be for God is "disobedience in the form of obedience; it is *the will to power in the form of service*."[103] In contrast, the Apostle Paul's wildly unreligious willingness to be "cursed and cut off" if it means winning for others communion with God is an example of an act recorded in scripture that "constitutes the most complete obedience and not disobedience" because it participates in the form of the crucified God (Rom. 9:1). Paradoxically, with his request, Paul "remains where he wishes God to ban him from, namely, in the most intimate community with God."[104]

Bonhoeffer describes two ways in which Christians dwell within a religious knowledge of good and evil and thereby establish their own will to be for God. First, he discusses inactivity that renounces public engagement altogether in the name of individual piety, and he says this primarily arises from "bourgeois existence." The inactivity of an affluent church-community results from Christians lavishing in their own prosperous or comfortable lot, such that spiritual focus rests on "a private realization of ethical ideals by which they see their own personal goodness guaranteed."[105] Bonhoeffer describes such narrowed, self-focus as "flight from public controversy... [into] the sanctuary of a *private virtuousness*." He says,

> Such people neither steal, nor murder, nor commit adultery, but do good according to their abilities. But in voluntarily renouncing public life, these people know exactly how to observe the permitted boundaries that shield them from conflict. They must close their eyes and ears to the injustice around them. Only at the cost of self-deception can they keep their private blamelessness clean from the stains of responsible action in the world.[106]

Bonhoeffer reminds the reader, though, that "ethical isolation" is a fiction.[107] Human beings are necessarily interdependent in guilt and in redemption, such that limiting oneself to one's own "closed circle of the pious" already disobediently denies Christ's call to respond to the needs of the neighbor and belong wholly to the world.[108] Thus, Bonhoeffer prefers the term "formation" over "sanctification," since reference to the latter too easily connotes an individualistic aim. He says, "The first task given to those who belong to the church of God is not to be something for themselves, for example, by creating a religious organization or leading a pious life, but to be witnesses of Jesus Christ to the world."[109]

Given the tendency among many Protestants in the United States to define witness in terms of moral righteousness, of greater concern for our theology of public witness is Bonhoeffer's criticism of religious Christians' "pseudo-doing," which he defines as "a particular expression" of the knowledge of good and evil. Describing religious individuals, he says, "It is not as if [they] do nothing, as if they were too lazy to do good works. Just the opposite is true. However, their doing is no genuine action," because it actually alienates and deepens disunion with other human beings.[110] Pseudo-doing is "self-deception" because it falsely "assumes that it is possible, even for a moment, to have the word of God other than by doing it" (James 1:22).[111] In other words, it assumes it is possible to proclaim Christ without taking the form of Christ's reconciling life. The good that takes the form of Christ "consists entirely in doing, not in judging. Judging another always entails an impediment in my own activity. Those who are judging never arrive at doing."[112] The pseudo-doing that best describes the United States context is that of religious Christians who engage in public discourse but whose voice bars reconciliation among human beings by monopolizing or proselytizing the public square, as depicted most explicitly in chapter 2 by the Religious Right. Religious Christians erroneously seek to be a witness for God by modeling and marketing their own pious devotion to ethical principles or religious standards that they demand the world adopt, but such self-focus and self-promotion never truly becomes free for the other—for the broader society which is "tired of Christian agendas" being thrust upon it.[113]

Pseudo-doing cannot be free for the other or belong wholly to the world because it does not participate in Christ but instead rests within an idea it calls Christian, which, as an ethical prescription, only deludes the religious community into being assured of its own goodness. Recall from the christology lectures that the living, incarnate God does not appear in the form of a static idea that may be possessed by the church and generally appropriated to any context. Ossifying Christ into an ethical system by which the church may justify itself and shape the world is congruent with misperceiving him "essentially as the teacher of a pious and good life."[114] Bonhoeffer writes, "Christ does not proclaim a system... which would be good today, here, and at all times. Christ does not teach an abstract ethic that must be carried out, cost what it may.[115] A church that assumes that its Christian responsibility is to deduce ethical principles in the vacuum of the pure ideal and then apply them to public life lacks Christ's regard for the lives of real human beings.[116] It refuses to "sacrifice a barren principle [for] a fruitful compromise" because the principle itself ensures Christians' "own untarnished conscience[s]" before each other and the rest of the world.[117] Therefore, Christians who establish themselves in the public square through a religious pseudo-doing arrive in the same sanctuary of private virtuousness and inactivity as those who refuse social and political engagement altogether.

Reprise: Repentance as the Alternative Mode of Being and Doing Good

Christians cannot possess the knowledge of good and evil without falling from their origin in Christ, yet if the church is to confess its own sin and take responsibility for the broader sin in which its everyday living participates, it must have some form of ethical reasoning through which it may identify behavior and forces in itself and society that harm others and cause or further injustice. In other words, the church must have some ethic or mode of being in the world that guides its public engagement. The church must function within some notion of the good through which it strives to make right that which is not and some understanding of sin such that it may recognize it in itself. We have already seen that a religious self-determination to be for God quickly devolves into being against God, because any attempt to be for God that is not christologically shaped is an expression of egocentrism. Instead, conformation to Christ necessitates belonging wholly to the world by being for human beings. Keeping in mind that Bonhoeffer introduces and establishes humanity's social existence as a central theological category, we may say that the good obtained through the form of Christ results in some measure of reconciliation among human beings and the sin concerning public witness is that which diminishes and destroys social flourishing. Instead of the knowledge of good and evil, which arises from the church constructing its own will to be for God and unfolds in explicit or implicit judgment on others, Bonhoeffer asserts that the church must gain its understanding of the good from "the knowledge of Jesus [which] consists entirely in doing the will of God."[118] Juxtaposing scripture's two garden scenes best depicts the difference between these two ethical frameworks.

The church participates in the goodness of the triune God by following the form of Jesus Christ, the form of a servant "who being in very nature with God did not consider equality with God something to be grasped" by exemplifying and enforcing the knowledge of good and evil, for example, but "humbled himself and became obedient to death—even death on a cross!" (Phil. 2:5–8). Conformation to Christ's cross rejects a religious reenactment of the Garden of Eden and instead places the church within the responsibility dramatized in the Garden of Gethsemane where Jesus says to Peter, James, and John, "'My soul is overwhelmed with sorrow to the point of death.'... Going a little farther, he fell with his face to the ground and prayed... 'My Father, if it is not possible for this cup to be taken away unless I drink it, may your will be done'" (Matt. 26:42).[119] Bonhoeffer says that instead of asking, "'How can I be good?' and 'How can I do something good?'" the church must, like Jesus, "ask the wholly other, completely different question: 'What is the will of God?'" A pious attempt to enact the tree of knowledge's good is a wholly different aim than seeking God's will in the contemporary moment since it cannot help but evade the will of God, which—as shown through the fallen flesh and cross of Christ—unexpectedly "embraces what is not God's will, sin and death."[120] God's will as expressed through Christ places the church directly into the center of fallen existence, into the midst of life's ethical ambiguities and unsolved dilemmas, which fundamentally unsettles moral certitude. A christologically shaped ethic constitutes not religious righteousness but repentance based on the penitent Christ, who performed the will of God by immersing himself fully into the messiness of sinful existence. Belonging wholly to the world through Christ redefines the good.

Discerning God's Will: Only by Participating in Reality Does the Church Share in the Good

The good that comes from discerning the will of God in the concrete moment (as distinct from that of the tree of knowledge) consists in the unity of two seemingly paradoxical claims: (1) "only by participating in reality do we share in the good" and (2) "everyone who acts responsibly" by participating in reality "becomes guilty."[121] In order to understand what Bonhoeffer means by sharing in the good through intimate participation in reality, we must unpack further the difference between Adam and Eve enacting their own will to be for God and Jesus obeying God's actual will. Juxtaposing Adam and Eve with Jesus raises the question of how exactly the church *knows* the will it is to obey without presumptuously possessing knowledge of the good.

A primary tension in the unfinished sections of *Ethics* is the relationship between direct obedience to God's command and the mediating task of discerning this concrete will of God. In *Ethics*, Bonhoeffer describes faithfulness to God's will as simple and direct obedience to the command of God in each historical moment.[122] He writes, "Just as specifically as God spoke to Abraham and Jacob and Moses and just as specifically as God spoke to Jesus Christ, to the disciples, and to the congregation through the apostles, so God speaks just as specifically to us or God does not speak at all."[123] This command "leaves the human being no room for application and interpretation but only for obedience or disobedience."[124] The call to single-minded obedience means "that there is no longer one possibility among many, but rather one option, what is real, the will of God."[125] Alongside this call to immediate obedience to the one will of God is Bonhoeffer's assertion that God's will "must be discerned again and again" in each new situation.[126] The process of discernment seems to contradict the call to immediate obedience, though, since discernment requires interpretation, which is fallible.

Bonhoeffer's description of immediate obedience to the command of God in the concrete moment also seems to presume a religious ability to know the good, since it seems to imply that, to some degree, Christians have an unmediated capacity to hear God's command.[127] Anticipating critiques that his framework warrants Christians some privileged status or ability to hear God speak directly to them, he says, "Does this mean that in every moment of our lives we could come to know the will of God through some kind of special, direct, divine inspiration, that in every moment God would unmistakably and unambiguously mark a specific action as willed by God? . . . No. . . . For the concreteness of the divine commandment consists in its historicity; it encounters us in historical form."[128] The church must live into the will of God as it immerses itself in the historical situation.

But the question remains: How can Bonhoeffer so strictly assert that the church knows the one will of God to which it must faithfully respond with immediate "simple obedience" and also uphold the necessity of discernment, which includes within it the possibility of misinterpretation, error, and disobedience?[129] My theology of public witness has constructed an interpretive path through the unfinished texts of *Ethics* and defines the will of God, to which the church has access, as nothing other than the form of the crucified Christ who accepts responsibility for sin. Bonhoeffer says, "The question of the will of God is not asking about something hidden or unfulfilled, but about what has been revealed and fulfilled. . . . It is itself already reality in the self-revelation of God in Jesus Christ."[130] The will of God "is nothing other than the realization of Christ-reality among us and in our world."[131] Given Bonhoeffer's depiction of the world's new ontology as Christ-reality, his maxim may be rephrased as, "Only by participating in Christ-reality do we share in the good," that is, only by living according to the redemptive threefold pattern of the incarnate, crucified, and risen God by taking Christ's form in the world. We may interpret Bonhoeffer's striking certainty (that for the church-community that has overcome the knowledge of good and evil "there is no longer a choice among various possibilities but always only one option of being elected to do the one will of God in simplicity") as confidence that the church enacts the will of God when it confesses sin through repentant activity in the midst of historical reality.[132] Put more simply, the church knows God's will when it takes responsibility for the sin in which it is always already enmeshed.

Although Christ reveals God's will for the church through his crucified form, Bonhoeffer recognizes that God's will "remains a question insofar as I, together with the world around me, am placed into this question by the answer given."[133] The answer given is the form of the crucified Christ that finds the church-community in its specific locus and historicity—in situations in which the church must evaluate particular sin and perform responsible repentance. Bonhoeffer says, "Responsible action takes place in the sphere of relativity. . . . It takes place in the midst of countless perspectives from which every phenomenon is seen."[134] God's speech is incarnate—is fleshed out—and so occurs "in the ambiguity of historical situations," within the particular times and places in which historical human beings are bound, such that Christians listen for the command of God "in the facts themselves," as he says in his prison correspondence.[135] The will of the living God who is active in history arises anew every moment in conjunction with an ever-unfolding reality. Enacting the will of God necessitates that the church-community be already immersed within life's ethical ambiguities and unsolved dilemmas in order to discern the signs of the times—the facts that stage responsible action. Because discernment is not foolproof, the church-community that confesses sin unto repentance, then, enacts the good without possessing knowledge of the good. Intimate participation in the ambiguity of the historical situation overcomes the knowledge of good and evil because life's ambiguity disallows any certainty of the church-community's own ethical correctness. Instead, "We can seek and find what is genuinely good only in the risk of action itself."[136]

Responsible action is a risk in that the church-community does not know if and how its attempts at repentance will heal the situation at hand, because the consequences of all action, good or bad, "are hidden in the historical situation."[137] Because our very activity may instigate further unseen injury, responsible action "has to observe, weigh, evaluate, and decide, and . . . do all that with limited human understanding. We must have the courage to look into the immediate future; we must seriously consider the consequences of our actions; and must attempt seriously to examine our own motives and our own hearts," says Bonhoeffer.[138] By acknowledging the ambiguity of the historical situation, Bonhoeffer is neither inviting a "blatant license to commit evil" nor negating the distinction between better and worse action.[139] The church-community must do everything in its power to act wisely and to bring about human reconciliation and social flourishing—must make educated, thoughtful decisions, keeping in mind that the lives of real human beings are at stake—and so it does not proceed by cavalierly presuming that God's grace will undo or erase sin's serious repercussions. Precisely because it understands itself as the body immeasurably responsible, the church-community labors within the world to the rhythm of the sinner's prayer, "God, have mercy on me, a sinner" (Luke 18:13). The community continues to throw itself on God's mercy not to deny responsibility but to offer its work to God as it confesses its own inadequacy to the one who promises to work all things together for good (Rom. 8:28). The church participates in the good when it lives according to the threefold structure of Christ-reality, because, by doing so, it prepares the way for Christ's concrete redemption.

Everyone Who Acts Responsibly Becomes Guilty

Bonhoeffer not only says that the church shares in the good by living according to Christ-reality, but also that everyone who acts responsibly by living according to Christ-reality becomes guilty. In other words, the church not only confesses sin but also opens itself up to further guilt through responsible repentance. Even if it discerns wisely, the church that risks attempts at transformative action within life's ethical complexities will become guilty to some degree, because, limited by its creatureliness, the church cannot ever enact perfect justice and healing.[140] The imperfect character of all human endeavors is precisely why the church's public activity must "be grounded in God's own action" through Christ.[141] Bonhoeffer writes in *Ethics*, "Nothing but God makes human action in history good. What is good in history is God's action alone. Human historical action is good only insofar as God draws it into God's own action and as the human agent completely surrenders all to God's action without claiming any other justification."[142] In *Discipleship* he says, "God alone knows our good works, while we know only God's good work," the work of the crucified Christ who accomplishes reconciliation through a repentance that belongs wholly to the world. "We journey under God's grace, we walk in God's commandments, and we sin," he says.[143]

In the face of certain guilt and the risk of further harm, the church is tempted toward passivity. Recall, however, that religious moralists cannot escape guilt through inactivity and pseudo-doing, but actually alienate themselves from Christ by refusing to take responsibility for sin. Bonhoeffer writes,

> Those who, in acting responsibly, seek to avoid becoming guilty, divorce themselves from the ultimate reality of history, that is, from the redeeming mystery of the sinless bearing of guilt by Jesus Christ, and have no part in the divine justification that attends this event. They place their personal innocence above their responsibility for other human beings and are blind to the fact that precisely in so doing they become even more egregiously guilty. They are blind to the fact that genuine guiltlessness is demonstrated precisely by entering into community with the guilt of other human beings for their sake.[144]

Our everyday living makes us complicit in sin as members of a common humanity, and such sin and injustice are too pervasive for us to extricate ourselves entirely from, in part because of the structural and intergenerational nature of sin and in part because of the tightly interwoven character of all aspects of human life. Economic, environmental, agricultural, technological, racial, class, national, and international sin and injustice form a tight web within which we live and move and have our being, and in a powerful or affluent society, our lives effortlessly benefit in countless, unrecognized ways from some or all of these structures. And yet, these are the realities comprising Christ-reality, that same reality in which humanity lives and moves and has its being, and in which the church harmonizes its activity with the christological pattern of redemption by accepting responsibility for injustice and suffering in the world (Acts 17:28). The church only shares in the goodness of Christ by participating in his form, which has transformed all of reality such that accepting responsibility through repentance ushers forth concrete redemption.

Because human beings share in the good by living according to Christ-reality, this-worldly living is not tragic. "The essence of Greek tragedy" is that "life's intrinsic structure is transgression against the laws of gods," Bonhoeffer says; in contrast, the guilt born from a community acting responsibly is a guilt already reconciled to Christ. The commandment of God breaks through the seemingly stark picture of certain sin and "commands freedom," placing the church-community made up of finite human beings into the redemptive flow of God's life and love.[145] Bonhoeffer says, "Thus a profound mystery of history is disclosed to us: those who act in the freedom of their responsibility see their action as flowing into and springing from [God]."[146] Unlike the social ethics of Reinhold Niebuhr, in which there is "eternal conflict between the necessities of historical action and the ethic of Jesus," Bonhoeffer's ethic of christological conformation "is not crushed by conflicts of principle but springs instead from an already accomplished reconciliation of the world with God."[147] Because reality is now structured after the pattern of Christ's life, death, and resurrection, the church may risk responsible action and be "actually on the way" as participants in Christ's transformative activity (even at the risk of further sin), instead of "standing perpetually at the crossroads, struggling forever to make the right decision... worn out by conflicting duties."[148] The church-community that, taking Christ's form, confesses sin, accepts further guilt, and repents, stands before God like Jesus "as the obedient one and as the free one [who] does the will of the Father." Bonhoeffer says,

> Obedience without freedom is slavery. Freedom without obedience is arbitrariness. Obedience [to the form of Christ] makes clear to human beings that they have been *told* what is good and what the Lord requires of them (Micah 6:8) ["to do justice, and to love mercy, and to walk humbly with your God"].... Freedom dares to act and leaves the judgment about good and evil up to God.[149]

Thus, responsible, repentant action based on the form of Christ "is bound yet creative."[150] The responsible church-community obeys the command of God as expressed through the form of Christ, but within a creative process it freely discerns, first, the content of its confession (the particular sin/s it is convicted of) and, then, its ensuing repentant activity, which together become the church-community's specific vocation of redemptive public engagement.[151]

■ CONFESSION UNTO REPENTANCE AS THE ECCLESIAL GUIDE FOR PUBLIC VOCATION

The driving concern of this book is how the church may offer a nontriumphal witness to the lordship of Christ in a pluralistic society. How can the church-community offer a particular and transformative witness to Christ without being arrogantly authoritarian and without falling into the trap of partisan politics? Given its disagreements, disunity, and sin, how may the church manifest concrete redemption? I have argued thus far that the church faithfully witnesses to Christ in public life when its mode of being in the world is confession unto repentance based on the form of the crucified God. This final section attempts greater detail about the ecclesial outworking of this form by showing how confession unto repentance guides the church into specific social and political engagement.

Limited Vocation, Boundless Responsibility

The dynamic of being at once bound yet open-ended characterizes the command of God in the concrete moment and the church's response to that command.[152] The command of God is limitless since it "embraces the whole of reality" and "is the total and complete claim of human beings by the merciful and holy God in Jesus Christ." It is also specific since it is answered "with our whole life as it is realized in activities in particular cases," in the times and places that "concern us, that we experience, that are realities for us, that pose concrete questions to us." Bonhoeffer continues, "Grace seeks out and finds human beings in their place... and claims them precisely there. It is a place that in every case and in every respect is burdened with sin and guilt."[153] Likewise, the church-community's specific vocation in public life is at once bound through obedience to the form of the crucified Christ in a specific place and time and open-ended in such a way that invites creative activity. Bonhoeffer writes, "We ask about the good... in the midst of a situation of our life that is both determined in a particular way and yet still incomplete, unique and yet already in transition."[154]

By reading Bonhoeffer's discussion of God's will and the structure of a responsible life through the lens of confession unto repentance, we can construct a framework for church-communities' public vocations that reflect the limited and limitless character of the command of God. A church-community's specific vocation may arise from conviction over a particular sin that it has committed as a local body, such as past racism. The process of confessing this sin and repenting may lead the community not only to repentant activity regarding its specific sin but also to a wider engagement with issues surrounding race on both a local and broader scale.[155] More likely, however, individual members within a church-body may become convicted of a broad-reaching social/structural sin within the local or global community that they bring before the body to help bear. The church-community may accept responsibility for a specific unjust structure of life, confessing the sin, as exemplified in part III, of environmental, racial, or socioeconomic injustice and may turn their attention toward ways in which they, as interdependent individuals within community, may begin to live within their local, national, and/or global context in a manner that resists these larger powers through redemptive, constructive repentance. Or it may be that the church-community is not a local worshipping congregation as such but a group of Christians, like those at the Southeast White House, who have come together around a common work. Given that the universal church is a body comprising many parts, the specific, primary vocations of particular church-communities will vary (1 Cor. 12); yet together as "genuine Christian responsibility, [they will encompass] all activity within the world."[156]

The church's vocational reach is broad not only because it is a body comprising many parts but also because "the call of Jesus Christ knows no bounds" and thus breaks through barriers such as race, class, and nation.[157] Bonhoeffer writes, "The Bible is loud and clear in its instruction to do whatever is right in front of us (Eccl. 9:10)," but we must also "guard the command to love the neighbor against any false limitation, and thus to preserve the freedom that the gospel gives to the concept of vocation."[158] As the Latin American liberation theologian Gustavo Gutiérrez argues, a community's vocation may actually involve embarking on a search for the neighbor, if injustice has pushed an oppressed people to the margins of society where their needs are hidden and silenced.[159] Similarly, in *Ethics*, Bonhoeffer endorses Nietzsche's criticism that neighbor love is ultimately self-love if it does not seek out those who are different from oneself. Nietzsche writes, "My brothers love the neighbor I do not recommend to you: I recommend to you love the farthest."[160] Whoever does not attend to the person who is most remote from a privileged circle of neighbors, friends, colleagues, and family "does not serve the neighbor but themselves."[161] Bonhoeffer says, "The call of Jesus Christ is the call to belong to Christ completely... vocation... requires "a definite field of activity" [but] by being related to Jesus Christ, [it] is set free from any isolation.... I remain aware of my responsibility towards the whole, and only thus fulfill my vocation."[162]

The church sustains awareness of its responsibility to the whole of life when it tries to make sense of all the factors at play in a complex issue, yet the church-community's actual repentant activity has "a limited scope." Bonhoeffer writes,

> Christ did not cause the world to cease being world, and every action that seeks to confuse the world with the kingdom of God is a denial of both Christ and the world.... No one has the responsibility of turning the world into the kingdom of God, but only of taking the next necessary step... Every transgression of this boundary leads to catastrophe. The task is not to turn the world upside down but in a given place, to do what, from the perspective of reality is necessary objectively and to really carry it out. But even in a given place, responsible action cannot always do what is ultimately right. It has to proceed step by step, ask what is possible, and entrust the ultimate step, and thus the ultimate responsibility, to another hand.[163]

It is because the ultimate responsibility to redeem belongs to God that Bonhoeffer refers to this-worldly action, as we saw in the previous chapter, as penultimate and as a *preparation* of the way for Christ's unfolding redemption. The church-community's activity may only be partially redemptive at best, for Christians who attempt to correct a complex situation all at once most likely are operating out of a moral principle with little regard for the cost to real human beings. For Bonhoeffer, the structure of a responsible life necessitates actions "in accord with reality." Because the responsible church-community really acts as it is intimately involved in some specific area of life, it cannot let itself be "worn down while eagerly but powerlessly confronting all injustice and misery in the world."[164] The local church-community recognizes, rather, "another limit" which is "that other people encountered" inside and outside the visible Christian community "must be regarded as responsible as well."[165]

Respecting other human beings as agents actually enhances the church-community's redemptive preparation as it enters into interdependent partnership with other Christians as well as with groups and individuals who do not self-describe as Christian. It is likely that a church-community becomes convicted of a particular sin by listening to grassroots workers or specialists not necessarily associated with the church, who understand, for example, the intricacies related to poverty or environmental crises. This necessitates that church-communities humbly respect the insights of others. Bonhoeffer says that "from its vantage point Christianity has something specific to say about worldly things," yet the essential task of the church does not consist is providing answers "to *all* social and political questions of the world, so that one would only have to listen to these answers to put the world in order."[166] Although Christianity addresses "certain economic and social attitudes and conditions that hinder faith in Jesus Christ," the nontriumphant church recognizes that it has often failed in its response to social, economic, and political concerns and "through its own fault has given offense, which hinders people from believing its message."[167] The church's failures exemplify its need to listen to and partner with others.

Humble recognition of the church's failures need not squelch the church's prophetic voice, however, for the heart of prophetic work as displayed in scripture is collective self-critique. A church-community that humbly recognizes its limit may challenge other Christians to support its work by inviting self-reflection through prophetic social criticism. Although our pluralistic, democratic country is not, nor should be considered, a Christian nation, the way of transformation opened up for ancient Israel by the Hebrew prophets could unfold in a similar manner in the United States when church-communities help each other discern their sin prophetically, reminding themselves that the cross is God's truth about the church.[168] In a nation where over three-fourths of the population are self-proclaimed Christians, confession of, and repentance for, specific injustice that destroys and diminishes others could produce significant social healing.[169] The high percentage of Christians in the United States provides a far-reaching audience for the call to repent, with a faithful response enabling significant, redemptive human flourishing on many levels within society. In order to avoid judging those outside the visible church, the church's prophetic criticism must be directed at itself; still, because Christians are simultaneously a portion of "We the People," repentant activity will challenge the life of the nation and the global order in numerous ways. The church's response to its own sin will propel it into democratic responsibility, but in order to avoid falling into a knowledge of good and evil, the church would do well not to condemn the nation for sin it refuses to acknowledge and address in its own institutional and communal life.

Only in Repentance May the Church Hope

Christians in the United States will likely continue to disagree on the purchase particularistic belief makes on believer's public lives in a pluralistic democracy and will likely persist for some time in polarizing politics. The church will remain a messy, broken revelation hidden in the humiliation of its sin and division, and this is a fact that followers of Christ must bear in sorrow. The authentic church, after all, is that "of Peter," the church that weeps for its own continuous sin.[170] Still, by participating in the form of Christ, who accepted responsibility for sin, suffering, and injustice, church-communities may prepare the way for Christ's unfolding redemption. Thus, followers of Christ may also bear their sorrow in hope; for, "only in repentance may we hope" that Christians in the United States may recognize that political and social divides do not delimit the manner in which the church is called to enact its public witness.[171] Instead, by taking the form of Christ in humility before each other and the rest of the world, church-communities have the theological foundation of Christ-reality upon which they may demonstrate and proclaim that Christ has accepted, judged, and reconciled the whole world to himself. The church that numbers itself with the transgressors may transcend the options that American social and political culture lay before it and may challenge each other to discern the will of God in the concrete moment in ultimate honesty about itself. By doing so, "the genuine community of the cross of Jesus Christ" not only has the character of vulnerability and weakness as it wears "the rags of confession and repentance," but also is a community of strength, precisely because it is not isolated in sin but is a fellowship defined by courageous participation in God's concrete redemption.[172] The community of the cross is a community of strength as the body that loves life, belongs wholly to this world, and is held together by a common vocation of redemptive repentance. Herein lies the evangelistic impulse of the witness. The redemptive force of confession and repentance draws human beings together, inviting others into the redeeming community of the cross that prepares the way for Christ. I turn now to two communities that embody this witness and to a hope generated by their living illustrations of communal work that exemplify ecclesial commitments and practices born out of a disposition of confession and repentance.

PART THREE

Contours of a Repenting Church

LOCATING THEOLOGY WITHIN REPENTING COMMUNITIES

Part II constructed a theological foundation upon which confession and repentance makes sense as public witness. Laying this foundation consequently has expanded our imaginations about what repentance encompasses and entails. At the same time, the christological redescription has altered common understandings: Repentance is not the private, self-focused aim of the individual before God but is participation in the Christ event and thus existence for others and a sharing in God's kingdom come. As a response to the new era inaugurated and embodied in Christ, repentance is definitively social and political. It is the politically intelligible expression of the liturgy of confession of sin; the communal, public proclamation of the all-embracing lordship of Christ; and the church's reorientation toward this world.

Whereas part II emphasized the central importance of renewed theological thinking for transformative Christian practice, part III reminds the theologian that all systematic thinking has a limit and that for theology that limit is the church, or "Christ existing as community." In *Act and Being*, Bonhoeffer writes:

> The fact is that, as a theologian, I cannot resist the lure of intellectual works righteousness except by locating my theology within the community of faith (which is the theologian's humility), allowing the community of faith to allocate its place and bestow meaning upon it. Thinking, including theological thinking, will always be "systematic" by nature and can, therefore, never grasp the living person of Christ unto itself. Yet, there is obedient and disobedient thinking (2 Cor. 10:5). It is obedient when it does not detach itself from the church, which alone can "upset" it as "systematic" thinking and in which alone thinking has meaning.... Think boldly, but more boldly still, believe and rejoice in Christ.[1]

Theology obedient to the living Christ locates itself within the community of faith and receives into itself all the messiness, complexity, and imperfection intrinsic to the actual church and to this-worldly living. Thus, in order to gain clarity about how the church offers a nontriumphal witness to the lordship of Christ, a theology of public witness must open itself up to existing church-communities attempting to do just that. The theologian must guard against constructing a closed system by welcoming lessons learned from an enfleshed church.

This is not to say, however, that one should first construct a system and then test its merits on a community. The relationship between formal theological reflection and insights gained through the practice of engaged communities is, at its richest, more circular than linear. As mentioned in the introduction, the influence of the Southeast White House on my theological thinking preceded any formal theological education. This book grows out of my experience there, where I first raised questions about the church's identity and mission in society. While working at the Southeast White House for two years in between undergraduate and graduate school (1999–2001), I also became an acquaintance of Tim Clayton, who at the time was working at the Falls Church Episcopal, the church I was attending in the Washington metropolitan area, and I became intrigued by his vision for Eleuthero. Thus, my relationship to the Southeast White House and, arguably, the Eleuthero Community is best described in a dual manner as participant-observer, not only in the scholarly sense as one who enters fully into the life of the community she is studying but also "participant" in a more ordinary sense, as one who chose to be an intern at the Southeast White House and as one who shares the social location of Eleuthero and would have felt quite at home as a congregant in that worshipping community.

Eleuthero's members are mostly white, well-educated, and artistically inclined professionals who, in their first year, ranged in age from mid-twenties to mid-forties. In that year the core members of Eleuthero consisted of Tim and Cheryl Clayton with their three children, Loren and Kelly Ayer with their two children, and Janelle and Craig Banta, all of whom moved in 2005 from the Washington, D.C., metropolitan area where they already were worshipping together at Kairos, a community within the Falls Church Episcopal that focused on social engagement under the leadership of Bill Haley and Tim Clayton. These couples, who were drawn to the vision of Eleuthero and had ties to New England through family or prior employment, joined two other families living in Portland, Maine, who had met Tim when he visited the area in preparation for the move: Sarrah and David Stankiewicz and Evan and Kathryn Pillsbury and their two children. Having found the job market a challenge in Maine, the core members of Eleuthero, all of whom were middle- to upper-middle-class in the Washington metropolitan area, are middle- to lower-middle-class in Portland, with many of the members underemployed and some on public assistance.

The Southeast White House includes a vastly diverse group of people, and this reflects the intention of the cofounders, Sammie Morrison, an African American, and Scott Dimock, a Caucasian, whose interracial partnership symbolizes the reconciliation the ministry wishes to foster. Sammie is a retired deputy chief of the D.C. Metropolitan Police Department who had previously served in the U.S. Army, and Scott is a retired staff member of the nondenominational high school ministry Young Life, through which he was ordained in the Evangelical Church Alliance. The reconciliation the Southeast White House represents and desires to cultivate, though, encompasses more than race. There is a wide range of diversity among the staff in terms of socioeconomic class, education level, family make-up, work experience, and political leanings, with many of these differences defying class and race stereotypes. Furthermore, the Southeast White House, as well as Eleuthero, is ecumenical, with the majority of denominational affiliations falling under the broad rubric of evangelicalism. In this regard, both are communities that felt familiar to me as one who grew up in an evangelical subculture and participated in evangelical para-church groups, has an ecumenical theological perspective, and, for the past decade, has worshipped in diverse Episcopal congregations ranging from the evangelical Falls Church Episcopal (which in recent years has decided to leave the Episcopal Church USA) to the historically Black and presently interracial Trinity Episcopal Church in Charlottesville, Virginia (which is quite content in this mainline denomination).

■ VARYING EMBODIMENTS OF CONFESSION UNTO REPENTANCE

Eleuthero and the Southeast White House are communities that seek to offer a nontriumphal witness to the lordship of Christ and that exemplify ecclesial commitments and practices born out of a disposition of confession and repentance. They not only show how public witness conformed to the incarnate, crucified, and risen Christ may unfold in lived reality, but also demonstrate through each community's particularity that confession and repentance may be embodied communally in various ways. There are, for example, a few key differences between Eleuthero and the Southeast White House that contribute to the varying ways they inhabit repentance. Eleuthero is a recently founded worshipping congregation set within the predominantly unchurched culture of Portland, Maine. Its eucharist-centered worship reflects a commitment to see the world—and its work and witness in the world—in a sacramental manner, and it draws on the liturgies of the Church of England, the Episcopal Church, and the Iona Community in Scotland to help shape that vision and form them as a people.[2] Eleuthero is a model of a community that is at once newly created in response to conviction about specific sin and also rooted in liturgical traditions; thus it is innovative but has resonance with the institutional church. In fact, because the community was so new (with my research on Eleuthero occurring at the end of its first year in fall 2006), one congregant, Dave Stankiewicz, joked that there would not be a lot for me to observe "since they haven't done much yet." Eleuthero's initial work of repentance involved a renewing of minds—an unlearning and learning anew the central messages of scripture—and so the chapter focuses a good deal on Tim's teaching and preparatory groundwork. The Eleuthero members look to Tim for guidance because, while neither they nor he assumes a top-down authoritative approach to community, his career as a pastor-theologian has afforded him the necessary time and space to do the demanding intellectual and psychological work of dismantling the theological apparatus bolstering a triumphal witness and of untangling the theological messages contemporary evangelicals have inherited. The strength of this case study is that it depicts a church-community whose repentance involves deliberately rearticulating the gospel in relation to their embedded theologies, and it depicts a community at the beginning stages of discerning the details of a vocation based on conviction about structural sin.[3] Because I am arguing that churches need to rethink their identity and public vocation in this way and because I want to provide a realistic depiction of the difficult yet vital steps of discernment and action that a reorientation of ecclesial witness demands, I focus my chapter on that first year.

The Southeast White House, on the other hand, is more established (having celebrated its ten-year anniversary in 2006, the year I conducted interviews to augment both the experience I had as a staff member from 1999–2001 and the research I had obtained for a seminar paper in fall 2001). Unlike Eleuthero, the Southeast White House is situated within a culture where belief in the Christian God is the norm and where the "hypocrisy" and "self-righteousness" of churchgoers is often noted by nonchurchgoing neighbors. Furthermore, although the Southeast White House sees itself more as a church-community than a nonprofit organization that provides various programs and services, it is not trying to be a formal or traditional worship community and refers to itself on occasion as an "outreach arm for congregations."[4] It provides space for vivid Christian witness as it relies heavily on volunteers from various churches to carry out its mission. Still, it is not beyond the scope of its identity, mission, and resources to provide a Sunday evening worship service similar to household gatherings described in the New Testament. In fact, a worship opportunity that does not conflict with other ecclesial commitments would center and strengthen the staff, volunteers, and neighbors' life together and would complement the ongoing Bible studies the Southeast White House provides—the power of which stems from the fact that the insights garnered from scripture are concrete since they arise from a common work. By functioning as an "outreach arm," the Southeast White House provides a vital service to the broader church body, with a few congregations in the metropolitan area and beyond partnering with the House to varying degrees by committing significant amounts of volunteer support and material resources. At the same time, however, the Southeast White House also reveals a deficiency in the way a variety of churches understand their identity and purpose when individuals who become participants in the House's work do so because their home congregations lack a transformative public witness rooted in redemptive social engagement.

Given that the church's public witness should conform to the incarnate, crucified, and risen Christ as opposed to other church-communities, I offer Eleuthero and the Southeast White House not as blueprint plans all churches should follow but as theologically rich and gloriously messy examples of public witness that faithfully demonstrate the person and work of Christ. In other words, my primary goal is to offer a fresh theological vision and to show how I have seen this vision enacted in two different communities, not to suggest that churches must structure themselves in these exact ways in order to live out a vocation based on confession and repentance. Every congregation has the resources and the call to enact repentance in public life, and my intent is to provide a compelling frame of reference for all kinds of Christian communities and congregations.

Discerning public vocation, though, most likely will require rethinking a church's identity, priorities, and organizational structure, and each denominational entity or community of believers has to do this for itself. Still, given that the identity and function of congregations traditionally revolves around worship, Eleuthero and the Southeast White House have something to teach us about the nature of true devotion as communities organized around a common work of repentance. As the prophet Isaiah boldly asserts, even the most intentionally designed and emotionally earnest worship, if disconnected from repentant action in the midst of the world, is to God pious self-deception and vain repetition:

> Day after day they seek me/ and delight to know my ways,/ as if they were a [people] that practiced righteousness/ and did not forsake the ordinance of their God; they ask of me righteous judgments,/ they delight to draw near to God..../ Look, you serve your own interest on your fast day,/ and oppress all your workers..../ Such fasting as you do today/ will not make your voice heard on high....
>
> Is not this the fast that I chose:/ to loose the bonds of injustice,/ to undo the thongs of the yoke,/ to let the oppressed go free,/ and to break every yoke?/ Is it not to share your bread with the hungry,/ and bring the homeless poor into your house;/ when you see the naked, to cover them,/ and not to hide yourself from your own kin?/ Then your light shall break forth like the dawn,/ and your healing shall spring up quickly;/ your vindication shall go before you,/ and the glory of the Lord shall be your rear guard./ Then you shall call, and the Lord will answer;/ you shall cry for help, and he will say, Here I am:
>
> If you remove the yoke from among you,/ the pointing of the finger.../ if you offer your food to the hungry/ and satisfy the needs of the afflicted, / then your light shall rise in the darkness... / and you shall be like a watered garden,/ like a spring of water,/ whose waters never fail./ Your ancient ruins shall be rebuilt;/ you shall raise up the foundations of many generations;/ you shall be called repairer of the breach,/ the restorer of streets to live in (Isaiah 58).

The worship—the praying, singing, preaching, listening, confessing, studying, serving, bearing, feasting—of a repenting community stems from a common work of existence for the oppressed, the abused, the prisoner, the homeless, the disabled, the immigrant, the exploited worker, the prostituted, the marginalized, the underserved, the forgotten, the estranged, and the hated. True worship pleasing to God cannot be outsourced or an add-on. It is praise and devotion arising from and found within responsible repentance that transforms society by satisfying the needs of the afflicted, rebuilding ruins, raising up foundations, and restoring streets to live in. The Eleuthero Community and the Southeast White House invite us, each in its own way, to reconsider congregational life through the lens of such responsible repentance. Now, in recognition of theology's limit and the impossibility of offering a foolproof systematic strategy for public engagement, we turn to Eleuthero asking that, as an imperfect and finite community of faith, it "bestow meaning" on a theology of public witness.

6 The Eleuthero Community

Confession and Repentance through Unlearning and Learning Anew

REPENTANCE AS REORIENTATION TOWARD THE WORLD AND THE YES TO EARTHLY LIFE

The back stairs of the 1782 Historic Jeremiah Buxton Tavern, now home to Tim and Cheryl Clayton and their three children, opens up to a room-turned-worship-space for the year-old Eleuthero Community. Side walls are lined with candle sconces and with windows overlooking a modest organic garden and the North Yarmouth, Maine, countryside. At the front on the old, wide, white pine floor-boards sits an altar area crafted from a small antique wooden table, a eucharistic clay chalice, and a striking Coptic cross, a gift that a friend brought back from Ethiopia. At the back stands an expansive and sophisticated collection of well-worn theological works from Saint Augustine and Martin Luther to Simone Weil, Abraham Joshua Heschel, Martin Luther King Jr., and Dietrich Bonhoeffer. Still to find are a couple of old church pews as well as pieces of stained glass to further set the space apart.

The small Eleuthero Community that gathers in this space consists of Christians whose faith compels them to affirm the world, to turn toward the world in gratitude and repentance, with the vision being that "Christian faith becomes a robust, recognized resource and inspiration for the care and dignifying of the natural world and of vulnerable populations." The world is affirmed because it is divine gift; its "underlying reality" is, as Archbishop Rowan Williams says, "God's giving... God's... self-sharing love" that "animates every object and structure and situation in the world."[5] Inherent within Eleuthero's affirmative orientation toward the world, though, is self-critique and confession of sin: "We find ourselves living in a sharp irony," the Web site reads; "As a culture arguably we have more—stuff, power, and success—than any people who have ever lived. Yet it is not at all clear that the way we are on is sustainable. It is not at all clear that the way we are on is life-giving to the world's poor and vulnerable. Indeed, it is not at all clear that stuff, power, and success feed our own souls, should we take the time to stop and look inside." As a community whose identity and mission grow out of its disposition of confession and repentance, Eleuthero recognizes that repentance includes but encompasses more than renunciation of sin. Aware of the christological pattern of reality—that divine affirmation of the world includes divine judgment, and ecclesial acceptance of judgment leads to this-worldly transformation—Eleuthero views its communal repentance as an active response to God's promise to redeem.

Instead of unsustainable living, members of Eleuthero are turning toward simplicity and sustainability; instead of cultural and political dominance, they seek service as obedience to the concrete will of God in Portland, Maine, and the surrounding area; instead of overlooking the environmental neglect and damage U.S. Christians and citizens persist in, the Eleuthero Community is turning toward and courageously facing their own responsibility. In order to carry this out, the community is taking steps "to found a retreat and study center for the exploration and development in solitude, in conversation, [and] in community the nexus of Christian spirituality with ecological care and social justice. Core members of Eleuthero will live into the vision by practicing lives of simplicity and wonder, community, spiritual disciplines, ecological care, and relationship with marginalized populations." The mission statement continues with an affirmative Yes to earthly life:

> Eleuthero is formed of a people who want to live deeply, in authentic community and with a depth of soul and a realization of the worth of every day, every person, every creature, every bit of what is. Eleuthero is the Greek verb meaning "to set free"; we believe that there are soul resources in Christian spirituality and theology that lead to freedom and life—for ourselves, for the vulnerable, and for the world into the future.[6]

The members of Eleuthero have come together, from D.C. and Portland, to belong wholly to the world: to acknowledge their complicity in the excesses of American culture, to learn from the ecologically astute culture of Maine, and to seek as a community sustainable ways of living.

■ REPENTANCE AS THE RENEWING OF MINDS

A common thread drawing into the Eleuthero vision those members already living in Portland is a felt need to unlearn and learn anew the heart of Christian witness—to be transformed into a new form by the renewing of minds (Rom. 12:2)—a daunting task for individuals to embark on outside the context of a community of supportive believers who are following similar lines of faith-seeking-understanding. One central component that attracts the couples living in Portland to Eleuthero is Tim's ability both to articulate what they have been intuiting for a while about the failures of Christian witness and this-worldly engagement and to help craft an alternative understanding of ecclesial mission and public witness. For example, Sarrah Stankiewicz, who works for Maine Audubon, "feels extremely convinced that it is our job as Christians to care for the earth" by, for example, using renewable energy and preserving the natural environment. She has felt "jaded," "disgusted," and "disillusioned" by the evangelical Christianity modeled by her home church in Massachusetts and recently went through "a whole period of change where [she] felt very distant from the faith because [she] needed to figure out... what the core emphasis was and so see that the way many evangelicals feel politically is not really built into Christian faith." The period when the Claytons, Ayers, and Bantas had just moved to Maine and were beginning their corporate worship together coincided with her "starting to figure out what Christianity was really about. They were reflecting these things," Sarrah says, "and Tim's sermons were reflecting these things." She continues, "What I saw in Eleuthero were people who were not into a commercialism [that markets Christian belief], who were not necessarily Republicans because they believed in Jesus, who were open minded and less fearfully filled with easy answers that made them feel secure." As a member of Eleuthero, Sarrah now feels "okay and comfortable with being a Christian" because she has found "common ground" not only with other committed Christians but with Christians whose faith explicitly seeks common ground with people outside the church.[7] For example, Eleuthero has fostered "space for discussion to emerge" through public lectures on ecology and theology led by Dave Stankiewicz and Tim Clayton and through two seminars at the Munjoy Hill community center around Martin Luther King's birthday on the spirituality that motivated the civil rights leader. The intent is for those inside and outside the Christian tradition to, in the words of Evan Pillsbury, "meet in the middle and allow relationships to develop through a common work and concern, through shared values such as a shared planet."[8]

Sarrah and Evan are both grateful that the Eleuthero Community fosters discussion and is open and ready to hear truths spoken from people who do not self-describe as Christian. In this way, Eleuthero manifests a nontriumphalism and demonstrates that being a witness is not the same as setting oneself up as possessor and disseminator of truth. Likewise, instead of responding to society in the judgment, condemnation, and fear that she observed throughout her Christian upbringing, Sarrah appreciates that Christians within the Eleuthero Community are "compelled by [their] faith" to take seriously warnings about human practices leading to environmental damage like global warming, and that as responsible human beings, they believe they can "actually do something about it."[9] Eleuthero's disposition of confession and repentance is thus marked by a desire to take responsibility for sin against the earth and—rejecting a dualistic rendering of the church and world—is marked by solidarity and mutually beneficial partnerships with others who share similar ecological concerns.

The Eleuthero "vision instantly appealed" to Sarrah's husband, Dave, a professor at Southern Maine Community College who has graduate degrees in theology and creative writing as well as an interest in environmental science. "One of the first things Tim said to me is that we are not here to be culture warriors in the sense of fighting the surrounding society, and I liked that the second he said it," Dave says. Having spent his adolescence and early adulthood in evangelical congregations and then college, Dave was "not at all interested in the knee-jerk conservatism of a lot of the evangelical church." Along with Eleuthero's commitment to scripture as the authoritative word of God, its conviction that the gospel applies to all aspects of life, its worship centered on liturgy and the eucharist, and its ecumenical/collaborative spirit, Dave says that "one of the best things about the community is that it is not trying to fit into already existing categories. Yet, at the same time—mostly through Tim's leadership—we are very aware of existing categories through which we are astutely navigating, such as the rather paralyzing liberal/conservative labels that try to characterize both theology and politics," he says. Although neither Sarrah nor Dave uses the specific language of confession and repentance to describe the community's process of unlearning and learning anew, it is clear that what draws them to Eleuthero is the community's constructive criticism of ecclesial witness and the corresponding vision of developing a theology and praxis that sees practices of sustainability as a mode of repentance and "environmental issues as central to the gospel and calling of faith."[10]

Like the Stankiewicz, Evan and Kathryn Pillsbury appreciate that Eleuthero seeks to "engage the culture in a positive way." Evan, a musician and staff member of InterVarsity Christian Fellowship, says, "My family has been in Maine for generations and in my lifetime I have never seen an effective engagement with the culture in any church or para-church ministry." While "creation care" was not what drew Evan to Eleuthero but rather the "local sense of mission to the city of Portland and the region of Maine," he says that he was open to growing in ecological understanding and that he is, in surprising ways, undergoing a "conversion." He says, "I am seeing new aspects of myself. [Being a part of Eleuthero] has changed the way we eat, shop.... We are going through a lot of turnover as a family. What this community has provided me is not necessarily all the answers but it has helped me to start to see what the questions are. I don't think I was expecting that sort of change."[11] Evan's account of being awakened to new questions and his description of the disruption and difficulty of transforming a lifestyle exemplifies the process of continuous conversion inherent within a life of discipleship characterized by repentance.

Kathryn Pillsbury, who also grew up in the church, appreciates that the Eleuthero Community cultivates patience for living within the difficult questions of Christian faith and witness. Together the community listened to a series of sermons by the New Testament scholar N. T. Wright, and discussing these sermons was a highlight for her because it helped relationships form among the members as it laid a theological foundation, absent in her former churches, that "God is redeeming the whole world and cares about the whole creation." She says:

> I get really depressed when I hear sermons that do not emphasize that the whole world matters to God and instead imply that it's just going to blow up. I'm still sorting through lots of questions, like what heaven is, and I'm not comfortable giving my children the answers that I grew up with. I'm more comfortable saying to them, "Well, we don't know exactly." I don't want them to grow up with that kind of thinking that you have to know the right answer and you have to understand, because that puts a lot of pressure on us to understand things we just can't understand. That's what I appreciate about Tim—that he says, "I don't know." He tells us what he has thought about and doesn't pretend to have all the answers. I think the whole group is like that. We ask, "Is this really what the Bible is trying to communicate?"[12]

Kathryn's reflection demonstrates that repentance as the renewing of minds includes honestly and courageously reflecting on one's inherited and embedded theology. Public witness arising from the renewing of minds stands in opposition, then, to the commonly held understanding, discussed in chapter 2, that witness entails distributing prepackaged answers to complex questions about God, the world, and the Christian life. Recall that in a prison letter describing the nature of God's presence in a world come of age, Bonhoeffer makes a similar connection between witness and authentic inquiry, deeming repentance "ultimate honesty."[13] In his outline for a book sketched in prison that same month, he asks a question that speaks to Kathryn's concern, "What do we really believe? I mean, believe in such a way that we stake our lives on it? . . . [We] evade [this] honest question . . . [and] that is why the air is not quite fresh."[14] Kathryn is grateful that Eleuthero is "committed to supporting each other as like-minded Christians" who seek answers to these honest questions "while working together to care for the environment and the poor."[15] As Kathryn's comment suggests, the renewing of minds is itself a concrete act of repentance when it arises out of being engaged in an embodied manner in the complexities and concerns of the world.

Repentance as Accepting Responsibility

The formal inauguration of the Eleuthero community occurred in its upstairs sanctuary at an evening worship and prayer service in fall 2005, in which Tim, who was nearing the final stages of ordination into the Episcopal priesthood, described the context out of which the community's worship and work was being shaped. He describes the very house in which they gather as a kind of living witness to a cultural transformation spanning 225 years: from the Great Awakening that came up the road a quarter of a mile to Walnut Hill shortly after the house was built, in which New Light preachers ventured into the wilderness that is now Maine declaring that individuals must be "born again" and believed that Christians were called by God to secure the land for the New Jerusalem, to "a strikingly different time in which Christian faith is not the unifying [or] motivating thought or impulse in New England culture," with Maine in particular having the lowest church attendance in the United States. Even though the description of Westerners entering a religionless era still appears far from accurate for much of the nation, for the majority of Maine's citizens, the institutional church—and with it, Christian faith—certainly lacks credence. Eleuthero exists to a certain extent "to meet this moment," and so Tim asks how we arrived at a point in which a Christian narrative of life has no rightful place in Maine.[16]

Instead of blaming society for its secularization or bemoaning it, in Eleuthero's opening sermon Tim offers an explanation that directs the church-community toward self-critique and responsible repentance in society. He bases this call on the Gospel reading for the night: Luke 4:14–30, the "paradigm-setting moment," the dramatic climax in Luke's biography where Jesus reaches adulthood and defines his public ministry before those gathered in the synagogue. Jesus reads from the scroll of Isaiah handed to him that promises favor and restoration and that exile will not last forever. "The Spirit of the Lord is on me," the Nazarene begins, "because he has anointed me to bring good news to the poor. He has sent me to proclaim release to the captives and recovery of sight to the blind, to let the oppressed go free, to proclaim the year of the Lord's favor." Jesus then "sits down claiming that in him this would become real." Tim emphasizes, however, that he stops reading before a natural concluding point. Instead of continuing to the promise of God's vengeance against those who have harmed the people of God, Jesus shows that the prophet's words are "as much *directed at* them as *for* them. Because, of course, the 'year of the Lord's favor' is the Sabbath and Jubilee year, the instructions from God" about economics and social ordering "that they had failed to put into practice." Isaiah was hearkening back to the Sabbath practices and the standards for sustainable living given to Moses in Leviticus 25:1–12, where "the poor [were] never to [fall] too far behind, the rich [were] never to [get] too powerful, beasts were to be respected, and the land never got exhausted."[17] Positioning the community as collectively responsible for inter- and intragenerational sin and directing Jesus' public proclamation toward contemporary Christians who sustain and spread prevailing cultural mindsets, Tim says:

> Remember our big question for tonight: How did we come to this moment?... Perhaps, just maybe... we've presumed upon God and thought it was about us—God and country—when of course it wasn't.... We've gotten too comfy and too protective of what we deem our own, and we've neglected justice for expedience.... Jesus' call in this programmatic passage was for his followers to be people who stand for justice... as a powerful people, as a privileged people, we have found this calling to be difficult.[18]

The formal inauguration of the Eleuthero Community begins with its pastor's admonition that "we have fallen short"; still, "once this is on the table" Tim reflects that his responsibility is "to sow seeds of hope" within the community and "move forward," which entails giving the full narrative of scripture its due. In essence, as priest of this community, Tim confesses that white American evangelicals have told fractured, false stories leading to triumphalism and disobedience and so his calling as pastor-theologian entails constructing, through teaching and through the life of the community, "a holistic biblical narrative, still wanting to be told, that can handle all of life." In other words, confession of sin unto repentance expresses itself in the Eleuthero Community first through a process of "unlearning" and learning anew: unlearning a theological perspective that evades divine judgment by positioning the church as specially favored and learning anew a theology that recognizes that the church, in its sin and redemption, belongs wholly to this world. Tim reflects, "The church has to be led by [constructive] teaching; otherwise [the critique of one's theological thinking] becomes a destructive thing" for Christians because it destabilizes and disorients without offering a new foundation and clear direction forward. "This is the mistake I have made in the past as a pastor," he says. "It is easier to tear down people's shallow ideas" than "build an intelligible structure of theology from scripture (which is certainly there)" that people can live into. "If repentance is turning," Christians cannot repent unless they "have somewhere else to go."[19]

Tim emphasizes that journeying forward through repentance also entails continuing to "celebrate the good things" about an evangelical faith like the commitment to scripture as the authoritative word of God, the conviction that Jesus is historically unique, the need for a vibrant prayer life and a living relationship with the Triune God, and a dependence on the movement of the Holy Spirit.[20] He also acknowledges that his "frustration with the shortcomings of evangelicalism" seems to be greater than the majority of the core members, and so he more readily views the nature of the community's work in terms of confession of sin and repentance. He says that his experience as a pastor in Washington, D.C., "was partly one of having to learn how to steward that feeling and conviction. The conviction [that we need to confess our sin before the world] is real and strong," but Tim found that while "I was telling people in the pew that we need to be confessing, I wasn't necessarily helping them get to a place that had taken me a long time to get to. I expected them to get there tonight and they were not going to get there in one night because it is too emotional and difficult" to understand the weight of North American evangelicals' failed witness in various areas of public life. Tim says, "I have also had to work on my own heart and my own sense of anger about what we have neglected and the shallowness of our theology in the past . . . of how we have been *fighting against* the people we should be *witnessing to* . . . I guess like a grieving person, my first reaction was anger."[21] Like Sarrah's comment above, Tim's use of "witness" demonstrates that repentance as renewing of minds necessitates that the church shed its antagonism toward the world as it recognizes its complicity—or put another way, its solidarity—with the rest of society in its sin against the earth. Whereas some Christians in the Washington, D.C., parish in which he served were defensive, wanting to argue that evangelicals have been involved in environmental activism and that to say otherwise is "a gross stereotype," Eleuthero begins the conversation as people "on the same page who can talk without fighting over the givens." Tim says, "I want a community where our evangelical friends from Washington who come up and aren't sure global warming is a reality can come into a place where you don't even debate that because that's been assumed a long time ago. Instead, we get right to the discussion of our responsibility for justice for the earth as Christians. The whole set of questions has changed and moved on."[22] Therefore, as Eleuthero enacts its confession and repentance through unlearning some of its inherited theology and then learning anew a holistic biblical narrative, a significant aspect of its work "is reaching out to *convert Christians*" to a life of responsible repentance as the members undergo continuous conversion themselves through Eleuthero's communal and incarnate telling.[23]

Repentance as Constructing a Holistic Biblical Narrative

Constructing a holistic narrative that can handle all of life is itself repentance—a renewing of minds based on preaching, hearing, discussing, and performing the Word—and such a narrative may be told in a variety of ways. For a community whose public vocation centers on ecological care and serving vulnerable populations, a holistic narrative emphasizes the interconnection of Luke 4 (and the Hebrew scriptures it echoes) with the "bookends to the story that need to be picked back up." In an early sermon Tim points to the richness of the creation stories in Genesis in which the self-sufficient God creates ex nihilo, "purely because of the joy of enacting this great drama of reality," which extends into the book of Revelation to "the return of the king and the consummation of the cosmos." The creation stories in Genesis repeatedly proclaim that " 'It is good.' . . . Creation is affirmed; life is made sustainable; the earth itself, the plants, the animals, all are given . . . 'agency' to take their roles in the creation and to continue it. They in a sense become analogous to us; they are given a kind of freedom under the sovereignty of God."[24] Having been created in the image of God, human beings are also good: "All human beings, everywhere, anytime in history, whatever status or race or ethnicity, are dignified with inherent worth," Tim says.[25] "But of course the story continues" with the sin "that blurs or mars or crushes down life . . . and sets us in a trajectory where these realities are covered, hidden, denied, or abused." As a result, humanity's intended "pastoral and easy relationship" with creation is now characterized by "threat or strain." Earthquakes, tsunamis, and hurricanes take human life and destroy human flourishing, and "we contribute our part back to it as well."[26] Tim draws on a recent example of a report following Hurricane Katrina:

> The Bush administration's policy of turning over wetlands to developers almost certainly also contributed to the heightened level of the storm surge . . . Bush had promised "no net loss" of wetlands, a policy launched by his father's administration and bolstered by President Clinton. But he reversed his approach in 2003, unleashing the developers. The Army Corps of Engineers and the Environmental Protection Agency then announced they could no longer protect wetlands unless they were somehow related to interstate commerce.[27]

Tim continues, " 'It is good' still," but as Romans 8 tells us, "creation is under frustration, is longing for release even as we are."[28] The bondage to which Romans 8 refers arises from human beings breaking our limit as creatures with each other and with the natural environment, and over time in complex ways this:

> works itself into castes and racism and oppression, which in its turn leads to what Simone Weil calls . . . the afflicted . . . those whose life is so tough, so hard, so hopeless, and every day the same and everyday unsure, that there is no open but only a closed horizon. . . . And this kind of thing is all too easy to illustrate in our world: the literally hundreds of thousands of children without a home, without parents, without schedule,

> without security or rhythm to life because of war, HIV, economic globalization, the vast numbers of people living out their days in bonded labor, sexual slavery, or maybe simply an employee in a sweat shop.[29]

Tim sows "seeds of hope" through this sobering sketch of a biblical and contemporary narrative of sin and suffering by promoting a spirituality that begins with Genesis and ends with Revelation's restoration and transformation of this world. He laments that evangelicals in the United States often emphasize otherwordliness, highlight the discontinuity in Revelation between this world and eternity, and interpret it "in dualisms that separate 'them' and 'us,' thus removing the critique of us." He says, "It is not surprising that [Christians in] the richest and most powerful nation in the world would take something like the book of Revelation and... remove its [socioeconomic] critique. If you simply follow how Babylon the Great is described, about the commerce and what that meant in the ancient world, what sort of structure was required economically, it's the same game as our consumer culture today." Instead of reading dualistically "so that its critique doesn't hit us," Tim places the book of Revelation in continuity with scripture's witness to a redeemed world. The questions Christians should be bringing to the text of Revelation, Tim argues, are those that "recapture the imagination" about this promised new world: "How does the continuity of Revelation work together with the cosmological implications of Romans 8," the "eager expectation" of "liberation from the bondage of decay" for the whole creation? How do Revelation and "Jesus' miracles of restoration to wholeness of life" together depict "the story of consummation?" For example, Tim refers to John 9 where Jesus spits on the earth, makes the mud, and places it on the eyes of a man blind from birth. Of significance is neither the man's individual sin nor the morality of his parents but that "Jesus takes him back to the creative moment by using the 'dust of the earth' and gives him full creation."[30] As this brief summary of a comprehensive biblical narrative shows, reading the New Testament holistically in light of Hebrew scripture leads not to an otherworldly, self-focused "religious" hope that confines repentance to an individual private act; rather it leads to a robust, transformative, earthly hope with social and political consequence.

Tim's retelling of the biblical narrative draws heavily on the British theologian and New Testament scholar N. T. Wright and so the community listens together to one of Wright's lecture series, "New Creation in Action: Spirituality, Justice, and Beauty." Tim says that he "was listening to this series and thought, 'Wow, this is the package.' Someone has synthesized the thoughts that have been swirling around in my head for a long time." Framing scripture with its "bookends," Wright reaffirmed for Tim that "the message of the New Testament in the book of Acts and the Gospels is not so much what [white evangelicals in North America] have assumed, that your eternal soul can now be saved and there might be some trickle-down effect to some other things, maybe." Rather, the actual proclamation reverses this emphasis and focuses on the resurrection of the body and the redemption of the material world: "Jesus is proclaimed as the first fruits of the new creation, so the new creation is the central image... with God doing this total and complete redemption project." The church then participates in God's redemption by "living expectantly into the world that will be by being a person of justice now," by living in right relationship with the earth and other human beings in recognition that "a bit of God's future meets us in the present." Energized by this earthly hope, the Christian community courageously "takes on the pain of all that is but also looks to a fulfilled day" by engaging in tasks in the present. Moreover, the Wright lectures were helpful to Eleuthero because they emphasized that the hope characterizing Christian ethics is fueled by the beauty and wonder experienced in this life. Sabbath/Jubilee practices not only manifest justice but also affirm creation as a gift that "feeds the soul." Echoing our earlier insight that a nontriumphal witness conformed to Christ allows the church to belong wholly to this world, the Eleuthero Community describes the Wright lectures as "terribly refreshing" because the focus on prayer and worship, doing justice, and experiencing the wonder of nature gave them "permission to live." Since a holistic reading of this sort was so rarely (if ever) heard or emphasized in the various churches and Christian subcultures in which Eleuthero members were raised, the series was important for the community because it gave them confidence "that we are not making this stuff up"; rather, Eleuthero's mission reflects the witness of scripture.[31]

Repentance as Preparing the Way through the Form of Christ

Constructing a holistic narrative that attends to the realities that claim Eleuthero in their historical moment and pose concrete questions for them involves not only preaching and teaching but also response and responsibility. Built into Tim's sermons is a call for Eleuthero to respond to the narrative with their lives by taking the form of Christ, "living the way of Jesus" in their particular time and place. In the inaugural sermon he says:

> The great question for the postmodern world is "Why?—Why suffering?" Viscerally, this is the thing that people cannot get around. The great thing about the book of Revelation is it changes the question. It acknowledges the reality of suffering but it changes the question from "Why?" to "How Long?" That is a question the church can live into. The church cannot live into the "Why?" question because no one can really understand evil and suffering. But the church can live into the "How long?" question by worshipping, praying, expecting the return, *by living the way of Jesus in this time*. The church is about bringing the eschatological reality into the present, and in that sense we say to the rest of the world, "*Let us in our embodied life together show you some of what the future is that we are looking towards.*"[32]

A spirituality and ethics that begins with Genesis and ends with Revelation necessitates "living in the humility of our finitude," which means living as creatures who know our limit before God, each other, and the earth on which we dwell, all the while "believing in the future," making "an attempt to follow" the Jesus of the Gospels "in a whole-hearted, wholly devoted passionate way... to see God show up and to struggle to ask and to live what is possible."[33] Belief in the future is, for Eleuthero, trust in Christ's present and future lordship over the entire cosmos that leads to "living now, as much as we can, as if the world God will bring will in fact be. Because it will. It is about living as if that is true, as if we are *forerunners*" preparing the way for "that wonderful world. Because we are. And because God is, and because he will do it, because he has already done it," says Tim.[34] Eleuthero is called to be forerunners, "to set the course" by carrying a special burden to care for the natural world and the poor, and preparing the way for the new creation inaugurated and embodied in Christ means "most of all" that Christ be "formed in us as individuals and as a people."[35]

In order for Eleuthero to grasp the full significance of the form of Christ in a manner similar to the early church, the community, Tim says, must "adopt an attitude of sobriety [toward] solutions of power and privilege." He says that conformation to Christ "will mean that we will be a people who learn how Jesus is redeeming, how his work on the cross brings, births, and nurtures new life—in the real world, how his kingdom comes and his will is done [on earth as it is in heaven]. And though we may not know the answers yet, nonetheless we will not settle for empire power bringing a veneer of order as being good enough, real enough, or deep enough."[36] For a community focused on ecological care, rejecting solutions of power and privilege necessitates countering, with their lives, the theology of dominion popular within U.S. Christianity. A theology of dominion is based, Eleuthero contends, on a misreading of Genesis 1:26–28 that places environmental destruction as other than, or secondary to, the perceived needs of human society. Michael Northcott, a Christian ethicist who has influenced Eleuthero's thinking and serves on Eleuthero's advisory board, argues that a Christian claim to dominion over creation is a denial of the lordship of Christ and thus an impediment to a faithful witness to Christ. He writes:

> Both prophets and apostles in the Bible resist claims to human dominion on earth because when human empires and kings, and even Israel herself, has claimed to exercise dominion, it has produced not a more fruitful earth or a more righteous society but quite the opposite—misrule, unrighteousness, corruption, and idolatry.... [A claim to dominion] sustains an attitude of control over history, and manifests an imperial desire to determine the destiny of the earth itself, which is directly contrary to the claim in the New Testament that Jesus alone is Lord of all.[37]

The Christian solution to the ecological crisis, according to Northcott and Eleuthero, is confession of sin unto repentance. Christians should confess before the world that "the fundamental cause of the modern ecological crisis is not at heart a fault of science or technology or economics or management—though these may all be implicated. At the heart of the ecological crisis is a spiritual crisis" implicating Christians who have falsely understood ourselves as masters over, not creatures alongside, nature.[38]

Therefore, during Eleuthero's first Lenten season together—that time in the Christian year when self-examination, confession of sin, and repentance takes on heightened significance as the church looks to Holy Week and Jesus' crucifixion and resurrection—the community meditates on the seven sayings of Jesus from the cross in order to learn how to take the shape of Christ in the world, and they derive personal and communal disciplines from them. For example, they discuss how Jesus' cry, "My God, my God, why have you forsaken me?" both shows that he has consciousness about what he is accomplishing (given that Psalm 22, which he quotes, describes his circumstances in a prophetic way) and is real and visceral as a human being who knows suffering at its worst. In turn the community reflects on the need to live within the tensions Jesus embodies, to face the world's pain while also living as a people of hope. The specific disciplines the community derives from their Holy Week reflection include consistent reading of the psalms with emphasis on the emotion embedded in them, educating themselves about the ecological crisis and its effects on people across the globe, as well as seeking out various peace activists, asking if they have some sort of faith that motivates them and how they engage not just critically but constructively. "If we are going to become people who can realize change in the world," Tim says, "people of real hope in our psychological depth and maturity, we need to be people who have Jesus formed in us.... Christ being formed in us is the unifying ground of the community" as well as the witness, "the thing we want to give out to the world."[39] This desire to take the form of Christ in the world—this understanding of witness as being a sign of things to come—is of one piece with Eleuthero's intentionally sacramental character.

Repentance as Life Together

In Eleuthero's inaugural sermon Tim invites members to prepare the way for Christ's complete redemption—or in the words of John the Baptist, to make "a straight path," to make Christ's person and work intelligible to the world—by demonstrating through their "embodied life together... some of what the future is we are looking towards." Cheryl Clayton says explicitly what Tim's words imply: preparing the way by taking the form of Christ necessitates community, specifically "Christ working through the community." The kind of repentance that transforms the church and society is too comprehensive to enact alone, and Eleuthero's dual and overlapping vocation of care for the natural world and care for vulnerable populations requires community as it reflects the all-encompassing, broad-reaching call of the gospel. Cheryl says:

> When Tim and I were dating we just started dreaming about what it would be like to be a community or church that really embodied all of the things that Jesus talks about—

really caring for all of creation, for vulnerable populations, for living into community and the implications that would have for life. So over the years as we were growing in our marriage, we were traveling to third world countries and seeing the impact that bad environmental decisions had on the poor, and we recognized that those experiences were having an impact on us and our vision for coming to New England one day and starting a community.

Complementing the conviction of the Pillsbury and Stankiewicz families that a community of like-minded believers is necessary for undergoing the difficult process of unlearning and learning anew, Cheryl emphasizes the necessity of community for carrying out the convictions born from and nurtured by a renewing of minds. She continues:

> St. Paul talks a lot about the significance of community. Christ working through the community is really what makes change in the world possible. Very early on, Tim and I said, "You know, we can feel these things and have these passions but there is absolutely no way that we can do this outside the context of community." What we are talking about is such a radical way of living in America that you need support; you need encouragement; you need people admonishing you. There is so much that comes out of community that enables you to live that out. And I really believe that Christ works in this way.... Outside of this context, I don't think this would be possible. I think this is intentional.... We need one another and we cannot live in isolation.

Cheryl argues that living in accordance with the new era Jesus brings is so radical in comparison to the typical lifestyle of most middle- to upper-middle-class U.S. Christians that it must be built into the very structure of the church-community. She believes that one can point to Christians and non-Christians alike who are "looking for something different from what American consumer culture offers"; for, in the midst of a magnitude of comfort and possessions, "people are not appeased; they are not happy, even as they live the American dream." Although there are people who want to live more radically for others, "typical evangelical churches are just not set up for caring for the poor, the widow, the orphan, the immigrant, and the environment in a way that really motivates drastic change in people and in the world." While there are "a lot of great models in other countries of people and communities consciously making some significant sacrifices with their time, money, and families," which have deeply encouraged Eleuthero and "have enabled us to have a bigger vision," Cheryl observes that this seems to be a very young movement in the United States.[40] She laments, "If you look at most middle-class Christians, they don't look very different from the rest of Americans. They have big beautiful homes with every amenity you could possibly imagine. How are their lives changed [by the gospel]? Where is the cost of discipleship—is there even a cost? This is what we are trying to do and we struggle everyday with the choices we make, the purchases we make, what we teach our children." Eleuthero's prayer, she says, "is that the Lord would put it on our hearts every day to willingly make the sacrifices."[41] Cheryl's reflections demonstrate that christological belonging refers not to "shallow and banal this-worldliness" characterized by comfort but to "profound this-worldliness" characterized by discipleship.[42]

Similar to Jesus' admonition that "it is easier for a camel to go through the eye of a needle than for someone who is rich to enter the kingdom of God" (Matt 19:24), Cheryl argues that U.S. Christians—themselves included—are growing at best in ecological care through "baby steps." She compares the lessons she teaches her children with the lessons they are trying to learn themselves as a community. With the children, Cheryl researches practices of companies like the Nestle Corporation, which is notorious for advertising their formula to women in developing countries who cannot afford it and who would be better off continuing to breastfeed instead of watering down, and thus contaminating, the formula that they are led to believe is better for their infants. She explains to the children that although Nestle makes great hot chocolate, "we can't buy it because of what they do in the world." She says:

> We show our children that as we read scripture, Jesus tells us that we need to love all people and that we need to be responsible with what we do with our time and money, and here is a company that is doing something very bad and unjust in the world.... On a child's scale not drinking that good hot chocolate is a sacrifice and the hope is that they would live more radically when they grow up. But I think that often this is where we are too as Americans—growing through baby steps, just starting with small things as an example of the changes to come.[43]

While all members of the community have sacrificed something, be it a larger sense of stability or specific career paths, to participate in the communal life and work of Eleuthero, one considerable risk for the Claytons involves providing financially for the needs of their children, two of whom have significant vision problems involving expensive therapy. On the other hand, Cheryl thinks that "as much as we can point to sacrifices that we have made...to use the word 'sacrifice' sounds outrageous" because the costs seem relative to their experience of God's provision.[44]

Not only is communal life necessary for enacting responsible repentance in society, a community like Eleuthero is itself an embodiment of repentance as existence for others—as existence for each other as well as existence for people who do not have a support structure similar to a Christian fellowship. Like Kathryn and Evan Pillsbury, Kelly and Loren Ayer's primary draw to Eleuthero was not ecological concern, rather the Ayers desired to resist the individualistic and insular forces influencing both the church and society. Loren shares how, prior to the Claytons' moving to D.C. and articulating the vision of Eleuthero, couples who were a part of the Falls Church group Kairos "discerned a corporate calling" that their "lives would be bound together for a lifetime even if [they] ended up living in different areas." Then after getting to know Tim and Cheryl, the Ayers felt called to the Claytons themselves and thus called to help fulfill the Clayton's ecclesial vision of care for the environment and vulnerable populations. The Ayers had been contemplating moving closer to Kelly's family in Maine but did not think it would be wise to do so "independent of community because [their] lives could get very inward focused" if it centered primarily on family.[45] In turn, it was this collective calling of the Kairos discernment group that gave the Claytons that necessary "next level of real community" that enabled them to make the move and venture further into their sense of calling.[46]

One striking aspect of Eleuthero's communal life, which mirrors the Ayers' conviction above, is the welcoming inclusion of children in such a way that avoids idolizing family and resists the insular infrastructure of many Christian churches. Cheryl says of Eleuthero, which has many children relative to the size of the group, "We seem to have attracted people with kids, and that's great, but we have a broader vision. We would like more diversity especially in terms of ethnicity, marital status, and education level... but at the moment this is what God has given us, so we are trying to be sensitive to and responsible for the children (and kids are invited to almost everything we do) while knowing that our primary goal is not, for example, to have an up-and-running Sunday school program." As shown in chapter 2, the top priority of most middle- to upper-middle-class churches in the United States is to serve the needs of its own congregants, for example, by providing opportunities for social gatherings in a "family-like atmosphere." In contrast, as a community whose existence is rooted in repentance, Eleuthero demonstrates that when a church decides first to exist for others, its own needs get met in unanticipated and profound ways. Although the focus is not the children, Cheryl stresses that she "feels very much that they are growing. They are growing vicariously as the vision and ministry grows." For example, a handful of times after church services at the Parkside Community Center (where Eleuthero's Sunday night worship began to meet in rotation with the Claytons' home in order to have a presence in the city), the adults and children have taken bread and soup left over from their communal meal to homeless men living on the streets surrounding the Parkside Community Center. Cheryl takes these opportunities to teach the children "about systems in America and how these are not bad men, how they may have made some bad choices but they deserve a second chance," lessons they "wouldn't hear in Sunday school." Cheryl says that "the children are listening and seeing all sorts of things that don't humanly seem possible because of our limitations and restrictions" as a family and as a community. For example, the Clayton children "have played a significant role in the ministry" by helping to provide hospitality to the myriad visitors who, enthralled by the vision, pilgrimage up to Maine. Surprised and overwhelmed by the outpouring of visitors, Cheryl says, "This summer our kitchen has put out probably 450 extra plates of food in just two and a half months; we've hosted over sixty people overnight during that time span, and so our whole family has really gotten caught up in serving the people that come." She concludes, "We didn't intend for the children to be a major part of the ministry, but I think God is working through how this plays out, too, by providing all kinds of opportunities for them to learn through things that are happening through the community. So, there is no formal way that families are involved, but because couples [in Eleuthero] have children, this is becoming a part of our life together."[47]

■ PUBLIC CONFESSION AND PUBLIC REPENTANCE

Repentance as a Readiness to Partner and Learn from Others

Central to Eleuthero's founding in Maine was the desire to learn about ecological care from the surrounding secular culture. Thus, built into Eleuthero's witness is a nontriumphal confidence in Christ's expansive lordship that shines out into the world, enabling non-Christians to be reflectors of Christ's truth to Christians. It is this confidence in the brilliancy and reach of Christ's light that disallows triumphalistic Christianity. As the primary one who has been laying the foundation for Eleuthero's repentant public engagement in the region of Portland, much of Tim's work before moving to Maine and continuing into this first year has been connecting with ecological professionals, learning from them and exploring what partnerships could be formed. Tim has reached out to both secular and Christian groups and has received positive responses from a variety of potential partners: a University of Southern Maine umbrella organization for different eco groups in the Casco Bay; Oceanside Conservation Trust; the political advocacy group Environmental Maine; the Winter Cache Project; a church-community forming in Lewiston, Maine; the International Church and its Central Africa Mission; and, through Evan's InterVarsity work with art students, InterVarsity Christian Fellowship at the University of Southern Maine and Maine College of Arts.

When Tim contacts an environmental scientist or activist he tries "to make the point somewhere relatively subtly but pretty early in the conversation that we [Christians] have not paid enough attention to this but that we would like to and would like to learn." Tim finds that even if he does not immediately bring up the failure of Christians to care for the environment, "it always comes up."[48] Although the ecological professionals with whom he speaks are well aware of the failures of Christians in this regard, Tim describes how a disposition of confession unto repentance, which is "the most basic aspect of being a Christian," is surprising to his hearers. In this way it manifests the new public language Bonhoeffer writes about in prison that is both traditional and revolutionary. A redemptive public witness does not employ the old language of religious righteousness that positions Christians as specially favored but the new language of Christ's righteousness and truth, the alternative righteousness of repentance that proclaims God's peace and the coming of God's kingdom.[49] Tim describes this dynamic in his first meeting with a biologist at the U.S. Fish and Wildlife Service, with whom he met in order to see whether or not there were any habitat values on the island property that Eleuthero is hoping to buy and preserve. He recalls,

> So I called her up out of the blue and gave her my one-sentence spiel about how we are trying to start this Christian community that looks at the interaction between Christianity and the earth. (I typically leave out the vision for the poor because it is too large to summarize and put all the pieces together, so I gave her that). There is this long silence on the other end. You can hear that she is irritated and she said, "Well, it's about time you Christians did something about this":
>
> So I went to meet her and sat down at the table and the next thing she said was, "Okay, I'll talk to you but don't you dare talk to me about the Bible." And you know, my sense that we need to confess is very useful, because I just kind of laughed and smiled and said, "You are absolutely right. I'm not hurt, just to let you know, because what you say is true."[50]

This exchange in turn led to a productive conversation that Tim attributes to the fact that confession and repentance "is very disarming in the way that Christianity should be disarming."[51] His experience of confessing sin in conversation with environmental professionals exemplifies how, as a nontriumphal witness to Christ, confession unto repentance opens up new possibilities for reconciliation and redemption.

Tim has found that "with every new audience" it is important "to re-establish the reality" that Christians have much to confess and repent for; still, "typically people don't want to dwell there." He says, "This is where I have had to learn. They appreciate the realness of the moment, but they don't want to know reasons." Being an "analytical thinker," this is where Tim says "he has messed up," particularly in a phone interview with a producer of the PBS program *Bill Moyers Journal*. Tim says:

> [A] Bill Moyers [producer] called me one day and upon reflection I think I blew that conversation because my mind immediately [thought] the easiest thing to do is tell him what's been wrong with what evangelicals have done and why they haven't cared about this in the past. Now, I think that everything I said is true. I think it is pretty easy to say why we haven't cared in the past, but he wasn't so much interested in that as he was in how people are engaging now. That's part of my personality—I want to clear the ground, cover the bases, and then start building up. But they just wanted to hear about the building.[52]

What Tim learned from this interview is that, although confession of sin may itself be public witness, it can also fall flat if not followed by constructive public engagement. Recognizing this dynamic, Eleuthero members express at an end-of-the-year meeting that they are "chomping at the bit," ready to use the first year's work of constructing a holistic narrative and building a life together as a springboard propelling them into the next level of more direct activity as a community.[53] The first year has been a "relationship building year" as the families who moved from Washington, D.C., have transitioned into new neighborhoods, jobs, and family schedules, and as the community as a whole has been intentional about getting to know one another, mostly through Sunday evening worship, dinner, and weekend outdoor activities. What is clear to every member is that they now need "a lived manifestation of their vision."[54]

Fostering a More Concrete Witness: Pursuing Public Space

A significant focal point for Eleuthero as it has envisioned its concrete public engagement has been the possibility of preserving a property on Little Diamond Island in the Casco Bay, a ten-minute ferry ride from downtown, Old Port Portland. The Sisters of Mercy's old, dilapidated orphanage and retreat for girls is for sale along with its surrounding woodlands and a 700-foot shoreline referred to affectionately by the Little Diamond home owners as "the Sisters' Beach." Given the rapid development on all the islands in the Bay, this property is the only one of its kind that could be a retreat for public use and is enhanced by its two existing structures that Eleuthero seeks to conserve and restore according to green building principles.[55] However, developers are attempting to clear the land and parcel it into multiple vacation-home lots, a land which is a significant habitat for almost a third of the declining species in Maine's Gulf.[56] While there are other island preservation sites in the Casco Bay, this would be the only space in which public teaching could occur and would be the first time a faith group has pursued guidance from, and a potential partnership with, the major local conservation organization Oceanside Conservation Trust.

The pursuit of the island property has been quite the emotional rollercoaster for the Eleuthero community as the contract has slid in and out of the developers' hands. Eleuthero's prayer has been, "Lord, keep this property for your kingdom work, and if it pleases you for us to inherit it to continue this work, let it be." At their "End of the First Year Check-up" meeting, Tim reflects that "God has given us this place in our hearts and minds"—a place that seems ideal to carry out the interconnected work of environmental care and relationships with vulnerable populations as it would provide retreat and community for the growing number of Sudanese refugees and other African immigrants moving to Portland, would be a place to house year-long or seasonal interns, engage college students, and host collaborative meetings with ecological professionals. "But if this is not to be, please, God, give us something that fulfills our calling. We are ready for the next step of service," they pray.[57]

Whether or not Eleuthero will be able to conserve the island property, the community stresses the importance of public space at this end-of-the-year meeting. The idea of an island property came four years before from a Washington D.C. friend of the Claytons and supporter of Eleuthero, Brad Noyes, who suggested that such a property would maximize the attraction of participating in Eleuthero's vision with its beauty and its spirit of retreat and renewal. In other words, a good space would "carry the weight of the [community's] message." The more beautiful and peaceful the space the less need to convince others to adopt ecological concerns and the less need for programmatic or "contrived" engagement with vulnerable populations. Furthermore, Eleuthero believes that the island would "stabilize" the community's calling.[58] Cheryl, who ran an impressive English as a Second Language program in Northern Virginia, dreams of bringing an ESL class she hopes to begin in Portland to the island, of hosting an international feast in which diverse peoples could meet and work with refugees, and of providing housing for potential interns from Nairobi Chapel in Kenya, who have offered their services to Eleuthero's work.[59] While acknowledging that they do not need the specific island property to carry out their mission, the members see this space as "truly matching up to their calling" since it is removed enough and close enough to Portland, has a public quality to it, and conveys a sense of being safe and sacred. The Clayton's home has served as this space to some degree during its first year, but Tim emphasizes that the space "has to be public" because they do not want to communicate that they are a church seeking to separate themselves from broader society. Eleuthero is trying to make their witness public in any way they can this first year, "but it is a challenge given how new and small" they are. Tim says, "We are trying very hard to be public merely by our presence," which means participating in protests, immigration rallies, and the advocacy work of environmental organizations; speaking at nearby colleges; and offering a prophetic voice at citizens' meetings.[60]

A public space would also "keep the church's identity concrete." Because Eleuthero is not a community of scientists or ecological experts, their primary contribution to ecological work is "doing the biblical witness justice" out of a desire "to get people who love Jesus to care about the earth and to ask those who love the earth to take an honest look at Jesus" and the resources within Christian faith.[61] The community imagines the island being a space out of which it may facilitate public discussions about spirituality and ecology similar to those it has hosted at various community centers. Such a space could convene ecological professionals and activists of any or no faith tradition and also could provide an opportunity both to "confess where we haven't been and learn from other people... but without pitching our conviction about the uniqueness of Jesus out the window." Tim says, "We need to learn from science while also doing some work of integration. By convening the meeting we can bring some people's imaginations around these things that otherwise would not happen, because," he says, "who else is going to do it?"

As a community trying to witness to the lordship of Christ in ways that move beyond commonly held assumptions, though, Eleuthero is forging an identity and mission that has the potential to be found suspect by those both inside and outside North American evangelicalism. Tim says:

> I have to be careful when [environmental professionals or activists] define me as friend and then assume that I must be the only kind of friendly Christian they have ever met—the kind that assumes that all stories wash out to the same thing. I don't believe that at all, and so it is very challenging to keep the uniqueness of Jesus piece and learn how to

> steward that conviction in these conversations, especially when it is brought up by the other person early on, when there hasn't been time for much relational depth to unfold between us.[62]

On the other hand, when Tim speaks with evangelicals about God and the environment, a common response is, "Aren't you trying to convert people?" All the while, Tim says, those who do not place themselves within the Christian tradition are oftentimes afraid that he *is* trying to convert them. Tim's attitude is, "I am trying to convert everybody, including myself!" While holding onto Christian distinctiveness, Eleuthero wants "to positively challenge people in a way that is respectful to who they are and what they are about," Tim says. He continues, "I think oftentimes folks simply cannot imagine that the Christian God could connect to what else they know and care about."[63] Although Eleuthero understands discipleship as a narrow road (Matt. 7:14) that is costly since it takes the form of the incarnate and crucified Christ, the holistic biblical narrative that it publically proclaims in word and deed opens wide the good news of the gospel to people who otherwise would not recognize the invitation to join ecclesial life as one they could accept. For example, one woman who read an article in the *Portland Press Herald* about Eleuthero and contacted the community has had a sense of conversion that she describes to the Claytons as now finding herself on the inside of the Christian story. This woman's conversion—her finding an entrance into this holistic biblical narrative—exemplifies the evangelistic import of a witness born out of a disposition of confession and repentance.

Repentance as Existence for Others: Connecting Ecological Care with Vulnerable Populations

The "Sister's Beach" connected to the island property looks out over the Casco Bay directly to Portland's eastern point, to a neighborhood called Munjoy Hill where two Eleuthero families, the Ayers and the Bantas, live. The placement of the island property and Munjoy Hill, each looking out toward the other, reflects the expansive vision of Eleuthero in a poignant way, that vision being the interconnected work of responsible care for the earth and for other human beings as participation in "God's total restoration project." Munjoy Hill and the surrounding neighborhoods have become home for a large number of Sudanese refugees (many from the Darfur region) fleeing genocide and civil war. In the state with the highest percentage of white residents in the country (96.5 percent), this section of Portland largely accounts for its small percentage of diversity. Along with a sizable community from Sudan, immigrants from Congo, Rwanda, Ethiopia, Serbo-Croatia, and approximately fourteen other, mostly African, countries fill the local schools and neighborhoods in and around Munjoy Hill.[64] Although the City of Portland has been welcoming to these refugees and immigrants, the neighborhood carries a stigma introduced generations before. *U.S. News and World Report* called it one of the largest white slums in the country, and, according to Kelly Ayer, "Many people used to and still do" caution not to "go over there to Munjoy Hill."[65] With a desire to be in relationship with diverse peoples, especially those who are vulnerable in transition and often get overlooked, Kelly "really love[s] living in this neighborhood" with its international market, "mix of countries, classes, and races," subsidized housing, colorful row homes, community garden, new elementary school constructed according to green building principles, and beautiful park and promenade overlooking the bay. The neighborhood also houses Central Africa Vision, a local Christian microfinance organization started by African immigrants with whom Eleuthero has begun a relationship. Portland residents are beginning to recognize Munjoy Hill's property value and so the patterns of displacement that adversely affect vulnerable populations are likely to ensue. Aware of this reality, Kelly hopes that "the heart" of the neighborhood "won't go away."[66]

Down the hill lies Parkside Community, the low-income housing complex where the Pillsbury family lives among many Sudanese neighbors and where Eleuthero's Sunday night worship meets in the community center. In spring 2006, after National Public Radio featured a story on Sudanese refugees, Eleuthero began praying that they "would be of some real use to that community."[67] The following Sunday Isaac Wani, a Sudanese refugee, met Evan on the sidewalk and shared that he was looking for Christians with whom to pray and share fellowship. Isaac worshipped with Eleuthero and came to other gatherings for about a month before disappearing. Eleuthero "did a little poking around" and found out that he had been taken to the county jail. The Eleuthero newsletter tells the story Isaac asked them to share for prayer, a story that "has been an education for us, to say the least, and continues to be a heart-rending situation for him":

> Isaac came to the US via three years in a UN camp in Cairo, having left Sudan after the death of his parents. His mother died in a UN camp in Uganda after his father was abducted from home late one night in 1988 and has never been seen again. Isaac worked for a time surveying for a multi-national oil company but was kidnapped by rebel forces before being captured by government forces, interrogated, and beaten. Finally, he escaped from the hospital and a priest helped him get from Khartoum to Cairo. His three sisters are in Khartoum, Sudan, and look to him for support. He came here with his wife, and here they had a son. Long story, but eventually she left him and would not let him see the child. He started to drink, ended up with a string of charges around some irresponsible (thank the Lord, not violent) behavior, and spent some time in jail. He got out on bail, went back to work, was in counseling, and was trying to get his life back in order (this is when he found us) when he was picked up again, apparently for some sort of violation of his probation agreement.[68]

Members of Eleuthero view Isaac's honesty with them about the details of his situation as "a privilege and a responsibility"; for not only does it reveal the suffering and courage of their new friend but also it "has all the pain that is typically associated with fleeing a situation like that in Sudan."[69] Father Joseph Bizimana, an African priest in Portland, laments with Tim that Isaac's situation "is all too common—the stresses of the grief, the losses, the new life and myriad changes, a heavy work load—and people sometimes break. Then, a small matter, but they are scared, their language skills aren't great, the jails are crowded, the courts are in a hurry, and they get lost. They get out and they are still broken and hurting, so it happens again and gets worse each time."[70] Lacking a strong relational network, many refugees have no support during the transition to the United States, much less someone to visit them should they wind up in jail. The Eleuthero Community became Isaac's weekly visitors, and they encouraged him to memorize Psalms so that he could pray and recite them when he felt particularly alone and afraid. Tim reflects on his visits in the July 2006 newsletter that "Matthew 25 is real, and Jesus is there. But what will [Isaac's] future be?"[71]

In early September 2006 Isaac was released from jail, and members of Eleuthero celebrated by taking him out for ice cream. About a month later in an e-mail prayer update, Tim writes that Isaac "reminded me very much of a deacon from Acts last night." While visiting him in jail, Tim had met another Sudanese man who asked him to visit his family. Isaac accompanied Tim to the small apartment where the wife, six children, and two grandchildren currently live. "The situation is challenging to say the least," Tim writes, "and I feel deeply inadequate to be of any real use. It was so good to have Isaac there, to translate not only language but also cultural customs. But even more, it was great to see Isaac now in ministry to those who have suffered some of the pain he has suffered."[72] While the Eleuthero community understandably feels inadequate when facing such hurting human beings who have unimaginable past and present hardships, they have been of real use in seemingly small but significant ways. For example, while Isaac was in jail Tim "ended up being his advocate" in what Tim jokingly calls "a ministry of Holy Annoyance." He says, "Basically I would wear my collar and just go and annoy people about him.... There was simply a lot of information that he did not get, or he got but not in a way that he could understand. And his English is not bad.... He is sharp of mind and wants to know" but he did not know who his lawyer was, when the lawyer would contact him, and the scheduled date of his court appearance. So Tim would visit Isaac and then go straight to the lawyer's office. "Finally I learned that it was simple overwork," Tim says. "People just had too much on their desks so if I simply showed up and asked about Isaac, they would then remember him."[73]

Affirming the dignity of Isaac and other refugees and immigrants not only involves sharing in their sufferings, by, for example, asking others to "remember" them, but also necessitates honoring the contributions they can make to the local community. Eleuthero desires to include refugees in its mutually supportive, communal life as well as be "a bridge" or "dot connector" between Portland's environmental work and the skills of refugees and immigrants. At the end-of-the-year meeting, Kelly Ayer reflects on how the community needs to be mindful about not having a one-way attitude of charity in which "*we* serve *them*" but instead may respect what many refugees and immigrants may already know about gardening, for example, by setting them up as teachers.[74] While Kelly and Kathryn garden at the community spot on Munjoy Hill and in an informal manner have begun to get to know some of the immigrants there, Eleuthero also imagines bringing these new friends to the Winter Cache Project (WCP), a small nonprofit that walks people through an entire gardening season and canning process in order to achieve some measure of self-sustainability outside the global market. Eleuthero reasons that immigrants who have come from more traditional cultures and rural settings have most likely done at least a small amount of gardening, while most of the Caucasians participating in the Winter Cache Project have little to no experience. Thus, the immigrants could potentially lead alongside the WCP teachers while also providing food for themselves without much expense. Eleuthero has suggested the idea to immigrant pastors who are interested but did not know about the Winter Cache Project. It hopes that by bringing the Caucasian "earthy, crunchy crowd" and the Sudanese refugees together through WCP, "relationships would happen naturally" with Eleuthero simply being "the glue" that brings them together. Eleuthero also imagines more clearly uniting its dual and overlapping vision of care for the earth and care for vulnerable populations by initiating an "urban clean-up" project whose goal would be removing harmful lead out of the soil in Portland's more industrialized areas. Immigrants tend to be poor and end up living in areas where the soil is damaged "so there's a real possibility of connection there," says Tim, "but we haven't found our way into that project yet."[75]

Repentance as Immeasurable Responsibility and Utter Humility

At the end-of-the-first-year meeting, the community discusses how to navigate the tension between humility and responsibility, in other words how to be attentive to their own limits while faithful to a vocation that recognizes the artificiality of compartmentalizing life. Demonstrating repentance as utter humility, Tim emphasizes that "there is a larger picture happening all around us and we are simply a tiny seed." Still, Eleuthero's vision and sense of responsibility is not tiny, and while the mission of participating in "God's consummation of the cosmos" is attractive in its all-encompassing hope and in its invitation for human beings to be agents of, and participants in, God's redemptive work, its boundless nature is overwhelming for the members as well. The community's common practical concern and constructive criticism at the end of the first year is that while the vision is clear, the specific tasks in the present are not. They have been too focused on the possibility of the island property such that much of the work they have imagined as a community seems to necessitate that specific space. Furthermore, while Tim has connected to a great number of diverse professionals and organizations, those relationships have "not trickled down to the community" in many tangible ways.

"Tim has great ideas and has forged exciting relationships, but how do we translate these into communal engagement?" the members ask themselves.[76] Some even wonder if the vision is too ideal and too huge to live into. The extensive nature of the calling and the ensuing risks of faith have been a challenge for Cheryl as well, who together with Tim, has envisioned the work of Eleuthero for seventeen years:

> Unfortunately or fortunately, I don't know which, God has only given us little steps at a time, and this has been real difficult for us.... We are trying to be focused on what the Lord has given us, and since he hasn't given us everything, it has caused us to question what we are doing. Tim and I certainly have questioned, but every time we start to, God gives us another step and that is really helpful.[77]

Addressing the concern that Eleuthero's vision is too ideal, Tim says, "Of course we are going to fall short and of course we know that all the time.... However small we are and whatever bits we do, if even to some small degree we do see God's kingdom come on earth as it is in heaven, then that is real and it counts. We may just be tiny, tiny pieces of sand on the beach of what God is going to do, but still, at least we are not shards of glass or nothing at all."[78] Eleuthero is discovering that the life and labor of a finite repenting church will be fragmentary, but, in the words of Bonhoeffer, "this very fragmentariness may, in fact, point towards a fulfillment beyond the limits of human achievement."[79] The community may rejoice in the glory of its imperfection because God weaves the unfinished work into the mosaic of Christ's consummation.

Eleuthero is trying to keep "their hearts and their minds" in tune with "God's boundless work" through which "the kingdom is being made new in the world," all the while "accepting limits... simply as a matter of who we are as embodied beings," says Tim. Even Jesus, whose form Eleuthero is trying to incarnate in the world, "had limitations as a human who got tired and thirsty." Tim further reflects that limitation need not be seen as a failure but may actually parallel the nature of goodness itself. He says:

> So many of Jesus' kingdom parables are organic farming examples that imply growth and process such that Jesus seems to reveal the organic nature of good versus the more immediate possibility of achieving evil. Since evil has no true ontology of its own and is only a tearing down of the good created from the beginning, it is possible to do a whole lot of evil in one day and it is very difficult to [construct] a whole lot of good in one day. So there is something about the fact that goodness will abide in ways that evil cannot that also makes goodness organic, slower to achieve. This process makes us more aware of our limits.[80]

Tim readily admits his limits. He can cast the vision (with the island as a focal point) and can follow these steps toward partnerships and public speaking events that have been unfolding before him as a priest, but he has not been as clear about "the middle steps" for Eleuthero's communal work in the world. While each member contributes to the vision through individual work and relationships, such as Sarrah's work at Maine Audubon or Janelle Banta's internship with Catholic Charity's Refugee and Immigration Services, the end-of-the-first-year meeting revealed that Eleuthero "needs a clearer sense of what [they] are inviting people into" in the present. This sense of lack drives the members to devise a number of concrete ways forward based on what "God has already given us," such as becoming more involved with refugee neighbors in the Parkside apartment complex and in the activities of its community center.[81] Notably, even as the community learns not to regard limitation as failure and finitude as sinful but to recognize limits as a positive aspect of what it means to be a creature before God, humble awareness of the incomplete character of their repentant action leads them deeper into responsible repentance. Here repentance is stimulated not by a subjective sense of sinfulness but by a desire that the community exists, like Christ, more concretely for others.

■ CONCLUSION

Tim summarizes that Eleuthero is "a people who are sometimes explicitly and always implicitly aware that we are unlearning some things and that we are learning new things, getting excited about them and then trying to figure out ways to bring other Christians along" this path of continuous conversion to the life of Christ and to a full witness of scripture.[82] Eleuthero's unlearning and learning anew demonstrates the central role the renewing of minds must play in a nontriumphant public witness; for, as previously shown, a nontriumphal witness today demands that Christians rethink dominant assumptions about Christ, the world, the church, and even repentance itself. Eleuthero's witness highlights that the renewing of minds is a definitive dimension of communal repentance and is necessary for social and political change. As they unlearn and learn anew a holistic biblical narrative that can handle all of life, Eleuthero members are undergoing various degrees of transformation, transitioning out of a theology and practice that is "shallow" because it has not been embedded in a deep this-worldliness and hence not in the cross of Christ rooted, as Bonhoeffer says, in "the depths of the earth."[83]

The narrative Eleuthero seeks to tell with their lives is bathed in a disposition of confession and is enacted through a repentance that fashions right relationships with the earth and with vulnerable human beings. As an exemplification of the polyphonic character of repentance, Eleuthero is wholly present to the joys and hardships of the work, which in turn necessitates, as Kelly Ayer says, "a life of prayer woven into all that we do."[84] As they prepare the way for Christ's consummating work, Eleuthero shows that repentance in public life serves as a politically intelligible expression of the liturgy of confession of sin. They confess through the eucharistic prayers "what we have done and what we have left undone," and out of sorrow for their own sin, the failures of evangelical Christianity, and the sin of the nation, they "humbly repent."[85] Eleuthero is one example of a community seeking to offer a nontriumphal witness to the lordship of Christ through a disposition of confession and repentance, which is made manifest through prayer, doing justice, and fostering community among diverse populations. In doing so, Eleuthero manifests its namesake. The church-community is "set free" to belong wholly to the world in its particular locus and historicity, and in joyful expectation of this-worldly restoration, Eleuthero prays the liturgy, "Lord by your power, Your Kingdom come."

7 The Southeast White House

A Local Presence in a Neglected Neighborhood

THE INITIAL ACT OF REPENTANCE: INCARNATE PRESENCE AND EXISTENCE FOR OTHERS

Driving down Pennsylvania Avenue SE, with the nation's Capitol building in the rear view mirror, the scenery of Capitol Hill—the Starbucks coffee shop, the Bank of America, the Bread and Chocolate Company, and well-kept townhouses—changes twelve blocks down to a McDonald's, used car lots, and homes protected by steel bars. Another six blocks brings the Anacostia River, a geographical barrier separating the most powerful section of the country from one of the most powerless, "the forgotten quadrant of the city" in terms of public services and resources.[1] To an unaccustomed outsider, the sight of poverty, loitering, and garbage scattered across the sidewalks and streets could be frightening. The proximity of abandoned shops, Checks Cashed Here stations, and liquor stores to each other indicates that one is now "east of the river." Still, within another block, the setting slightly alters again. Large leyland cyprus and oak trees, symbols of life and beauty in the Randle Highlands neighborhood, line the avenue, obscuring the decrepit apartments and abandoned buildings permeating the side streets and alleys. While not technically within its borders, this section of the city holds the stigma of Anacostia, which is notorious for drug related crime and young adult violence. However, unlike Anacostia proper, it is socioeconomically diverse within a one-mile radius, with pockets of poverty adjacent to tree-hidden ridges holding half-million dollar homes. Two-thirds of the children in this working poor African American neighborhood live in single-parent homes, and one-third of the families qualify for public assistance.[2]

Directly off the avenue, upon a hill, stands the inner-city community ministry the Southeast White House (SEWH), a historic turn-of-the-century manor home dubbed by the neighbors "the Little White House" because of its similar architecture and placement on "the other Pennsylvania Avenue." The house sits amid a pocket of poverty as "a house on the hill for all people," and in particular as

(i) a place of reconciliation for all that divides the city and the city from the rest of the world;
(ii) a refuge and resource center serving the needs of the Randle Highlands, Hill Crest, Penn Branch, Congress Heights, and Fort Dupont communities in Southeast Washington, D.C.;
(iii) a base for mentoring and other forms of support to the local youth population;

(iv) a gathering place for individuals and groups working with the poor and disenfranchised of the District of Columbia and the Washington metropolitan area;

(v) and a training ground for those seeking greater exposure to the inner city and related urban issues.[3]

Working alongside local congregations, nonprofits, civic organizations, and other community groups serving lower-income residents in Southeast D.C., the house "hosts" those who come in need of "lifestyle changes, jobs, fellowship, volunteer opportunities, friendship, and love" through such activities as mentoring and tutoring programs, athletic and arts programs, "Mom's Night Out" life skills and parenting classes, the People's House (an information database connecting people with specific needs to service providers), prayer breakfasts and Bible studies, and neighborhood barbecues.[4]

Cofounders Sammie Morrison and Scott Dimock say that first and foremost "the house is here to be the presence of Jesus" in a community that has been isolated, overlooked, and underserved.[5] In other words, the SEWH was established by these seasoned residents of metropolitan D.C. simply to be a presence—to exist for others—and the heart of its ongoing witness is its incarnate presence, specifically in a part of the city that most Washingtonians and suburbanites avoid. Its public witness entails both sharing life with its neighbors and inviting into this space those who would not otherwise come to this section of the city. In a "Companion Guide to Experiential Learning into the Heart of Southeast D.C.," mentor and author of the guide, Kristi Kiger, quotes Jonathan Kozol's *Savage Inequalities*: "There are 'two worlds of Washington,' the *Wall Street Journal* writes. One is the Washington of 'cherry blossoms, the sparkling white monuments, the magisterial buildings of government . . . of politics and power.' . . . Just over a mile away, the other world is known as Anacostia."[6] This guide for volunteers and "urban plunge" groups reads, "Here we want to tell you a little bit about Washington D.C. that is not often written about in guidebooks or explored on tour buses. We're taking you off the map . . . literally! At Barnes & Nobles and Borders bookstores, out of nearly 20 Washington D.C. maps, none of them include the areas east of the river that we are about to introduce you to."[7]

The Southeast White House ministers as place—as "refuge," "base," "gathering place," "training ground"—and as a local presence it is consciously responding to, and taking responsibility for, society's neglect. Scott says that he, Sammie, and other friends supporting the effort wanted a community ministry or "hospitality house" in Southeast precisely because "this is the area split off from the rest of the city." Sammie says, "We moved into the Southeast White House in 1996 with absolutely no preconceived notions as to how to use it. *We just knew where we wanted to be*, that we wanted to be used, and that God would tell us how to go forward."[8] Although no one at the Southeast White House uses the terms "confession" and "repentance" to describe the impetus behind their work, the ministry's very presence in the neighborhood stems from an initial act of repentance as Scott and Sammie turned toward the forgotten quadrant of Washington, D.C., and moved into the neighborhood in order to encounter the neglected neighbor.[9] Because the SEWH's very existence is based on a desire to live for others, especially those on the margins of the city, it epitomizes christological repentance. Even though the ministry qua ministry is not conscious that its communal work exemplifies confession and repentance, Scott says, "Every person involved [in the heart of the work] is a true believer in the sense that they understand that following Christ means repenting for sin and reaching out to others. We are applying personal repentance in a communal way and this moves us towards reconciliation with our neighbors."[10] Scott's description of the SEWH's communal repentance mirrors the orientation of *metanoia* in the Synoptic Gospels, in Acts, and in the Christ event itself—namely, toward other human beings. Recall that during the first century the term *metanoia* principally referred to human relations with one another and that John the Baptist and Jesus' call to repentance reveals its social and political import since they both associate repentance with God's kingdom come. Oriented toward relationship with others, the SEWH's communal repentance embodies christological repentance. By moving "towards reconciliation with [its] neighbors," the ministry takes the form of Christ's own reconciling life.

When Scott or Sammie speak of reconciliation, they specifically mean cultivating mutually encouraging and beneficial relationships across the various boundaries that divide human beings, with their own partnership symbolizing racial healing.[11] As "a place of reconciliation" the SEWH serves as "an environment where suburban and urban, rich and poor, black and white, young and old, religious and nonreligious can come together," and it "strives to offer every person that passes through its doors an opportunity to know that they are a friend held in high regard" [sic].[12] The SEWH refuses to abide, then, by the dualisms that normally divide human beings, and in this regard the ministry also manifests repentance, that pattern of thinking (discussed in chapter 4) that places Christians in solidarity with the whole world reconciled to Christ. By taking the form of Christ through a disposition of repentance, the SEWH has become, in their words, a "presence for Jesus" in this forgotten quadrant, "a house on the hill for *all* people."[13]

■ INHABITING REPENTANCE: FOSTERING RIGHT RELATIONSHIPS

Repentance as Belonging to the Neighborhood through Prayer and Interdependence

Not only was the SEWH inaugurated by an act of repentance as Scott and Sammie turned toward the neglected neighborhood, the ministry's work should be viewed as ongoing repentant activity as it fosters relationships and draws others into its communal life together, connecting people normally divided by race, religion, politics, economics, social standing, geography, and culture. By moving into the neighborhood and accepting responsibility for the neglect of Southeast D.C., the SEWH positioned itself as a "path" upon which relationships with diverse peoples could be cultivated and sustained, in turn opening up space for those outside the neighborhood to enter into the work of repentance and be transformed themselves.[14] By serving as a path of transformation, the SEWH demonstrates that repentance is not simply the singular act of an individual turning toward Christ and coming to faith; rather, repentance is discipleship itself. Sammie, a retired D.C. metropolitan police officer who lives five blocks from the SEWH, understands the house simultaneously as a "path" of transformation and a "gateway" for resources to enter the quadrant's isolated pockets of poverty; for, the SEWH is unique in its unwavering conviction that the resources come into the community not through disembodied financial donations supporting the programs the house establishes but through mutually beneficial relationships the house helps foster. Marilyn Dimock, who has been involved in the vision and ministry of the SEWH since its inception, says, "All that the house does comes out of a sense of relationship. Every human being needs relationship, and we want to provide relationships both for this community and the people who are bringing material possessions and resources to it."[15]

The emphasis on reciprocal relationship is crucial for a ministry attending to the needs of lower-income families living in a depressed and isolated area, because it guards against a pseudo-repentance that turns toward the neighbor yet reinforces divides through paternalistic charity. Scott addresses this concern through his oft-repeated line, "We came here with no plans or programs except to listen to the needs of the neighborhood and be a presence for Jesus."[16] In other words, they came without agenda, desiring to learn about the community from the neighbors themselves. Still, listening to the needs of the neighbors does not in and of itself guard against an imbalance of power if the neighborhood is in the position of need and the ministry in the position of provision. Although it understands itself as a gateway through which resources enter, the SEWH avoids a static power relation by belonging wholly to the neighborhood through a solidarity that recognizes its interdependence with others and that consciously places its ministry at the mercy of answered prayer. At the SEWH, prayer is central to the work of fostering right relationships and "has been the hallmark of the house from the beginning."[17] Hilary Barnett, who was part of the inaugural group of full-time mentors, says that "the leadership of the SEWH relies on prayer and promotes prayer among the workers as the primary way to be led.... There [is] a sense of being in an attitude of prayer and trusting God's leading in decision making."[18]

The SEWH's dependence on prayer establishes its dependence on human relationship with people inside and outside the neighborhood. The ministry refuses to meet its needs through traditional fund-raising and looks instead to scripture's promise that "when two or three agree on specific needs, pray, and wait for provision, God supplies the need" (Matt. 18:20). These communal prayers are offered by staff, volunteers, and neighbors alike who share a common dependence on God. Human relationship, then, is both the indispensable framework through which prayer is offered (when two or three gather) and is the vehicle through which prayers are answered. Marilyn says:

> Money in and of itself is not the primary need. People and the resources they bring are the need. When someone walks in with a sewing machine or says I'll give you $500 to start a little league for the children, we suggest that she brings the sewing machine and a friend and that they work together with the neighbors, or that the person offering money be the organizer or coach of the sports team. Our answered prayers are embodied in action.

Furthermore, not only are needs met through the form of relationship but also the content of the answered prayer includes new friendship. Marilyn continues:

> We are not trying to raise money; rather, we are trying to open up ways for others to have a generous heart like it says in Paul's letters. We want the giver's life to be affected in the same way as the recipient's. So, for example, people in the community learn how to sew but what also happens for these two women is that their lives become far fuller—they are rejoicing in new relationships.[19]

Both the ministry as a whole and the individual staff workers consciously place themselves in positions of financial interdependence. While many who serve at the house volunteer their time and resources, even the core team of staff who sustain the ministry and its programs also see themselves as a "staff of volunteers" in that the ministry does not operate out of a traditional payroll. Instead, each staff member working full-time at the house obtains funding through an outside source, be it a grant, retirement funds, or congregational support. The neighborhood quickly realized that the SEWH lacks wealth and that as a ministry it "lives by faith" through its dependence on prayer and relationships. While the neighbors could have been suspicious of this interracial ministry moving into this predominantly poor, black neighborhood and operating out of what appears to be an upper-middle-class home, Sammie credits the neighbors' immediate openness to the SEWH to the wisdom of God, whose will for the house, he says, was revealed through its lack of finances. When the house was purchased, it was in need of much restoration yet depended on contributions from others around the city and nation. For the past decade, the house has been renovated gradually by volunteer church and college groups who share home-repair skills, donate supplies, and involve willing neighbors in the reconstruction. Sammie says:

> At the beginning of making improvements, we had made friends with some of the neighbors who would come over regularly and eat with us. In one instance, a gentleman said, "I am sure glad that you waited to get to know the neighborhood before you started improving this place beyond what we have and embarrassing the whole rest of the community, and that you have included me in what you are doing. I feel really good about this house, and I know the rest of the neighborhood feels the same." So because we

> didn't have the money and the Lord is wiser than us, we were forced to wait on improvements. That was pleasing to the community. Now that we have received more help and are making more and more improvements, we remember that lesson of inclusion.[20]

Scott concludes, "Prayer is everything to us in that we have no resources generated other than by prayer. We are always in prayer and ask the Lord to take care of the needs of the SEWH. Over the ten years that we have been here, we have never had an abundance of finances but we have never been completely out of money either."[21]

Oftentimes unexpected new opportunities for inhabiting repentance arise as the house prays for its own operational needs and the needs of the neighborhood and "waits to see how God is going to provide." For example, in 1999 there was a period of time when the SEWH could not afford electricity. As Scott and Sammie paid the monthly bills out of their own pockets, they knew that they "had a responsibility to be in prayer about it and trust in God's provision."[22] During that time an artist, Margie Quinn, from Northwest D.C. came to the house and asked if she could use a room as a studio for three months to paint a series depicting life in Southeast and to prepare for an art exhibit, Anacostia: A Place of Spirit. Sammie and Scott agreed, warning her that "the lights might be cut off, but until that happens, you are welcome to be with us." Margie offered to pay the electricity bill, and years later her participation in the ministry includes not only keeping the lights on but also implementing and running a weekly Gracious Arts Program for the children in Southeast who previously had no opportunity to learn performing and visual arts. The SEWH was pleased to be a part of the Anacostia: A Place of Spirit show because it melded with the ministry's mission of boundary-crossing. The show brought 600–700 people from around the metropolitan area across the geographical barrier of the Anacostia River into this isolated community. Moreover, the paintings themselves have become a public witness to the reconciliation occurring at the SEWH, as they have been included in shows at Union Station during Black History Month and around the world in places like St. Petersburg, Russia, and the Van Gogh Museum in Amsterdam. When they are not displayed in art museums, Margie's paintings reside at the SEWH. "They adorn our walls and tell our story because they depict our luncheons, our father and son meals, an intern cooking, working, and serving, and a pastor and a family fellowshipping at the SEWH," says Sammie. Regarding answered prayers, he says, "How could we have thought up an artist who wanted to be here for three months but winds up staying for seven years?"[23]

The SEWH also relies on prayer as the means through which it is led deeper into its vocation of existence for others. Exemplifying the insight discussed in chapter 5 that God's will is made known to church-communities living out of a disposition of repentance as they listen for God's command through the various situations that present themselves, Sammie says that although the original purpose of the house simply was to provide a place for fellowship for those residing inside and outside Southeast, "The Lord immediately pushed something in front of us, and that had to do with mentoring children."[24] During the first year of operation, a group of college students used the SEWH as a base for a week long "urban plunge" trip, and the house facilitated a clean-up project in a building adjacent to Randle Highlands Elementary School. The group of white students wondered what the community would think and how they would react to their community service: Would it be seen as paternalistic charity? Would the group be deemed outsiders? The answer came when "a young inquisitive boy" asked to help, "and herein lies the beauty of this story," Sammie says. As the child worked alongside the group, the college students "showed him lots of love and when they broke for lunch, they brought this child back to the SEWH, a block and a half from the school, for a peanut butter and jelly sandwich." Over the course of the week, the one child recruited another child and another until there were so many children that the university group started organizing activities for them—water-balloon-throwing contests, three-legged races, and capture-the-flag games each afternoon. Sammie says, "They built relationships with these kids in one week, and when the [college] group left, the children kept coming back for PB&Js."[25]

The SEWH observed that "the children were always hungry and often dirty" and these factors pointed to the fact that these six-, seven-, and eight-year-olds "were really on their own." Participating in the sufferings of God in the world through christological repentance includes the acceptance of children, and by inviting them to the house for peanut butter and jelly sandwiches, the ministry was taking responsibility for the children's well-being. The SEWH then formally welcomed them into their lives by replicating a successful mentoring program from Portland Oregon called Friends of the Children. The Oregon director, Duncan Campbell, taught a group of newly instituted, full-time mentors their methods and gave them access to their research and resources. Through the combined efforts of the parents, teachers, and Friends, the program selected the most "at-risk" children in the first grade to be mentored in a one-on-one setting, four hours a week throughout elementary, junior high, and high school. The mentors work toward goals agreed on by the parents, teachers, and children and in doing so partner with the schools and families. These goals include school performance but also expand into "learning to meet and greet someone," "broadening horizons," and "making wise decisions."[26] Virtually every child in the neighborhood wants a mentor, and so the SEWH created a "Siblings Program," which utilizes volunteer mentors by pairing them first with the siblings of these children and then with the many other children in the neighborhood who desire this kind of friendship.

By placing themselves in positions of interdependence through prayer and relationship, the staff (whose social, educational, and economic backgrounds vary) do not claim socioeconomic solidarity with their neighbors; rather, they connect the neighborhood to social networks and the resources the neighborhood itself lacks. In *Not All of Us Are Saints: A Doctor's Journey with the Poor*, Dr. David Hilfiker writes about living and working in Christ House, a medical recovery shelter for homeless men in Northwest Washington, D.C., and argues that those who are privileged socially and economically are "irredeemably middle-class." One's experiences, expectations, education, social networks, sense of entitlement, and secure psychological make-up fostered through stable and trusting relationships bar one from ever being able to claim social solidarity with those who are poor. It is important, then, to distinguish between socioeconomic solidarity and the SEWH's repentant act of movement toward others that first sent the ministry into the neglected community and sustains them there. Hilfiker says:

> The poverty of inner-city Washington is not to be sought. The spiritual discipline of "voluntary poverty" has nothing in common with the oppression and despair of the ghetto. There is nothing beautiful or romantic... in lives crushed by the weight of indifferent history and cultural negligence. The poverty of the inner city is evil, and we betray those caught in its web by romanticizing it or imagining that we—by divesting ourselves of some bits of our privilege—can choose to enter into it.[27]

Still, the SEWH is in solidarity with its neighbors in the vital sense described above, as existence with and for others through a reconciliation that resists dualisms that destroy community. Hilfiker acknowledges that although the irredeemably middle class cannot claim socioeconomic solidarity, sharing life with a neglected population will lead to personal transformation. He says, "While the landscape of poverty is inaccessible to most of us... neither is it possible to live as a privileged person within the world of the very poor without undergoing changes."[28] Therefore, that initial act of repentance, through which Sammie and Scott took responsibility for the neglected neighborhood and invited others into the ministry, enables solidarity in that the act opened up the way for staff and volunteers to dwell within repentance.

Repentance as Taking the Shape of Christ in the World

The irredeemably middle-class SEWH neither views itself in socioeconomic solidarity with its neighbors nor does it define itself as the neighborhood benefactor; rather, "the primary work of the house," according to Marilyn, "is to believe what Jesus says in the Gospels about himself and the kingdom of God and to pray in that light." The SEWH's mission is rooted in John 6:28–29 where a crowd of followers ask Jesus, "What must we do to perform the works of God?" and Jesus answers, "This is the work of God: that you believe in him whom he has sent." Ultimately the work of believing in the one God has sent means that the church-community anticipates concrete redemption for itself and for others. The church-community believes all things (1 Cor. 13:7), and for the SEWH this specifically means believing that the neglected and isolated neighborhoods comprising the forgotten quadrant have been reconciled to Christ. The SEWH is energized by this expansive belief, and its presence with the neighbors also strengthens them to believe—to have eyes to see—that the new has come (2 Cor. 5:17). The belief in

Christ's all-encompassing reconciliation in turn strengthens them to act creatively in light of that vision. Marilyn explains that believing what Jesus said about himself and the kingdom, specifically that the kingdom already is fulfilled in him, necessitates simultaneously praying what Jesus prayed—"Our Father who art in heaven, hallowed be thy name. *Thy kingdom come*, thy will be done *on earth*"—and living how Jesus lived, because "to believe Jesus means to live Jesus."[29] Exemplifying the this-worldly character of christological existence for others, Marilyn says, "It is fascinating that 80 percent of the good news of the Gospels is what Jesus did on earth.... If we are to believe Christ, are to have the thoughts and prayers of Christ, are to live Christ, then most of our work has to be actively attending to need." Attending to need occurs, as we will soon see, within a process of mutual transformation that empowers those living inside and outside of Southeast D.C.

The SEWH prays and does what Jesus says to do in the Gospels "in an attempt to be a picture of the kingdom of God on earth," to take the shape and be "a presence of Jesus in the neighborhood." The house is a picture and presence of the kingdom Jesus embodies in that it facilitates many ways to care for children "because Jesus loved children," hosts weekly meals that conform to Jesus' description in Luke 14 in which a host invites a marginalized population to a banquet, houses a database containing information on social service agencies in the Washington metropolitan area in order to attend to the needs described in Matthew 25, and prays that all who enter would experience peace "because Jesus' main promise between the resurrection and ascension was that his presence would be known through peace."[30] The staff believes that as they take the form of Christ or "live in the spirit of Jesus," this spirit pervades the house in such a way that gives significance to the ministry as place. In other words, as the staff and volunteers live in the spirit of Jesus, the place—the house itself—takes sacramental, christological form.[31] Sammie understands the house's sacramental character this way: "We put Jesus before everything...and we try to have an environment in which Christ in us does the speaking."[32] Christ speaks, Sammie and Scott have learned, through the presence of peace in the house; for, this is the most frequent comment about the SEWH, namely that people feel this peace, a peace that radiates even through the organized chaos of its after-school programs. Scott shares this story:

> One day an African American woman came to the door...on a mission. She was a street smart author who had served some time in jail. She was working for the *Washington Post* and came...to write an article on the fact that many whites were at the Southeast White House in an area that is 97 percent African American. As she charged through the front door, she shook my hand and barked at me, "Who owns this place?" followed by a tirade of questions only a reporter would ask. The associate who met her at the door with me quickly answered the first question—"Jesus does." My thought was "right answer, wrong timing." So for the next fifteen minutes I answered the questions the best I could while touring her through the...house. [Toward the end] she grabbed my elbow, looked me eye to eye, and said, "I owe you an apology. I am really sorry that I came in here with a real attitude."

With a chuckle Scott says that he told her that he "noticed" and that he "forgave her" at which point she said, "I have not felt peace in my twenty years in Washington as I am feeling right now."[33] This incident was for Scott "a confirmation that Jesus is present" and that God is revealing Godself through the SEWH. Sammie confirms, "We don't wear Jesus on our chest but in our heart and [our faith] comes out in our spirit. We walk around with a sense of joy and we treat each other like family and every new person is made to feel like family as well. That is where the sense of the peace of Christ comes in."[34] The SEWH's emphasis on letting the environment witness to Christ reflects the insight discussed in chapter 2 that the first confession of faith the Christian community "makes before the world is its action. It interprets itself."[35] As Marilyn explains, "To proclaim Jesus in action" means "to think as Francis of Assisi thought: speak Jesus always but only use words when necessary... The thing people sense [at the house] is a spirit of love and then out of that spirit they learn who Jesus is."[36] Scott concludes, "The intent of the house is to be a place where people can find love and peace. The New Testament says that when Jesus was in the upper room with his disciples he says, 'Peace I leave with you.' He says it three times to emphasize the point. So where peace is, Jesus is present."[37] As a place of peace, the SEWH exemplifies how a witness conformed to Christ makes Jesus' nearness and contemporaneity concrete. As a community whose presence stems from that initial repentant act of taking responsibility for the neglect of the neighborhood, the SEWH also demonstrates that repentance prepares the way for the kingdom of God, for those spaces within which peace and right relationships may reign through the lordship of Christ.

"Christ in us does the speaking" not only through the peace of the house but also through the relationships fostered in that space. Marilyn contends that Jesus' life on earth shows that God relates to God's creation through relationship, such that after Jesus' ascension, God continues to relate to human beings in "relationship through community." She argues that in the North American evangelical subculture, the term "relationship" has been defined too individualistically as "my relationship with Jesus," but relationship with, in, and through Christ necessitates other human beings. Because Christ exists as relationship, God's reconciliation with all of humanity is demonstrated and proclaimed at the SEWH as the ministry fosters unlikely relationships between diverse human beings. In doing so, it emphasizes inclusion, that Christ's reconciling work encompasses the totality of human beings. Marilyn says, "Jesus was on earth for *all* people and gave all people opportunities to come together." Because the SEWH has taken the form of Christ by existing for others, participation in the being of Christ occurs simply by entering into the narrow space of the house, regardless of whether those who come to fellowship and serve consider themselves inside or outside the Christian tradition.[38]

The SEWH avoids the religious distinctions and dualisms that position human beings against one another (discussed in chapter 4) by focusing on the person of

Christ more than on one's identity as "Christian," because, Marilyn says, "the word has become associated in many people's minds with negative things" and oftentimes obscures a clear picture of Christ.[39] Former mentor Hilary Barnett, who describes the SEWH as faith-based, nondenominational, and ecumenical, says, "The idea is to be a safe and welcoming place for people of all religions or no religion. The Christ-centered influence is apparent when people pray and discuss their interests over lunch. I think the idea is for the people working or volunteering to 'be' Christ to those they are serving and to each other. Therefore, their behavior is the evidence of Christ at the SEWH."[40] Scott shares how the SEWH's identity and mission—its identity around the person of Christ and its mission of taking Christ's shape in the world—enables people of other faith traditions or no faith tradition to feel a sense of belonging and to participate in the work. He describes a recent lunch conversation about Jesus' parables with a Muslim student from Baghdad, who was representing Iraq at a conference and was hoping to attend Georgetown as an undergraduate. Excited by the connection he and the student made through a discussion of Jesus' teachings, Scott says, "He had a great time here and when he left he called his mother and told her he needed to come to Georgetown because he had found a home."[41] Because participating at the SEWH does not necessitate a specific statement of faith, "there is room," says Marilyn, for people inside and outside the Christian tradition to participate in the reconciling work of Christ.[42]

By refusing to view itself as religiously privileged and abide by religious dualisms, the SEWH shows that participation in the being of Christ—in Christ's reconciling work—is open to all regardless of religious affiliation. In this way, the SEWH manifests a disposition of repentance in that it rejects a religious righteousness that promotes itself and positions itself as specially favored. One way the ministry demonstrates christological righteousness instead is by intentionally choosing "not to advertise or sell itself."[43] While the SEWH is public as "a house on the hill for all people," those inside and outside the neighborhood hear about the SEWH not through self-promotion but through word of mouth or "interpersonal communication." The SEWH's reasoning for this is in line with the discussion of Christ's hidden character in chapter 3. As I argue there, repentance as Christ's righteousness is an expression of the incognito, an alternative mode of being and doing good that stands in opposition to a triumphal presence. By taking the form of the christological incognito through a disposition of repentance that rejects religious righteousness, dualisms, and special favor, the SEWH offers a nontriumphal witness to the lordship of Christ.

The SEWH also takes the form of the christological incognito through the informal partnerships it has with all the various groups serving the lower-income population in Southeast. Informal partnerships with the various nonprofits, civic organizations, and local congregations allow the SEWH to carry out its primary mission of being a "gathering place," "place of reconciliation," "refuge and resource center," "base for . . . youth programs," and "training ground" without taking credit for the good works it facilitates. (Indeed, the impact of the SEWH's presence and work is hard to quantify and often is evidenced in the details and "small success stories" of slowly transforming lives, which the broader public is not privy to see).[44] The SEWH is incognito as it desires to promote not itself but the work of these groups and to assist them in that work in whatever way possible.

Repentance as Feast: The SEWH's Reconciliation Meals

Christ exists as relationship at the SEWH—right relationships are created and sustained—because the ministry first took the form of Christ by turning toward the forgotten quadrant and accepting responsibility for its neglect. The SEWH's ongoing repentant activity—the cultivation of right relationships by connecting people normally estranged from one another—occurs organically during the weekly Wednesday Reconciliation Luncheon and Tuesday Fellowship Breakfast. The original intent of the SEWH was to be a house of hospitality, and over the last decade, hospitality occurs most consistently around the dining room table. The meals draw Southeast residents, mentored children, clergy, executive directors and nonprofit workers, politician spouses and civil servants, and the average suburbanite from Virginia or Maryland to a table set for a feast. Fine china, fresh flowers, and cloth napkins accompany the often extravagant home-cooked meal, creating the banquet scene in Luke 14 where those who are marginalized are the honored guests.[45] Introductions and an innocuous get-to-know-you question weave around the table following the prayer, with a rousing chorus of table taps applauding any declaration that one is a native Washingtonian.

The SEWH hospitable meal cultivates right relationships first by fostering dignity in the neighbors through the extravagance of the meal itself. Denise Speed, whose apartment was located a quarter of a mile from the SEWH and who lived in the neighborhood for eighteen years, learned that the SEWH was present for the sake of the community when she was on the way to the bus stop and heard swing music coming from the top of the hill. The house was hosting a wedding reception for one of its volunteer mentors. "They were partying," Denise says, "and curiosity got the best of me." She was instantly invited to join the celebration, but declined only to return for a luncheon where she received the same festive welcome. She candidly depicts the now regular experience:

> Coming from the background I have—and it wasn't a bad background—but I have had some misfortunes. I've had to eat in some situations where I was around some people who were questionable, because I stayed in a shelter one time. There it is communal style and everyone eats together. I was around folks that have drug problems and alcohol problems and mental problems. My situation was purely economic. I was trying to save some money to get an apartment. But never in a million years did I think that I would eat in a place like [the SEWH]. You know, most places give you paper plates, some plastic utensils, and paper napkins. They take your plate and tell you to hit the road—beat it—just like that. But here you actually get to sit down at a decent

> tablecloth, candles no less, decent china—not plastic plates, not paper plates, not Styrofoam—but china with silver edges, fresh flowers on the table cut by Wilma, napkins that are cloth and laundered everyday, nice silverware. And the menu—food that I know in an average restaurant you are going to pay some serious money to eat. I've never experienced that before in my life. I think I have the pounds to show for it! I eat very well here, thank you; yes I do, gourmet meals, thank you. I eat better here than I have ever eaten, even if I went and paid for it. Yes, the meals here are legendary. Everybody in the neighborhood knows it. They treat their guests, from the neighborhood or not, the same, no matter what. Everybody's the same. Nobody's ostracized or told they are eating too much of this, or "put that back." I've experienced that too. And they always serve you coffee, tea, and some desert. I get my daily four food groups when I come up here—four food groups and then some. Some days I feel like tipping the folks here. That's how it is.[46]

Wilma Mpelo, who serves as hostess, confirms Denise's experience, specifically, that there is an intentional message in how and what the SEWH serves at a meal. She remembers a neighbor commenting after a typically large gathering where the dining room table expanded to folding tables stretching across the living room, "All these dishes. Why don't you just use paper plates? They make really pretty paper plates." However, Wilma insists that her company is treated with utmost dignity. She stresses that coming to a meal at the SEWH may be the only time a neighbor eats beef burgundy marinated in *real* burgundy wine. "The other thing," Wilma adds, "is that the meal sends a message that you are worth it because you are not being treated differently than anyone else."[47] Sammie agrees, "We try to make everyone who comes here feel important, because they are. They are children of God. And it is important that we put on our best. If not, who are we saving it for?"[48]

While Denise appreciates the quality of the food and the setting, what she highlights most about the mealtime is this sense of equality around the table. She enjoys "the togetherness aspect of it," where she meets and interacts with people to whom she has not previously been exposed, "people I would never have a conversation with, much less break bread at the same table," she says.[49] Summer Dye, who served as a full-time mentor for four years, describes the barriers the SEWH tries to overcome and in doing so reveals that being involved in the work fosters transformation even in the minds and hearts of the committed staff:

> When you have a situation where there is a socioeconomic distinction between people, the individual coming from a lower socioeconomic level may be accustomed to the government helping financially and, therefore, that person gets used to being viewed as a project. Now, the SEWH is wonderful because the separations and distinctions between people aren't felt as much.... It is important that we constantly throw our elitist attitude out the window. I have come a long way and so have a lot of people who work and volunteer here. I want to see people as God sees them—as always equal. We want to embrace everyone... and exude love not judgment.

According to Summer, the meal fosters equality because it allows for reciprocity, in which distinctions between giver and receiver fade. Summer says, "An individual is either cooking and serving or sitting and eating. We have done a good job of having most people (especially those who come repeatedly) be each. Sometimes God blesses you to be a giver and server, and sometimes God blesses you to be a receiver.... Whether they are serving or being served they are given a chance to know love—a love that they so need, that all of us so need."[50] Creating opportunities to serve dignifies the neighbor, according to Summer, because it establishes a medium through which one may express gratitude and practice love. By serving, the neighbor becomes host, plays an active role in the SEWH family, and reinforces her sense of belonging. As Sammie is prone to say, "The first time you come you are a guest. The second time, you're family."[51]

Louis Robertson, a maintenance worker at Randle Highlands Elementary School, says that the meals foster dignity and equality as "people develop one another." After meeting one of the mentors at the elementary school, Louis started spending time at the SEWH and "began to find ways to help out around the house, like by taking the trash to the dumpster" on his way to work. Louis was struck by how the house empowered many of the people volunteering "who were also being helped themselves." Quoting Sammie, Louis says that the meals create space "where need and provision meet" and says that he has never seen that happen "anywhere but here." Louis says:

> Sammie and Scott encourage people to share needs as they introduce themselves around the table, and at first someone's pride might not allow him to share, but some people—and I have seen it—share a need for a job and then a person passes a piece of paper inviting him to come by his office. So the need can be met that quick.... This same person may find that he has abilities to offer another person in need.... I'm proud to say that one breakfast I was the one who had a provision. A teacher's aid came through here looking for a job and I spoke to the coordinator running the aftercare program at Randle. He got an interview and was hired, so I felt very good that I was here and heard the need.... I continue to keep my eyes and ears open to people who would benefit from coming to this meal.

Louis explains that initially he would only bring people to the SEWH that he "could be proud of," but he says that "Sammie quickly let me know that this is a place that welcomes everyone." As a body conformed to the crucified Christ, the SEWH seeks not to set itself up as judge, presumptuously distinguishing between the dignified and the undignified; rather, the house welcomes and loves the real human being. Now Louis keeps his "eyes and ears open" for people to invite to the meal, like one man he met "who had been laid off from his job" and "was doing some painting at Union Station." Louis says, "Right away it hit me that this person is down (I could tell by his countenance), and since I was going to have a scrumptious meal, I invited him along. He brought his paintings and Margie worked with him, and now he is a part of the family." Louis concludes that the SEWH is "like church" in that "a person can come for the meal and wind up with a home."[52] According to Louis, the luncheons are also a picture of the kingdom of heaven. He says, "In heaven you will be rubbing shoulders with all sorts of people, like presidents of countries; you're gonna be dealing with queens, but in heaven, a president will be just like me. The House is a place where none of that matters. We all come here with one common goal: to fellowship and help one another."[53] The reconciliation luncheon is a picture of the kingdom of God, says Louis, a beautiful foreshadowing of the wedding festival in the eschaton where individuals, regardless of merit and status, feast at the eternal wedding supper of the Lamb (Rev. 19:9). Louis' comments reveal that the SEWH is a community of joy and strength as it encourages relationship and mutual empowerment. As a mode of repentance, the meal fosters right relationships between people normally estranged from one another, and its festive character exemplifies that repentance includes joy. Activity arising from a disposition of repentance participates in the christological pattern of life, thus witnessing not only to Christ's judging No to the sin that destroys community but also to Christ's affirmative Yes to life and this-worldly belonging.

Mentor John Johnson explains that through the hospitality meals, the SEWH functions not only as home where diverse peoples become a part of one family but it also functions as public space. Reinforcing the SEWH's mission to build relationships, John says:

> We have very few sit-down restaurants in Southeast. Around the table is where ideas are exchanged and relationships are formed, so if you go to a carry-out—those stores with bullet-proof glass—and just go, pay, and take the food home, you never get to break bread with folks around you and ask questions, folks you don't know. I think this place serves as that sit-down restaurant, and that's important. That really impacts a community because we live in these different pockets. The community doesn't know itself and that causes conflict. At any given time when someone does something, you assume they do things out of malice but if you sit and eat with them then you can talk with them. I think everything is built on relationships.... The SEWH exists to build community.[54]

Sammie also implies that the SEWH serves the double function of home and public space. He says:

> There is a need for a place where resources are gained and people are developed just by meeting other people. Wouldn't it be wonderful to go to a meeting looking for a house and then sit next to a real estate broker or a person across the table looking to sell his house? The SEWH provides a place where chance things like that actually are thought up by the Master long before we got here. We just want to put people together, allow them to become friends, and watch how that friendship extends into what Jesus can do in neighborhoods and communities. There is a hospitality element that allows for this. So much is done on the golf course and at the dinner table—and we have the dinner table.

By fostering right relationships and connecting people whose paths otherwise would not cross, the SEWH prepares the way for Christ's transformation, for "what Jesus can do in neighborhoods and communities."[55]

The communal strength exemplified at the luncheons and breakfasts extends beyond these meals. Because the SEWH serves as both family home and public space, it provides the staff and volunteers who encounter strangers in need (both in the neighborhood and in other parts of the metropolitan area) a safe community to bring the stranger into and a group who together can help bear a particular burden. Sammie describes how one Christmas season one of the mentors met a seventeen-year-old woman heading from Florida to Minnesota who was stranded at the bus station because she had lost her ticket. Sammie says, "This mentor loves the Lord and loves children and invited the young lady to the SEWH. At first this lady was hesitant to take the ride and to leave the safety of the bus station, but because she had no more money, because there was no way for her to assert that she had purchased a ticket, and because the sister she was visiting did not have a phone in her apartment, she was destitute." Sammie explains that the mentor brought the woman to the house, called friends associated with the SEWH, and was able to get enough money for a ticket home. Four years after the encounter, the SEWH received an e-mail from the woman who shared how the experience "helped her understand the importance of family and appreciate God."[56]

Encounters like these happen more regularly through the People's House, a referral center in the basement of the SEWH that contains information on over thirty-five hundred social service agencies in the metropolitan D.C. area. The People's House was created by councilmen and congressmen associated with the SEWH (such as Kevin Chavis, Tony Hall, and Frank Wolf, among others), some of whom had traveled to Peru and learned about the *caso de pueblo*, the house for the people, situated in every village. Scott explains, "Someone hung out there to take care of needs in that little town. So if you needed a loaf of bread, he'd take you to the baker. We tried to figure out how to replicate this in a big city like D.C. and came up with a database organized in twenty-seven human need categories. People can call the toll free number and have a three way conversation with the person in need, the provider, and us, or a person can just walk in."[57] Jennifer Lowery, former director of the People's House, made relationship-building between herself and her client a priority and explains how this service connects to the other aspects of the house. When a client would come to the People's House during lunch hours, Jennifer would invite them to the luncheon. Almost all of her visitors came again to participate in future luncheons, to seek volunteer opportunities around the house toward a means of reciprocity or job-skill development, or to seek Jennifer's wise counsel and prayer.[58]

Scott shares that the weakness of the People's House is that over the years there have not been enough volunteers to receive the calls. Because of this lack, the People's House best serves the families whose children are in the "Friends of the Children" or "Siblings" mentoring programs. Sammie says, "While the mentors focus on developing the child, People's House finds resources to help these families buy food, pay rent and utilities, get to work, find clothing for interviews, or enter rehab facilities." As with every other aspect of the ministry, the SEWH understands the strength and usefulness of the database in terms of relationships. Sammie says, "These agencies get to know us and give us the best service possible. They rely on our information about a client to be factual. I'm sure they have the same heart to help everyone, but our relationships with these agencies make it easier for all involved."[59]

Repentance as Bridging Divides and Mutual Transformation

The SEWH serves as a "bridge" connecting people normally divided or, in Bonhoeffer's words, a "narrow space" in the world through which reconciliation with and through Christ is demonstrated and proclaimed. The image of bridging people and communities estranged from one another is central to the SEWH's self-understanding, and many of the staff refer to the ministry, as well as their individual sense of calling, as being a bridge between communities. Being a bridge is another way of saying that the house inhabits repentance by fostering right relationships, as exemplified through the reconciliation meals, the mentoring programs, and even the Anacostia: A Place of Spirit art show. The metaphor of "bridge" is apropos in that it attends to the neighborhood's isolation in the forgotten quadrant of the city and connotes the double movement of people coming into the neighborhood and neighbors moving beyond the limits and cycles of poverty through a broadening of horizons. Sammie describes the poverty in Southeast as a "whole cycle of making do from one day to another." He says that the community as a whole "isn't interested in going too broad or too far; it has no experience with that and so is not attracted to it." According to Sammie, when the neighbors only know this one neighborhood, they "become blind to certain things, like the fact that cars are better suited than houses, like the number of men standing on the corner not working and that there are few men in the households with women." When the neighbors travel beyond the neighborhood, "they see a different America. So when they see more and have enjoyed more, they begin to care about more." Sammie says a similar broadening of vision occurs for people coming to the SEWH. He says, "Because many of the circles our staff travels in are faith-based circles, the people who hear about the house and choose to volunteer here are doing so out of a desire to serve. When they come, they see a people who are not violent but they heard about a people who are violent; they see a people who are grateful but they heard about a people who are ungrateful. So there is a reality that takes place that erases some of the lines of division based on color, culture, and economics. Both sides learn from one another."[60] Scott echoes Sammie's sentiments: "We are here to expose the neighbors to life beyond the neighborhood but also for suburban people to feel comfortable enough to come here and learn about urban culture. There are African Americans who have no white friends and white people who have no black friends, and now friendships are developing because this is a neutral spot, a loving, caring place, where people feel a sense of comfort enough to share who they are and what they are all about."[61]

Hilary also calls the SEWH "a bridge-building place where people that are different can spend time together on a daily basis." She describes the limited options and sense of hopelessness in a community so poor and homogeneous and describes the SEWH as "a place of hope," particularly in relation to the girls she mentored. She says:

> For my girls, I wanted to break the bubble of limited expectations by showing that there is hope and endless possibilities in life. I wanted to show them life in other parts of the city and the country so that they could realize what else is out there. I always tried to connect these other ways of life to choices they could make in their present situation—like working hard in school, making plans for college, considering living outside of Southeast D.C. I also laughed a lot and helped them learn to deal with struggle and crisis with humor, faith, and prayer. I tried to help them dream bigger than working at McDonalds and going to cosmetology school.[62]

Scott, who also describes the work as "building bridges," says, "We empower people here whether by helping them find a job or by giving them a voice in the decisions of the house and its ministry to the community. We have so many stories where real changes and growth occur in the lives of the children and adults."[63] Iris Lamberson, whose daughter Kiosha became a mentee in the Friends of the Children program in the first grade, describes the opportunities the SEWH has provided for her children and herself. She says that because of the influence of the SEWH, her teenage daughter "is into different cultures and trying new things. She's not afraid to go out of town and meet new people. In fact, she likes that. The White House opened her eyes to a lot of different things that she can advance into as she gets older." Iris, who chaperones children's trips, helps with the Tuesday breakfasts, and cooks for Mom's Night Out programs, also has benefited from "living right around the corner" and calls the SEWH her "backbone." She says, "I am looking for a new job and the White House told me I could come up whenever I need to and stay as long as I want to use the computers and printers. They are doing whatever they can to help me find a job; they have even given me leads." Echoing that the SEWH is a unique combination of home and public space, Iris continues, "When you go to other places you feel pressured that you are taking too long, but the SEWH has taught me how to use the computer, how to set up a resume, write a cover letter. They have been like a big family. I just love the Little White House. As long as this building is up and running, I will be here to help out."[64]

Like Hilary, John Johnson describes his role as "being an alternative to what the children already have, to be a friend, exactly what our organization's name is, Friends of the Children, not to be their teacher, their mom or dad, but to be the person whose job it is to expose them to different things." John says, "I always use the analogy that most of us are raised to think that two plus two equals four, which is right, but so does three plus one, so does five minus one. So I am here to give them those other equations and let them choose which one works best for them." John, who holds an undergraduate degree in theater and writes poetry and plays, says that developing creativity in his boys is central to his work, not simply through art but also by teaching them to see the world in new ways. He says that he teaches them to "*create* a different way." John explains that often "someone with an abundance of resources looks at someone without an abundance of resources and says, 'You need to think like me,'" but he teaches his mentees that although they must expand their knowledge, they do not have to support the status quo.[65]

Thinking creatively necessitates education, and the boys John mentors are reminded of this every time they call his cell phone and hear John's Monopoly-inspired poem recited on the answering machine: "Education is important/ That's why we all need to take a ride on the reading railroad/ Because many of us can't pass Go or collect 200 dollars a week from minimum wage jobs/ so we go directly to jail." Drawing a connection between lack of opportunity and the threat of drug culture, John shares that as he and his boys were driving on the highway around the National Mall, he discovered that they did not know whether the monuments and buildings were located in Virginia, Maryland, or D.C. John says, "Our kids need to know that congressmen and the president live in the same city they live in, just a couple of miles away, and that they have the potential to be congressmen, senators, and presidents. They need to see the Capitol, Smithsonian museums, and monuments as part of their neighborhood. They need to be able to make informed decisions about their lives and not make decisions just based upon their block or what is going on in their household." With a laugh, John says that his aim is simple: "My goal is to get them to understand that this world has people in it and you should meet them—ask questions, learn from them, and then make decisions based on all that information. Don't rely on a myopic point of view. Explore your world."[66]

A recent trip to an area near New Orleans, still devastated from Hurricane Katrina, gave twenty junior high and high school students from Southeast an opportunity to do just that. John describes how important it was for the teenagers he mentors to see how people in other areas suffering hardship are working toward change. He says, "They actually got to see the way people in another state cope with tragedy. They got to volunteer in a community where they didn't know anybody but they also could relate to much of what they were seeing, like dilapidated buildings."[67] Mike Wingfield, who first built a number of relationships with the boys in the neighborhood by coaching basketball, also says that this trip to Waven, Mississippi, was significant because it showed the teenagers that they had the power to help change conditions. Mike, who seeks to "provide the boys with the tools for self-determination," says:

> Just this past April, we took a group of kids down to Mississippi to do a service project. We have a number of groups that come into this neighborhood to do the same, and typically they do not have the same skin tone; they are Caucasian or some other race. They are

> out in the community cleaning up and so we said that we need to go and show that we don't just have folks come into our community, but we have the same spirit of service and can go help others. As it turned out—and we didn't know this [beforehand]—we served in a predominantly white neighborhood, with some wealthy folks, some poor folks, and some middle-income folks, but needless to say, all of them had lost their homes.

Exemplifying the bridging work of the SEWH, Mike continues, "It was an enlightening, eye-opening experience for the kids and I think it changed them. I also think it changed the people we served because they saw a different image of young blacks."[68]

As bridge, the SEWH facilitates a double movement—neighbors' horizons are expanded as they participate in activities and engage communities beyond Southeast and people who formerly had no impetus to come into the neighborhood have the opportunity to be transformed through new relationships. The guidebook explains the double movement this way: "We believe in mutual transformation"; when diverse populations are brought together, "everyone learns from one another and [is] strengthened."[69] John says that mutual transformation is intrinsic to his role as Friend. "Friendship is a two way street, so my boys are teaching me," and just as the neighbors are grafted into the SEWH family, the boys' families are welcoming John "into their day to day operations." John, who had little interaction with anyone other than African Americans until graduating from college, shares that transformation and racial understanding is also occurring among the mentors themselves "through the commonality of the work." The mentors have grown closer as they have watched each other grapple with issues affecting their mentees and over time have grown comfortable discussing these struggles with one another. John says, "There is a whole lot I've had to do to grow and I've by no means arrived, but I've learned to respect other people through our conversations."[70]

As John's testimony demonstrates, the staff members are far from neutral observers or mere facilitators of the mutual transformation occurring at the SEWH; rather they are undergoing *metanoia* themselves as they live unreservedly in the problems of the neighborhood. Interestingly, Hilary and Kristi both describe this transformation in terms of their capacity to be more effective bridge-builders. Hilary, who started mentoring six girls in the first grade and followed them through junior high school, describes how her work in Southeast has transformed her into "a better spokesperson for the true realities of the poor to the calloused, indifferent, or confused upper classes." She says, "I was on such a different path before I came to the SEWH. I was deeply moved by the problem of racism and the plight of poor children, but I had no first-hand experience and no real knowledge of the factors involved. I didn't know how to get at the problems from my side of the fence, so to speak. The SEWH gave me the chance to get involved directly." Sharing how her faith led her to the work and echoing the insight that as a mode of discipleship repentance is a response made with one's whole life, she continues:

I felt called [to the SEWH] and remained there in obedience to that calling. On a daily basis I relied on the grace that is offered through Christ to forgive myself and to find hope in desolate places. I threw my whole self into being in Southeast and learning through experience what [life in the neighborhood] is all about. Being around Scott and Sammie was a tremendous help. I benefited from their decades of experience and their mentoring. I learned how ignorant I was and how privileged I am. I realized that the quality of my life is due almost entirely to the heritage I have."

As a "spokesperson" for Southeast, Hilary finds that many Christians are concerned about poor populations but have little understanding about systemic and intergenerational factors surrounding poverty. She says:

A classic example has been the focus (sometimes sick fascination) on children born out of wedlock and the number of children that are born to one woman with different fathers. The suburban folk are so fixated on the traditional definition of family that they cannot get past the paternity issues to see the humanity of the situation. I can't tell you how many times I was asked about the fathers of my girls. I wanted to talk about the virtues of the girls and the progress that their families were making and how we could all work together towards a better life for them.

Although "the judgment that [she] often sensed was an obstacle to productive conversation," Hilary's hope for the girls and confidence in God's movement in their lives remains strong.[71] As Bonhoeffer says, "How can success make us arrogant, or failure lead us astray, when we share in God's sufferings through a life of this kind?"[72]

Mentor Kristi Kiger describes a similar transformation of "learning how to operate in both worlds" and the "long process of learning a lot of [the] factors" surrounding poverty in the inner city. She, too, describes herself now as a spokesperson or "walking advocate for D.C." Given her exposure to international poverty through travel and short-term projects, Kristi has had to "shift [her] understanding of poverty and recognize [her] mistake of saying 'well, this isn't real poverty.'" She recalls people in villages she visited "scrounging through trash to find material to build a house," and although this is not characteristic of poverty in North American inner cities, she says she now sees firsthand that the developed world has "very real poverty" with its own particular difficulties and its own destructive character. In the guidebook to experiential learning in Southeast, Kristi quotes David Shipler's *The Working Poor* in order to highlight the complex, interconnected factors shaping poverty in the United States. Shipler writes:

For practically every family... the ingredients of poverty are part financial and part psychological, part personal and part societal, part past and part present. Every problem magnifies the impact of others, and all are so tightly interlocked that one reversal can produce a chain reaction with results far distant from the original cause. A run-down apartment can exacerbate a child's asthma, which leads to a call for an ambulance, which generates a medical bill that cannot be paid, which ruins a credit record, which hikes the

> interest rate on an auto loan, which forces the purchase of an unreliable used car, which jeopardizes a mother's punctuality at work, which limits her promotions and earning capacity, which confines her to poor housing.[73]

Kristi explains that as a "walking advocate" she wants to break down stereotypes and presuppositions that she herself held and others hold about inner-city poverty. She admits that the factors are complicated and sometimes sharing a small piece of the puzzle with those outside the community risks reinforcing stereotypes, "so that is where education comes in," she says; "even if some things are confirmed in the minds of people I am sharing with, at least I can help them take another step and look at why things are the way they are and the challenges these families face."[74] Kristi's own transformation demonstrates how vital the renewing of minds is to a witness born out of a disposition of repentance.

Repentance as Renewing of Minds: Transformation through Experiential Learning

Given its placement in Washington, D.C., the house draws both a myriad of energetic young professionals and seasoned pastors and workers into its ministry through its meals and mentoring programs and welcomes workgroups from around the country who seek to learn more about the full spectrum of life in their nation's capitol. "Since local issues reflect national trends," Kristi says that the SEWH "hopes both to educate people around the country and influence people who are working on the systems in D.C." Kristi wants to effect broader change by "bringing everyone [she knows] into this realm" through written updates on the progress of her girls that are sent to family and friends around the country and by inviting people at her church "to volunteer here and get to know us."[75]

In 2006 Kristi authored "The Southeast White House Guidebook," a "companion" to the experiential learning individual volunteers and college or church groups undergo while serving at the SEWH. The guidebook covers seven key factors that impact the Southeast community (business and finances; diversity, division, and unity; employment; education; housing, shelters, and home ownership; health and recreation; and safety and security) and helps volunteers inhabit repentance by "*provid[ing]* information, *provoke[ing]* questions, and *prompt[ing]* new actions." Each lesson opens with "a story from the streets of Southeast" and space for personal reflection. Kristi encourages the reader to "write down your raw thoughts" and "not deny stereotypes you might hold" because "the more you are aware of your own perspective, the more ready you will be to take on the perspective of another." The lesson then focuses on "gaining understanding" through reflection on "past history," "current happenings," and "future hope." Kristi writes:

> The Scriptures constantly call God's people to *remember*, not neglecting their past but learning from it and applying it to their current situation. Likewise, we must understand the past of a community in order to serve it more effectively in the present. Furthermore,

> Jesus urges his disciples to be able to interpret the "signs of the times." They are to be aware of the current world that they are living in and minister to it accordingly. Prophets...spent most of their ministries speaking truth to the situation at hand. We must understand the times if we are to speak prophetically into our 21st century society. Finally, Jesus brings...hope.... He will renew all things, and we are to seek His Kingdom "on earth as it is in heaven." Thus, our hope is in Jesus' resurrection and the redemption of our communities, and we can see glimpses even now of the things that He is using to bring about restoration.

Each lesson then offers a "biblical meditation" that includes but also goes beyond a call to attend to the personal needs of poor populations by addressing "the ways we govern society" in relation to each topic. The guidebook concludes with the statement that the factors influencing poverty are interconnected, and each issue, in and of itself, is "complex with no easy answers"; yet if the problems are interlocking, then the solutions must be holistic as well. While Kristi warns at the beginning of the guidebook that "this is not a solution manual to urban ministry—answers are not given," she concludes the book with an invitation to live within these difficult questions through continued responsible engagement in the neighborhood. She says, "We want to dream big dreams and pursue grand visions! Dream with us about the ways that the whole Body of Christ can be involved in the redeeming work of Jesus in our communities." Kristi commissions the volunteers to take the information and experiential knowledge gained at the SEWH back to their homes, schools, churches, and workplaces, and she ends the guidebook with a vision of what will be: "Then I saw a new heaven and a new earth...for the old order of things has passed away" (Rev. 21:1–4).[76]

Repentance as Preparing the Way While Navigating Limits

By taking responsibility for the neglect of Southeast D.C., the SEWH embarked on a search for a marginalized population and thereby guarded the command to love the neighbor against false limitation. Responsibility to the call of Jesus "knows no bounds" in the sense that it breaks through barriers of religion, race, gender, class, and culture.[77] In this regard, the SEWH's specific vocation may be summarized as the call to breach false limits as it fosters right relationships among human beings.

As the SEWH breaks through false limits, it also confronts its own human limitations since a church-community's activity in the world cannot help but be finite and limited. Still, the nature of the church's limits is not always obvious. Is faithfulness to Christ characterized by resting in what it understands its limits to be or proactively attempting to forge beyond them? For example, because the SEWH centrally focuses on building bridges across divides—including political divides—its prime "weak spot," according to Hilary, is that it does not take a more "aggressive, activist stance" on particular issues and policies affecting the community. In a town so brutally partisan, the SEWH offers a fresh opportunity for conversations across political divides and for common ground to be sought—an accomplishment of no small value. At the same time, the SEWH's congenial approach lessens its ability to speak that prophetic (and, thus, likely divisive) word Kristi hints at in the guidebook. On occasion the SEWH has an opportunity to take a more direct approach to political issues in its own space when a congressional staffer or Senator's spouse comes to a reconciliation lunch or breakfast, yet the SEWH understands its role more passively as fostering "encounters" that may bring about transformation. A congressional staffer may sit next to a woman on welfare and as a result have a new understanding of poverty, for example. The staff person "hears a real story and meets a real person, and we hope that this will affect the way she sees the world and the policies she encourages," says Kristi. Although the SEWH "does not track these," it hopes "that these kinds of encounters are a part of the toolkit for those people who are working on the structures."[78] The mutual transformation the house hopes to foster includes "bringing people in power into awareness" of the issues affecting lower-income communities because, Marilyn says:

> When you look back at the Old Testament, it wasn't the prophets or teachers but the rulers who actually had to let the people go, so while we are trying to empower those in the neighborhood, it is important that transformation also occurs in the lives of the people with the power. We think the best way for people to understand the issues is to be in relationships with the people who are in need. If this is true then it really matters that the governing body in the House, Supreme Court, and Executive Branch understand the totality of the population."[79]

Hilary says the reality, though, is that while local pastors and other leaders of civic organizations and nonprofits are affected and strengthened by their time at the SEWH, the effect the SEWH has on federal leaders, local politicians, and staffers who hear about the SEWH and visit on occasion is "remote at best," for D.C. policies have not changed dramatically in ways that help lower-income communities. A change in policies, Hilary says, would be "a natural outcome" of a leader or staffer transformed by spending time at the SEWH.

Furthermore, Hilary worries that the focus on "presence" emphasizes "being" with the community at the expense of "doing" things that would directly prompt structural change. For example, the SEWH often points to the one grocery store in Southeast as evidence of the community's lack of resources, but the ministry has not demanded another store. Hilary thinks the SEWH is missing an opportunity to mobilize people toward addressing more structural problems and points to the "abundance" of young, energetic "movers and shakers in our city" who want to serve but do not all feel comfortable volunteering in the mentoring program.[80] Still, while the SEWH is not mobilizing these volunteers, it certainly welcomes them. Scott says that because the SEWH is aware of the many needs in the community and cannot address them all, they are open to all who work for the good of the community. If a group with community organizing skills wants to address structural change, Scott says the SEWH's response would be, "Right on!

We'll help you!" His main concern, though, is finding enough volunteer interns just "to keep the place going." He says, "The interns are the ones who keep the spirit alive here, from my perspective, in how they approach their relationship to God and show it through their work."[81] Whether the need is interns, mentors, or other people working toward change in the neighborhood, "there is a void between need and availability," says Sammie.[82]

Acknowledging that the SEWH does not directly address systemic injustice, Kristi says that the ministry cannot claim to be a community development organization like the many ministries that fall under John Perkin's Christian Community Development Association that are buying blocks of homes and offering affordable housing in neighborhoods being gentrified.[83] A number of the SEWH staff members and volunteers mention a looming threat of gentrification as developers have recently turned toward Southeast, and Scott and Marilyn both agree that "we should have been sharper on buying the building next door and putting in low cost housing."[84] John Johnson also speaks of the neighborhood's likely transition from an isolated community into a gentrified one as developers build high-end condos, which raises property tax and pushes families across the Maryland state line into Prince George's County. John says, "The families who have been here through the drug deals and the killings won't get to benefit from the change in infrastructure and that's sad."[85] Kristi explains that for various reasons only two of the girls she mentors live in D.C. now, even though they all began at the neighborhood elementary school. She says, "They want to be back in the community that they are familiar with but their families have not been able to [move back] because of the housing market. So [the SEWH] has to address what we are going to do in ten to fifteen years when lower-income folks will no longer be around us. Some people would love it if we were addressing housing issues, but that isn't our specialty. It's part of the bigger picture." Describing herself as someone who wants simultaneously to "see the big picture and be involved in the details of the children's lives from homework to tying shoes," Kristi says, "I have the big systemic issues in mind, but I also really do believe in the power of that one-on-one relationship. When it comes down to it, my role as a Friend is one-on-one relationships with six girls and their families. We need people working on the systems but we also cannot neglect the people suffering within these systems."[86]

Limits are apparent, too, as the SEWH attends to their neighbors who are suffering within unjust structures. Mike says that "at a micro level we are able to address particular individuals but the problems are so large.... There are some issues we can only begin to address. Certainly, we are involved with families but the problems within families are so deeply rooted."[87] Sammie echoes Mike, "There are many needs in the community. The government can't provide it all and the People's House can't find it all, *but we take it as our responsibility to stay engaged*."[88]

The SEWH sees its work as preparing the way "for what Jesus can do in neighborhoods and communities" and recognizes that this preparation must be done in humble acknowledgment of its limits. The church is the body that recognizes the penultimate's dependence on the ultimate and so, while "preparing the way is indeed a matter of concrete intervention," says Bonhoeffer, its impetus behind responsible, repentant activity is extravagant trust in Christ's coming transformation that breaks into our present.[89] Scott says that the role of the SEWH is depicted well in the parable of the sower; the SEWH prepares the way for Christ "by preparing the ground to accept seeds and then cultivating the ground to produce crops" (Mark 4:1–20). Preparing the ground and recognizing the ministry's own limits leads to partnerships with other organizations and groups. Notably, a number of these organizations would not be serving in Southeast were the SEWH not already present there. Preparing the ground both leads to partnerships and to a prayerful awareness that the ultimate responsibility for redemption belongs to God.

Reprise: Repentance as Incarnate Presence

Scott says that offering a clear and concise description of the SEWH's work is "just impossible; it has to be experienced." What is clear is that the ministry began because Scott and Sammie "knew where [they] wanted to be"—that they wanted to take responsibility for the neglect of the community by being "a presence of Jesus." In those first few weeks, they sat on two folding chairs in an empty manor house and prayed that God would use them in that neglected neighborhood and "would tell [them] how to go forward." Over half a century ago while providing a public witness that differs from the SEWH's in interesting and important ways,[90] Dorothy Day described the unplanned Catholic Worker movement in words that nevertheless strikingly capture the spirit and witness of the Southeast White House, a ministry whose sense of christological responsibility has led to it being a presence "there" in the midst of the world and a grateful and awe-filled participant in God's ever-unfolding redemption:

> We were just sitting there talking.... We were just sitting there talking when lines of people began to form, saying, "We need bread." We could not say, "Go, be thou filled." If there were six small loaves and a few fishes, we had to divide them. There was always bread.
>
> We were just sitting there talking and people moved in on us.... And somehow the walls expanded....
>
> It was as casual as all that, I often think. It just came about. It just happened....
>
> The most significant thing...is poverty, some say. The most significant thing is community, others say. We are not alone anymore.
>
> But the final word is love.... We cannot love God unless we love each other, and to love we must know each other. We know Him in the breaking of the bread, and we know each other in the breaking of bread, and we are not alone anymore. Heaven is a banquet and life is a banquet, too, even with a crust, where there is companionship.

> We have all known the long loneliness and we have learned that the only solution is love and that love comes with community.
>
> It all happened while we sat there talking, and it is still going on.[91]

Because christological repentance is defined not by being consumed with one's own sin and need but by existence for others, the SEWH's very presence in the neighborhood is a mode of repentance. Its repentance is its incarnate presence for others, its hospitality that draws people normally divided into the reconciliation of Christ. While living in a house of hospitality, Dorothy Day concluded that "the final word is love," and this is true for christological repentance at the SEWH as well. The final word for repentance is love, as shown by Jesus, who took responsibility for sin out of obedience to the Father and love for real human beings. "We cannot love God unless we love each other," Day said, and John Johnson echoes, to love we must "know" each other; we must "break bread with folks... eat with them so that [we] can talk with them." Repentance is a banquet where, in the words of Louis, we "fellowship and help one another," and life is a banquet, even with "some dessert," says Denise, where there is "togetherness"—where the walls and tables expand to include an ever-enlarging new humanity.[92] The SEWH witnesses to the fact that we all know the long loneliness (some of us are more aware of it than others), that it is not simply the forgotten quadrant that is in need but those who live outside neglected neighborhoods also require healing and wholeness, those promises of God that are made real and visible only through concrete repentance. The SEWH inhabits repentance by fostering right relationships that lead to mutual transformation because "the only solution is love" and love comes with relationship. Its nontriumphal public witness expressed through its christological refusal to abide by dualisms and religious favor opens up relationship and belonging to all, regardless of religion, race, class, politics, geography, or culture. This all happened—the way was prepared—by Sammie and Scott first being a presence for Jesus, simply sitting there talking on those two folding chairs, and it is still going on.

Conclusion

Concrete Implications of an Ecclesial Witness Based on Repentance

Part III, "Contours of a Repenting Church," examined the identity and mission of two church-communities in order to open our imaginations to what the theology of public witness constructed in part II might look like in lived experience. Through theological ethnography, part III invited Eleuthero and the Southeast White House to bestow tangible meaning on a theology of public witness that establishes confession unto repentance as the church's primary mode of being in the world. The case studies have served as a guard against confining this theology to a closed system abstracted from the creative struggles of actual church-communities seeking to offer a nontriumphal witness to the lordship of Christ in our pluralistic democracy; for, such systematizing could never grasp the dynamic movement of the living God and the manifold vocations of church-communities responding to sin, suffering, and injustice in specific contexts. Therefore, Eleuthero and the Southeast White House serve as examples but not blueprint plans or exhaustive accounts of Christian social and political engagement. As case studies, they leave open the question of what a disposition of confession unto repentance would mean for other communities and congregations. At the same time, they intend to stimulate reflection on a church's self-understanding, purpose and priorities, organizational structure, and shape it takes in the world. Toward this end, I highlight a few defining characteristics of a church-community witnessing to Christ's lordship in a nontriumphal manner. The presentation below is not meant to exhaust but to generate further consideration on the concrete implications of a public witness based on a disposition of repentance that may be discerned from these communities and from the theology of public witness they embody.

After demonstrating in part I that the triumphalistic and compromising tendencies of Christian public presence today require a renewed understanding of witness as conformation to Christ, part II grounded a disposition of confession unto repentance in Jesus' public presence and in the work of the incarnate, crucified, and risen God. The church witnesses to both the person and work of Christ through repentance—to the person of Christ by taking the form of the penitent and crucified one in public life and to the work of Christ by belonging wholly to the world through a disposition of repentance that aligns the church with the christological pattern of life, with the theological reality that divine affirmation of the world includes divine judgment and that the acceptance of divine judgment leads to this-worldly redemption. Specifically the church takes the form of Christ and witnesses to the work of Christ by affirming humanity and being in solidarity with humanity instead of setting itself apart as dispenser of truth, moral exemplar, and judge; by receiving and accepting God's judgment on itself; and by demonstrating God's reconciliation with the world through acts of concrete redemption rooted in responsible repentance. The threefold witness to divine affirmation, judgment, and reconciliation is interwoven into the life and work of the church-community such that embodied proclamations of God's affirmation overlap with those of God's judgment of the world and reconciliation with the world, embodied proclamations of God's judgment overlap with messages of affirmation and reconciliation, and so on. For the purpose of utmost clarity, however, I will describe in turn characteristics of a redemptive public witness that demonstrates that God in Christ affirms the world, judges the world, and has reconciled the world to God. These features constitute a witness that is simultaneously bold and humble as it demonstrates the lordship of Christ in a nontriumphal manner, and that is redemptive as it leads to healing transformation for both the church and society. Furthermore, because these characteristics of a redemptive public witness are based on christological repentance (repentance defined by and participating in the person and work of Christ), they also serve as a synopsis of what a nonreligious interpretation of repentance encompasses and entails.

■ CHARACTERISTICS OF ECCLESIAL WITNESS DEMONSTRATING CHRIST'S AFFIRMATION

We have seen that God's affirmation of humanity is made manifest by God's presence in the world as the real human being in fallen flesh. God's work in Christ may be understood through the category of repentance since Jesus was intimately involved with sin through his bodily encounter with fallen existence. Christ affirms not just humanity but fallen humanity, not just the created world but the fallen world, by drawing near in solidarity with sinners, with real human beings. In his ministry, Jesus' solidarity is seen most poignantly in his first public act when he responds to John's call to repent by numbering himself with transgressors in his Jordan River baptism, and the event of Jesus' baptism introduces repentance as an activity defining God's love and righteousness and God's outworking of redemption. Repentance that participates in the affirming power of the Christ event necessitates existence with and for others, to which the fallen flesh of the incarnation and the baptismal response of the sinless Jesus testify.

The most basic feature of a public witness demonstrating Christ's affirmation of the world is, therefore, *existence with and for others* through the church-community's *incarnate presence in its own sinful flesh*. The repentant community immerses itself physically and unreservedly into a particular situation of concern, not arrogantly as if the church has answers to particular problems already sorted out but as a people committed to being engaged, listening, and learning from others. "We moved into the Southeast White House in 1996 with absolutely no preconceived notions as to how to use it. We just knew where we wanted to be, that we wanted to be used," says Sammie Morrison.[1] "We came here with no plans or programs except to listen to the needs of the neighborhood and be a presence for Jesus," echoes Scott Dimock.[2] The Southeast White House's incarnate presence, as previously shown, is a mode of repentance that witnesses to Christ's affirmation of humanity because it is based on the House's desire to exist for others and to listen and learn from them, especially those deemed the outcasts of society who are pushed to the margins of the city. Because incarnate presence in situations of social concern or injustice is vital for witnessing to Christ's affirmation of humanity, a public witness faithful to Christ cannot be based on ideology, be it political or theological. Ideologues and commentators on the sidelines cannot offer a redemptive public witness because they set themselves up as judge, the form that stands in total opposition to the shape of Christ in the world. We see Christians take the form of judge not only when their public proclamations about social and political matters are made from an armchair, but also through the pseudo-doing described in chapter 5, through political activism that is bodily in the sense that it may involve leg-work, mass organization, and political protest, yet nevertheless contradicts the incarnation because it is driven by moral principles and religious standards that promote the church over against the world. Christ was engaged bodily in the concerns of the world not as a moral exemplar but as one in solidarity with fallen humanity. Incarnate presence means public engagement as one numbered with transgressors.

As a community that counts itself among current transgressors, the church cannot disassociate from the sinful world. The church demonstrates Christ's affirmation of this world when it *refuses to take a defensive stance against it*. "One of the first things that Tim said to me is that we are not here to be culture warriors in the sense of fighting the surrounding society," Dave Stankiewicz says, "and I liked that the second he said it."[3] Indeed, the very impetus behind Eleuthero's incarnate presence in Portland, Maine, was to learn ecological care from the surrounding secular culture out of confidence in Christ's expansive lordship, which shines out into the world allowing non-Christians to be reflectors of Christ's truth to Christians. While a defensive stance stems from the presumption that Christians possess the truth and the knowledge of good and evil and thus protecting these from assault depends on them, the repentant community, in contrast, witnesses to Christ's affirmation of the world when it, like Eleuthero, assumes not special favor but rather that it must listen and learn from the insights and actions of others. The repentant community recognizes that engaging culture in a positive, open, and constructive manner is faithful to Christ, who belonged wholly to this world. It also recognizes that Christians are historical, contextual beings—that this is part of the gift of being human—and that like everyone else, Christians are necessarily formed by cultural forces and societal trends, both positive and negative. This means that instead of arrogantly and blindly understanding itself in stark opposition to the surrounding culture, the repentant church in solidarity with humanity may cultivate an awareness about the ways the church has been affected by negative cultural trends (like the consumerist mentality, discussed in chapter 2, that shapes the exclusive Christians' understanding of salvation) and may be receptive enough to alter dominant assumptions it previously held. Refusing to take a defensive stance against the world does not mean that the church sheds its distinctive identity as the body of Christ in the world. It means that its identity is not defined in opposition to the rest of humanity. Like Christ, the repentant church demonstrates in action and speech that it is for, not against, the world.

Finally, the repentant church demonstrates Christ's affirmation of this world when it displays *a love for this life* through commitment to present historical reality *driven by this-worldly hope for restoration* rather than a religious hope preoccupied with individualistic and other-worldly notions of salvation. Other-worldly preoccupation inadvertently renounces Christ's lordship over this world and risks framing matters of life and death in terms of eternal destiny to the detriment of attending to the serious effects of dehumanization and diminution in this life. This is especially dangerous when concern for eternal souls is coupled with fatalistic resignation to the inevitability of evil in a fallen world that in turn acquiesces to unjust structures. Other-worldly preoccupation misses the gift of the polyphony of life that bids the church be swept up into an earthly love that rushes headlong into the beauty and sorrow of this life because it finds Christ there. In contrast to the world-denying influences within the Christian religion, christological hope for this-worldly restoration gives the church, in the words of Eleuthero, "permission to live."[4] As Bonhoeffer writes, "It is only when one loves life and the earth so much that without them everything seems to be over that one may believe in the resurrection and the new world."[5] Love for this life will cause the repentant community to become deeply enmeshed in the places of struggle and distress out of a sense of urgency for restoration. Love for life is shown, though, not simply through hard work and toil but also through playfulness and festivity that invites others into an inclusive celebration. "They were partying," Denise Speed says of her first encounter at the Southeast White House, "and curiosity got the best of me."[6] As we saw, the Southeast White House witnesses to Christ's affirmation regularly at their weekly luncheons through good food and fellowship, and the feast both manifests and cultivates this-worldly hope and love by affirming human dignity and instilling a sense of belonging.

■ CHARACTERISTICS OF ECCLESIAL WITNESS DEMONSTRATING DIVINE JUDGMENT

We have seen in part II that Christ's affirmation of humanity includes God's judgment on humanity. The Christ event declares a simultaneous divine acceptance and protest, God's Yes and No continuously proclaimed upon the whole world, including the church. Christ's Yes includes the No, since Christ's affirmation of the world is not divine blessing on the sin and injustice that runs rampant in the world. God's judgment upon humanity is made manifest through Christ's cross, where

God receives divine judgment by accepting guilt and taking responsibility for sin. In other words, Christ demonstrates God's judgment on the sin that destroys community and diminishes human beings by directing that judgment to himself.

The most basic way the church demonstrates God's judgment on humanity, then, is also by directing it toward itself. Conformed to the crucified Christ, the repentant church acknowledges God's rightful judgment by *accepting responsibility* for sin, suffering, and injustice *through repentant activity* in the midst of the world. Accepting responsibility for sin will lead to the incarnate presence discussed above, to the church existing for others by immersing itself in the places of struggle and distress and in the problems of social and political life while acknowledging its present complicity in the sin of society with which it is intimately interconnected. By exposing sin in itself—in its own communal life and in its relationship with other human beings and with society as a whole—the church exposes sin in the world. Because the church's exposed sin is integral to its witness, public engagement based on confession unto repentance avoids triumphalism. At the same time, making sin visible through repentant action that brings social healing witnesses to Christ's present and future lordship over the various realms of sociopolitical life. The Southeast White House's initial act of repentance—its move into the neighborhood to encounter the neglected neighbor—witnesses to Christ's lordship over the forgotten quadrant of the nation's capital, and taking responsibility for this neglect through repentant action prepares the way for Christ's concrete redemption. Likewise, Eleuthero's confession of complicity in the excesses of American culture and its repentant activity in the form of learning and applying practices of sustainability witnesses to Christ's lordship over the environment; its ecological care participates in and prepares the way for Christ's total restoration of the natural world. Thus, the church that accepts responsibility for sin not only witnesses to God's judgment on humanity but also demonstrates the nature and purpose of that judgment, namely healing transformation and concrete redemption. The notion of divine judgment has come to connote punishment, as seen through its use in the public arena by leaders of the Religious Right, who now and again gain publicity through outrageous claims identifying catastrophe with God's judgment over groups of people they deem immoral. The judgment of God is misconstrued, though, when understood as punishment, whether in political or religious spheres, since divine judgment is in the service of divine promise. The judgment of God is real and severe—it is crisis—because it holds a mirror up to the sin in us and in the structures of which we are a part and for which we are responsible. The judgment of God is severe but is severe not as punishment but as love—a love intent on bringing wholeness to humanity and this world, which can occur only when we courageously face ourselves: our dualistic mindsets, shallow theologies and easy answers, commitments and lack thereof, our fears of others and the unknown, of being responsible, of losing privilege, comfort, and a sense of control.

Thus, a repentant church receiving God's judgment on itself will be marked by *honesty* and *courage*. It will be honest as it searches out the truth about itself, about its blind spots, preoccupations, and religious idolatries, about the ways the church has harmed others, perhaps in the form of dogma or rigid biblical interpretation, perhaps because it lacks traditional practices of Christian hospitality that welcome the stranger, the outcast, and the despised. It will be courageous as it refuses to hide behind those things that make it feel safe and secure, be it a notion of religious favor, assurance that one's group possesses the truth, or adherence to moral principles. The repentant church is the courageous church as it seeks to be continuously reawakened to the ways it remains complicit in oppressive thought and action, in the myriad structural evils of our political, social, religious, and economic systems. It is courageous as it stands before the living God, open and receptive to divine disruption and criticism, which may be articulated through voices the church is used to dismissing and would rather ignore. The courage and honesty of Eleuthero and the Southeast White House is seen most clearly through their determination, each in their own way, to *undergo continuous conversion* as they *dwell within repentance*, as these communities remain present and engaged while being led deeper into their specific vocations. As we saw, the Southeast White House inhabits repentance as it fosters relationships among people normally divided and draws others into its communal life together. Eleuthero undergoes continuous conversion through the renewing of minds as the members honestly and courageously reflect on their own inherited and embedded theologies and invite other Christians to do the same.

While the case study of Eleuthero highlights the central role the renewing of minds plays in a nontriumphant public witness, rethinking dominant assumptions is integral to the work of both Eleuthero and the Southeast White House. Each community illustrates that a concrete implication of a repentant church demonstrating God's judgment is *the renewing of minds*. As argued in the introduction, the triumphalistic tendencies of public witness today demand that Christians rethink dominant assumptions about Christ, the world, the church, repentance, and even the notion of witness itself. Both Eleuthero and the Southeast White House show that inhabiting repentance unsettles patterns of thinking, even those that are allegedly Christian, and both promote an education rooted in lived experience, in what Tim Clayton calls an attempt "to struggle to ask and to live what is possible."[7] As we saw, Eleuthero's confession unto repentance is inaugurated by and requires unlearning and learning anew, and the Southeast White House invites all involved in the work (whether volunteer mentors, urban plunge groups, or guests at a reconciliation luncheon) into a transformation *fueled by experiential learning*. A guidebook meant to provoke new thinking and prompt new action reinforces the experiential learning and challenges its readers to live within difficult questions through responsible engagement with the issues and the people they affect. Continuous conversion through the renewing of minds occurs in the lives of the staff and committed "family" members as well. Louis Robertson is convicted of pride and learns from Sammie "that this is a place that welcomes everyone"; Hilary Barnett learned "how ignorant I was and how privileged I am... that the quality of my life is due almost entirely to the heritage I have"; Kristi Kiger shifts her understanding of poverty in the developed world and "realizes the mistake of saying, 'well, this isn't real poverty.'"[8] A posture of openness toward divine disruption, as exemplified by Louis, Hilary, and Kristi, requires that one remain within the difficult questions of faith and discipleship, that one practices a faith-seeking-understanding open to continuous conversion, even and especially when the process of rethinking is painful. God's spirit awakens and convicts, shatters conventions, and searches out hidden traces of racism, sexism, or blinding stereotypes in a church-community inhabiting repentance. In turn, the repentant community witnessing to divine judgment in this way cannot help but disavow any claim to goodness. It cannot lift itself up as a model of moral righteousness because it deems itself responsible for sin.

■ CHARACTERISTICS OF ECCLESIAL WITNESS DEMONSTRATING CHRIST'S RECONCILIATION

We have seen that it is precisely by belonging wholly to the world by accepting guilt and taking responsibility for sin that Christ has reconciled humanity to God and has transformed the world's ontology. The world's identity is no longer narrowed to its fallen structure; rather, in its sin and in the unfolding of redemption, the world is definitively reconciled to Christ. Because the world has been reconciled to God through Christ, though not demonstratively redeemed, the church is called to witness to this already accomplished reconciliation by being a concrete redemptive presence through responsible acts of repentance. The church community demonstrates Christ's reconciliation, then, *when its repentant activity prepares the way for or leads to concrete redemption*. Restoration and healing may be newsworthy and have a broad public reach yet more likely will be found in those "small success stories" of slowly transforming lives of which Scott Dimock speaks.[9]

The repentant community demonstrates Christ's reconciliation with the world and makes Christ's redemption concrete by *fostering right relationships* with creation and other human beings. The Southeast White House fosters mutually transformative relationships across the various boundaries that divide human beings by positioning itself as a path upon which unlikely encounters occur and relationships with diverse populations are cultivated and sustained. By cultivating unlikely relationships, it witnesses to the inclusive and expansive nature of Christ's reconciling work that encompasses the totality of humanity. The Southeast White House witnesses to Christ's reconciliation every time an improbable group of people share a meal around the dining room table and a mentor spends time with a child. As the community shares life with an "at-risk" child or a stranger who normally would not be welcome at such a gathering, the Southeast White House witnesses to the social flourishing inherent in the kingdom of God that Christ inaugurates and embodies. The House understands itself as a "bridge" connecting people normally divided, and as bridge it facilitates double movement or mutual redemption in both the neighbors and those who formerly had no impetus to come into the neighborhood. The Eleuthero Community witnesses to Christ's reconciliation by fostering right relationships as well, specifically with the earth and with a vulnerable population of African immigrants. It also understands itself as a bridge as it seeks to be a "dot connector," or "glue" between diverse people like the Sudanese refugees and the Caucasians involved in the Winter Cache sustainability project.[10]

Tim Clayton calls potential connections like the one above a "work of integration" because it gathers people together around a shared concern or need.[11] The repentant community demonstrates Christ's reconciliation, then, not only when it serves as a bridge fostering right relationships but also when it *partners with others around a common work*. Indeed, the shared work likely will be precisely what facilitates authentic and mutually transformative relationships, both within the community and with those who do not self-describe as Christian. Evan Pillsbury says, for example, that the public lectures on theology and ecology and on the spirituality of Martin Luther King offered "space for discussion to emerge" where people inside and outside the Christian tradition could "meet in the middle and allow relationships to develop through a common work and concern, through shared values such as a shared planet."[12] Similarly, Tim Clayton's meetings with environmental professionals and activists with which Eleuthero hoped to partner opened up new possibilities for reconciliation and concrete redemption as Tim broke down barriers by beginning these conversations with confession of the church's past and present sin that has hindered ecological care. By welcoming all who seek the good of the community, the Southeast White House also exemplifies reconciliation around a common concern. As a "house on the hill for all people," it opens up participation in Christ's reconciling work to all who struggle for the flourishing of the neighborhood regardless of whether they consider themselves inside or outside the church. By refusing to view itself as specially favored and to abide by religious dualisms, the Southeast White House respects the integrity of everyone who comes to share in the work of the House; "there is room" to participate in the being and activity of Christ, according to Marilyn Dimock, regardless of religious affiliation or lack thereof.[13] Borrowing Tim's words about Eleuthero, the Southeast White House invites people into the work in "a way that is respectful to who they are and what they are about" without necessitating that they become Christian.[14] Moreover, redemptive partnerships occur not simply between the repentant community and other groups or individuals but also among the community members themselves. John Johnson's comments about the growth of interracial relationships among the full-time mentors, who are learning to trust one another as they grapple with issues affecting their mentees, exemplifies the kind of authentic reconciliation that may emerge *within* the repentant community around a shared concern.

Finally, the repentant community demonstrates Christ's reconciliation and makes redemption concrete through its *embodied life together* that grows into an ever-enlarging new humanity. For the Southeast White House this means sharing life with its neighbors and inviting into its space those who would otherwise avoid this section of the city. As the staff and volunteers "live in the spirit of Jesus," a sense of peace and love pervade the house, and the house itself takes sacramental form and draws others into its redemptive space.[15] The House witnesses to the lordship of Christ precisely because it has become a place within which peace, love, right relationships, and a sense of belonging reign; it has become, in other words, a picture and presence of the kingdom of God. The evangelistic import of the witness lies in the fact that the repentant church's "embodied life together" shows the world the promises of God, or in the words of Tim Clayton, "some of what the future is that we are looking towards."[16] As the repentant church keeps Christ's total restoration of this world in view, its communal existence enables all who enter into the life of the community to live more in accordance with the kingdom come. Cheryl Clayton contends that the radical and alternative form of life that becomes a picture and presence of God's kingdom must be built into the very structure of community, which would necessitate rethinking the constitution of local churches. "What we are talking about is such a radical way of living in America that you need support; you need encouragement; you need people admonishing you," she says, "and I really believe that Christ works [through community]. Outside of this context, I don't think it would be possible."[17] Reconsidering how United States Protestants "do church" does not necessarily mean an overhaul of denominations (although our "Protestantism without Reformation" would benefit from ecumenical collaboration), but it would mean resisting the insular infrastructure of most churches by structuring congregations, as suggested above, around a common work or need in the world, with worship, Bible study, prayer, and fellowship growing out of this common vocation. The repentant community ordered around a common work demonstrates the reconciliation of Christ and makes Christ's being concrete when its life together ushers forth social flourishing.

As this presentation suggests, a communal life of repentance is a life of abundance. To witness to divine affirmation, judgment, and reconciliation is to share in the life and love of Christ and thus to be truly human and belong wholly to this world. The church-community that belongs to this world has ears to hear God convict it of its complicity in social/structural sin and has the liturgy and prayers of confession to face and name that sin. Confession of specific sin leads the church into its particular vocation, into social and political action full of the significance and purpose of Christ, characterized by the disposition of repentance described above. The church witnesses in a nontriumphal manner to Christ's lordship precisely through this engagement—the form it takes in the world—which both speaks for itself and nurtures a new language, granting the repentant community a new public voice at once theological and intelligible to a pluralistic society because it constitutes words not of superiority and division but of solidarity in sin and redemption. And the public proclamation in word and deed is this: God is for human beings, for the world, and if God is for us who can be against us?

NOTES

Preface and Acknowledgments

1. Bonhoeffer, *Life Together*, Vol. 5 of *Dietrich Bonhoeffer Works*, 16 vols. (Minneapolis: Fortress Press, 2010), 82, italics in original.

2. Annie Dillard, *The Writing Life* (New York: HarperPerennial, 1990), 58–59.

Chapter 1

1. Tim Clayton, interview with author, April 24, 2006; e-mail, April 21, 2006. The meeting was taped and sent to the town's congressional representative.

2. Ibid.

3. By "public" I mean the social and the political broadly construed. In *A Theology of Public Life*, Charles Mathewes defines "public life" in a way helpful to my project. He says that "public" does not simply refer to politics; rather, "it includes everything concerned with the 'public good'" (1). See Charles Mathewes, *A Theology of Public Life* (Cambridge: Cambridge University Press, 2007).

4. I borrow this understanding of a theology of glory from Larry Rasmussen. See *Dietrich Bonhoeffer: His Significance for North Americans* (Minneapolis: Fortress Press, 1990), 173.

5. Tim Clayton, e-mail, April 21, 2006.

6. The idea of a nontriumphal lordship is rooted in the New Testament, where the term "lordship" is used both to signify Christ's uniqueness and primacy and to overturn the common Roman understanding of lordship, in which the patriarch imposes his will on his household. Even given the biblical overturning of common understandings of lordship, second-wave feminists such as Carol P. Christ, Mary Daly, and Rosemary Radford Ruether were particularly concerned with the use of the term "lordship" in the 1970s. For more contemporary accounts see Elisabeth Schüssler Fiorenza's idea of kyriarchy in *Rhetoric and Ethic: The Politics of Biblical Studies* (Minneapolis: Fortress Press, 1999) and Sallie McFague's discussion of "models" or metaphors we use to talk about God in *Models of God: Theology for an Ecological Nuclear Age* (London: SCM, 1987). McFague argues that the problem is not the metaphor itself but the exclusive use of a certain metaphor at the expense of others that also speak of God's identity and character. I base my understanding of "lordship" on the exclusive and inclusive character of Christ as the one Word of God and the one and only Light of Life, as will be developed in the next chapter, and so I use the term confidently here because it is precisely the expansive lordship of Christ that charges Christians to listen to all voices inside and outside the church with great seriousness, to voices and ideas perhaps unfamiliar and initially threatening to many Christians. John W. de Gruchy responds to lordship language in the Barmen Declaration in a similar manner in *Bonhoeffer and South Africa: Theologies in Dialogue* (Grand Rapids: Eerdmans, 1984), 127–131.

7. Edwin H. Robertson, ed., *No Rusty Swords: Letters, Lectures and Notes 1928–1936, from the Collected Works of Dietrich Bonhoeffer* (New York: Harper & Row, 1965), 161–162.

8. When translating the Bible, Luther refused to use the term *Kirche* (institutional church) and instead used *Gemeinde* (community).

9. In *Letters and Papers from Prison*, Bonhoeffer refers to "revelation theology," and his habilitation thesis, *Act and Being*, as a whole may be described as a theology of revelation because it is centrally concerned with the nature of revelation. See Dietrich Bonhoeffer, *Letters and Papers from Prison*, ed. John W. de Gruchy, trans. Isabel Best et al., Vol. 8 of *Dietrich Bonhoeffer Works*, 16 vols. (Minneapolis: Fortress Press, 2010), 500. The polished draft of my manuscript was completed before the publication of DBWE 8, so I relied on Dietrich Bonhoeffer, *Letters and Papers from Prison*, trans. Reginald Fuller et al. (New York: Touchstone, 1997). However, I have replaced most of the Touchstone translations with those of the Fortress Press edition.

10. See the preface of Dietrich Bonhoeffer, *Sanctorum Communio: A Theological Study of the Sociology of the Church*, ed. Clifford J. Green, trans. Reinhard Krauss and Nancy Lukens, Vol. 1 of *Dietrich Bonhoeffer Works*, 16 vols. (Minneapolis: Fortress Press, 1998), 21.

11. See the editors' introduction of Bonhoeffer, *Sanctorum Communio* DBWE 1, 14–19.

12. I recognize the importance of speaking of "churches" in the plural and I do this when speaking about sociological realities. I also speak of "the church" in the singular as a theological reality unified in all its differences through Christ.

13. The opening example of the Tim Clayton's public witness still falls within the realm of my ecclesiological concern, given that as a priest he is not simply an individual Christian but a representative of the church.

14. Bonhoeffer, *Letters and Papers* DBWE 8, 479–480.

15. Classical secularization theorists include Max Weber and Emile Durkheim, and second-generation theoreticians include Peter Berger, Harvey Cox, and A. F. C. Wallace. See Kevin M. Shultz, "Secularization: A Bibliographic Essay," in "After Secularization," special issue, *Hedgehog Review: Critical Reflections on Contemporary Culture* 8, no. 1–2 (2006): 170–177. Also see Peter L. Berger et al., *The Desecularization of Religion: Resurgent Religion and World Politics* (Grand Rapids, Mich.: Eerdmans, 1999); James Davidson Hunter and Jennifer L. Geddes, eds. "After Secularization," special issue, *Hedgehog Review: Critical Reflections on Contemporary Culture* 8, no. 1–2 (2006); Charles Mathewes and Christopher McKnight Nichols, *Prophecies of Godlessness: Predictions of America's Imminent Secularization, from the Puritans to Postmodernity* (New York: Oxford University Press, 2008); and Charles Taylor, *A Secular Age* (Cambridge, Mass.: Belknap Press of Harvard University Press, 2007).

16. More than nine-in-ten Americans (92%) believe in the existence of God or a universal spirit. See the Pew Forum on Religion and Public Life, U.S. Religious Landscape Survey: Summary of Key Findings, http://religions.pewforum.org/pdf/report2religious-landscape-study-key-findings.pdf.

17. For a recent study that treats Bonhoeffer's "world come of age" in a different manner, arguing that the concept does apply to the North American context, see Jeffrey C. Pugh, *Religionless Christianity: Dietrich Bonhoeffer in Troubled Times* (New York: T&T Clark, 2008).

18. For an account of secular "tradition," see Jeffrey Stout's *Democracy and Tradition* (Princeton, N.J.: Princeton University Press, 2004). The term "pluralism" has many different connotations and meanings. What I mean by pluralism is heterogeneity. Kristen Deede Johnson defines pluralism in a helpful way as a descriptive term referring to "the co-existence of distinct faiths, cultures, ethnicities, races, and ideologies within one society." See *Theology, Political Theory, and Pluralism: Beyond Tolerance and Difference* (Cambridge: Cambridge University Press, 2007), 1. I will use the term "pluralism," even though it is

loaded with various meanings, rather than "heterogeneity," because "pluralism" is a term commonly associated with our democratic context.

19. See Ronald F. Thiemann, *Religion in Public Life: A Dilemma for Democracy* (Washington, D.C.: Georgetown University Press, 1996), 42–71, for an analysis of this "misleading metaphor" and for a fuller discussion of the relationship between religious and secular forces in the public realm.

20. Bonhoeffer, *Letters and Papers* (Touchstone edition), 383. DBWE 8 translates "exists for others" as "being there for others" (503).

21. On guilt as an ethical concept in Bonhoeffer, see Christine Schliesser, *Everyone Who Acts Responsibly Becomes Guilty. The Concept of Accepting Guilt in Dietrich Bonhoeffer: Reconstruction and Critical Assessment* (Neukirchen, Germany: Neukirchener-Verlag, 2006), 52–54.

22. Abraham Joshua Heschel, *The Prophets: An Introduction* (New York: Harper & Row, 1969), 16.

23. See Wafik Wahba, "Middle Eastern Perspectives and Expressions of Christian Repentance," in *Repentance in Christian Theology*, ed. Mark J. Boda and Gordon T. Smith (Collegeville, Minn.: Liturgical Press, 2006).

24. Cheryl Bridges Johns, "Yielding to the Spirit: A Pentecostal Understanding," in Boda and Smith, *Repentance in Christian Theology* (see note 23), 295.

25. Michael Battle, "Penitence as Practice in African/African American Christian Spirituality," in Boda and Smith, *Repentance in Christian Theology* (see note 23), 329–330, 341. For an example of a confession that challenges the emphasis on forgiveness of the oppressor, see "The Black Paper" confession of black Methodists in James H. Cone, *Black Theology and Black Power* (Maryknoll, N.Y.: Orbis Books, 1997), 109–110.

26. See the seminal work, Kelly Brown Douglas, *Sexuality and the Black Church: A Womanist Perspective* (Maryknoll, N.Y.: Orbis Books, 1999).

27. For example, see Willis Jenkins and Jennifer M. McBride, *Bonhoeffer and King: Their Legacies and Import for Christian Social Thought* (Minneapolis: Fortress Press, 2010).

28. John W. de Gruchy, "A Concrete Ethic of the Cross: Interpreting Bonhoeffer's Ethics in North America's Backyard," *Union Seminary Quarterly Review* 58.1–2 (2004): 43–45. The phrase "beyond Bonhoeffer" comes from Harvey G. Cox, "Beyond Bonhoeffer: The Future of Religionless Christianity," *Secular City Debate*, ed. Daniel Callahan (New York: Macmillan, 1966), 205–214. De Gruchy writes about Cox in his essay and speaks of going *beyond* and *with* Bonhoeffer.

29. Larry Rasmussen's *Dietrich Bonhoeffer: His Significance for North Americans* arises out of two earlier works, *Dietrich Bonhoeffer: Reality and Resistance* (New York: Abingdon, 1972), his pioneering study of the christological ethics of responsibility grounding Bonhoeffer's resistance activity, and *The Predicament of the Prosperous* (Philadelphia: Westminster Press, 1978), a constructive critique cowritten with Bruce C. Birch on the role North American affluence has played in shaping the nature of Christian faith in the United States. In *His Significance for North Americans*, Rasmussen unpacks various relevant themes in Bonhoeffer's writings, such as the character of Christian patriotism and resistance, with the thesis guiding the second half of the book coinciding most directly with my concerns. Rasmussen insists that the North American church's public vocation be rooted in a theology of the cross. He argues that a "conversion" to a theology of the cross, which fosters an ecclesial "ethic of the cross," is vital for a transformative public witness in the United States (144–173). He observes that many North American church-communities lack a "distinct ecclesiology"

and "clear ethic" shaping their identity and mission in the world, says that Bonhoeffer's understanding of ethics as christological conformation is "the most promising and under-developed dimension of the theology of the cross," and suggests that Bonhoeffer's corresponding notion of responsibility is the most significant ethical category for the North American Protestant church today (165, 143–144). By placing Bonhoeffer's insights in the service of our U.S. context, Rasmussen paves the way for such a project, but he leaves the task of developing a more detailed and concrete ethic up to scholars who come after him. Confession and repentance are also at the center of de Gruchy's work on Bonhoeffer's significance for South Africa. See *Bonhoeffer and South Africa: Theology in Dialogue* (Grand Rapids, Mich.: Eerdmans, 1984) and "Confessing Guilt in South Africa Today in Dialogue with Dietrich Bonhoeffer," *Journal of Theology for Southern Africa* 67 (1989): 37–45. De Gruchy weaves into his description and analysis of the church struggle during and after apartheid theological claims that are central to the ethic of confession and repentance that I will construct, namely the promise of a theology of the cross, the intrinsic connection between confessing sin and confessing the lordship of Christ, confession of sin as an all-embracing confession of guilt, confession of guilt as the essence of the church's witness, and the necessity of concrete acts of repentance. Thus, De Gruchy and Rasmussen—each constructing a theology from Bonhoeffer that informs his own context—both indicate that acceptance of guilt and repentance are requisite for a redemptive witness.

30. Ernst Feil's seminal 1971 work, *Die Theologie Dietrich Bonhoeffers: Hermeneutik, Christologie, Weltverständnis* (Munich, Germany: Chr. Kaiser and Matthias Grünewald, 1971) provides a compelling portrayal of the unity of thought across Bonhoeffer's writings, even as the dimensions of his theology progress. In some detail Feil traces the historical development of Bonhoeffer's work in ways that draw attention to its essential unity; my own proposal proceeds from Feil's careful study of that unity. (See also the 1985 Fortress Press English translation).

31. See Dietrich Bonhoeffer, *Ethics*, trans. Reinhold Krauss, et al., Vol. 6 of *Dietrich Bonhoeffer Works*, 16 vols. (Minneapolis: Fortress Press, 2005), 134–145.

32. See Christine Schliesser, *Everyone Who Acts Responsibly Becomes Guilty*, 159. In her introduction, Schliesser writes that it is surprising that Bonhoeffer's notion of "acceptance of guilt" has not been examined systematically by previous scholars, given that it is such a central concept in Bonhoeffer's theology and directly tied to other central concepts like "responsibility" that have received adequate attention. The scholars that do include the notion of "acceptance of guilt" in their scholarship do so only in passing and merely offer a description instead of an examination of its grounding, methodology, and utilization.

33. Ibid., 189–190, and "Editors' Introduction" in Bonhoeffer, *Ethics* DBWE 6, 35. Larry Rasmussen makes this same observation in *Dietrich Bonhoeffer: Reality and Resistance* (New York: Abingdon Press, 1972), 54, footnote 111.

34. Bonhoeffer, *Letters and Papers* DBWE 8, 41. The essay is best known by its Touchstone title, "After Ten Years," although the DBWE 8 entitles the essay, "An Account at the Turn of the Year 1942–1943." For recent scholarship on the nature of Bonhoeffer's participation in the conspiracy circle, see Sabine Dramm, *Dietrich Bonhoeffer and the Resistance*, trans. Margaret Kohl (Minneapolis: Fortress Press, 2009). Dramm argues that Bonhoeffer's actual participation in the conspiracy was not as substantial as is usually assumed and that his role is best described as "intellectual pastoral care" (240).

35. Schliesser, *Everyone Who Acts Responsibly Becomes Guilty*, 91–92, 180–186.

36. Ibid., 180–181. The editors of the *Dietrich Bonhoeffer Works* translate Bonhoeffer's term *fremde Schuld* as "taking on another's guilt," while Schliesser translates it more directly as "foreign guilt." *Fremde* may mean strange, foreign, unknown, unfamiliar, or unaccustomed.

37. Dietrich Bonhoeffer, *Life Together* and *Prayerbook of the Bible*, ed. Geffrey B. Kelly, trans. Daniel W. Bloesch and James H. Burtness, Vol. 5 of *Dietrich Bonhoeffer Works*, 16 vols. (Minneapolis: Fortress Press, 1996), 100–102.

38. See Mark J. Boda and Gordon T. Smith, eds., *Repentance in Christian Theology* (Collegeville, Minn.: Liturgical Press, 2006).

39. Gerhard Kittel, ed., *Theological Dictionary of the New Testament*, Vol. 4 (Grand Rapids: Eerdmans, 1967), 626–629.

40. Dietrich Bonhoeffer, *Discipleship*, eds. Geffrey B. Kelly and John D. Godsey, trans. Barbara Green and Reinhard Krauss, Vol. 4 of *Dietrich Bonhoeffer Works*, 16 vols. (Minneapolis: Fortress Press, 2003), 247. See editors' footnote 78.

41. Bonhoeffer, *Letters and Papers* (Touchstone, 1997), 369.

42. Bonhoeffer, *Letters and Papers* DBWE 8, 486.

43. Bonhoeffer, *Ethics* DBWE 6, 164 (emphasis mine).

44. For a helpful summary of 1960s and 1970s scholarship, see Stephen R. Haynes, *The Bonhoeffer Phenomenon: Portraits of a Protestant Saint* (Minneapolis: Fortress Press, 2004), 13–35.

45. See Ralf K. Wüstenberg, *A Theology of Life: Dietrich Bonhoeffer's Religionless Christianity*, trans. Doug Stott (Grand Rapids, Mich.: Eerdmans, 1996).

46. Bonhoeffer, *Letters and Papers* DBWE 8, 373.

47. Bonhoeffer, *Letters and Papers* DBWE 8, 501–502.

48. Wayne Whitson Floyd Jr., "Style and the Critique of Metaphysics: The Letter as Form in Bonhoeffer and Adorno," *Union Seminary Quarterly Review* 46, no.1–4 (1992): 247.

49. Ibid.

50. Hanfried Müller, "Concerning the Reception and Interpretation of Dietrich Bonhoeffer," in *World Come of Age*, ed. Ronald Gregor Smith (Philadelphia: Fortress Press, 1967), 183–184. Quoted in Floyd.

51. Floyd, "Style and the Critique of Metaphysics," 249. Floyd takes the image of lightning flashes from Walter Benjamin, who says, "In the fields of which we are concerned, knowledge exists only in lightning flashes. The text is a thunder rolling long afterward."

52. Bonhoeffer, *Discipleship* DBWE 4, 44.

53. In *Discipleship* Bonhoeffer further says, in the chapter "Costly Grace," that cheap grace is "forgiveness of sin as a general truth," in other words, as an intellectual assent to this truth without discipleship (43). Bonhoeffer draws on Kierkegaard and describes how a sentence may be true as a conclusion but may be self-deceptive as a presupposition: "Only those who in following Christ leave everything they have can stand and say that they are justified solely by grace" (51).

54. Bonhoeffer, *Letters and Papers* DBWE 8, 364.

55. Dietrich Bonhoeffer, *Barcelona, Berlin, New York: 1928–1931*, ed. Clifford J. Green, trans. Douglas W. Stott, Vol. 10 of *Dietrich Bonhoeffer Works*, 16 vols. (Minneapolis: Fortress Press, 2008), 186.

56. Conversely, a church-community may gain self-understanding when a scholar presents a theological narrative of its work, drawing from the myriad resources within the traditions of philosophical theology, theological ethics, and related disciplines. See Jennifer M. McBride, "Bestowing Meaning: A Reflection on Philosophical Theology and

Ethnography," *Practical Matters: A Transdisciplinary, Multimedia Journal of Religious Practices and Practical Theology* (Issue 3). Online. Available: http://www.practicalmattersjournal.org. I appeal not to a textualism that reduces lived experience to linguistics but to what Manuel A. Vásquez refers to as Paul Ricoeur's "softer use of the analogy of text." Even so, I recognize that there are good reasons to move beyond Ricoeur's metaphor since it does not adequately capture the performative quality of lived communities. I refer to communities as theological texts here in order to emphasize their theological authority within a subfield where abstract discourse is the norm. See Manuel A. Vásquez, *More Than Belief: A Materialist Theory of Religion* (Oxford: Oxford University Press, 2011), 216.

57. Listening to the communities helped me construct the categories central to my theology of public witness. For example, only after observing these communities did I notice how Bonhoeffer's insistence on the threefold nature of Christ's work could influence a theology of public witness; in turn, I began to see repentance as the linchpin that holds together a witness to Christ's affirmation, judgment, and reconciliation with the world.

■ Chapter 2

1. Bonhoeffer, *Letters and Papers from Prison*, ed. John W. de Gruchy, trans. Isabel Best et al., Vol. 8 of *Dietrich Bonhoeffer Works*, 16 vols. (Minneapolis: Fortress Press, 2010), 364.

2. Rick Warren appeals to this idea in the Pew Forum conversation, "Myths of a Mega-Church," *The Pew Forum on Religion and Public Life*, May 23, 2005, available: http://pewforum.org/events/. What many evangelicals insinuate when they say Christianity "is not a religion but a relationship" is that they are not susceptible to the faults of "religion" as they define them such as compartmentalizing faith or trying to earn one's way to God. In addition, when evangelicals deny that Christianity is a religion, they often diminish the importance of formal liturgy and knowledge of tradition, which Bonhoeffer's notion of religionless Christianity certainly does not do.

3. For a fuller discussion of Bonhoeffer's critique of religion in a world come of age, see Clifford J. Green, *A Theology of Sociality* (Grand Rapids, Mich.: Eerdmans, 1999), 263–265.

4. The scholar arguably most associated with discussions regarding ecclesial witness in the United States today is the postliberal, theological ethicist Stanley Hauerwas. Hauerwas is the contemporary interlocutor most relevant to my project of constructing a theology of public witness because his theology focuses on the visible church that has a distinctive identity and mission in the world; he speaks of witness as formation, particularly as being formed by the life, death, and resurrection of Christ; and he, too, appeals to Barth and Bonhoeffer. I value his focus on witness yet think his theology does not address with sufficient clarity the faltering witness of Protestant churches in the United States. In order for the witness Hauerwas proposes to be intelligible to the world, his project needs to be challenged and corrected in two interrelated ways.

First, Hauerwas defines witness as obedient peaceableness based on the church's understanding of itself as forgiven sinners, but it is not clear how this self-understanding makes evident God's love for the world and demonstrates Christ's transformative, concrete redemption of the world to those outside the Christian tradition. Peaceableness, as Hauerwas describes it, does not amount to actions that exemplify Bonhoeffer's "deed which interprets itself," a concept that Hauerwas quotes and endorses in his engagement with Bonhoeffer in *Performing the Faith: Bonhoeffer and the Practice of Nonviolence* (Grand Rapids, Mich.: Brazos Press, 2004). Hauerwas's proposal for ecclesial witness would be more compelling if he grounded peaceableness not simply in the church's forgiven sin but in public activities characterized by confession and repentance. A theology of public witness based on confession and repentance paints a more realistic picture of the visible church by incorporating the church's exposed failures into the logic of witness itself.

Second, the church's public witness should clearly communicate that Christ (and the body of Christ) is for, not against, the world. Hauerwas's project does not communicate this to the extent he intends; his rhetoric of the church as peaceable and the world as violent positions the church and the world as fundamentally antagonistic. At root, Hauerwas's theology lacks an appreciation for the christological fact that the world, like the church, stands under God's judgment and mercy. The functional antagonism between the church and the world is most clearly articulated in Hauerwas's description of democratic liberalism, which he defines as a totalizing and coercive reality. My theology of public witness serves as a corrective and shows that the church need not define itself against liberalism's (real or imagined) totalizing attempts because Christ encompasses divine and human reality in its totality—and Christ does so in a way that defies totalizing dominance. Bonhoeffer's theology places the church in the midst of the world both as a community visibly distinct because it has the language and activity of confession unto repentance and as one in open solidarity with the world because of its shared sin and redemption. Such solidarity reveals the permeability between the church and the world that allows and necessitates shared public activity, while the singular dimension of Hauerwas's model more strictly delimits boundaries and exposes him to criticisms of sectarianism.

In *Performing the Faith*, Hauerwas brings more explicitly into the conversation about nonviolence the fact that the Christian community "may be implicated... in forms of violence we have not recognized or have chosen to ignore," and he mentions that acknowledging this may witness to the violence present within all of our lives (180–181, 208). Still, according to Hauerwas, the church's primary truthful witness is not the confession of its complicity in sin and violence but is the "peaceableness" itself. The truthfulness of Christian claims about the kingdom of God must be evidenced by lives lived truthfully in accordance with that peace. Bonhoeffer, in contrast, refers to "ultimate honesty," or the church's most truthful witness, as confession of sin leading to repentance. Both Bonhoeffer and Hauerwas share a desire for the recovery of the political significance of a visible church, and it is to this concern that Hauerwas points when denying criticism of sectarianism. Hauerwas, however, misinterprets witness and the thrust of Bonhoeffer's call for a visible church as the church's capacity to make *God* visible (44–45). Although Bonhoeffer highlights the necessity of a visible church, he does not equate this with God's visibility nor with Christian holiness but with the willingness to enter directly into the world's suffering, confess sin, and repent by accepting responsibility for injustice.

5. Dietrich Bonhoeffer, *Berlin: 1932–1933*, ed. Larry L. Rasmussen, trans. Isabel Best and David Higgins, Vol. 12 of *Dietrich Bonhoeffer Works*, 16 vols. (Minneapolis: Fortress Press, 1996), 302.

6. Bonhoeffer, *Ökumene, Universität, Pfarramt 1931–1932*, eds. Eberhard Amelung and Christoph Strohm, Vol. 11 of *Dietrich Bonhoeffer Works*, 16 vols. (Minneapolis: Fortress Press, 1994), 459.

7. See Hunsinger, *How to Read Karl Barth: The Shape of His Theology* (New York: Oxford University Press, 1991), 234–280.

8. Andreas Pangritz argues that Barth and Bonhoeffer's later theologies are each governed by Colossians 1:17, which testifies to an expansive inclusivity that takes seriously the

integrity of a realm outside the Christian religion. Even though Barth does not directly reference Bonhoeffer, Barth agrees most substantially with Bonhoeffer's theology in the section explored below, "The Glory of the Mediator." See Andreas Pangritz, *Karl Barth in the Theology of Dietrich Bonhoeffer*, trans. Barbara and Martin Rumsheidt (Grand Rapids, Mich.: Eerdmans, 2000), 134–137.

9. Karl Barth, *Church Dogmatics* IV/3: *The Doctrine of Reconciliation*, ed. G. W. Bromiley and T. F. Torrance, trans. G. W. Bromiley et al. (Edinburgh, Scotland: T&T Clark, 1976), 135. Hereafter "*CD*" replaces *Church Dogmatics* in the notes.

10. For a complete text of the Barmen Declaration see the appendix of Arthur C. Cochrane, *The Church's Confession under Hitler* (Philadelphia: Westminster Press, 1962).

11. Barth, *CD* IV/3, 87. In this section I draw significantly from Hunsinger's study, "Secular plurals of the Truth" in *How to Read Karl Barth*. Hunsinger describes the "normativity, superiority and singularity" of the one Word of God on pages 247–253.

12. Barth *CD* IV/3, 87, 91.

13. Ibid., 99.

14. Ibid., 111.

15. Ibid., 91.

16. Ibid., 46, 75.

17. Ibid., 86.

18. Ibid., 46, 77.

19. Ibid., 46.

20. Ibid., 96, 107.

21. Ibid., 130, 126.

22. Ibid., 114. Barth also speaks of the church as "witness to truth" or "witnesses of witnesses" in his address, "The Word of God and the Task of Ministry," *The Word of God and the Word of Man* (Gloucester, Mass.: Peter Smith, 1978), 209, 216.

23. Barth, *CD* IV/3, 98.

24. Ibid., 123.

25. Ibid., 114–115. Barth's category of witness sheds some light on how Bonhoeffer can assert that his context of a world come of age provides a fresh perspective on the Christian God. In Barth's language, the world come of age is a secular parable of the kingdom that unwittingly witnesses to Christ letting himself "be pushed out of the world and onto the cross" (Bonhoeffer, *Letters and Papers* DBWE 8, 479).

26. For discussions of Barth's understanding of Christianity's unique relationship to Judaism see Eugene F. Rogers, "Supplementing Barth on Jews and Gender: Identifying God by Anagogy and the Spirit," *Modern Theology* 14, no. 1 (1998): 43–81; and Eberhard Busch, *Unter dem Bogen des einen Bundes: Karl Barth und die Juden 1933–1945* (Neukirchen-Vluyn, Germany: Neukirchner Verlag, 1996).

27. Hunsinger, *How to Read Karl Barth*, 270.

28. Barth, *CD* IV/3, 110, 122–127.

29. Ibid., 129.

30. Robert Wuthnow, *America and the Challenges of Religious Diversity* (Princeton, N.J.: Princeton University Press, 2005), 6.

31. The study conducted in-depth personal interviews in fourteen metropolitan areas in various regions of the country. The Christians interviewed for Wuthnow's book vary in denominational affiliation; the only demographic factor common to all the Christians interviewed is that they are members of a church whose building is within the immediate

vicinity of a mosque, temple, or synagogue. See Wuthnow, *America and the Challenges of Religious Diversity*, 5–7, and notes on pages 315–316.

32. There is an interesting academic subfield arising around "theologies of religious pluralism," but it has not yet filtered down into a conversation in which the average churchgoer participates. These works include Mark S. Heim, *The Depth of the Riches: A Trinitarian Theology of Religious Ends* (Grand Rapids, Mich.: Eerdmans, 2001); Paul J. Griffiths, *Christianity through Non-Christian Eyes* (Maryknoll, N.Y.: Orbis Books, 1990); Gavin D'Costa, *Christianity and World Religions* (Oxford: Wiley-Blackwell, 2009); and Paul Hedges and Alan Race, eds., *Christian Approaches to Other Faiths* (London: SCM, 2008). See also David H. Jensen, "Religionless Christianity and Vulnerable Discipleship: The Interfaith Promise of Bonhoeffer's Theology," *Journal of Ecumenical Studies* 38, no. 2–3 (2001): 151–167, for an examination of the interfaith resources in Bonhoeffer's theology.

33. For examples of scriptures in which the persons of the Trinity witness to one another, see Mark 1:11, John 5:37, John 8:18, John 15:26, 1 John 5:6–9.

34. See N. T. Wright, *Surprised by Hope: Rethinking Heaven, the Resurrection, and the Mission of the Church* (New York: HarperOne, 2008) for an argument that Christian understandings of salvation have been more influenced by a platonic notion of disembodied souls going to heaven than by the biblical witness of the resurrection of the body and the coming of God's kingdom.

35. Wuthnow, *America and the Challenges of Religious Diversity*, 149.

36. Ibid., 156.

37. For a full description of what Wuthnow means by "spiritual shopper" see ibid., pages 106–129.

38. Wuthnow, *America and the Challenges of Religious Diversity*, 143–158.

39. Ibid., 159.

40. An important exception is the Presbyterian Church of America, whose pastors are often trained at Westminster Theological Seminary (which broke in 1929 from the Theological Seminary of the Presbyterian Church, now named Princeton Theological Seminary, largely over what they deemed "modernist influences" like Karl Barth's theology). See http://www.wts.edu/about/history.html. The question for Christians who rightly acknowledge that faith is divine gift is whether Pauline theology and the whole witness of scripture points toward limited atonement or universal redemption. See Bruce McCormack's essay, "So That He May Be Merciful to All: Karl Barth and the Problem of Universalism," presented at the 2007 Second Annual Conference on Karl Barth at Princeton Theological Seminary, "Karl Barth and American Evangelicals: Friends or Foes?" and published in *Karl Barth and American Evangelicalism*, ed. Bruce L. McCormack and Clifford B. Anderson (Grand Rapids, Mich.: Eerdmans, 2011). McCormack argues that there is an unresolved tension in Paul's letters between a limited and universal understanding of atonement and so the church should neither promote a *doctrine* of limited atonement nor a *doctrine* of universal salvation; either doctrine restricts the freedom of God. Although I agree that a doctrine of universal salvation is unsubstantiated in scripture, the church is called, I argue, to witness to the truly good news of expansive redemption.

41. Wuthnow, *America and the Challenges of Religious Diversity*, 170.

42. Ibid., 177. I examine Paul's apocalyptic theology in chapter four. For a helpful discussion of passages in scripture that point toward a narrower view of salvation, see Hans Urs von Balthasar, *Dare We Hope: "That All Men Be Saved"?* trans. David Kipp (San Francisco: Ignatius, 1988).

43. Wuthnow, *America and the Challenges of Religious Diversity*, 177.

44. Ibid., 176.

45. Ibid., 183.

46. Ibid., 159, 175.

47. See note 33.

48. Wuthnow, *America and the Challenges of Religious Diversity*, 187.

49. Paul A. Bramadat, *The Church on the World's Turf: An Evangelical Christian Group at a Secular University* (New York: Oxford University Press, 2000), 12.

50. Ibid., 66.

51. Ibid., 119–138.

52. Ibid., 25.

53. Ibid., 128.

54. Addressing the idea of "mission fields" Bramadat says, "All faculty and students are, in a manner of speaking, witnessing 'targets'" (120–122). While Bramadat does not say that the students refer to others as "targets," interestingly, a similar evangelical fellowship group, Campus Crusade for Christ (along with its high school offshoot, Student Venture) does specifically teach students to find "target groups"—the clubs or sports teams in which they are involved that serve as their primary "mission fields."

55. Bramadat, *The Church on the World's Turf*, 135–136 (emphasis mine).

56. Wuthnow also speaks of "witnessing opportunities." Wuthnow, *America and the Challenges of Religious Diversity*, 171.

57. Bramadat, *The Church on the World's Turf*, 120, 58–59.

58. Marsha G. Witten, *All Is Forgiven: The Secular Message in American Protestantism* (Princeton, N.J.: Princeton University Press, 1993), 106–134; 125, 134.

59. Bramadat, *The Church on the World's Turf*, 135.

60. IVCF as well as other evangelical student groups like Campus Crusade for Christ stress obedience to the "Great Commission," where Jesus says, "All authority in heaven and on earth has been given to me. Therefore, go and make disciples of all nations, baptizing them in the name of the Father and of the Son and of the Holy Spirit and teaching them to obey everything I have commanded you" (Matt. 28:16–20). Based on their understanding of witness, these campus groups interpret the activities of making disciples and baptizing them as leading others "to make a decision for Christ." In other words, discipleship refers not to following the life and teachings of Jesus in the Gospels but to strategic action aimed at saving individual souls. See Bramadat, *The Church on the World's Turf*, 122.

61. Karl Barth, *CD* II/2: *The Doctrine of God*, ed. G. W. Bromiley and T. F. Torrance, trans. G. W. Bromiley (Edinburgh, Scotland: T&T Clark, 2001), §28, 273.

62. Bonhoeffer falls into the trap of unreflectively assuming whiteness as the norm; thus he critiques North American theology in the essay "Protestantism without Reformation" when what he clearly means, given his praise of African American sermons and worship, is white theology.

63. Eberhard Bethge, *Dietrich Bonhoeffer: A Biography*, ed. Victoria J. Barnett (Minneapolis: Augsburg Fortress, 2000), 160.

64. Dietrich Bonhoeffer, "Protestantism without Reformation," *No Rusty Swords: Letters, Lectures and Notes 1928–1936 from the Collected Works of Dietrich Bonhoeffer*, ed. Edwin H. Robertson (New York: Harper & Row, 1965), 113. Also see Josiah U. Young, "Dietrich Bonhoeffer and Reinhold Niebuhr: Their Ethics, Views on Karl Barth, and Perspectives on African-Americans," *Bonhoeffer's Intellectual Formation: Theology and Philosophy in His*

Thought, ed. Peter Frick (Tübingen, Germany: Mohr Siebeck, 2008), 292–300; and Josiah U. Young, *No Difference in Fare: Dietrich Bonhoeffer and the Problem of Racism* (Grand Rapids, Mich.: Eerdmans, 1998).

65. Bonhoeffer, "Protestantism without Reformation," 116.

66. Bethge, *Dietrich Bonhoeffer: A Biography*, 658.

67. Ibid., 166.

68. Bonhoeffer, "Protestantism without Reformation," 116–117.

69. Stephen R. Haynes and Lori Brandt Hale, *Bonhoeffer for Armchair Theologians* (Louisville, Ky.: Westminster John Knox, 2009), 11.

70. Dietrich Bonhoeffer, *Barcelona, Berlin, New York: 1928–1931*, ed. Clifford J. Green, trans. Douglas W. Stott, Vol. 10 of *Dietrich Bonhoeffer Works*, 16 vols. (Minneapolis: Fortress Press, 2008), 353–354.

71. Karl Barth, *The Word of God and the Word of Man* (Gloucester, Mass.: Peter Smith, 1978), 18–19 (emphasis mine).

72. Karl Barth, *The Epistle to the Romans*, trans. Edwyn C. Hoskyns, 6th ed. (Oxford: Oxford University Press, 1968), 56, 38.

73. Luther also views repentance as a guard against false comfort. See theses 92 and 95 of his 1517 "Disputation on the Power and Efficacy of Indulgences," in Timothy F. Lull, ed., *Martin Luther's Basic Theological Writings*, 2nd ed. (Minneapolis: Fortress Press, 2005), 46.

74. Barth, *The Word of God and the Word of Man*, 67.

75. Ibid., 68, 74.

76. Ibid., 87.

77. Ibid., 20, 39, 41.

78. Ibid., 37–39.

79. Ibid., 33, 39–40, 45 (emphasis mine).

80. The Roman Catholic theologian Karl Adam first used the imagery of a bomb dropping on the playground in the June 1926 issue of the *Hochland*. It was later quoted by John McConnadine in his article, "The Teachings of Karl Barth: A Positive Movement in German Theology," *Hibbert Journal* 25 (1927): 385–386. This imagery is common knowledge in theological circles, although the reference is often not cited. I borrow this footnote from Hauerwas, *With the Grain of the Universe*, 152, note 27.

81. Barth, *The Word of God and the Word of Man*, 196. See McCormack, *Karl Barth's Critically Realistic Dialectical Theology*, 31–125, for further discussion on the nature of Barth's break with liberal theology. My text honors gender inclusivity. In the spirit of preserving the integrity of the work of other authors like Barth and Kierkegaard, though, I will retain their original language. The Fortress Press *Dietrich Bonhoeffer Works* English Language Edition has incorporated gender inclusivity into its translations, with the exception of reference to God. When I use translations that have not done so, I adapt the language in the quote to adhere to gender inclusivity.

82. Barth, *The Word of God and the Word of Man*, 170–171.

83. Barth, *The Epistle to the Romans*, 110. See Job 42.

84. Ibid., 40, 85.

85. Barth, *The Epistle to the Romans*, 90. Barth refers to Kierkegaard's "infinite qualitative distinction" in the "Preface to the Second Edition" of *The Epistle to the Romans*, 10.

86. Ibid., 45.

87. Barth, *The Epistle to the Romans*, 48–49.

88. In "Biographical Context," *New Studies in Bonhoeffer's Ethics*, ed. William J. Peck (Lewiston, N.Y.: Edwin Mellen Press, 1987), Robin W. Lovin argues that *Ethics* is, in part, Bonhoeffer's proposal for a Christian ethic in light of Barth's radical critique of human morality. See pages 69–74.

89. See McCormack, *Karl Barth's Critically Realistic Dialectical Theology* for a discussion of how Barth seems not to have an ethic (170–173) and on Barth's critical negation of all human ethics (273–280). McCormack argues that Barth's discussion of ethics is a main weakness in *The Epistle to the Romans* (179–180) and that "witness" is the primary ethical category for Barth in *Church Dogmatics* (277).

90. Barth, *The Epistle to the Romans*, 97.

91. Barth, *The Word of God and the Word of Man*, 82.

92. Barth, *The Epistle to the Romans*, 41, 59, 68, 106.

93. Barth, *CD* IV/2 §66.3, 552.

94. Jesus also refuses to claim innocence before Pilate, "But he gave him no answer, not even to a single charge, so that the governor was greatly amazed" (Matt. 27:11–13; see also Mark 15:1–5), and only speaks words that condemn himself, "All of them asked, 'Are you, then, the Son of God?' He said to them, 'You say that I am.' Then they said, 'What further testimony do we need? We have heard it ourselves from his own lips'" (Luke 22:66–71).

95. Because I rely on sociological studies for my examples, I employ the studies' definitions of each subgroup being depicted.

96. Falwell's Moral Majority and Robertson's Christian Coalition should not be conflated, given the doctrinal differences among their followers. Most notably, Falwell appealed to fundamentalist and evangelical Christians and Robertson reaches Pentecostal and charismatic Christians. For a fuller discussion of differences, see Susan Friend Harding, *The Book of Jerry Falwell: Fundamentalist Language and Politics* (Princeton, N.J.: Princeton University Press, 2000), 18–19.

97. Harding, *The Book of Jerry Falwell*, 10–11.

98. Joshua Yates, "11/9/1989 to 9/11/2001 and Beyond: The Return of Jeremiad and the Specter of Secularization," *Prophesies of Godlessness: Predictions of America's Imminent Secularization from the Puritans to the Present Day*, eds. Charles Mathewes and Christopher McKnight Nichols (New York: Oxford University Press, 2008), 217–218.

99. Harding, *The Book of Jerry Falwell*, 10–11. The Christian Coalition activist is quoted in Yates, "The Return of Jeremiad and the Specter of Secularization," 219.

100. Harding, *The Book of Jerry Falwell*, 14–15.

101. Quoted in Yates, "The Return of the Jeremiad and the Specter of Secularization," 219.

102. Ibid., 211–212, 229.

103. Ibid., 212.

104. See Mark A. Noll, Nathan O. Hatch, and George M. Marsden, *The Search for Christian America* (Westchester, Ill.: Crossway Books, 1983) for an argument that early America was not "uniquely, distinctly or predominantly Christian" such that there is a "lost golden age" from which Christians can measure present society (17).

105. Yates, "The Return of Jeremiad and the Specter of Secularization," 212–213.

106. For some recent critiques of the Religious Right see Randall Balmer, *Thy Kingdom Come: How the Religious Right Distorts the Faith and Threatens America, An Evangelical's Lament* (New York: Basic Books 2006); John Clifford Green, *The Values Campaign: The Christian Right and the 2004 Elections* (Washington, D.C.: Georgetown University Press,

2006); Sam Harris, *Letter to a Christian Nation* (New York: Knopf, 2006); Michael Lerner, *The Left Hand of God: Taking Back Our Country from the Religious Right* (San Francisco: HarperSanFrancisco, 2006); Chris Hedges, *American Fascists: The Christian Right and the War on America* (New York: Free Press, 2007); and Charles Marsh, *Wayward Christian Soldiers* (New York: Oxford University Press, 2007).

107. Barth, *Word of God and Word of Man*, 67.

108. Yates, "The Return of Jeremiad and the Specter of Secularization," 213.

109. Christian Smith, *Christian America? What Evangelicals Really Want* (Berkeley: University of California Press, 2000), 2–9, 13, 18. Smith's study of "ordinary evangelicals" does not distinguish black or other minority conservative Christians from white conservative Christians. Black churches fall under all headings: fundamentalist, evangelical, Pentecostal, and mainline (13). Wuthnow and Evans's edited volume, *The Quiet Hand of God*, shows that 9 percent of all mainline Christians are members of a minority group (12).

110. Smith, *Christian America?* 18, 21, 45.

111. Bramadat, *The Church on the World's Turf*, 120–121.

112. Smith, *Christian America?* 48.

113. Ibid., 115. Indeed, at least one influential evangelical para-church ministry, Bill Bright's Campus Crusade for Christ, interprets discipleship primarily in terms of verbal evangelism (until recently perhaps; see *God's Politics*, 357–361, about Wallis's influence on Bright). Also see Nancy Tatom Ammerman, *Pillars of Faith: American Congregations and Their Partners* (Berkeley: University of California Press, 2005), 116–131, for a discussion about the conservative Christian concern that focus on physical needs will distract from the more important task of saving souls.

114. In *The Presence of the Kingdom*, trans. Olive Wyon (Colorado Springs: Helmers & Howard, 1989), Jacques Ellul argues against interpreting "salt of the earth" and "light of the world" as a call to be moral or adhere to certain moral principles. Instead Ellul describes being salt and light as being a witness to Christ in a manner quite similar to Barth. See chapter 1, "The Christian in the World," 1–20.

115. Smith, *Christian America?* 109, 158–159.

116. Ibid., 18, 99.

117. Ibid., 48, 60.

118. Ronald J. Sider, *The Chicago Declaration* (Carol Stream, Ill.: Creation House, 1974), 1–3.

119. Brantley Gasaway, "An Alternative Soul of Politics: The Rise of Contemporary Progressive Evangelicals," Ph.D. diss., University of North Carolina, 2007. For an example of a contemporary progressive evangelical movement linked to the work of Jim Wallis that emphasizes conversation and avoids the pitfalls of morality discourse, see the Web site of New Monasticism, http://www.newmonasticism.org/, led in part by Jonathan Wilson-Hartgrove.

120. Jim Wallis, *The Call to Conversion: Why Faith Is Always Personal but Never Private* (New York: HarperCollins, 2005), xi.

121. Jim Wallis, *God's Politics: Why the Right Gets It Wrong and the Left Doesn't Get It* (New York: HarperCollins, 2005), xix, 4–5.

122. Ibid., 3.

123. Ibid., 75 and cover jacket.

124. Ibid., 18–19.

125. Ibid., xviii, 97, 105, 144, 150, 153, 157, 145.

126. Ibid., xix, xxi, xxiii.

127. Ibid., 73–74.

128. Ibid., 87, 241, 295 (emphasis mine).

129. For examples of how Wallis equates moral and theological thinking see pages 13, 32, 60, 212.

130. See Jennifer Ayres, "'With an Urgency Born of This Hope...': A Constructive Practical Theology of Reformed Social Witness Practice," Ph.D. diss., Emory University, 2007. Ayers argues that biblical mandates may be used to orient the content of Christian behavior but that appealing to mandates should not replace engagement in sustained theological reflection, which is central to the practice of social witness itself. She argues that, in this sense, Christians need to "get beyond loose ties to Scripture."

131. Wallis, *God's Politics*, 47, 68.

132. Jim Wallis, *The Great Awakening: Reviving Faith and Politics in a Post-Religious Right America* (New York: HarperOne, 2008).

133. For example, Wallis's critique that George W. Bush makes international policy a "moral battle between good and evil" loses its prophetic edge when Wallis himself advocates the use of morality discourse. In *God's Politics*, Wallis also criticizes the former president's blasphemous use of the Gospel of John on the first anniversary of 9/11. Bush said, "This ideal of America is the hope of all mankind... That hope still lights our way. And the light shines in the darkness. And the darkness has not overcome it." Wallis certainly has the capacity for more sophisticated christological thinking than he displays as a popular public figure. Here he reminds the readers that the light in the darkness is "the Word of God and the light of Christ. It's not about America and its values" (142).

134. For an example of morality discourse among politically liberal Christians see the March 2007 statement against the Iraq War, "Ending the War Is a Moral Not a Political Issue," on the National Council of Church's Internet advocacy site, http://www.faithfulamerica.org. While Faithful America often avoids the kind of morality discourse I have been describing and offers instead more nuanced explanations about why they think people of faith should take a particular stand on certain issues, this example shows how easy it is to fall into a superficial call to do what is "moral." As the example of Jim Wallis and *Sojourners* shows, the content of a message may be prophetic while the language appeals to a flattened sense of morality. When this happens, the rhetoric reduces the prophetic power of the message.

135. Mainline Protestants may also be distinguished from more conservative Christians by their denominations' participation in the twentieth century's progressive ecumenical movement through the Federal Council of Churches, which emphasized international and national civic responsibility. The Federal Council of Churches changed its name in 1950 to the National Council of Churches and continues its ecumenical advocacy work. The NCC's work is perhaps most visible today through its Internet advocacy interfaith community, Faithful America. Mainline WASPs (white Anglo-Saxon Protestants) may also seem more liberal than evangelicals given that, to a limited extent, a minority of white mainline leaders became active in the civil rights movement and Vietnam War protests. Liberal Protestants often articulate a progressive vision although efforts at racial equality today are "largely symbolic." Mainline Christians look with nostalgia to the Civil Rights Movement as the "peak of liberal social activism" even though white liberal congregations were no more willing to sacrifice their control over society than conservative churches. See Wuthnow and Evans, "Introduction"; Laura R. Olson, "Mainline Protestant Washington Offices and the Political Lives of Clergy"; and Bradford Verter, "Furthering the Freedom Struggle," in *The*

Quiet Hand of God: Faith Based Activism and the Public Role of Mainline Protestantism, eds. Robert Wuthnow and John H. Evans (Berkeley: University of California Press, 2002), 77, 183, 186.

136. Wuthnow and Evans, "Introduction," 15; Olson, "Mainline Protestant Washington Offices and the Political Lives of Clergy," 55.

137. Wuthnow and Evans, "Introduction," 21.

138. Mark Chaves, Helen M. Giesel, and William Tsitsos, "Religious Variations in Public Presence: Evidence from the National Congregations Study," in *The Quiet Hand of God: Faith Based Activism and the Public Role of Mainline Protestantism*, eds. Robert Wuthnow and John H. Evans (Berkeley: University of California Press, 2002), 122.

139. Wuthnow and Evans, "Introduction," 5.

140. Robert Wuthnow, "Beyond Quiet Influence? Possibilities for the Protestant Mainline," in *The Quiet Hand of God: Faith Based Activism and the Public Role of Mainline Protestantism*, eds. Robert Wuthnow and John H. Evans (Berkeley: University of California Press, 2002), 398.

141. Wuthnow and Evans, "Introduction," 11–18.

142. Chaves, Giesel, and Tsitsos, "Religious Variations in Public Presence," 122–124.

143. Wuthnow, "Beyond Quiet Influence?" 401.

144. Wuthnow and Evans, "Introduction," 16.

145. Chaves, Giesel, and Tsitsos, "Religious Variations in Public Presence," 108; Wuthnow, "Beyond Quiet Influence?" 385.

146. Nancy T. Ammerman, "Connecting Mainline Protestant Churches with Public Life," in *The Quiet Hand of God: Faith Based Activism and the Public Role of Mainline Protestantism*, eds. Robert Wuthnow and John H. Evans (Berkeley: University of California Press, 2002), 77, 148.

147. Mark Chaves, *Congregations in America* (Cambridge, Mass.: Harvard University Press, 2004), 59–60.

148. Chaves, *Congregation in America*, 46–50, 56; Ammerman, "Connecting Mainline Protestant Churches" 131; Wuthnow, "Beyond Quiet Influence?" 393.

149. Chaves, *Congregation in America*, 51. See Wuthnow, "Beyond Quiet Influence?" 390, for an overview of all the public activities in which mainline congregations are involved (table 15.4).

150. Ammerman, "Connecting Mainline Protestant Churches," 131.

151. "Form" or *Gestalt* is a significant category in Bonhoeffer's theology. For example, the christology lectures speak of the "form of Christ" as word, sacrament, and church, and of Christ taking the form of a sinner in the likeness of sinful flesh (*Berlin: 1932–1933* DBWE 12, 315–323). In *Discipleship* Bonhoeffer speaks of the church's imitation of Christ as conformation to Christ (see DBWE 4, chapter 13, "The Image of Christ," 281–288). In *Ethics*, Bonhoeffer also defines Christian ethics as conformation to Christ (see "Ethics as Conformation," DBWE 6, 76–102).

152. Bonhoeffer, *Letters and Papers* DBWE 8, 362–364.

153. Ibid., 389.

154. Clifford Green, *Bonhoeffer: A Theology of Sociology*, 269.

155. Bonhoeffer's inquiry in prison into a "nonreligious interpretation" of biblical concepts arose, in part, from engaging with Rudolf Bultmann's program of demythologization, the process of preserving the essential message of the New Testament, the *kerygma*, for the scientifically and technologically sophisticated modern individual by freeing it from its

"apocalyptic" and "mythological" backdrop. Bultmann asserts that much of the New Testament is meaningless for rational, modern persons who are open to the kerygmatic essence but closed to the "mythical view" of the world, such as a three-storied cosmology that shapes doctrines and creeds. Instead of discarding these elements, Bultmann seeks to reinterpret them in order to discover their deeper existential and universal meaning.

156. Contrary to the majority of German scholarship at the time, Ernst Feil rightly observed this in his 1971 study.

157. See Ernst Feil, *The Theology of Dietrich Bonhoeffer*, trans. Martin Rumscheidt (Philadelphia: Fortress Press, 1985), 192–194. Quote from Dietrich Bonhoeffer, *Gesammelte Schriften*, vol. 3, ed. Eberhard Bethge, 6 vols. (Munich, Germany: Chr. Kaiser Verlag, 1958–1974), 41. Translated in Feil, *The Theology of Dietrich Bonhoeffer*, 200.

158. Bonhoeffer, *Letters and Papers* DBWE 8, 389.

159. Ibid. Translation mine.

160. Ibid., 365, 373.

161. See Eberhard Bethge, *Dietrich Bonhoeffer: A Biography*, ed. Victoria Barnett, trans. Eric Mosbacher et al. (Minneapolis: Augsburg Fortress, 2000), 880–884. For more on the arcane discipline see John W. Matthews, "Responsible Sharing of the Mystery of Christian Faith: *Disciplina Arcani* in the Life and Theology of Dietrich Bonhoeffer," *Dialog* 25, no. 1 (1986): 19–25; also published in Geffrey B. Kelly and C. John Weborg, eds., *Reflections on Bonhoeffer: Essays in Honor of F. Burton Nelson* (Chicago: Covenant Publications, 1999), 114–128. See Roger Poole, "Bonhoeffer and the Arcane Discipline," in *Ethical Responsibility: Bonhoeffer's Legacy to the Churches*, eds., John D. Godsey and Geffrey B. Kelly (New York: Edwin Mellen Press, 1982), 271–291. See also Kenneth Surin, "*Contemptus Mundi* and the Disenchanted World: Bonhoeffer's 'Secret Discipline' and Adorno's 'Strategy of Hibernation,'" *Journal of the American Academy of Religion* 53, no. 3 (1985): 383–410; and Barry Harvey, "The Body Politic of Christ: Theology, Social Analysis, and Bonhoeffer's Arcane Discipline," *Modern Theology* 13, no. 3 (1997): 319–346.

162. Bonhoeffer, *Letters and Papers* DBWE 8, 390, and Dietrich Bonhoeffer, *Letters and Papers from Prison*, trans. Reginald Fuller et al. (New York: Touchstone, 1997), 300. For a superb study of Bonhoeffer's use of the secret disciple, see Jonathan Malesic, *Secret Faith in the Public Square: An Argument for the Concealment of Christian Identity* (Grand Rapids, Mich.: Brazos Press, 2009). On the surface, Malesic's argument for the concealment of Christian identity in public life and my concern for a particular and distinct Christian witness based on confession and repentance may seem diametrically opposed. However, given the nature of confession unto repentance as public witness, Malesic and my arguments generally agree more than they disagree in that we both call for a humble Christian witness in public life grounded in an understanding of christological hiddenness (see my chapter 3). For another use of Bonhoeffer's secret discipline for the U.S. context see Marsh, *Wayward Christian Soldiers*, 147–150.

163. Geffrey B. Kelly and F. Burton Nelson, *A Testament to Freedom: The Essential Writings of Dietrich Bonhoeffer* (New York: HarperCollins, 1995), 86.

Chapter 3

1. Ernst Feil argues in *The Theology of Dietrich Bonhoeffer* (Philadelphia: Fortress Press, 1985), 61–64, that *Sanctorum Communio* lacks an explicit christology. In this work, Bonhoeffer examines the church as "Christ existing as community," but the dissertation's point of departure is not shaped by christology, Feil says. Still, *Sanctorum Communio* offers

insight into the progression of Bonhoeffer's christology in that the dissertation examines the extent to which the reality of God's revelation in Christ simultaneously establishes the church as a component of revelation.

2. For more on witness within the life of the Trinity see Eugene F. Rogers Jr., *Sexuality and the Christian Body* (Oxford: Blackwell, 1999), 269–275.

3. Rowan D. Williams, "The Body's Grace," in *Our Selves, Our Souls and Bodies*, ed. Charles Hefling (Boston: Cowley Publications, 1996), 58–68. Cited in Rogers, *Sexuality and the Christian Body*.

4. For a helpful essay on the topic, see Clifford Green, "Trinity and Christology in Bonhoeffer and Barth," *Union Seminary Quarterly Review* 60, no. 1–2 (2006): 1–22.

5. Dietrich Bonhoeffer, *Berlin: 1932–1933*, ed. Larry L. Rasmussen, trans. Isabel Best and David Higgins, Vol. 12 of *Dietrich Bonhoeffer Works*, 16 vols. (Minneapolis: Fortress Press, 1996), 302–303. I utilize both DBWE 12 and *Christ the Center* in my discussion of Bonhoeffer's christology lectures. For a helpful note describing the reasons for discrepancies in these texts, see DBWE 12, 299, footnote 1.

6. Thus, Bonhoeffer's theology asserts what the seventeenth-century Lutheran scholastics rejected—being human really impacts the Son of God. For a helpful discussion of the *genus tapeinoticum* (genus of humility), which Lutheran scholastics rejected, see Bruce McCormack, "Karl Barth's Christology as a Resource for a Reformed Version of Kenoticism," *International Journal of Systematic Theology* 8, no. 3 (2006): 243–251.

7. Bonhoeffer says in *Discipleship*, "This is why Jesus accepted sinners (Luke 15:2): he bore them in his own body." Dietrich Bonhoeffer, *Discipleship*, ed. Geffrey B. Kelly and John D. Godsey, trans. Barbara Green and Reinhard Krauss, Vol. 4 of *Dietrich Bonhoeffer Works*, 16 vols. (Minneapolis: Fortress Press, 2003), 215. Barth's theology affirms this even more poignantly in *Church Dogmatics* IV/1, ed. G. W. Bromiley and T. F. Torrance, trans. G. W. Bromiley (Edinburgh, Scotland: T&T Clark, 1980), §59. Barth says, "God goes into the far country for this to happen. He becomes what he had not previously been. He takes into unity with His divine being a quite different, a creaturely, and indeed a sinful being.... He does not deny, let alone abandon and leave behind or even diminish His Godhead to do this" (203). God remains God while taking into Godself sinful humanity, because, Barth says earlier in §59, "The humility in which He dwells and acts in Jesus Christ is not alien to him, but proper to him... He is among us in humility, our God, God for us, as that which He is in Himself, in the most inward depth of His Godhead" (193).

8. Dietrich Bonhoeffer, *Letters and Papers from Prison*, ed. John W. de Gruchy, trans. Isabel Best et al., Vol. 8 of *Dietrich Bonhoeffer Works*, 16 vols. (Minneapolis: Fortress Press, 2010), 362.

9. Ibid., 364, 373.

10. I say that Bonhoeffer's theology finds "support" and not "precedent" in Barth because the influence of Barth and Bonhoeffer on one another is at times difficult to unravel in detail. Certainly Barth's early theology first influenced Bonhoeffer. There are also traces of Bonhoeffer's theology in Barth's later theology, which was published after Bonhoeffer's death. For studies that show the interconnection of Bonhoeffer and Barth's theologies, see Andreas Pangritz, *Karl Barth in the Theology of Dietrich Bonhoeffer*, trans. Barbara and Martin Rumscheidt (Grand Rapids, Mich.: Eerdmans, 2000) and Charles Marsh, *Reclaiming Dietrich Bonhoeffer: The Promise of His Theology* (New York: Oxford University Press, 1994).

11. Markus Wriedt, "Luther's Theology," trans. Katharina Gustavs, in *The Cambridge Companion to Martin Luther*, ed. Donald K. McKim (Cambridge: Cambridge University Press, 2003), 94.

12. Timothy F. Lull, *Martin Luther's Basic Theological Writings*, 2nd ed. (Minneapolis: Fortress Press, 2005), 41. The Latin form *poenitentiam agite* and the German phrase *tut Busse* may be translated either "repent" or "do penance." See editor's footnote 3.

13. Bonhoeffer, *Letters and Papers* DBWE 8, 480.

14. Lull, *Martin Luther's Basic Theological Writings*, 41.

15. Lull, *Martin Luther's Basic Theological Writings*, 326 (from *The Small Catechism*). See Jane E. Strohl, "Luther's Spiritual Journey," in *The Cambridge Companion to Martin Luther*, ed. Donald K. McKim (Cambridge: Cambridge University Press, 2003), 153–155. Also see Ronald K. Rittgers, "Private Confession in the German Reformation," and Andrew Purves, "A Confessing Faith: Assent and Penitence in the Reformation Traditions of Luther, Calvin, and Bucer," in *Repentance in Christian Theology*, ed. Mark J. Boda and Gordon T. Smith (Collegeville, Minn.: Liturgical Press, 2006), 189–207, 251–266. Bonhoeffer cites Luther on this in *Discipleship* DBWE 4, 209, 221, 271, and in *Ethics*, trans. Reinhold Krauss, et al., Vol. 6 of *Dietrich Bonhoeffer Works*, 16 vols. (Minneapolis: Fortress Press, 2005), 95.

16. Lull, *Martin Luther's Basic Theological Writings*, 326.

17. Bonhoeffer, *Ethics* DBWE 6, 136. This phrase is from the Catholic Latin Mass and is spoken in the *confiteon*, the confession of sin. It has traditionally been translated "through my fault, through my fault, through my most grievous fault." See page 136, editor's footnote [80].

18. See Wolf Krötke, "Dietrich Bonhoeffer and Martin Luther," in *Bonhoeffer's Intellectual Formation: Theology and Philosophy in His Thought*, ed. Peter Frick (Tübingen, Germany: Mohr Siebeck, 2008), 53–82. See also Heinz Joachim Held, "Schuldübernahme als Ausdruck der Christusnachfolge bei Martin Luther und Dietrich Bonhoeffer," in *Konsequenzen: Dietrich Bonhoeffers Kirchenverständnis heute*, ed. Ernst Feil and Ilse Tödt (Munich, Germany: Kaiser, 1980), 140–168. Held examines the concept of accepting guilt as discipleship in Luther and Bonhoeffer. See Hans-Jürgen Abromeit, *Das Geheimnis Christi: Dietrich Bonhoeffers erfahrungsbezogene Christologie* (Neukirchen-Vluyn, Germany: Neukirckener Verlag, 1991), 349–352. Abromeit also argues that Bonhoeffer gets his notion of the acceptance of guilt from Luther, especially from Luther's understanding of the identity of the church as the body of Christ. Also see Klaus Grünwaldt, Chrstiane Tietz, and Udo Hahn, *Bonhoeffer und Luther: Zentrale Themen inhrer Theologie* (Hanover, Germany: VELKD, 2007).

19. Karl Barth, *CD* IV/1, 172 (emphasis mine).

20. Ibid.

21. See Karl Barth, *Church Dogmatics* IV/2, ed. G. W. Bromiley and T. F. Torrance, trans. G. W. Bromiley (Edinburgh, Scotland: T&T Clark, 1978) §66.4, "The Awakening to Conversion," 566–567.

22. Ibid.

23. Ibid., 555, 560, 582.

24. Ibid., 564.

25. Bonhoeffer, *Letters and Papers* (New York: Touchstone, 1997), 369–370.

26. Barth, *CD* IV/2 §66.4, 583–584 (emphasis mine). Interestingly, Calvin, like Barth after him, alludes to the Christian's participation in Christ's vicarious penance; see Purves, "A Confessing Faith," 256.

27. Barth, *CD* IV/2 §66.4, 577–581.

28. Dietrich Bonhoeffer, *Christ the Center*, trans. Edwin H. Robertson (New York: Harper Collins, 1978), 60.

29. Stanley E. Porter, "Penitence and Repentance in the Epistles," in *Repentance in Christian Theology*, ed. Mark J. Boda and Gordon T. Smith (Collegeville, Minn.: Liturgical Press, 2006), 149–150.

30. Guy Dale Nave Jr., "'Repent, for the Kingdom of God Is at Hand': Repentance in the Synoptic Gospels and Acts," in *Repentance in Christian Theology*, ed. Mark J. Boda and Gordon T. Smith (Collegeville, Minn.: Liturgical Press, 2006), 87–103. Nave builds on William Chamberlain's study, *The Meaning of Repentance* (Philadelphia: Westminster, 1943), 17. Also see Edith M. Humphrey, "'And I Shall Heal Them': Repentance, Turning, and Penitence in the Johannine Writings," in *Repentance in Christian Theology*, ed. Mark J. Boda and Gordon T. Smith (Collegeville, Minn.: Liturgical Press, 2006), 118.

31. Nave, "'Repent, for the Kingdom of God Is at Hand,'" 87–89.

32. Porter, "Penitence and Repentance in the Epistles," 142–145.

33. Nave, "'Repent, for the Kingdom of God Is at Hand,'" 89 (emphasis mine).

34. Ibid.

35. Ibid., 98. For example, Nave argues that those who reject Jesus in the synagogue in Luke 4:18–30, reject God's inclusive acceptance of all people. He says, "The acceptance of Gentiles into the community of God's people required a fundamental change in thinking on the part of those who considered themselves God's chosen ones" (98). This parallels the argument in chapter 2 of this volume that a basic rethinking of Christ's identity and mission is needed among Protestant Christians in the United States that will challenge the church's understanding of its chosen status.

36. Ibid., 90–91.

37. Humphrey, "'And I Shall Heal Them,'" 107, 120–121. Humphrey further argues that the book of Revelation also casts judgment and repentance in the larger drama of the world's redemption. She poignantly writes, "Side by side with the indictment, however, sounds the call for repentance. Here is the paradox: that deaf ears, blind eyes, and hard hearts should be healed.... To the One by whose will all exist and were created... unceasing worship sounds in the City whose gates remain confidently open. Despite the specter of judgment, in the final vision there is no slamming of the holy gates. Instead, we hear the persistent invitation of the Spirit: 'Come'" (120).

38. See footnote 45 below about Bonhoeffer's use of the "right road."

39. Bonhoeffer, *Letters and Papers* DBWE 8, 480.

40. Bonhoeffer, *Letters and Papers* (Touchstone, 1997), 361–362 (emphasis mine).

41. Bonhoeffer, *Letters and Papers* DBWE 8, 482. Scholars examining *Letters and Papers from Prison* tend to interpret Bonhoeffer's writings about faith in a world come of age as a call to human strength but pay less attention to Bonhoeffer's call to participate in Christ's redemptive powerlessness. I will show that a witness based on repentance is both participation in Christ's redemptive powerlessness and a call to strong, responsible action in the world.

42. Geffrey B. Kelly and F. Burton Nelson, *A Testament to Freedom: The Essential Writings of Dietrich Bonhoeffer* (New York: HarperCollins, 1995), 440.

43. Larry L. Rasmussen, *Dietrich Bonhoeffer: Reality and Resistance* (New York: Abingdon Press, 1972), 56.

44. Ibid.

45. Scholars are right to emphasize that a proper interpretation of Bonhoeffer's theology necessitates attention to his historical context. Still, a theology of public witness

rooted within Bonhoeffer's theology and characterized by confession of sin unto repentance embraces more than the highly exceptional circumstances of Bonhoeffer's life. It would only add confusion to digress into how Bonhoeffer's participation in the conspiracy amounts to "sharing in God's sufferings in the worldly life" or to attempt to answer the many questions his historical context raises. For an excellent study of the theological ethics of Bonhoeffer's participation in the conspiracy and an explanation of the historical circumstances surrounding his decisions, see Rasmussen's *Dietrich Bonhoeffer: Reality and Resistance*. Also see Robin W. Lovin, "Biographical Context," *New Studies in Bonhoeffer's Ethics*, ed. William J. Peck (Lewiston, N.Y.: Edwin Mellen Press, 1987), 67–103; and Sabine Dramm, *Dietrich Bonhoeffer and the Resistance*. Still, it is worth mentioning Bonhoeffer's references to his resistance activity as repentance, because it shows how his use of the term progresses.

In the January 1938 circular letter, "To the Young Brothers of the Church in Pomerania," Bonhoeffer appeals to repentance in a manner familiar to Protestants, as the act that places Christians back on the "right road." His use of "penitence" in the 1938 letter is not as innovative as in his reflections from prison, in which repentance is not merely the act of turning but is the right road itself, in other words, is participation in the way of Christ. Still, in the circular letter, Bonhoeffer is already thinking creatively about repentance. He expands the concept beyond an individual Christian's relationship to God and positions it as a communal act. The passage above continues, "Even if the obedience of penitence is harder now than it was then, because we are hardened in our guilt—it is the only way by which God will help us back to the right road" (Kelly and Nelson, *A Testament to Freedom*, 440). Bonhoeffer views the very existence of the Confessing Church as a proclamation of the gospel. Yet, as the "witness" of the Confessing Church grows "weaker and weaker" with members beginning to question whether or not resisting the national church was necessary, Bonhoeffer exhorts the Confessing Church to view the struggle as a repentance that would restore the church to its faithful witness (Ibid., 439).

The Confessing Church's resistance continues to dwindle, though, and in February 1938 Bonhoeffer's first contacts with the leaders of the military resistance to Hitler are made. In August 1939 Bonhoeffer becomes a civilian agent of the *Abwehr*, the German military intelligence agency, marking the beginning of his involvement in the conspiracy against Hitler. Rasmussen argues that Bonhoeffer viewed his secular colleagues in the resistance movement as a brotherhood that had taken the form of Christ by accepting the burden of guilt that, in turn, opened up space for redemption and renewal. In other words, during his involvement in the *Abwehr*, Bonhoeffer came to associate repentance with the form of Christ, responsible action, and the free acceptance of divine judgment.

46. Bonhoeffer, *Letters and Papers* (Touchstone, 1997), 361.

47. See Rowan Williams's sermon on the presence of the suffering Christ in Gethsemene delivered at the one hundredth anniversary of Bonhoeffer's birth at St. Matthäus Church, Berlin, on February 5, 2006. An English translation of the sermon may be found at http://www.archbishopofcanterbury.org/307?q=Bonhoeffer+2006.

48. Barth, *CD* IV/1 §59, 165. Barth also says that Jesus' baptism "is a clear anticipation of the passion."

49. Bonhoeffer, *Letters and Papers* (Touchstone, 1997), 361.

50. Nave, "Repent, for the Kingdom of God Is at Hand," 101.

51. Bonhoeffer, *Letters and Papers* DBWE 8, 501, and *Letters and Papers* (Touchstone 1997), 381 (combined translation).

52. Bonhoeffer emphasizes in prison that the incarnation bestows worth upon a broad expanse of human experience, for "the polyphony of life" (life's various experiences ranging from joy to hardship) is a "christological fact," he says (*Letters and Papers* DBWE 8, 393–394). A fuller discussion of "polyphony" occurs in the next chapter of this volume.

53. Bonhoeffer, *Letters and Papers* DBWE 8, 501.

54. Robert W. Jenson, "Luther's Contemporary Theological Significance," *The Cambridge Companion to Martin Luther*, ed. Donald K. McKim (Cambridge: Cambridge University Press, 2003), 277. Citation from Martin Luther, *D. Martin Luthers Werke: Kristische Gesamtausgaber [Schriften]*. vol. 26. (Weimar, Germany: H. Böhlau, 1883–1993), 332. Bonhoeffer paraphrases Luther's line in the christology lectures, *Christ the Center*, 52, and again in *Discipleship* DBWE 4, 225.

55. Jenson, "Luther's Contemporary Theological Significance," 277. See Bernd Wannenwetsch, "Luther's Moral Theology," in *The Cambridge Companion to Martin Luther*, ed. Donald K. McKim (Cambridge: Cambridge University Press, 2003), 134. In *Freedom of a Christian*, Luther speaks of Christian life as "form." See Timothy F. Lull, ed., *Martin Luther's Basic Theological Writings* (Minneapolis: Augsburg Fortress, 2005), 405.

56. See B. A. Gerrish, "'To the Unknown God': Luther and Calvin on the Hiddenness of God," *The Journal of Religion* 53, no. 3 (1973): 265; and Hilton C. Oswald, ed., *Luther's Works*, vol. 10, *First Lectures on the Psalms* (Saint Louis, Mo.: Concordia Publishing House, 1974), 119–120. In *First Lectures on the Psalms* and in the *Heidelberg Disputation*, Luther refers to God revealed in God's hiddenness. In his 1525 text, *Bondage of the Will*, however, Luther does make a distinction between light inaccessible (God's hiddenness outside revelation) and the incarnation (God's hiddenness inside revelation).

57. Gerrish, "'To the Unknown God,'" 263–293.

58. Lull, *Martin Luther's Basic Theological Writings*, 58.

59. Ibid., 57.

60. In *Bonhoeffer's Theology: Classical and Revolutionary* (Nashville: Abingdon Press, 1970), James W. Woelfel argues that "Religionless Christianity is Bonhoeffer's final expression of Luther's *simul justus et peccator* dialectic" (82). Woelfel argues that Bonhoeffer's reflections on religionless Christianity express his concern with the dialectic of justification and obedient discipleship as seen, for example, in his contrast between cheap and costly grace in *Discipleship*. Also see Regin Prenter's seminal article, "Bonhoeffer and the Young Luther," in *World Come of Age*, ed. Ronald Gregor Smith (Philadelphia: Fortress Press, 1967), 161–181. Along with making a significant contribution early in the religionless Christianity debates by arguing that Bonhoeffer's writings should be interpreted christologically, Prenter argues more specifically that through a theology of the cross, Bonhoeffer, like Luther, tries to protect a theology of the Word against becoming a principle that discourages obedient discipleship. Prenter writes, "Both the young Luther and Bonhoeffer combat such a theology of the Word with their *theologia crucis*... Only on this basis does it seem to me that we can fully understand those thoughts of the later Bonhoeffer on the non-religious interpretation of the gospel in a world come of age" (168).

61. Bonhoeffer, *Letters and Papers* DBWE 8, 479–480.

62. Ibid., 478–480.

63. Ibid., 367.

64. Bonhoeffer, *Letters and Papers* (Touchstone, 1997), 362.

65. Ibid., 360. In *Creation and Fall*, Bonhoeffer says, "That means that God accepts [human beings] as they are, as fallen. He affirms them as fallen... God's action does not

break through the new laws of earth and [humanity], it enters into them." See Dietrich Bonhoeffer, *Creation and Fall* and *Temptation*, trans. John C. Fletcher (New York: Touchstone, 1997), 100.

66. Bonhoeffer, *Letters and Papers* DBWE 8, 406.

67. Bonhoeffer, *Christ the Center*, 46. See also *Berlin* DBWE 12, 313.

68. Bonhoeffer, *Christ the Center*, 45–46, 106–110. See also *Berlin* DBWE 12, 313–314, 356.

69. Bonhoeffer, *Berlin* DBWE 12, 346–347.

70. Ibid., 355, 359.

71. Ibid., 355.

72. Ibid.

73. Bonhoeffer, *Christ the Center*, 106–107.

74. Søren Kierkegaard, *Philosophical Fragments*, rev. trans. Howard V. Hong (Princeton, N.J.: Princeton University Press, 1974), 37–43.

75. See Dietrich Bonhoeffer, *Love Letters from Cell 92: The Correspondence between Dietrich Bonhoeffer and Maria von Wedemeyer, 1943–45* (Nashville: Abingdon Press, 1995), 185–186. For a discussion of Kierkegaard's influence on Bonhoeffer, see Geffrey B. Kelly, "Kierkegaard as 'Antidote' and as Impact on Dietrich Bonhoeffer's Concept of Christian Discipleship," in *Bonhoeffer's Intellectual Formation: Theology and Philosophy in His Thought*, ed. Peter Frick (Tübingen, Germany: Mohr Siebeck, 2008), 145–165. Interestingly, Kelly does not examine the section in *Training in Christianity* about the christological incognito, although he does cite the reference above in *Philosophical Fragments.*

76. Søren Kierkegaard, *Training in Christianity and the Edifying Discourse Which "Accompanied" It*, trans. Walter Lowrie (Princeton, N.J.: Princeton University Press, 1944), 127.

77. Ibid., 131–132.

78. Ibid., 134.

79. Kierkegaard, *Training in Christianity*, 129. In Plato's *Republic*, book 2, Plato argues that an act must be hidden to be perfectly just.

80. Bonhoeffer, *Christ the Center*, 107.

81. Ibid., 108 (emphasis mine). Following Paul, Bonhoeffer never separates the incarnation and crucifixion; thus Jesus "was really made sin for us" not only on the cross, Bonhoeffer argues in his christology lectures, but also throughout his earthly life. The Revised English translation makes more clear the connection between 2 Cor. 5:21 and Rom. 8:3 (discussed below). It reads, "for our sake God made him one with human sinfulness."

82. See Bonhoeffer, *Christ the Center*, 108 and DBWE 12, 357.

83. Bonhoeffer, *Berlin* DBWE 12, 356.

84. Vincent P. Branick, "The Sinful Flesh of the Son of God (Rom 8:3): A Key Image of Pauline Theology," *Catholic Biblical Quarterly* 47 (1985), 253–254.

85. Bonhoeffer, *Berlin* DBWE 12, 356. Bonhoeffer, *Ethics* DBWE 6, 85. I get the phrase "intrinsically damaged" from Ian A. McFarland. For a study of how Christian theologians have dealt with the question of the fallenness of Christ's human nature and for an argument that Christ's assumption of fallen human nature does not necessitate that he himself sinned, see Ian A. McFarland, "Fallen or Unfallen? Christ's Human Nature and the Ontology of Human Sinfulness," *International Journal of Systematic Theology* 10, no. 4 (October 2008), 399–415.

86. Ivor J. Davidson, "Pondering the Sinlessness of Jesus Christ: Moral Christologies and the Witness of Scripture," *International Journal of Systematic Theology* 10, no. 4 (October 2008), 386. Also see Branick, "The Sinful Flesh," 246–262.

87. Bonhoeffer, *Christ the Center*, 108.

88. McFarland, "Fallen or Unfallen?" 411–413. McFarland writes:

> Therefore, whereas in all other human being the nature and hypostasis are inseparable (so that if the former is fallen, the latter is sinful), the divine hypostasis of Christ preexists—and thus is not bound by—his human nature by virtue of its eternal subsistence in the divine nature.... A careful analysis of the question of Christ's human nature allows a clear distinction to be drawn between *fallenness* and *sinfulness* as predicates in relation to the Chalcedonian categories of *nature* and *hypostasis*, respectively.... A nature can be damaged (and thus fallen); but a nature cannot sin, because sin is ascribed to agents, and thus is a matter of hypostasis. (412–413)

89. Branick argues that commentators often falsely impose on Paul their own theological presumption that only a pure, sinless Christ could affect atonement, and he argues that the description of Christ "not knowing sin" in 2 Cor. 5:21 does not necessarily refer to the earthly Jesus but could refer to the preexisting Christ, especially when related to Paul's theology of sinful flesh in Rom. 8:3. Branick writes, "One wonders if the concern to safeguard 'the moral supremacy and spotless purity' of Christ is not reading into the text a notion of sin different from that of Paul" (252–253); for Paul does not understand sin ethically nor "first of all [as] an individual act or condition" but rather as "a cosmic and aeonic perversion" in which Christ freely involves himself by taking a sinful nature (256–257). Although "Paul in fact gives us a picture of Christ that insists on his involvement with sin" this reading still "leaves room for the affirmation of Christ as sinless in a... personal sense" (246, 261).

90. Bonhoeffer, *Christ the Center*, 109.

91. Bonhoeffer, *Berlin* DBWE 12, 357.

92. Ibid., 350.

93. Bonhoeffer, *Christ the Center*, 104.

94. Bonhoeffer, *Berlin* DBWE 12, 342.

95. Ibid., 307.

96. Ibid., 302–308.

97. Bonhoeffer, *Christ the Center*, 112.

98. Bonhoeffer, *Berlin* DBWE 12, 359–360.

99. Lull, *Martin Luther's Basic Theological Writings*, 58.

100. In *Experiences in Theology: Ways and Forms of Christian Theology*, trans. Margaret Kohl (Minneapolis: Fortress Press, 2000), 15–17, Jürgen Moltmann parallels an atheist "protest theology" with a Christian theology of the cross. He writes, "Those who recognize God's presence in the face of the God-forsaken Christ have protest atheism within themselves—but as something they have overcome. So they well understand the atheists... Christian theology does not belong solely in the circle of the people who are 'insiders'... A Christian theologian... must know the godless too, for he belongs to them as well" (17).

101. For another study on contemporaneity in Bonhoeffer's christology lectures see Matt Jenson, "Real Presence," *Scottish Journal of Theology* 58, no. 2 (2005): 143–160.

102. Bonhoeffer, *Berlin* DBWE 12, 310.

103. Charles Marsh, *Reclaiming Dietrich Bonhoeffer*, 94.

104. Bonhoeffer, *Christ the Center*, 48.

105. Bonhoeffer, *Berlin* DBWE 12, 324. See Marsh's *Reclaiming Dietrich Bonhoeffer* for a fuller analysis of Bonhoeffer's theology of selfhood, especially "The Self for Others," 137–157.

106. Bonhoeffer, *Christ the Center*, 60–62. See also *Berlin* DBWE 12, 324–325.

107. Bonhoeffer, *Berlin* DBWE 12, 325.

108. Ibid., 302–305.

109. Bonhoeffer, *Christ the Center*, 50. See also *Berlin* DBWE 12, 315–318.

110. Bonhoeffer, *Berlin* DBWE 12, 318. See Fritz de Lange, *Waiting for the Word: Dietrich Bonhoeffer on Speaking about God*, trans. Martin N. Walton (Grand Rapids, Mich.: Eerdmans, 2000) for an examination of the possibilities and limits of speaking about God in the contemporary context of Western Europe.

111. Eberhard Bethge mentions that Bonhoeffer "instinctively disliked apologetics." See Bethge, *Dietrich Bonhoeffer: A Biography*, 44.

112. Kelly and Nelson, *A Testament to Freedom*, 86.

113. Bonhoeffer, *Berlin* DBWE 12, 316. The fact that scripture is truth spoken into the concrete moment to particular communities is most evident in the epistles, written to specific, local church-communities. Bonhoeffer's scriptural hermeneutics argues that God speaks through the New and Old Testaments just as concretely today. Thus, language in the Hebrew Bible is to be understood relationally rather than propositionally. Similarly, Hermann Cohen shows that the Hebrew word for "truth" is the same word for "faithfulness" and points to the covenant between God and Israel. See *Religion of Reason: Out of the Sources of Judaism*, trans. Simon Kaplan (New York: F. Ungar, 1972), 441–445. In *Concluding Unscientific Postscript*, Kierkegaard argues a similar point that truth is subjective in the sense that it involves personal relating. The meaning of scripture is misconstrued if the interpretation does not take into consideration the context of divine-human relationship.

114. Bonhoeffer, *Christ the Center*, 35.

115. Bonhoeffer, *Christ the Center*, 74 and *Berlin* DBWE 12, 331.

116. Bonhoeffer, *Berlin* DBWE 12, 322.

117. Bonhoeffer, *Christ the Center*, 57–58.

118. Ibid., 58. See also *Berlin* DBWE 12, 322–323.

119. Bonhoeffer, *Discipleship* DBWE 4, 216.

120. Rowan Williams, *Ray of Darkness: Sermons and Reflections* (Cambridge, Mass: Cowley, 1995), 34–36. In *Creation and Fall*, Bonhoeffer also connects the idea of "bodiliness" with "dependence" (41, 52).

121. Bonhoeffer, *Christ the Center*, 58.

122. Ibid., 59.

123. Ibid., 59, 113. Bonhoeffer was unable to complete his christology lectures, most likely because of the demands of the Church Struggle in 1933. See Bonhoeffer, *Discipleship* DBWE 4, 279 for a similar statement.

124. Barth, *CD* IV/1 §59, 172.

125. Bonhoeffer, *Ethics* DBWE 6, 83 (emphasis mine). In "Biographical Context," Robin W. Lovin argues that since Bonhoeffer wrote *Ethics* under varying circumstances, readers should approach it with an understanding of the unique historical and biographical influences on the text. The drafts of chapters collated into *Ethics* were written before and during his involvement with the *Abwehr* conspiracy, some at his parents' house in Berlin, at the Ruth von Kleist-Retzow estate, and at the Benedictine monastery in Ettal. The most complete chapters were written before the war and before his involvement with the conspiracy when he was able to devote more focused attention to his writing, while others were written in between his assignments as a courier for the *Abwehr*.

126. Bonhoeffer, *Christ the Center*, 103.

127. Bonhoeffer, *Ethics* DBWE 6, 88.

128. See Peter Frick, "Friedrich Nietzsche's Aphorisms and Dietrich Bonhoeffer's Theology," in *Bonhoeffer's Intellectual Formation: Theology and Philosophy in His Thought*, ed. Peter Frick (Tübingen, Germany: Mohr Siebeck, 2008) for a fuller description of Bonhoeffer's christological redescription and reversal of Nietzsche's thought and for important distinctions between Nietzsche's philosophy and Bonhoeffer's theology. Frick argues that we cannot be sure Bonhoeffer was referencing Nietzsche's autobiography with the term *Ecce Homo*; still, it is clear that in the section, "Ethics as Formation," Bonhoeffer counters Nietzsche's idea of *Übermenschentum* or superhumanity with Christ, who affirms not the superhuman but the real human being (94). Bonhoeffer's use of *Ecce Homo* most directly refers to Pilate's exclamation at Jesus' trial in the Gospel of John, "Here is the man!" (19:5). Bonhoeffer engaged Nietzsche's writings throughout his career, for he references *Beyond Good and Evil* and *Thus Spoke Zarathustra* in his 1929 Barcelona lecture "Basic Questions of a Christian Ethic," pages 363, 367. See Dietrich Bonhoeffer, *Barcelona, Berlin, New York: 1928–1931*, ed. Clifford J. Green, trans. Douglas W. Stott, Vol. 10 of *Dietrich Bonhoeffer Works*, 16 vols. (Minneapolis: Fortress Press, 2008), 359–378. Also see André Dumas, *Dietrich Bonhoeffer: Theologian of Reality*, trans. Robert McAfee Brown (New York: Macmillan, 1971), 161–162 for a comparison of Nietzsche and Bonhoeffer's work.

129. Taken from the editor's footnote (59) in Bonhoeffer, *Ethics* DBWE 6, 233. See the section, "Why I Am So Wise," in Friedrich Nietzsche, *Ecce Homo: How to Become What You Are*, trans. Duncan Large (Oxford: Oxford University Press, 2007).

130. Bonhoeffer, *Ethics* DBWE 6, 35.

131. Ibid., 234.

132. Bonhoeffer's observation that some of Nietzsche's insights help clarify Christian truth and highlight the radical nature of the gospel message echoes a paradox G. K. Chesterton observed about his own thinking: "I did try to found a heresy of my own; and when I had put the last touches to it, I discovered that it was orthodoxy." See G. K. Chesterton, *Orthodoxy* (Garden City, N.Y.: Doubleday, 1959), 12.

133. Bonhoeffer, *Discipleship* DBWE 4, 217.

134. Bonhoeffer, *Ethics* DBWE 6, 276. Whereas Anselm's substitutionary atonement theory places the moment of reconciliation at the cross, Bonhoeffer's soteriology includes both the cross and God's prior decision and act of becoming human (8).

135. Bonhoeffer, *Ethics* DBWE 6, 231–232, 248.

136. Ibid., 233.

137. Ibid., 235.

138. Ibid., 233.

139. Bonhoeffer, *Prayerbook of the Bible*, ed. Geffrey B Kelly, trans. Daniel W. Bloesch and James H. Burtness, Vol. 5 of *Dietrich Bonhoeffer Works*, 16 vols. (Minneapolis: Fortress Press, 1996), 158.

140. Ibid., 157. Following Luther, Bonhoeffer claims that Jesus prays the Psalms with Christians. This hermeneutic of reading Hebrew scripture christologically is problematic, however, if it disallows nonchristological, Jewish readings of scripture.

141. Ibid., 171.

142. Bonhoeffer, *Prayerbook of the Bible* DBWE 5, 172. In *Expositions on the Psalms* Augustine makes a similar argument. See *The Works of Saint Augustine: A Translation for the 21st Century*, Vol. 17, trans. Edmund Hill, ed. John E. Rotelle (Brooklyn, N.Y.: New City Press, 1997). See especially Augustine's comments on Psalm 22.

143. Bonhoeffer, *Ethics* DBWE 6, 261. Frick, "Friedrich Nietzsche's Aphorisms and Dietrich Bonhoeffer's Theology," 198.

144. Bonhoeffer, *Ethics* DBWE 6, 263.

145. Bonhoeffer, *Discipleship* DBWE 4, 60.

146. Ibid., 90; Bonhoeffer, *Letters and Papers* (Touchstone, 1997), 337.

147. Bonhoeffer, *Discipleship* DBWE 4, 90.

148. Bonhoeffer, *Ethics* DBWE 6, 82; Bonhoeffer, *Letters and Papers* DBWE 8, 541; Bonhoeffer, *Life Together* DBWE 5, 111.

149. Bonhoeffer, *Ethics* DBWE 6, 6–7. The editors of *Ethics* offer this insight about Bonhoeffer's focus on theological humanism. Bonhoeffer consistently uses the word *Menschwerdung* (becoming human) rather than the theological term *Inkarnation* (incarnation) in order to underscore that the significance of the incarnation for human beings is that participation in the being of Christ makes human beings more fully human. Of course, the patristic understanding that God became human so that human beings might become divine and Bonhoeffer's understanding that God became human so that human beings might become more fully human are not mutually exclusive statements, since they are united by the christological fact that Christ is both fully God and fully human. Bonhoeffer's emphasis on the human being is significant in that it speaks to our twenty-first-century need for a Christian witness concerned with human flourishing. This emphasis is seen not only in the *Dietrich Bonhoeffer Works* edition of *Ethics* but also in John de Gruchy's study, *Confessions of a Christian Humanist*. See especially John W. de Gruchy's chapter, "Being Human," in *Confessions of a Christian Humanist* (Minneapolis: Fortress Press, 2006), 33–53.

150. Bonhoeffer, *Ethics* DBWE 6, 232.

151. Being "in Christ" can refer to humanity as it does here, to the world's new ontology as I argue in the next chapter, and can refer more narrowly to the church.

152. Bonhoeffer speaks of this in *Discipleship* DBWE 4, 215.

153. Ibid., 215–216.

154. Bonhoeffer, *Ethics* DBWE 6, 253.

155. Ibid., 231–232.

156. Bonhoeffer, *Life Together* DBWE 5, 111.

157. Kelly and Nelson, *A Testament to Freedom*, 201.

158. See Bonhoeffer, *Creation and Fall*, 106–107.

■ Chapter 4

1. The terms "reconciliation" and "redemption" should be distinguished. Bonhoeffer's theology claims that the world already has been reconciled to God through Christ, not that the world is demonstratively redeemed. When I use the term "redemption," I am referring to the concrete redemption made manifest here and now.

2. See http://www.christianitytoday.com/tc/7r5/7r536b.html. Macmillan published the first English translation in paperback in 1963, and SCM Press published a second paperback version in 1964.

3. Dietrich Bonhoeffer, *Discipleship*, ed. Geffrey B. Kelly and John D. Godsey, trans. Barbara Green and Reinhard Krauss, Vol. 4 of *Dietrich Bonhoeffer Works*, 16 vols. (Minneapolis: Fortress Press, 2003), 32. While the editors' introduction provides some historical explanation, the afterword, taken from the German edition, is much more helpful for this than the introduction. I suggest that a North American reader turn to the afterword before reading Bonhoeffer's text.

4. Dietrich Bonhoeffer, *The Cost of Discipleship* (New York: Touchstone, 1995), 258; 267; 272–273; 278–280; 284 (emphasis mine).

5. Bonhoeffer, *Discipleship* DBWE 4, 236, 247, 253. The DBWE translation of the fourth quote may be found on pages 260–262 and the fifth on page 266.

6. See the German editor's comments on this in *Discipleship* DBWE 4, 306.

7. See Bonhoeffer's *Discipleship* DBWE 4, "The Visible Church-Community" and "The Saints," 225–280, especially 233, 253–254, 259, 261.

8. Ibid., 144–145. For Bonhoeffer's discussion in *Ethics* of the Sermon on the Mount, see Dietrich Bonhoeffer, *Ethics*, trans. Reinhold Krauss, et al., Vol. 6 of *Dietrich Bonhoeffer Works*, 16 vols. (Minneapolis: Fortress Press, 2005), 231, 235.

9. *Discipleship* DBWE 4, 95, 239.

10. Ibid., 247, 251.

11. Ibid., 174. Also see page 256, where he affirms that "God alone is righteous" and that Christians "do not possess our own righteousness."

12. Ibid., 149.

13. Ibid., 146–152.

14. Ernst Feil makes a similar argument in *The Theology of Dietrich Bonhoeffer* (Philadelphia: Fortress Press, 1985), 126–138.

15. Bonhoeffer, *Discipleship* DBWE 4, 86.

16. See Thomas Merton, "Apologies to an Unbeliever," *Faith and Violence: Christian Teaching and Christian Practice* (Notre Dame, Ind.: Notre Dame University Press, 1968), 205–214, for his discussion of self-assured Christians. For examples of campaigns to save Christmas see the Web site for Liberty Counsel at http://www.lc.org/helpsavechristmas/index.htm or "Help Save Christmas: Blogging the War against Christmas" at http://www.conservblogs.com/Christmas/. Also see *The War on Christmas: How the Liberal Plot to Ban the Sacred Christian Holiday Is Worse Than You Thought* (New York: Sentinel, 2005) by Fox News host, John Gibson.

17. Bonhoeffer, *Discipleship* DBWE 4, 249.

18. This popular phrase "being in the world but not of the world" comes from Jesus' prayer for his disciples in John 17:15–19, but it risks misconstruing Jesus' words as a call for Christians to endure existence in the fallen world rather than actively embrace this-worldly living through Christ.

19. Bonhoeffer, *Discipleship* DBWE 4, 37 (emphasis mine). The preface concludes, "Today it seems so difficult to walk with certainty the narrow path of the church's decision [not to incorporate into the Reich church] and yet to remain wide open to Christ's love for all people" (40).

20. Bonhoeffer completed the manuscript of *Discipleship* around the same time that the Gestapo closed the seminary. Once the book was published, he sent copies to the seminarians and wrote in a circular Christmas letter that "since the book appeared in print, I have often dedicated it in spirit to all of you. That I did not do so explicitly on the title page is due to the fact that I did not want to claim your support for my own thoughts and theology—our community has another foundation" (see "Editors' Afterword to the German Edition," *Discipleship* DBWE 4, 303).

21. See Victoria Barnett, *For the Soul of the People: Protestant Protest against Hitler* (New York: Oxford University Press), 1992. Many leaders and members tried to forge a middle ground that sought church independence from the "German Christian" Reich church while denouncing resistance that had the character of political protest against the state at large.

Barnett writes, "The irony is that the struggle of the Confessing Church to remain free of Nazi ideology was for many a struggle to remain apolitical." Disassociating ecclesial concerns from the social and political needs of the world, "They felt that the church, come what may, was called upon to be the church and nothing more" (73).

22. Bonhoeffer, *Discipleship* DBWE 4, 298.

23. For example, the German afterword in the *Dietrich Bonhoeffer Works* edition of *Discipleship* mentions Bonhoeffer's discussion of the phrase "but let me first" from Luke 9:57–62 as a direct reference to the seminarians who were tempted to become legalized. This point was argued in Hanfried Müller's 1961 doctoral dissertation. See Bonhoeffer, *Discipleship* DBWE 4, 311.

24. Bonhoeffer, *Discipleship* DBWE 4, 103. Compare this translation with the 1995 Touchstone paperback edition, 107. The *Dietrich Bonhoeffer Works* edition translates the phrases above in a manner that more directly mirrors the Nazi terminology from which Bonhoeffer was drawing.

25. Ibid., 112.

26. Explicit references to the Nazi totalitarian context are rare in Bonhoeffer's work. In *Authentic Faith: Bonhoeffer's Theological Ethics in Context*, ed. Ernst-Albert Scharffenorth, trans. David Stassen and Ilse Tödt (Grand Rapids, Mich.: Eerdmans, 2007), Heinz Eduard Tödt comments that when the manuscript to *Ethics* was found and read by the Nazis, they found no evidence of dissent because his references are so subtle. See Tödt, *Authentic Faith*, 18.

27. Bonhoeffer, *Discipleship* DBWE 4, 272.

28. Ibid., 40.

29. See Søren Kierkegaard, *Fear and Trembling*, trans. Alastair Hannay (London: Penguin, 1985) as an example of the teleological suspension of the ethical.

30. Bonhoeffer, *Discipleship* DBWE 4, 96–97 (emphasis mine). The Johannine texts are particularly susceptible to being misused to support an interpretation that condemns the world and places it in contrast to things eternal or spiritual. The author of 1 John writes, "Do not love the world or the things in the world. The love of the Father is not in those who love the world; for all that is in the world—the desire of the flesh, the desire of the eyes, the pride in riches—comes not from the Father but from the world. And the world and its desires are passing away, but those who do the will of God live forever" (1 John 2:15–17). However, this same epistle that appears to contrast the material world with the eternal Father opens with an appeal to the material reality of Christ and to his simultaneous identity with the everlasting God: "We declare to you what was from the beginning, what we have heard, what we have seen with our eyes, what we have looked at and touched with our hands, concerning the word of life—this life was revealed, and we have seen it and testify to it, and declare to you the eternal life that was with the Father and was revealed to us" (1 John 1:1–2). The letter's dominant message centers on the lesson that love for Christ remains merely abstract and thus unreal unless it is concretely embodied in one's love for fellow human beings, whom Christ loves. 2 John makes the significance of Christ's materiality even more apparent by associating a deceitful and false witness with the denial of the importance of Christ's fleshy existence (1:7).

31. Gerhard Kittel, ed., *Theological Dictionary of the New Testament*, Vol. 3 (Grand Rapids, Mich.: Eerdmans, 1964), 868–895.

32. Dietrich Bonhoeffer, *Letters and Papers from Prison*, ed. John W. de Gruchy, trans. Isabel Best et al., Vol. 8 of *Dietrich Bonhoeffer Works*, 16 vols. (Minneapolis: Fortress Press, 2010), 486.

33. For example, Bonhoeffer continues to affirm Christ as the bearer of sin and guilt, and in *Discipleship* he uses a phrase that in *Ethics* refers to Christ this-worldly character: that Christ is the one who drinks the earthly cup "to the dregs." See Bonhoeffer, *Discipleship* DBWE 4, 88, 90.

34. Bonhoeffer, *Discipleship* DBWE 4, 61–67.

35. Ibid., 62.

36. Bonhoeffer, *Letters and Papers* (Touchstone, 1997), 369.

37. Feil, *The Theology of Dietrich Bonhoeffer*, 133. Feil says that in *Discipleship* Bonhoeffer "turns the cross, and with it the community, into a ghetto" in which there is "no genuine relation of the cross to the world." He asks, "How is the world to be redeemed from [a ghetto]?"

38. Bonhoeffer, *Discipleship* DBWE 4, 309.

39. Before becoming a book, *Discipleship* was delivered as lectures at Finkenwalde.

40. Bonhoeffer, *Discipleship* DBWE 4, 205–212.

41. See especially Bonhoeffer, *Discipleship* DBWE 4, 225–280.

42. The letter to the Ephesians (6:12) says that Christians struggle not against flesh and blood, in other words not against other human beings, but against evil powers and principalities. Walter Wink's work on powers and principalities is helpful on this point: *Naming the Powers: The Language of Power in the New Testament* (Philadelphia: Fortress Press, 1984); *Unmasking the Powers: The Invisible Forces That Determine Human Existence* (Philadelphia: Fortress Press, 1986); *Engaging the Powers: Discernment and Resistance in a World of Domination* (Minneapolis: Fortress Press, 1992). Martyn reminds the reader that Paul does not identify the forces of oppression and dehumanization with particular groups of human beings (the struggle is not against flesh and blood), although the power of "the flesh" is expressed through particular destructive acts of human beings and groups. See J. Louis Martyn, *Theological Issues in the Letters of Paul* (Nashville: Abingdon Press, 1997), 286.

43. See J. Christiaan Beker, *Paul's Apocalyptic Gospel: The Coming Triumph of God* (Philadelphia: Fortress Press, 1982); J. Louis Martyn, *Galatians* (New York: Doubleday, 1997), Vol. 33A of the *Anchor Bible*; and Douglas A. Campbell, *The Deliverance of God: An Apocalyptic Reading of Justification in Paul* (Grand Rapids, Mich.: Eerdmans, 2009). See also Martinus C. de Boer, "Paul, Theologian of God's Apocalypse," *Interpretation* 56, no. 1 (2002). See Vincent P. Branick, "Apocalyptic Paul?" *Catholic Biblical Quarterly* 47 (1985): 664–675, on Beker's work as a significant (albeit, he argues, one-sided) breakthrough in Pauline studies.

44. Like Martyn, J. Christian Becker makes clear that Paul's cosmic dualism is not a Gnostic dualism that shows contempt for the world or that encourages otherworldliness. In *Paul's Apocalyptic Gospel*, Beker argues that for Paul, the Christ-event both modifies and intensifies the Jewish apocalyptic thought patterns he inherited. The incursion of Christ modifies a strict dualism or separation between "this age" and "the age to come," since with Christ come the powers of the new age and the in-breaking of the new creation into the old. The dualism between the powers of death and the powers of life are at the same time intensified, however, because Christ's "radical stance *for the world*" commissions the church "to do battle against... the value structures of the present world... through a hope that incarnates itself in a cruciform existence" (41, 44). See also J. Christian Becker, *Paul the Apostle* (Philadelphia: Fortress Press, 1980), 143–149.

45. There is a debate among New Testament scholars about how appropriate it is to refer to some of Paul's thinking as "apocalyptic." For example, see R. Barry Matlock, *Unveiling the Apocalyptic Paul: Paul's Interpreters and the Rhetoric of Criticism* (Sheffield,

UK: Sheffield Academic Press, 1996). Although the word is contested, it is the best one-word description of what New Testament scholars such as Beker, Martyn, and Campbell, construe is happening in Paul's thinking.

46. Philip G. Ziegler, "Dietrich Bonhoeffer—An Ethics of God's Apocalypse?" *Modern Theology* 23, no. 4 (October 2007): 579–594. Ziegler offers a survey of the brief literature on Bonhoeffer and apocalyptic thought, which includes Larry Rasmussen's qualified association of the two in *Dietrich Bonhoeffer: His Significance for North Americans* (Minneapolis: Fortress Press, 1990), 75–88, and Charles C. West's counterargument in West, "Review of *Dietrich Bonhoeffer: His Significance for North Americans*," *Theology Today* 47, no. 4 (1991): 471–473. Ziegler argues that Pauline apocalyptic logic is at work in *Ethics* as seen through Bonhoeffer's emphasis on the uncontingent character of God's in-breaking, the Christ-event as that which unsettles dualisms like good and evil, the cosmic scope of Christ's work that remakes reality, and the church as a body that necessarily stands in solidarity with the rest of the world.

47. Bonhoeffer, *Discipleship* DBWE 4, 207–208.

48. Beker, *Paul's Apocalyptic Gospel*, 9.

49. Ibid., 120.

50. See Ibid., 29–39. Also see Michael J. Gorman, *Cruciformity: Paul's Narrative Spirituality of the Cross* (Grand Rapids, Mich.: Eerdmans, 2001).

51. Martyn, *Theological Issues in the Letters of Paul*, 282.

52. Martyn, *Galatians*, 95–105.

53. Martyn, *Theological Issues in the Letters of Paul*, 295; Martyn, *Galatians*, 524–540.

54. Martyn, *Galations*, 95–105; Martyn, *Theological Issues in the Letters of Paul*, 281–284.

55. Martyn, *Galatians*, 530 (emphasis mine), 406–412, 524–540.

56. Martyn, *Theological Issues in the Letters of Paul*, 93–94.

57. Ibid.; Martyn, *Galations*, 408; see also 393–412, 478–479, 570–574. Also see Udo Schnelle, *Apostle Paul: His Life and Theology*, trans. M Eugene Boring (Grand Rapids, Mich.: Baker Academic, 2005). Schnelle shows that in 2 Cor. 5, Paul develops the ontological and cosmological dimensions of the cross event. He says, "As a universal event, God's reconciling act can be limited neither to the individual nor the church, for it overcomes the alienation between God and the world grounded in universal human sinfulness" (257).

58. Translation taken from Martyn, *Galations*, 402.

59. Ibid., 570–571.

60. See Bonhoeffer, *Discipleship* DBWE 4, 218.

61. Martyn, *Galatians*, 404–406.

62. Martyn, *Theological Issues in the Letters of Paul*, 79–82; Martyn, *Galations*, 37.

63. Martyn, *Galatians*, 163–164.

64. Ibid., 570.

65. Martyn, *Theological Issues in the Letters of Paul*, 286.

66. Ibid., 93–94.

67. Ibid., 93–94.

68. New International Version used here in place of the New Revised Standard Version.

69. Martyn, *Galatians*, 533, 536.

70. Ibid., 532–533.

71. Ibid., 532.

72. Ibid., 105.

73. Ibid., 564.

74. Protest atheism serves as one example of the inadequacy of a dualistic rendering of faith and unbelief. The "protest theology" of the atheist centered on anger at injustice shares, in some respects, the heart of God. In note 100 in chapter 3, I cited Jürgen Moltmann's discussion of parallels between the protest atheist and the theologian of the cross. Moltmann writes, "Those who recognize God's presence in the face of the God-forsaken Christ have protest atheism within themselves—but as something they have overcome. So they well understand the atheists.... Christian theology does not belong solely in the circle of the people who are 'insiders'.... A Christian theologian... must know the godless too, for he belongs to them as well." Jürgen Moltmann, *Experiences in Theology: Ways and Forms of Christian Theology*, trans. Margaret Kohl (Minneapolis: Fortress Press, 2000), 17.

75. See Richard B. Hays, *The Faith of Jesus Christ: An Investigation of the Narrative Substructure of Galatians 3:1–4:11* (Chico, Calif.: Scholars Press, 1983). See also Martyn, *Galatians*, 250–275.

76. Martyn, *Galatians*, 264. Even if one finds Martyn and Hays's arguments about the genitive construction unconvincing and thinks the phrase should be translated "faith in Christ," Reformed theology asserts that faith is a gift from God and not a human possibility; thus, there is still no theological validity in the Reformed tradition for Christians to operate within a religious dualism that I am calling "faith and unbelief."

77. Martyn, *Galatians*, 271.

78. Martyn, *Theological Issues in the Letters of Paul*, 289.

79. Martyn, *Galatians*, 478–479.

80. Ibid., 426–431, 478–479, 524–526, 570–574.

81. Dietrich Bonhoeffer, *Ethics*, trans. Reinhold Krauss, et al., Vol. 6 of *Dietrich Bonhoeffer Works*, 16 vols. (Minneapolis: Fortress Press, 2005), 66.

82. Ibid., 54–55.

83. Ibid., 58.

84. Ibid.

85. Ibid., 54. Bonhoeffer also writes, "The name Jesus embraces in itself the whole of humanity and the whole of God" (85).

86. Dumas's 1968 study examines the world's ontological structure and interprets Bonhoeffer's christology through this theme of structuring (*Gestaltung*). See André Dumas, *Dietrich Bonhoeffer: Theologian of Reality*, trans. Robert McAfee Brown (New York: Macmillan, 1971).

87. Larry L. Rasmussen, *Dietrich Bonhoeffer: Reality and Resistance* (New York: Abingdon Press, 1972), 16, 23. Rasmussen borrows the term "ontological coherence" from Eberhard Bethge in "The Challenge of Dietrich Bonhoeffer's Life and Theology," *Chicago Theological Seminary Register* 51, no. 2 (1961), 30.

88. Rasmussen, *Reality and Resistance*, 16.

89. Bonhoeffer, *Ethics* DBWE 6, 249–250.

90. Ibid., 83, 58.

91. Ibid., 66.

92. Ibid., 157.

93. Ibid., 94.

94. Ibid., 94–95.

95. Ibid., 263.

96. Ibid., 157.

97. Karl Barth, *Church Dogmatics* IV/1, ed. G. W. Bromiley and T. F. Torrance, trans. G. W. Bromiley (Edinburgh, Scotland: T&T Clark, 1980), §59, 158–159.

98. Bonhoeffer, *Ethics* DBWE 6, 251.

99. In *Life Together*, ed. Geffrey B Kelly, trans. Daniel W. Bloesch and James H. Burtness, Vol. 5 of *Dietrich Bonhoeffer Works*, 16 vols. (Minneapolis: Fortress Press, 1996), Bonhoeffer speaks of respecting the integrity of the "other" in the context of Christian community; still, his distinction between spiritual love and human or "self-centered" love also serves as an explanation for how God loves and respects the world, which is other, and as a guide for how Christians, in turn, are to love and respect others. Spiritual love is filtered through, or mediated by, Christ, while human love errs in that it desires to control and dominate that which is other. Human love errs even if its desire arises from good intentions. Bonhoeffer says, "Self-centered love... loves [the other]... not as free persons.... It wants to do everything it can to win and conquer; it puts pressure on the other person.... Self-centered love cannot love the enemy, that is to say, one who seriously and stubbornly resists it.... In the face of the enemy [human love] turns to hatred, contempt, and slander.... Genuine spiritual love... does not desire but serves.... Spiritual love... comes from Jesus Christ" (38–47).

100. Bonhoeffer, *Ethics* DBWE 6, 224, 264.

101. I take the term "diminution" from Rowan William's *Resurrection: Interpreting the Easter Gospel* (Cleveland, Ohio: Pilgrim Press, 2002) by which he means any behavior that diminishes another human being or oneself. See chapter 1, "The Judgment of Judgment: Easter in Jerusalem," 1–22. Bonhoeffer uses the mantra "origin, essence, and goal" again and again in *Ethics* DBWE 6. For example, see page 251.

102. Bonhoeffer, *Ethics* DBWE 6, 158.

103. Ibid., 251.

104. Ibid., 88, 91.

105. Ibid., 91.

106. Ibid., 65–67.

107. Ibid. Notice how this emphasis in *Ethics* differs from *Discipleship* as described in the previous sections of this chapter. There is no longer any need for the church to conquer territory for Christ because the entire world is already reconciled to God through Christ.

108. Ibid., 92.

109. Ibid., 251.

110. Ibid., 92.

111. Ibid., 251–252. For more on discipleship and joy, see Bonhoeffer's early essay that he wrote for von Harnack's seventy-fifth birthday, entitled, "'Joy' in Early Christianity: Commemorative Paper for Adolf von Harnack," found in Dietrich Bonhoeffer, *The Young Bonhoeffer, 1918–1927*, eds. Paul Duane Matheny et al., trans. Mary C. Nebelsick and Douglas W. Stott, Vol. 9 of *Dietrich Bonhoeffer Works*, 16 vols. (Minneapolis: Fortress Press, 2003), 370–385.

112. Terence E. Fretheim, "Repentance in the Former Prophets," in *Repentance in Christian Theology*, ed. Mark J. Boda and Gordon T. Smith (Collegeville, Minn.: Liturgical Press, 2006), 25–45, 36; Carol J. Dempsey, "'Turn Back, O People': Repentance in the Latter Prophets," in *Repentance in Christian Theology*, ed. Mark J. Boda and Gordon T. Smith. (Collegeville, Minn.: Liturgical Press, 2006), 47–66.

113. The Christian tradition that speaks most clearly about repentance as joyful expectation is Eastern Orthodoxy. In his chapter, "'Life in Abundance': Eastern Orthodox Perspectives on Repentance and Confession," in *Repentance in Christian Theology*, ed.

Mark J. Boda and Gordon T. Smith. (Collegeville, Minn.: Liturgical Press, 2006), 211–230, John Chryssavgis writes that U.S. Christians "have tended to lose sight of repentance as [this] fundamentally joyous, restorative return to life in its abundant fullness" (211–212). As "the resurrection unleashed," repentance's primary orientation, Chryssavgis argues, is toward the future coming kingdom (213). A historically significant theologian in North American Christianity who, perhaps surprisingly, shares the Eastern Orthodox understanding of repentance is Jonathan Edwards. Edwards, who is best known for the title of his sermon, "Sinners in the Hands of an Angry God," considers repentance to be a source of delight, deeming it "sweet sorrow" (272). See Wilson H. Kimnach, Kenneth P. Minkema, and Douglas A Sweeney, eds., *The Sermons of Jonathan Edwards: A Reader* (New Haven, CT: Yale University Press, 1999), 18–19. In his chapter "The Penitential: An Evangelical Perspective," Gordon T. Smith argues that although the penitential has historically been a central dimension of the evangelical tradition (as examined through the Puritans and seventeenth- and eighteenth-century Wesleyan renewal movements), it was "all too easily couched in a culture of guilt and fear," which contemporary evangelicals too often still dwell within, especially in relation to private sins. Gordon argues that there has been a "disappearance" of confession in worship in many evangelical and mainline churches, and he writes that evangelical churches have dispensed with a penitential focus in order to alleviate the culture of shame. Smith also makes the astute observation that "evangelicals are all too easily prone to indicate how they are accepted by God while at the same time condemning the society in which they live," and Smith implies that this may be linked to the lack of confession in worship. Gordon T. Smith, "The Penitential: An Evangelical Perspective," in *Repentance in Christian Theology*, ed. Mark J. Boda and Gordon T. Smith (Collegeville, Minn.: Liturgical Press, 2006), 267–286. Marsha G. Witten's *All Is Forgiven: The Secular Message in American Protestantism* (Princeton, N.J.: Princeton University Press, 1993) provides evidence for Smith's claim. Witten studies how a sample of Presbyterian USA and Southern Baptist pastors preach about the parable of the prodigal son (Luke 15:11–32) and shows that preachers use a variety of rhetorical strategies that avoid attending to the sin of the audience and instead use outsiders as examples. Witten describes such strategies as generalizing sin or speaking of sin in vague and abstract ways; deflecting sin to outsiders, even to a specific social group; and describing sin in therapeutic terms that lessen one's sense of responsibility (79–102).

114. Bonhoeffer, *Ethics* DBWE 6, 251.

115. Ibid., 252.

116. Heinz Eduard Tödt et al., eds. *Dietrich Bonhoeffer Werke*, Band 6, *Ethik* (Munich, Germany: Chr. Kaiser Verlag, 1992), 137–162.

117. See Bonhoeffer, *Ethics* DBWE 6, 146, editors' footnote (2).

118. Ján Liguš, "Dietrich Bonhoeffer: Ultimate, Penultimate and Their Impact, the Origin and the Essence of *Ethics*," in *Bonhoeffer's* Ethics*: Old Europe and New Frontiers*, ed. Guy Carter et al. (Kampen, Netherlands: Kok Pharos, 1991), 59–72. See Dietrich Bonhoeffer, *Gesammelte Schriften*, Vol. 5, ed. Eberhard Bethge (Munich, Germany: Chr. Kaiser Verlag, 1972), 452–457.

119. Bonhoeffer, *Letters and Papers* DBWE 8, 213.

120. Ibid., 222.

121. Dietrich Bonhoeffer, *Conspiracy and Imprisonment, 1940–1945*, ed. Mark S. Brocker, trans. Lisa E. Dahill, Vol. 16 of *Dietrich Bonhoeffer Works*, 16 vols. (Minneapolis: Fortress Press, 2006), 92.

122. Bonhoeffer, *Ethics* DBWE 6, 153.

123. Ibid.

124. Ibid., 342–343.

125. Ibid., 344.

126. Ibid., 154.

127. For example, see Hiroki Funamoto, "Penultimate and Ultimate in Dietrich Bonhoeffer's *Ethics*," in *Being and Truth*, ed. Alistair Kee and Eugene T. Long (London, UK: SCM, 1986), 376–392; See also John Godsey and Ján Liguš: John D. Godsey, *The Theology of Dietrich Bonhoeffer* (Philadelphia: Westminster Press, 1960), 277; Ján Liguš, "Dietrich Bonhoeffer: Ultimate, Penultimate and Their Impact, the Origin and the Essence of *Ethics*," in *Bonhoeffer's* Ethics*: Old Europe and New Frontiers*, 59–72. Liguš defines the ultimate in various ways such as "the justification of the sinner," "God's compassion on the sinner," "God's final word," "the whole Gospel," "the life and work of Jesus Christ," "God's mercy on the sinner," and the penultimate as "preparing the way for the Gospel message," "the acceptance of justification," "removing obstacles" for faith, and so forth. Liguš also defines the ultimate and penultimate in ways outside the context of law and gospel but does not show how these various definitions relate to one another. For example, he also defines the ultimate as "Christ" and "the eschaton" and the penultimate as "created reality given by God" and "the natural preserved for redemption."

128. In *Ethics* Bonhoeffer uses the categories of the ultimate and penultimate to reclaim the concept of the natural for Protestant ethics. Significantly, Bonhoeffer wrote the draft of the chapter "Ultimate and Penultimate Things," while in a Catholic monastery in Ettal. For a helpful discussion of the penultimate see Rachel Muers, *Keeping God's Silence: Towards a Theological Ethics of Communication* (Oxford: Blackwell, 2004), 86–91. Muers highlights that Bonhoeffer chooses to describe the world as the penultimate instead of as fallen creation because doing so avoids the presumption that the world remains unreconciled to Christ. In *Self and Salvation: Being Transformed* (Cambridge: Cambridge University Press, 1999), David Ford helpfully says that the concepts penultimate and ultimate "undermine...dualisms while preserving necessary distinctions" (262). For further scholarship on the ultimate and penultimate, see Stephen Plant, *Bonhoeffer* (London: Continuum, 2004), 113–118; Dumas, *Theologian of Reality*, 158–160; Feil, *The Theology of Dietrich Bonhoeffer*, 144–146. Finally, see Robin Lovin's use of Bonhoeffer's concepts of penultimate/ultimate and of the divine mandates for a twenty-first-century Christian realism in *Christian Realism and the New Realities* (Cambridge, Cambridge University Press, 2008).

129. I am grateful to Robin Lovin for discussing and researching this issue with me. Bonhoeffer connects these two chapters at the end of "Ultimate and Penultimate Things," DBWE 6, 168–170.

130. Dietrich Bonhoeffer, "Protestantism without Reformation," *No Rusty Swords: Letters, Lectures and Notes 1928–1936 from the Collected Works of Dietrich Bonhoeffer*, ed. Edwin H. Robertson (New York: Harper & Row, 1965), 116. See Reinhold Niebuhr, *The Nature and Destiny of Man*, 2 vols. (Louisville, Ky.: Westminster Knox Press, 1996).

131. Bonhoeffer, *Ethics* DBWE 6, 161.

132. Ibid., 162–163.

133. Ibid., 160.

134. Ibid., 164–165 (emphasis mine).

135. Ibid., 167.

136. Ibid., 163.

137. Ibid., 155.

138. Geffrey B. Kelly and F. Burton Nelson, *A Testament to Freedom: The Essential Writings of Dietrich Bonhoeffer* (New York: HarperCollins, 1995), 351.

139. Bonhoeffer, *Letters and Papers* DBWE 8, 485.

140. Bonhoeffer, *Letters and Papers* (Touchstone, 1997), 310.

141. Quoted in Ralf K. Wüstenberg, *A Theology of Life: Dietrich Bonhoeffer's Religionless Christianity*, trans. Doug Stott (Grand Rapids, Mich.: Eerdmans, 1996), 123. Varied translation in Bonhoeffer, *Letters and Papers* DBWE 8, 394. For other scholarship on polyphony see Wayne Whitson Floyd Jr., "Style and the Critique of Metaphysics: The Letter as Form in Bonhoeffer and Adorno," *Union Seminary Quarterly Review*: "Theology and the Practice of Responsibility: Essays on Dietrich Bonhoeffer," 46, no. 1–4 (1992): 247; Ford, *Self and Salvation*, 241–265; and Robert O. Smith, "Bonhoeffer and Musical Metaphor," *Word and World* 26, no. 2 (2006): 195–206. Also see Andreas Pangritz, "Point and Counterpoint: Resistance and Submission," in *Theology in Dialogue: The Impact of the Arts, Humanities, and Science on Contemporary Religious Thought*, ed. Lyn Holness and Ralf K. Wüstenberg (Grand Rapids, Mich.: Eerdmans, 2002); Jeremy S. Begbie, *Resounding Truth: Christian Wisdom in the World of Music* (Grand Rapids, Mich.: Baker, 2007).

142. Bonhoeffer, *Letters and Papers* DBWE 8, 342; Bonhoeffer, *Letters and Papers* (Touchstone, 1997), 215.

143. Bonhoeffer, *Letters and Papers* (Touchstone, 1997), 219, 216.

144. Bonhoeffer, *Letters and Papers* DBWE 8, 394.

145. Bonhoeffer, *Letters and Papers* (Touchstone, 1997), 157.

146. Ibid., 282, 157.

147. Ibid., 336.

148. Ibid., 374.

149. Bonhoeffer, *Letters and Papers* DBWE 8, 485.

150. Kelly and Nelson, *A Testament to Freedom*, 88–89.

151. Ibid., 89–90. We may think of "earth" as having an environmental connotation and "world" as having a political/social connotation, but Bonhoeffer uses these terms—as well as the words "humanity," "reality," and "life"—interchangeably. Moreover, by defining the earth christologically and granting it worth through the crucified Christ, Bonhoeffer reclaims the term "earth" from Nazi "blood and soil" mythology. The "earth" was a pregnant term in German Society in 1932, because it pointed to the Nazi belief that guarding the nation or land from non-Aryans was essential for preserving a "pure" German bloodline or racial identity.

152. Karl Barth, *The Word of God and the Word of Man* (Gloucester, Mass.: Peter Smith, 1978), 46–47.

153. Bonhoeffer, *Letters and Papers* DBWE 8, 372–373.

154. Bonhoeffer, *Letters and Papers* (Touchstone, 1997), 247. For a helpful essay on the power of Easter living, see Douglas John Hall, "*Ecclesia Crucis*: The Disciple Community and the Future of the Church in North America," *Union Seminary Quarterly Review*: "Theology and the Practice of Responsibility: Essays on Dietrich Bonhoeffer," 46, no. 1–4 (1992): 59–73. As Hall says, for Bonhoeffer "the resurrection means being sent back into the life of the world with a new exposure to its brokenness and a new concern for its mending" (69–70).

155. Rowan Williams, *Ray of Darkness: Sermons and Reflections* (Cambridge, Mass: Cowley, 1995), 64.

156. Ibid., 65.

157. Rowan Williams, *Resurrection: Interpreting the Easter Gospel* (Cleveland, Ohio: Pilgrim Press, 2004), 1–67.

158. Williams, *A Ray of Darkness*, 66–67.

159. Bonhoeffer, *Letters and Papers* DBWE 8, 181.

160. Bonhoeffer, *Letters and Papers* (Touchstone, 1997), 169.

161. Bonhoeffer, *Ethics* DBWE 6, 92.

162. Bonhoeffer, *Letters and Papers* (Touchstone, 1997), 169–171. See Irenaeus, *The Scandal of the Incarnation: Irenaeus against the Heresies*, trans. John Saward (San Francisco: Ignatius Press, 1990).

163. Bonhoeffer, *Letters and Papers* (Touchstone, 1997), 391.

164. Bonhoeffer, *Letters and Papers* DBWE 8, 181.

■ Chapter 5

1. Dietrich Bonhoeffer, *Sanctorum Communio: A Theological Study of the Sociology of the Church*, ed., Clifford J. Green, trans. Reinhard Krauss and Nancy Lukens, Vol. 1 of Dietrich Bonhoeffer Works. 16 vols. (Minneapolis: Fortress Press, 1998), 127.

2. Bonhoeffer also calls *Sanctorum Communio* a "Christian social philosophy" (21).

3. In *Bonhoeffer: A Theology of Sociality* (Grand Rapids, Mich.: Eerdmans, 1999), Clifford J. Green also observes that in *Sanctorum Communio* Bonhoeffer does not attend to the question of how his "*theological description* of the Christian community relates to the *actual religious institution* existing around him" (27).

4. Bonhoeffer, *Christ the Center*, trans. Edwin H. Robertson (New York: HarperCollins, 1978), 59.

5. Ibid., 58–59.

6. Ibid.

7. Ibid., 113.

8. Dietrich Bonhoeffer, *Ethics*, trans. Reinhold Krauss, et al., Vol. 6 of *Dietrich Bonhoeffer Works*, 16 vols. (Minneapolis: Fortress Press, 2005), 142.

9. Green, *A Theology of Sociality*, 23, 29–30.

10. Ibid., 52. See footnote 91 in Green.

11. Bonhoeffer, *Sanctorum Communio* DBWE 1, 139.

12. Ibid., 134.

13. Ibid., 126–127.

14. Ibid., 153.

15. Ibid., 130.

16. Green, *A Theology of Sociality*, 56–57.

17. Ibid., 21–28. Other strengths of the text include that it critically engages philosophical idealism's notion of *Geist* and replaces modern theology's epistemological subject-object framework with the sociological category of I-You relation, which respects otherness and preserves difference by grounding knowledge of the world in encounter not ego. Bonhoeffer does mention the importance of repentance in *Sanctorum Communio*, but he does not offer an account of how repentance establishes continuity between the church as a sinful body and Christ existing as community. See Bonhoeffer, *Sanctorum Communio* DBWE 1, 119–120, 214.

18. See note 4 in chapter 2 of this volume.

19. Green, *A Theology of Sociality*, 22.

20. Bonhoeffer, *Sanctorum Communio* DBWE 1, 140–141.

21. For example, Bonhoeffer's concern for concreteness is seen in his words:

> The church is God's new will and purpose for humanity. God's will is always directed towards the concrete, historical human being. But this means that it begins to be implemented *in history*. God's will must become visible and comprehensible at some point in history. But at the same point it must already be completed. Therefore, it must be revealed. Revelation of God's will is necessary because... where God speaks and [where] the word becomes deed and history through human beings is broken. (*Sanctorum Communio* DBWE 1, 141–142)

22. Bonhoeffer, *Sanctorum Communio* DBWE 1, 140. Bonhoeffer cites the following verses as examples where Paul identifies Christ and the church: 1 Cor. 12:12, 6:15, 1:13; verses where Christ is present in the body of Christ: 1 Cor. 1:30, 3:16, 2 Cor. 6:16, Col. 2:17, 3:11; verses where the church-community is a collective person called Christ: Gal. 3:28, Col. 3:10, Eph. 1:23; and verses where identification cannot be made since the church awaits Christ's coming: Eph. 4:8, 1 Thess. 4:16, Phil. 3:20, 1 Cor. 15:23.

23. Bonhoeffer, *Christ the Center*, 59.

24. Bonhoeffer, *Sanctorum Communio* DBWE 1, 149–150.

25. Charles Marsh, *Reclaiming Dietrich Bonhoeffer: The Promise of His Theology* (New York: Oxford University Press, 1994), 67–80.

26. Ibid., 80. Bonhoeffer's social ontology exemplifies that even in the early years of his theological thinking, before he speaks of a religionless Christianity that counters inwardness and metaphysics, he frees himself from the premises of metaphysics and insists instead on a theological framework of concrete worldliness.

27. For a helpful essay on cruciform community, see Stephen G. Ray Jr., "Embodying Redemption: King and the Engagement of Social Sin" in *Bonhoeffer and King: Their Legacies and Import for Christian Social Thought*, ed. Willis Jenkins and Jennifer M. McBride (Minneapolis: Fortress Press, 2010), 163–174.

28. Dietrich Bonhoeffer, *Act and Being: Transcendental Philosophy and Ontology in Systematic Theology*, ed. Wayne Whitson Floyd Jr., trans. H. Martin Rumscheidt, Vol. 2 of *Dietrich Bonhoeffer Works*, 16 vols. (Minneapolis: Fortress Press, 1996), 81.

29. Marsh, *Reclaiming Dietrich Bonhoeffer*, 7–20. Barth's early theology, which Bonhoeffer knew, emphasizes God's freedom from human beings, but his later theology shows that God's freedom is freedom for humanity. See Karl Barth, *Church Dogmatics* II/2: *The Doctrine of God*, ed. G. W. Bromiley and T. F. Torrance, trans. G. W. Bromiley (Edinburgh, Scotland: T&T Clark, 2001), §28, "The Being of God Is the One Who Loves in Freedom."

30. Bonhoeffer, *Act and Being* DBWE 2, 112.

31. See Martin Heidegger, *Being in Time*, trans. Joan Stambaugh (Albany: State University of New York Press, 1996); Marsh, *Reclaiming Dietrich Bonhoeffer*, 112–114. Bonhoeffer often speaks of Christ and the church being free for the other, but he does not reduce discipleship to this. Theologies concerned with the exploitation of vulnerable populations, such as feminist theologies, caution against defining discipleship strictly as being for the other. If one were to summarize Bonhoeffer's theology in this way, it would eclipse other aspects integral to his theology such as the polyphony of life. This book has placed being for others alongside belonging wholly to the world, which includes a recognition of life's polyphony and gives value to strength and fullness of life as much as weakness and suffering. Furthermore, as discussed in the introduction, my primary concern is the triumphal tendencies of

Christians and churches who maintain and benefit from the status quo; thus, a focus on being for others is an important corrective.

32. Bonhoeffer, *Act and Being* DBWE 2, 120.

33. Ibid., 120, 113.

34. Ibid., 120.

35. Bonhoeffer, *Sanctorum Communio* DBWE 1, 145.

36. Ibid., 150.

37. Bonhoeffer, *Act and Being* DBWE 2, 146–147.

38. The lectures were given in the winter term at the University of Berlin as "Creation and Sin" but published as *Creation and Fall.*

39. Dietrich Bonhoeffer, *Creation and Fall* and *Temptation*, trans. John C. Fletcher (New York: Touchstone, 1997), 84.

40. Mark J. Boda, "Renewal in Heart, Word, and Deed: Repentance in the Torah," in *Repentance in Christian Theology*, ed. Mark J. Boda and Gordon T. Smith (Collegeville, Minn.: Liturgical Press, 2006), 3–24, 17.

41. Ibid., 16, 21.

42. Bonhoeffer, *Sanctorum Communio* DBWE 1, 178–180.

43. Bonhoeffer, *Act and Being* DBWE 2, 121.

44. Bonhoeffer, *Letters and Papers* (Touchstone, 1997), 382.

45. Bonhoeffer, *Ethics* DBWE 6, 257–258.

46. See Christine Schliesser, *Everyone Who Acts Responsibly Becomes Guilty. The Concept of Accepting Guilt in Dietrich Bonhoeffer: Reconstruction and Critical Assessment* (Neukirchen-Vluyn, Germany: Neukirchener-Verlag, 2006), 39–41, 45–48, 70, 112, 125–131.

47. Bonhoeffer, *Ethics* DBWE 6, 258–259.

48. In his Bible study *Temptation*, which is published with the lectures *Creation and Fall*, Bonhoeffer first mentions "vicarious suffering for the world." Dietrich Bonhoeffer, *Creation and Fall* and *Temptation*, trans. John C. Fletcher (New York: Touchstone, 1997), 138.

49. Bonhoeffer, *Sanctorum Communio* DBWE 1, 182.

50. Ibid., 191, 146.

51. Bonhoeffer, *Act and Being* DBWE 2, 137, 150. Clifford Green argues against critics of *Sanctorum Communio* who say that Bonhoeffer's understanding of church in the dissertation is too sectarian and exclusive. See chapter 2, "Human Sociality and the New Humanity of Christ: *Sanctorum Communio*," specifically pages 60–61. My primary intention here is not to offer a critique of the dissertation but rather an observation that the description in *Ethics* of Christ-reality lays a foundation upon which a fresh perspective of the church's identity and mission may be constructed. The background for the shift toward his later understanding must be understood by the eventual collapse of the Confessing Church's resistance. This progression of thinking led to his idea of a religionless Christianity. For our context, the dualism of "in Adam" or "in Christ" also excludes constructive conversation with other faith traditions.

52. Bonhoeffer, *Act and Being* DBWE 2, 113. Bonhoeffer sums up the section, "Ethics as Formation," with this italicized line: "*The church is the place where Jesus Christ's taking form is proclaimed and where it happens*" (120).

53. Bonhoeffer, *Ethics* DBWE 6, 67–68 (emphasis mine).

54. Ibid., 63.

55. Ibid. Bonhoeffer also uses the imagery of Luke 2:27, "no place in the inn," in *Discipleship* to describe the visible church (DBWE 4, 225).

56. In order to witness to Christ's acceptance, judgment, and reconciliation with all of humanity, the church then must not (contra *The Cost of Discipleship*) "conquer territory for Christ" because all reality is already Christ-reality (258). Because all of reality is Christ-reality, the church need not fight for "its existence in the world" or for space to secure its own interests. Bonhoeffer says that the church should "desire no more space than it needs to serve the world with its witness . . . to the world's reconciliation with God through Christ" (*Ethics* DBWE 6, 63–64).

57. From Bonhoeffer, *Letters and Papers* DBWE 8, 389.

58. Fretheim, "Repentance in the Former Prophets," 25–45; Dempsey, "'Turn Back, O People': Repentance in the Latter Prophets," 47–66.

59. Bonhoeffer, *Ethics* DBWE 6, 142. As argued in chapter 3 in this volume, because repentance as nontriumphal witness is defined by the person and work of Christ, repentance should be understood as discipleship, following after Jesus by taking the form of Christ. This connection between repentance and discipleship is the key to understanding costly grace as something other than works righteousness.

60. Ibid., 68.

61. Ibid., 136.

62. Ibid.

63. Ibid., 66.

64. Ibid., 256.

65. Ibid., 135.

66. Bonhoeffer, *Discipleship* DBWE 4, 90.

67. In *Discipleship* Bonhoeffer specifically says, "Even though Jesus Christ has already accomplished all the vicarious suffering necessary for our redemption, his sufferings in this world are not finished yet. In his grace, he has left something unfinished in his suffering, which the church-community is to complete in this last period before his second coming" (DBWE 4, 222).

68. In *Church Dogmatics* IV/3: *The Doctrine of Reconciliation*, ed. G. W. Bromiley and T. F. Torrance, trans. G. W. Bromiley et al. (Edinburgh, Scotland: T&T Clark, 1976), Barth says, "The judgment of the world begins in the 'house of God' (1 Peter 4) and it is from there that it spreads to embrace the world around" (91). Bonhoeffer discusses 1 Peter 4:17–18 in *Temptation*, but his conclusion is quite different from the implication of the aforementioned passage in *Ethics* in which the "whole guilt of the world falls on the church . . . and because here it is confessed and not denied, the possibility of forgiveness is opened" (*Ethics* DBWE 6, 136). In *Temptation*, the church's acceptance of judgment frees the church from God's wrath that instead "fall[s] upon the godless" (*Creation and Fall*, 138).

69. Bonhoeffer, *Ethics* DBWE 6, 95.

70. "Christological fact" is Rasmussen's phrase meant to communicate that acceptance of guilt is intrinsic to Christ's identity. See Larry L. Rasmussen, *Dietrich Bonhoeffer: Reality and Resistance* (New York: Abingdon, 1972), 52.

71. Bonhoeffer, *Ethics* DBWE 6, 135.

72. Ibid., 136.

73. Ibid., 138–140.

74. See Dietrich Bonhoeffer, "Report on the Mass Deportation of Jewish Citizens," *Conspiracy and Imprisonment 1940–1945*, ed. Mark S. Brocker, trans. Lisa E. Dahill, Vol. 16 of *Dietrich Bonhoeffer Works*, 16 vols. (Minneapolis: Fortress Press, 2006), 225–229.

75. See Bonhoeffer, *Ethics* DBWE 6, 164–165.

76. Dietrich Bonhoeffer, *Life Together*, ed. Geffrey B Kelly, trans. Daniel W. Bloesch and James H. Burtness, Vol. 5 of *Dietrich Bonhoeffer Works*, 16 vols. (Minneapolis: Fortress Press, 1996), 111; Bonhoeffer, *Ethics* DBWE 6, 142.

77. Bonhoeffer, *Ethics* DBWE 6, 142.

78. Bonhoeffer, *Life Together* DBWE 5, 111.

79. Ibid., 108, 110.

80. Ibid., 113.

81. Ibid., 109, 113.

82. Ibid., 113.

83. Ibid., 112.

84. Ibid., 114, 116.

85. Ibid., 116.

86. Bonhoeffer, *Discipleship* DBWE 4, 169.

87. Bonhoeffer, *Ethics* DBWE 6, 141.

88. Ibid., 142 (emphasis mine).

89. Bonhoeffer, *Creation and Fall*, 58. By interpreting the tree of knowledge as grace, Bonhoeffer's reading of Genesis follows Luther, who argues that the law presupposes relationship with God, not a fall from God. The tree of knowledge gives Adam and Eve a concrete way to respond to God's love in obedience to a divine command. Luther says, "And so when Adam had been created in such a way that he was, so to speak, drunk with joy towards God, and rejoiced also in all other creatures, then a new tree was created for the distinction between good and evil, so that Adam might have a definite sign of worship and reverence towards God." See Bernd Wannenwetsch, "Luther's Moral Theology," in *The Cambridge Companion to Martin Luther*, ed. Donald K. McKim (Cambridge: Cambridge University Press, 2003), 125. From Martin Luther, *D. Martin Luthers Werke: Kritische Gesamtausgaber [Shriften]*, 65 vols. (Weimar, Germany: H. Böhlau, 1883–1993), 42, 71.

90. Bonhoeffer, *Creation and Fall*, 58.

91. Ibid., 59. For an examination of Bonhoeffer on the incomprehensibility of evil, see Charles T. Mathewes, "A Tale of Two Judgments: Bonhoeffer and Arendt on Evil, Understanding, and Limits, and the Limits of Understanding Evil," *Journal of Religion* 80, no. 3 (2000): 375–404.

92. Bonhoeffer, *Creation and Fall*, 107.

93. Ibid., 58. Bonhoeffer speaks of the cross as "the sign of perfection in the world" in Geffrey B. Kelly and F. Burton Nelson, *A Testament to Freedom: The Essential Writings of Dietrich Bonhoeffer* (New York: HarperCollins, 1995), 251.

94. Bonhoeffer, *Ethics* DBWE 6, 309.

95. Ibid., 134. Scripture and tradition refer to Christ as both judge and the one judged on humanity's behalf, or, as Barth says, "The Judge Judged in Our Place." Karl Barth, *Church Dogmatics* IV/1: *The Doctrine of Reconciliation*, ed. G. W. Bromiley and T. F. Torrance, trans. G. W. Bromiley (Edinburgh, Scotland: T&T Clark, 1980), §59.2. Bonhoeffer emphasizes that the church takes the form of the *crucified* Christ, the form of the one judged on humanity's behalf, not the form of Christ who sits on the right hand of God "to judge the quick and the dead" as the creed says. When the church presumes continuity with God as judge, it breaks its union with the crucified Christ. In other words, as fully God and fully human, Christ can be both confessor and judge of guilt, but the church cannot. The church's identity and mission stems from the crucified Christ.

96. Bonhoeffer, *Ethics* DBWE 6, 315.

97. Ibid., 84. This passage mirrors one in *Life Together* that was written within the context of Christian community. Bonhoeffer writes:

> God hates this wishful dreaming because it makes the dreamer proud and pretentious. Those who dream of this idealized community demand that it be fulfilled by God, by others, and by themselves. They enter the community of Christians with their demands, set up their own law, and judge one another and even God accordingly. They stand adamant, a living reproach to all others in the circle of the community. They act as if they have to create the Christian community, as if their visionary ideal binds the people together.... So they first become the accusers of other Christians in the community, then accusers of God, and finally the desperate accusers of themselves. (DBWE 5, 36)

98. Bonhoeffer, *Discipleship* DBWE 4, 169–175.
99. Ibid., 336.
100. See my note 99 in the previous chapter.
101. Bonhoeffer, *Creation and Fall*, 71, 73.
102. Ibid., 74. The church-community must examine whether it is acting out its own will to be for God or is truly living for others, because "there is a kind of confession of Christ" and action done on behalf of Christ "that Jesus rejects because it is in contradiction with doing the will of God" (Bonhoeffer, *Ethics* DBWE 6, 331. See Matt. 7:21).
103. Bonhoeffer, *Creation and Fall*, 81 (emphasis mine).
104. Bonhoeffer, *Sanctorum Communio* DBWE 1, 185.
105. Bonhoeffer, *Ethics* DBWE 6, 220.
106. Ibid., 80.
107. Ibid., 220.
108. Ibid., 155–156.
109. Ibid., 64.
110. Ibid., 314–315, 328–329. This passage in *Ethics* is about Pharisees in the New Testament whom Bonhoeffer depicts as a prototype for religious Christians today. However, scholars such as Victoria Barnett and Steven Haynes have shown how a derogatory use of Jewish sects to make Christian theological points under Nazism was dangerous for Jews then and damages attempts at post-Holocaust Jewish-Christian relations today.
111. Ibid., 329.
112. Ibid., 314.
113. Ibid., 92. Bonhoeffer continues, "Just as the form of Christ is misperceived where he is understood essentially as a teacher of a pious and good life, so formation of human beings is...wrongly understood where one sees it only as guidance for a pious and good life" (93–94). In "Protestantism without Reformation" Bonhoeffer says, "The claim to be the church of Jesus Christ [is]...a recognition which is humbling because it leads to repentance. The church is a church of sinners and not of the righteous" (100).
114. Ibid., 93–94.
115. Ibid., 98.
116. Ibid., 248. Bonhoeffer's concern for realistic social and political undertakings mirrors Aquinas' insight that a society should only construct and enforce policies and laws that real human beings in a specific time and place can effectively follow and under which they can successfully thrive. Aquinas writes in his *Summa Theologica*, "Law should be possible both according to nature and according to the customs of the country.... Now human law is framed for a number of human beings, the majority of whom are not perfect in

virtue. Wherefore human laws do not forbid all vices...but only the more grievous vices, from which it is possible for the majority to abstain; and chiefly those that are to the hurt of others." Thomas Aquinas, *Summa Theologica, Volume II*. Trans. Fathers of the English Dominican Province (Notre Dame, Ind.: Ave Maria, 1981), Q. 96 Art. 2.

117. Bonhoeffer, *Ethics* DBWE 6, 242, 79.

118. Ibid., 318.

119. I speak of the Garden of Gethsemane here to emphasize ecclesial posture, not to make a theological claim that the church was or was not with Christ in the Garden.

120. Kelly and Nelson, *A Testament to Freedom*, 455.

121. Bonhoeffer, *Ethics* DBWE 6, 47.

122. Ibid., 318.

123. Ibid., 379.

124. Ibid., 378.

125. Ibid., 313. For more on discerning the will of God see Luca Bagetto, "The Exemplification of Decision in Dietrich Bonhoeffer," *Union Seminary Quarterly Review* 46, no. 1–4 (1992): 197–204. See also Lisa E. Dahill, "Probing the Will of God: Bonhoeffer and Discernment," *Dialog* 41, no. 1 (2002): 42–49.

126. Bonhoeffer, *Ethics* DBWE 6, 321.

127. For a discussion on how Bonhoeffer reconciles an ethics of formation and command, see Plant, *Bonhoeffer*, 118–124.

128. Bonhoeffer, *Ethics* DBWE 6, 379.

129. Bonhoeffer, *Discipleship* DBWE 4, 77–83.

130. Bonhoeffer, *Ethics* DBWE 6, 74.

131. Ibid.

132. Ibid., 320.

133. Ibid., 74–75.

134. Ibid., 284.

135. Ibid. Bonhoeffer, *Letters and Papers* DBWE 8, 265.

136. Bonhoeffer, *Ethics* DBWE 6, 248.

137. Ibid., 221.

138. Ibid., 268.

139. Ibid., 227, 235.

140. Likewise, Augustine says in *The City of God* that true justice in this life only comes through the confession and forgiveness of sin. He writes, "Our righteousness itself, too, though genuine, in virtue of the genuine Ultimate Good to which it is referred, is nevertheless only such as to consist in the forgiveness of sins rather than in the perfection of virtues. The evidence for this is in the prayer of the whole City of God on pilgrimage in the world, which as we know, cries out to God through the lips of all its members: 'Forgive us our debts, as we forgive our debtors.' And this prayer is not effective for those whose 'faith, without works, is dead' but only for those whose 'faith is put into action through love'" (19.27). See Augustine, *Concerning the City of God against the Pagans*, trans. Henry Bettenson (London: Penguin, 1984), 892.

141. Bonhoeffer, *Ethics* DBWE 6, 226.

142. Ibid., 226–227.

143. Bonhoeffer, *Discipleship* DBWE 4, 279.

144. Bonhoeffer, *Ethics* DBWE 6, 234.

145. Ibid., 264–265, 382, 384.

146. Ibid., 226.

147. Ibid., 229, 238.

148. Ibid., 265, 385.

149. Ibid., 287–288.

150. Ibid., 288.

151. Bonhoeffer's discussion of the structure of responsible life leads to a section about the place of responsibility, which Bonhoeffer calls "vocation." See Bonhoeffer, *Ethics* DBWE 6, 289–298.

152. Bonhoeffer, *Ethics* DBWE 6, 254–255.

153. Ibid., 378, 74–75, 254–255, 290. While attuned to the whole, Bonhoeffer means to offer limits by focusing on concrete existence; however, the times and places that concern Christians in the United States can be quite overwhelming in our global context, in that as members of the universal body of Christ and as citizens of the world's leading power, "we have been placed objectively by our history," as Bonhoeffer says, not only within local communities but also on the international stage.

154. Bonhoeffer, *Ethics* DBWE 6, 246–247.

155. I am thinking here of a local Charlottesville congregation who entered a process of confession over four decades later for its participation in Massive Resistance to school desegregation in the late 1950s. See my essay, "Christ Episcopal Church amidst Massive Resistance: A Theological Examination of Christian Duty," for a history of, and challenge to, Christ Church's involvement www.livedtheology.org. Nothing has been written yet on the church's public confession and its attempt at reconciliation.

156. Bonhoeffer, *Ethics* DBWE 6, 239, 243.

157. Ibid., 291.

158. Ibid., 295–296.

159. See Gustavo Gutiérrez, *A Theology of Liberation: History, Politics, and Salvation*, trans. and ed. Caridad Inda and John Eagleson (New York: Orbis Books, 1988), 113.

160. Bonhoeffer *Ethics* 295. See Friedrich Wilhelm Nietzsche, *Thus Spoke Zarathustra* in: *The Portable Nietzsche*, trans. Walter Kaufmann (New York: Penguin, 1976), 174.

161. Bonhoeffer, *Ethics* DBWE 6, 294–295.

162. Ibid., 292–293.

163. Ibid., 224–225.

164. Ibid., 289. Although as a body, a local community most likely can only commit to engage deeply one or two concerns, individual Christians can be educated about a whole range of public issues that they can support through voting.

165. Bonhoeffer, *Ethics* DBWE 6, 269.

166. Ibid., 353.

167. Ibid., 361, 353. Bonhoeffer makes a connection here to Matt. 18:6.

168. Bonhoeffer, *Discipleship* DBWE 4, 131.

169. 76.1 percent of the United States population self-describe as Christian. See the Pew Forum's "U.S. Religious Landscape Survey," http://religions.pewforum.org/affiliations, which measures the size and demographic characteristics of religious groups in the United States. The percentage of adults that belong to evangelical Protestant churches is 26.3; to historically black churches is 6.9; to mainline Protestant churches is 18.1; to Catholic congregations is 23.9; to Eastern Orthodox congregations is 0.6, and to other Christian congregations is 0.3.

170. From "Peter and the Church Struggle" (church election sermon, July 23, 1933):

> Peter's church—this is not something which one can say with untroubled pride. Peter, the confessing, believing disciple, Peter denied his Lord on the same night as Judas betrayed him;...Peter's church, that is the church which shares these weaknesses, the church which itself again and again denies and falls, the unfaithful, the fainthearted, timid church which again neglects its charge...But Peter is also the man of whom we read: 'He went out and wept bitterly'....Peter's church is not only the church which confesses its faith, nor only the church which denies its Lord; it is the church which still can weep. (Kelly and Nelson, *A Testament to Freedom*, 215)

171. Kelly and Nelson, *A Testament to Freedom*, 276.

172. Bonhoeffer, *Life Together* DBWE 5, 111; Dietrich Bonhoeffer, *The Cost of Discipleship*, trans. R. H. Fuller (Touchstone: New York, 1995), 114. Bonhoeffer says that by wearing the rags of confession and repentance, the church "gives...strong witness to the injustice of the world" (Bonhoeffer, *Discipleship* DBWE 4, 110).

■ Introduction to Part III and Chapter 6

1. Dietrich Bonhoeffer, *Act and Being: Transcendental Philosophy and Ontology in Systematic Theology*, ed. Wayne Whitson Floyd Jr., trans. H. Martin Rumscheidt, Vol. 2 of *Dietrich Bonhoeffer Works*, 16 vols. (Minneapolis: Fortress Press, 1996), 132, 135.

2. For a description of the Iona Community, see http://www.iona.org.uk.

3. I borrow the term "embedded theology" from Howard W. Stone and James O. Duke, *How to Think Theologically* (Minneapolis: Fortress Press, 1996).

4. Scott Dimock, interview with author, November 6, 2006.

5. See www.eleutherocommunity.org. The Web site has been redesigned and revised since I accessed it during 2006–2008, although the pages mentioned here have been electronically stored by the Eleuthero Community and much of the same content and language may be found on the new site. Also see Rowan Williams, "Environmental Lecture: Changing the Myths We Live By," July 5, 2004. Available: http://www.archbishopofcanterbury.org/1064.

6. All quotes in paragraph from the "Vision and Mission" link of the original Web site, 2005–2008, and may be found in a slightly redacted version under the "Welcome" and "Our Calling" links of the revised site.

7. Sarrah Stankiewicz, interview with author, September 9, 2006.

8. Evan Pillsbury, interview with author, September 8, 2006. The lecture series includes "A Theology of Water" summer 2006 (with such talks as "Water, The Mediator of Life," "Water, The Mediator of God's Wide Love, God's Good Gift for All," "Water, The Mediator of Justice," and "Water, The Mediator of Existential Longing") and the "God over Guinness" Winter 2006/2007 series. Single lectures have included, "Christianity and Consumer Culture: Collusion or Critique?" and "The Anthropology of Wendell Berry."

9. Sarrah Stankiewicz, interview with author, September 9, 2006.

10. Dave Stankiewicz, interview with author, September 10, 2006.

11. Evan Pillsbury, interview with author, September 8, 2006.

12. Kathryn Pillsbury, interview with author, September 7, 2006.

13. Dietrich Bonhoeffer, *Letters and Papers from Prison*, ed. John W. de Gruchy, trans. Isabel Best et al., Vol. 8 of *Dietrich Bonhoeffer Works*, 16 vols. (Minneapolis: Fortress Press, 2010), 478.

14. Dietrich Bonhoeffer, *Letters and Papers from Prison*, trans. Reginald Fuller et al. (New York: Touchstone, 1997), 382. In a letter to Bethge, Bonhoeffer expands on this thought in a way that also correlates with Kathryn Pillsbury's comments above. Bonhoeffer writes, "The

church must come out of its stagnation. We must move out again into the open air of intellectual discussion with the world... if we are to get down to the serious problems of life" (378).

15. Kathryn Pillsbury, interview with author, September 7, 2006.

16. Tim Clayton, "Eleuthero Launch Talk," October 14, 2005.

17. Ibid.

18. Ibid.

19. Tim Clayton, interview with author, September 8–9, 2006.

20. Ibid.

21. Ibid.

22. Ibid.

23. Ibid.

24. Tim Clayton, "Staunch the Bleeding," November 4, 2005.

25. Ibid.

26. Ibid.

27. Ibid. See also Sidney Blumenthal, *Spiegel Online International*, "No One Can Say They Didn't See It Coming," August 31, 2005, http://www.spiegel.de/international/1,1518,372455,00.html.

28. Clayton, "Staunch the Bleeding," November 4, 2005.

29. Ibid.

30. Ibid.

31. Tim Clayton, interview with the author, September 8–9, 2006.

32. Clayton, "Eleuthero Launch Talk," October 14, 2005.

33. Ibid.

34. Tim Clayton, "Built into Creation," October 21, 2005.

35. Clayton, "Staunch the Bleeding," November 4, 2005; Clayton, "Eleuthero Launch Talk," October 14, 2005.

36. Clayton, "Staunch the Bleeding," November 4, 2005.

37. Michael Northcott, "The Dominion Lie: How Millennial Theology Erodes Creation Care," in *Diversity and Dominion: Dialogues in Ecology, Ethics, and Theology*, ed. Kyle S. Van Houtan and Michael S. Northcott (Eugene, Ore.: Cascade Books, 2010), 105.

38. Michael Northcott, "The Ecological Spirit: Being Church and Being Creatures," Jesus and the Earth: The Gospel and the Future of the Environment, University of Gloucestershire, February 8, 2003, http://www.jri.org.uk/resource/ecologicalspirit.htm, 7.

39. Tim Clayton, interview with author, September 8–9, 2006; Clayton, "Staunch the Bleeding," November 4, 2005.

40. One example is the work of Rt. Rev. James Jones, the Anglican Bishop of Liverpool, who has lent Eleuthero "his good name and support" and has helped Eleuthero cast its vision. In Liverpool, the Anglican diocese has been working with the city to start a new school where the whole curriculum centers on the environment, with the building itself constructed for experiential learning; it collects rain water and uses solar power, for instance. The bishop's public work and "public voice for justice" has influenced Tony Blair, who was present for the formal opening of the school. Not long before the school opening, in public speeches, Blair had challenged the government of the United Kingdom to realize the link between environmental degradation and the plight of the world's poor and had proposed that taxes should be determined by the consumption of raw materials rather than according to income. Another Christian organization that has greatly influenced Eleuthero's vision is A Rocha and its international director, Peter Harris; see www.arocha.org.

41. Cheryl Clayton, interview with author, September 10, 2006.

42. Bonhoeffer, *Letters and Papers* DBWE 8, 485.

43. Cheryl Clayton, interview with author, September 10, 2006.

44. Ibid.

45. Loren Ayer, interview with author, September 7, 2006.

46. Tim Clayton, interview with author, September 8–9, 2006.

47. Cheryl Clayton, interview with author, September 10, 2006.

48. Tim Clayton, interview with author, September 8–9, 2006.

49. See Bonhoeffer, *Letters and Papers* DBWE 8, 389–390.

50. Tim Clayton, interview with author, September 8–9, 2006.

51. Ibid. Tim offers another example of the redemptive power of an attitude of confession. He says, "There was an article that appeared in a scientific journal written by a biologist at Oberlin, and he was basically doing the standard lambasting of evangelicals. There were two responses written back to him. One of them involved my friend. He got international voices together to write, and while they didn't really apologize, they took a very conciliatory, 'we hear you' kind of approach. I thought, 'That's pretty good, although I'd like to see a little more but on the whole, that's pretty good'.... There was another response that went out in the journal written by a biologist at a Christian college and his argument was basically, 'You know, there is just a lot more going on than you are aware of. Now Christian colleges have environmental science programs and there are different Christian groups that care.' While there is some truth in what he is saying, it just seemed to me that he was pointing to a small amount of history to make up for a large amount of neglect, and he's acting like this other guy has the problem! And yet, again, isn't the ability to confess and repent the most basic aspect of Christian life? Why couldn't he just simply say, 'You are right. This has been a huge problem and we have been wrong, *but*...' (and he could do that in a short paragraph). Then he could say, 'But at least now these things are happening and they are exciting.' That then has a completely different spirit to it, and it allows other people to attach onto it. What actually ended up happening was the Oberlin scholar wrote back and interestingly enough, to the international voice he replied with 'I hear you; I wish you would do more, and could you be more public about that?' which I thought was a valid point. Then to the professor at the Christian college he was like, 'Don't even try to defend Christians,' and it was clear which response spoke to him. What was amazing though is that the Oberlin professor in his reply then used more scripture than had been previously used in this discussion. He pointed out the places where the prophets of the Lord had risked relationship, safety, and status, and had gone and told the people the word of the Lord that was not popular. He was basically saying to them, 'Aren't the prophets of the Lord to call the people to confession?'" (See David W. Orr, "Armageddon versus Extinction," *Conservation Biology* 19, no. 2 (April 2005): 290–292; "Conservation Theology for Conservation Biologists—a Reply to David Orr," *Conservation Biology* 19, no. 6 (December 2005): 1689–1692; Fred Van Dyke, "Between Heaven and Earth—Evangelical Engagement in Conservation," *Conservation Biology* (December 2005): 1693–1696; David. W. Orr, "A Response," *Conservation Biology* 19, no. 6 (December 2005): 1697–1698).

Tim also says that genuine confession demands repentance and he cites Pat Robertson's incomplete admission about the effects of global warming. He says, "Pat Robertson has come out in the past couple of months admitting that global warming seems to be real, and so Christians act like, well, okay, now we can sign up. But now that Christians have changed their minds, what ever happened to all the stuff that we have done in the past? Do we need to acknowledge that? Do we need to go and make amends? Isn't this just a basic Christian thing? Why do we skip that piece?"

52. Tim Clayton, interview with author, September 8–9, 2006. The Bill Moyers' show, "Is God Green," aired on PBS on October 11, 2006.

53. Cheryl Clayton, End of First Year Meeting, author present, September 8, 2006.

54. End of First Year Meeting, author present, September 8, 2006.

55. Tim Clayton, interview with the author, September 8–9, 2006.

56. From "Island Property" and "Support Eleuthero" links on the original Web site. For an explanation of what came of the island property and the pursuit of public space, see the forthcoming link, "Community Narrative" under "Community Resources," www.eleutherocommunity.org.

57. End of First Year Meeting, author present, September 8, 2006.

58. Loren Ayer, interview with author, September 7, 2006.

59. The Claytons' connection with the Nairobi Chapel was established through the Falls Church Episcopal in metropolitan Washington, D.C., where Tim previously served as a pastor.

60. Tim Clayton, interview with author, September 8–9, 2006.

61. Ibid.

62. Ibid.

63. Ibid.

64. "Sudanese Refugees Find New Home in Maine," *Weekend Edition Transcript, NPR News*, April 29, 2006.

65. A local ministry on Munjoy Hill, the Root Cellar, reports on their Web site, http://www.therootcellar.org, that *U.S. News and World Report* rated Portland's Munjoy Hill/Bayside/Kennedy Park community as the second largest white slum in America.

66. Kelly Ayer, interview with author, September 6, 2006.

67. Tim Clayton, "The Eleuthero Community Prayer Update Newsletter, Beginning of Summer 2006," e-mail, July 1, 2006.

68. Tim Clayton, "The Eleuthero Community Newsletter," e-mail, July 25, 2006. Quoted with permission from Isaac Wani (name changed).

69. Ibid; Evan Pillsbury, interview with author, September 8, 2006.

70. Tim Clayton, "The Eleuthero Community Newsletter," e-mail, July 25, 2006. This is Tim's paraphrase of the conversation with Father Bizimana.

71. Tim Clayton, "The Eleuthero Community Newsletter," e-mail, July 25, 2006.

72. Tim Clayton, "Prayer Update and Island News," e-mail, September 29, 2006.

73. Tim Clayton, interview with author, September 8–9, 2006.

74. End of First Year Meeting, author present, September 8, 2006.

75. Tim Clayton, interview with author, September 8–9, 2006.

76. End of First Year Meeting, author present, September 8, 2006.

77. Cheryl Clayton, interview with author, September 10, 2006.

78. Tim Clayton, interview with author, September 8–9, 2006.

79. Bonhoeffer, *Letters and Papers* (Touchstone, 1997), 215.

80. Tim Clayton, interview with author, September 8–9, 2006.

81. End of First Year Meeting, author present, September 8, 2006.

82. Tim Clayton, interview with author, September 8–9, 2006.

83. Geffrey B. Kelly and F. Burton Nelson, *A Testament to Freedom: The Essential Writings of Dietrich Bonhoeffer* (New York: HarperCollins, 1995), 351.

84. Kelly Ayer, interview with author, September 6, 2006.

85. Eleuthero's "Prayers and Holy Communion" service sheet has been adapted from the Iona Community, the Episcopal Church's Book of Common Prayer, and that of the Church of England. This line is from the Book of Common Prayer's prayer of confession. See *The Book of Common Prayer: According to the Use of the Episcopal Church* (New York: Oxford University Press, 1990).

■ Chapter 7

1. The Southeast White House information pamphlet.

2. See the profile of neighborhood cluster 34 at Neighborhood Info D.C., http://www.neighborhoodinfodc.org.

3. The Southeast White House information pamphlet.

4. Ibid.

5. Scott Dimock, interview with the author, October 16, 2006. Scott Dimock and Sammie Morrison founded the SEWH as a nonpartisan effort on behalf of national and municipal leaders who were concerned about lower income residents in Washington, D.C.

6. Jonathan Kozol, *Savage Inequalities: Children in America's Schools* (New York: Crown Publishers, 1991), 181.

7. Kristi Kiger, "The Southeast White House Guidebook: Companion Guide to an Experiential Learning Journey into the Heart of Southeast, D.C.," January 2006, 4.

8. Sammie Morrison, interview with the author, August 28, 2006 (emphasis mine).

9. For an example of an inner-city ministry that understands its relation to its neighbors in a similar way as the SEWH yet self-consciously describes its work as an act of repentance, see the description of Mark Gornik's work with Sandtown Habitat and New Song Community Ministries in Charles Marsh's *Beloved Community: How Faith Shapes Social Justice from the Civil Rights Movement to Today* (New York: Basic Books, 2005), 190–192. Adding the fourth "R" of repentance to John Perkin's model of "reconciliation, redistribution, and relocation," Gornik says, "We came here out of repentance, to learn from our neighbors and just be a part of the community.... When people would ask us, 'What are you doing here?' our answer was always the same: 'We are here to be neighbors'" (190). Also see Mark R. Gornik, *To Live in Peace: Biblical Faith and the Changing Inner City* (Grand Rapids, Mich.: Eerdmans, 2002).

10. Scott Dimock, interview with author, November 6, 2006.

11. Sammie describes his partnership with Scott as "a natural match for two people freed up by retirement and freed up by our will to follow Christ." Both Scott and Sammie have significant mentoring and urban ministry experience. As a retired officer of the Washington Metropolitan Police Department, Sammie has been particularly aware of the responsibility toward adolescent children inherent within his social power and influence. He describes a homicide scene in the early 1970s that instigated his "first dedicated move" toward taking responsibility for others through mentoring. Sammie says, "A young kid had just shot another kid when I arrived. I started thinking about the awesome power of a police officer who has responsibilities and power to carry out those responsibilities.... I thought if I had just simply been there before the shooting took place, then it wouldn't have happened, because I would have been a deterrent. So I thought, 'I need to get there five minutes before the bullet starts to move. Well, five minutes is cutting it close, so I need to be there fifteen minutes before the shooting occurs.' Fifteen minutes led me to thinking in terms of fifteen years. After that I joined Big Brothers and Big Sisters and since then have continued

mentoring young men in that model" (Sammie Morrison, interview with author, August 28, 2006). Scott spent a significant portion of his career working in urban ministry with the organization, Young Life, and his interest in race issues began as a white college student in Durham, North Carolina, where he participated in the civil rights movement.

12. Scott Dimock, interview with author, November 6, 2006; Southeast White House information pamphlet.

13. The Southeast White House information pamphlet.

14. Sammie Morrison, interview with author, August 28, 2006.

15. Marilyn Dimock, interview with author, October 16, 2006.

16. Scott Dimock, interview with author, October 16, 2006.

17. Ibid.

18. Hilary Barnett, interview with author, November 29, 2006.

19. Marilyn Dimock, interview with author, October 16, 2006. The SEWH turns to Mother Teresa as a guide for its emphasis on prayer. Marilyn says, "Throughout church history there are different people who have stood out as reflections of what is said in the Gospels and Mother Teresa is one of them. So the SEWH has looked to how she did her work in Calcutta as a picture of what that could be for us in the twenty-first century. Mother Teresa emphasized that prayer is the covering; prayer is the way for raising money; prayer is the way the house loves people and does not force them into anything even if they walk away. Mother Teresa also taught that caring for need has to be secondary to learning to love Jesus herself."

20. Sammie Morrison, interview with author, November 6, 2001.

21. Scott Dimock, interview with author, October 16, 2006.

22. Ibid.

23. Sammie Morrison, interview with author, August 28, 2006.

24. Ibid.

25. Ibid.

26. Ibid. Although all of the children began in Randle Highlands Elementary school, since 1996 they have moved to twenty-eight different schools within the metropolitan area. Sammie says, "History shows that children of our economic ilk move more times than most and so our intent is to be with them wherever they go."

27. David Hilfiker, *Not All of Us Are Saints: A Doctor's Journey with the Poor* (New York: Hill and Wang, 1994), 78–79.

28. Ibid., 79.

29. In *A Theology of Life: Dietrich Bonhoeffer's Religionless Christianity*, trans. Doug Stott (Grand Rapids, Mich.: Eerdmans, 1996), Ralf K. Wüstenberg sums up Bonhoeffer's concept of "religionless Christianity" with a phrase similar to Marilyn's: "to live as to believe" (160).

30. Marilyn Dimock, interview with author, October 16, 2006.

31. Ibid.

32. Sammie Morrison, interview with author, August 28, 2006.

33. "The Spirit of Social Hope: A Collection of Reflections," The Project on Lived Theology, April 26–27, 2006, 10–11; Scott Dimock, interview with author, October 16, 2006.

34. Sammie Morrison, interview with the author, August 28, 2006.

35. Geffrey B. Kelly and F. Burton Nelson, *A Testament to Freedom: The Essential Writings of Dietrich Bonhoeffer* (New York: HarperCollins, 1995), 86.

36. Marilyn Dimock, interview with author, October 16, 2006.

37. Scott Dimock, interview with author, October 16, 2006.

38. Marilyn Dimock, interview with author, October 16, 2006.
39. Ibid.
40. Hilary Barnett, interview with author, November 29, 2006.
41. Scott Dimock, interview with author, October 16, 2006.
42. Marilyn Dimock, interview with author, October 16, 2006.
43. Ibid.
44. Scott Dimock, interview with author, October 16, 2006.
45. See Jennifer M. McBride, "A Theology of the Southeast White House Hospitable Meal," December 2001. Available: http://www.livedtheology.org/pdfs/mcbride_hospitable.pdf.
46. Denise Speed, interview with author, November 6, 2001.
47. Wilma Mpelo, interview with author, November 6, 2001.
48. Sammie Morrison, interview with author, November 6, 2001.
49. Denise Speed, interview with author, October 17, 2006.
50. Summer Dye, interview with author, November 6, 2001.
51. Sammie Morrison, interview with author, August 28, 2006.
52. Louis Robertson, interview with author, October 18, 2006.
53. Ibid.
54. John Johnson, interview with author, October 17, 2006.
55. Sammie Morrison, interview with author, August 28, 2006.
56. Ibid.
57. Scott Dimock, interview with author, October 16, 2006.
58. Jennifer Lowery, interview with author, November 6, 2001.
59. Sammie Morrison, interview with author, August 28, 2006.
60. Ibid.
61. Scott Dimock, interview with author, October 16, 2006. The SEWH not only bridges people separated by the Anacostia River, but it also had the opportunity in 2005 to serve as a "neutral ground," where rival gangs held a truce summit that was led by local police.
62. Hilary Barnett, interview with author, November 29, 2006.
63. Scott Dimock, interview with author, October 16, 2006.
64. Iris Lamberson, interview with author, October 16, 2006.
65. John Johnson, interview with author, October 17, 2006.
66. Ibid.
67. Ibid.
68. Mike Wingfield, interview with author, October 17, 2006.
69. Kiger, "The Southeast White House Guidebook," 20.
70. John Johnson, interview with author, October 17, 2006.
71. Hilary Barnett, interview with author, November 29, 2006.
72. Bonhoeffer, *Letters and Papers* (Touchstone, 1997), 370.
73. David K. Shipler, *The Working Poor: Invisible in America* (New York: Random House, 2004), 11.
74. Kristi Kiger, interview with author, October 17, 2006.
75. Ibid.
76. Kiger, "The Southeast White House Guidebook," i, 1–2, 27.
77. Bonhoeffer, *Ethics* DBWE 6, 290–291.
78. Kristi Kiger, interview with author, October 17, 2006.
79. Marilyn Dimock, interview with author, October 16, 2006.

80. Hilary Barnett, interview with author, October 4, 2007. For an example of a lower-income community that has challenged its local grocery store, see Heidi B. Neumark's presentation at the 2006 Spring Institute on Lived Theology, www.livedtheology.org. Neumark describes how welfare moms dressed up as inspectors and demanded change. See Neumark, *Breathing Space: A Spiritual Journey in the South Bronx* (Boston: Beacon Press, 2003) for a fuller story of her work as a pastor in the Bronx.

81. Scott Dimock, interview with author, October 16, 2006.

82. Sammie Morrison, interview with author, August 28, 2006.

83. The SEWH as an organization does not belong to the CCDA, although a number of the individual staff members have been attending the annual CCDA conferences for years. See John M. Perkins, *Let Justice Roll Down* (Ventura, Calif.: Regal Books, 1976); *Beyond Charity: The Call to Christian Community Development* (Grand Rapids, Mich.: Baker Books, 1996); and most recently with Charles Marsh, *Welcoming Justice: God's Movement towards Beloved Community* (Downers Grove, Ill.: InterVarsity Press, 2009).

84. Scott Dimock, interview with author, October 16, 2006.

85. John Johnson, interview with author, October 17, 2006.

86. Kristi Kiger, interview with author, October 17, 2006.

87. Mike Wingfield, interview with author, October 17, 2006.

88. Sammie Morrison, interview with author, August 28, 2006 (emphasis mine).

89. Dietrich Bonhoeffer, *Ethics*, trans. Reinhold Krauss, et al., Vol. 6 of *Dietrich Bonhoeffer Works*, 16 vols. (Minneapolis: Fortress Press, 2005), 164–165.

90. The most obvious difference is that Dorothy Day, Peter Maurin, and members of the Catholic Worker movement lived (and live) in voluntary poverty with their neighbors.

91. Dorothy Day, *The Long Loneliness* (New York: HarperCollins, 1997), 285–286.

92. See interview information for Scott Dimock, Sammie Morrison, John Johnson, Louis Robertson, and Denise Speed.

■ Conclusion

1. Sammie Morrison, interview with author, August 28, 2006.
2. Scott Dimock, interview with author, October 16, 2006.
3. Dave Stankiewicz, interview with author, September 10, 2006.
4. Tim Clayton, interview with author, September 8–9, 2006.
5. Dietrich Bonhoeffer, *Letters and Papers from Prison*, trans. Reginald Fuller et al. (New York: Touchstone, 1997).
6. Denise Speed, interview with author, November 6, 2001.
7. Clayton, "Eleuthero Launch Talk," October 14, 2005.
8. Louis Robertson, interview with author, October 18, 2006; Hilary Barnett, interview with author, November 29, 2006; Kristi Kiger, interview with author, October 17, 2006.
9. Scott Dimock, interview with author, October 16, 2006.
10. Tim Clayton, interview with author, September 8–9, 2006.
11. Ibid.
12. Evan Pillsbury, interview with author, September 8, 2006.
13. Marilyn Dimock, interview with author, October 16, 2006.
14. Tim Clayton, interview with author, September 8–9, 2006.
15. Marilyn Dimock, interview with author, October 16, 2006.
16. Clayton, "Eleuthero Launch Talk," October 14, 2005.
17. Cheryl Clayton, interview with author, September 10, 2006.

BIBLIOGRAPHY

SELECTED BIBLIOGRAPHY

Abromeit, Hans-Jürgen. *Das Geheimnis Christi: Dietrich Bonhoeffers erfahrungsbezogene Christologie*. Neukirchen-Vluyn: Neukirchener Verlag, 1991.

Ammerman, Nancy Tatom. *Pillars of Faith: American Congregations and Their Partners*. Berkeley: University of California Press, 2005.

———. "Connecting Mainline Protestant Churches with Public Life." In *The Quiet Hand of God: Faith Based Activism and the Public Role of Mainline Protestantism*, ed. Robert Wuthnow and John H. Evans, 129–158. Berkeley: University of California Press, 2002.

Aquinas, Thomas. *Summa Theologica, Volume II*. Trans. Fathers of the English Dominican Province. Notre Dame, Ind.: Ave Maria, 1981.

Augustine. *Concerning the City of God against the Pagans*. Trans. Henry Bettenson. London: Penguin, 1984.

Ayres, Jennifer. "'With an Urgency Born of This Hope...': A Constructive Practical Theology of Reformed Social Witness Practice." Ph.D. diss., Emory University, 2007.

Bagetto, Luca. "The Exemplification of Decision in Dietrich Bonhoeffer." *Union Seminary Quarterly Review*: "Theology and the Practice of Responsibility: Essays on Dietrich Bonhoeffer." 46, no. 1–4 (1992): 197–204.

Balmer, Randall Herbert. *Thy Kingdom Come: How the Religious Right Distorts the Faith and Threatens America, An Evangelical's Lament*. New York: Basic Books, 2006.

Barnett, Victoria. *For the Soul of the People: Protestant Protest against Hitler*. New York: Oxford University Press, 1992.

Barth, Karl. *Church Dogmatics* II/2: *The Doctrine of God*. Ed. G. W. Bromiley and T. F. Torrance. Trans. G. W. Bromiley. Edinburgh, Scotland: T&T Clark, 2001.

———. *Church Dogmatics* IV/1: *The Doctrine of Reconciliation*. Ed. G. W. Bromiley and T. F. Torrance. Trans. G. W. Bromiley. Edinburgh, Scotland: T&T Clark, 1980.

———. *Church Dogmatics* IV/2: *The Doctrine of Reconciliation*. Ed. G. W. Bromiley and T. F. Torrance. Trans. G. W. Bromiley. Edinburgh, Scotland: T&T Clark, 1978.

———. *Church Dogmatics* IV/3: *The Doctrine of Reconciliation*. Ed. G. W. Bromiley and T. F. Torrance. Trans. G. W. Bromiley, et al. Edinburgh, Scotland: T&T Clark, 1976.

———. *The Epistle to the Romans*. Trans. Edwyn C. Hoskyns. Oxford: Oxford University Press, 1968.

———. *Evangelical Theology: An Introduction*. Trans. Grover Foley. New York: Holt, 1963.

———. *The Humanity of God*. Trans. John Newton Thomas and Thomas Wieser. Louisville, Ky.: Westminster John Knox Press, 1960.

———. *The Word of God and the Word of Man*. Gloucester, Mass.: Peter Smith, 1978.

Battle, Michael. "Penitence as Practice in African/African American Christian Spirituality." In *Repentance in Christian Theology*, ed. Mark J. Boda and Gordon T. Smith, 329–343. Collegeville, Minn.: Liturgical Press, 2006.

Beker, J. Christiaan. *Paul's Apocalyptic Gospel: The Coming Triumph of God*. Philadelphia: Fortress Press, 1982.

———. *Paul the Apostle*. Philadelphia: Fortress Press, 1980.

Begbie, Jeremy S. *Resounding Truth: Christian Wisdom in the World of Music.* Grand Rapids, Mich.: Baker, 2007.

Berger, Peter L., et al. *The Desecularization of Religion: Resurgent Religion and World Politics.* Grand Rapids, Mich.: Eerdmans, 1999.

Bertram, Robert. "The Authority to be (Culpably) Inclusive: A Mark of Bonhoeffer's *Confessio*." Eighth International Bonhoeffer Congress. Berlin, Germany. 2000.

Bethge, Eberhard. "The Challenge of Dietrich Bonhoeffer's Life and Theology." *Chicago Theological Seminary Register* 51, no. 2 (February 1961): 1–38.

———. "The Church Confessing, Then and Now: The Barmen Declaration 1934–84." *Union News* 2 (September 1984): 6a–6b, 6k–6l.

———. *Dietrich Bonhoeffer: A Biography.* Ed. Victoria J. Barnett. Trans. Eric Mosbacher et al. Minneapolis: Augsburg Fortress, 2000.

———. "The Legacy of the Confessing Church." *Church and Society* 85 (1995): 78–92.

———, ed. *Prayer and Righteous Action in the Life of Dietrich Bonhoeffer.* Ottawa, Ont.: Canterbury House, 1979.

———. "Schuld Bei Dietrich Bonhoeffer." In *Am gegebenen Ort: Aufsätze und redden 1970–1979.* Ed. Eberhard Bethge. Munich, Germany: Chr. Kaiser Verlag, 1979.

Birch, Bruce C., and Larry L. Rasmussen. *The Predicament of the Prosperous.* Philadelphia: Westminster Press, 1978.

Bischoff, Paul. "*Participation*: Ecclesial Praxis with a Crucified God for the World." *Journal for Christian Theological Research* 8 (2003): 19–36.

Boda, Mark J. "Renewal in Heart, Word, and Deed: Repentance in the Torah." In *Repentance in Christian Theology*, ed. Mark J. Boda and Gordon T. Smith, 3–24. Collegeville, Minn.: Liturgical Press, 2006.

Boda, Mark J. and Gordon T. Smith, eds. *Repentance in Christian Theology.* Collegeville, Minn.: Liturgical Press, 2006.

Bonhoeffer, Dietrich. *Act and Being: Transcendental Philosophy and Ontology in Systematic Theology.* Ed. Wayne Whitson Floyd Jr. Trans. H. Martin Rumscheidt. Vol. 2 of *Dietrich Bonhoeffer Works.* 16 vols. Minneapolis: Fortress Press, 1996.

———. *Barcelona, Berlin, New York: 1928–1931.* Ed. Clifford J. Green. Trans. Douglas W. Stott. Vol. 10 of *Dietrich Bonhoeffer Works.* 16 vols. Minneapolis: Fortress Press, 2008.

———. *Berlin: 1932–1933.* Ed. Larry L. Rasmussen. Trans. Isabel Best and David Higgins. Vol. 12 of *Dietrich Bonhoeffer Works.* 16 vols. Minneapolis: Fortress Press, 1996.

———. *Christ the Center.* Trans. Edwin H. Robertson. New York: HarperCollins, 1978.

———. *Conspiracy and Imprisonment: 1940–1945.* Ed. Mark S. Brocker. Trans. Lisa E. Dahill. Vol. 16 of *Dietrich Bonhoeffer Works*, 16 vols. Minneapolis: Fortress Press, 2006.

———. *The Cost of Discipleship.* Trans. R. H. Fuller. Touchstone: New York, 1995.

———. *Creation and Fall* and *Temptation.* Trans. John C. Fletcher. New York: Touchstone, 1997.

———. *Discipleship.* Ed. Geffrey B. Kelly and John D. Godsey. Trans. Barbara Green and Reinhard Krauss. Vol. 4 of *Dietrich Bonhoeffer Works.* 16 vols. Minneapolis: Fortress Press, 2003.

———. *Ethics.* Trans. Reinhold Krauss, et al. Vol. 2 of *Dietrich Bonhoeffer Works.* 16 vols. Minneapolis: Fortress Press, 2005.

———. *Gesammelte Schriften.* Vol. 3. Ed. Eberhard Bethge. Munich, Germany: Chr. Kaiser Verlag, 1968. 6 vols.

———. *Gesammelte Schriften*. Vol. 5. Ed. Eberhard Bethge. Munich, Germany: Chr. Kaiser Verlag, 1972. 6 vols.

———. *Letters and Papers from Prison*. Ed. John W. de Gruchy. Trans. Isabel Best et al, Vol. 8 of *Dietrich Bonhoeffer Works*. 16 vols. Minneapolis: Fortress Press, 2010.

———. *Letters and Papers from Prison*. Trans. Reginald Fuller et al. New York: Touchstone, 1997.

———. *Life Together* and *Prayerbook of the Bible*. Ed. Geffrey B Kelly. Trans. Daniel W. Bloesch and James H. Burtness. Vol. 5 of *Dietrich Bonhoeffer Works*. 16 vols. Minneapolis: Fortress Press, 1996.

———. *Love Letters from Cell 92: The Correspondence between Dietrich Bonhoeffer and Maria von Wedemeyer, 1943–45*. Ed. Ruth-Alice von Bismarck and Ulrich Kabitz. Trans. John Brownjohn. Nashville: Abingdon Press, 1995.

———. "Protestantism without Reformation." In *No Rusty Swords: Letters, Lectures, and Notes, 1928–1936 from the Collected Works of Dietrich Bonhoeffer*, ed. Edwin H. Robertson, 92–118. New York: Harper & Row, 1965.

———. *Sanctorum Communio: A Theological Study of the Sociology of the Church*. Ed. Clifford J. Green. Trans. Reinhard Krauss and Nancy Lukens. Vol. 1 of *Dietrich Bonhoeffer Works*. 16 vols. Minneapolis: Fortress Press, 1998.

———. *The Young Bonhoeffer: 1918–1927*. Ed. Paul Duane Matheny et al. Trans. Mary C. Nebelsick and Douglas W. Stott. Vol. 9 of *Dietrich Bonhoeffer Works*, 16 vols. Minneapolis: Fortress Press, 2003.

Bramadat, Paul A. *The Church on the World's Turf: An Evangelical Christian Group at a Secular University*. New York: Oxford University Press, 2000.

Branick, Vincent P. "The Sinful Flesh of the Son of God (Rom 8:3): A Key Image of Pauline Theology." *Catholic Biblical Quarterly* 47 (1985): 246–262.

———. "Apocalyptic Paul?" *Catholic Biblical Quarterly* 47 (1985): 664–675.

Brocker, Mark S. "Bonhoeffer's Appeal for Ethical Humility." In *Reflections on Bonhoeffer: Essays in Honor of F. Burton Nelson*, ed. Geoffrey B. Kelly and C. John Weborg, 290–298. Chicago: Covenant Publications, 1999.

Bultmann, Rudolf. "New Testament and Mythology: The Mythological Element in the Message of the New Testament and the Problem of Its Re-interpretation." In *Kerygma and Myth: A Theological Debate*, ed. Hans Werner Bartsch, trans. Reginald H. Fuller, 1–44. New York: Harper and Row, 1961.

Burtness, James H. *Shaping the Future: The Ethics of Dietrich Bonhoeffer*. Philadelphia: Fortress Press, 1985.

Busch, Eberhard. *Unter dem Bogen des einen Bundes: Karl Barth und die Juden 1933–1945*. Neukirchen-Vluyn, Germany: Neukirchener Verlag, 1996.

Campbell, Douglas A. *The Deliverance of God: An Apocalyptic Reading of Justification in Paul*. Grand Rapids, Mich.: Eerdmans, 2009.

Carson, Ronald A. "The Motifs of *Kenosis* and *Imitatio* in the Work of Dietrich Bonhoeffer, with an Excursus on the *Communicatio Idiomatum*." *Journal of the American Academy of Religion* 43, no. 3 (1975): 542–553.

Chaves, Mark. *Congregations in America*. Cambridge, Mass.: Harvard University, 2004.

Chaves, Mark, Helen M. Giesel, and William Tsitsos. "Religious Variations in Public Presence: Evidence from the National Congregations Study." In *The Quiet Hand of God: Faith Based Activism and the Public Role of Mainline Protestantism*, ed. Robert Wuthnow and John H. Evans, 108–128. Berkeley: University of California Press, 2002.

Chesterton, G. K. *Orthodoxy*. Garden City, N.Y.: Doubleday, 1959.

Chryssavgis, John. "'Life in Abundance': Eastern Orthodox Perspectives on Repentance and Confession." In *Repentance in Christian Theology*, ed. Mark J. Boda and Gordon T. Smith, 211–230. Collegeville, Minn.: Liturgical Press, 2006.

Clements, Keith W. *What Freedom? The Persistent Challenge of Dietrich Bonhoeffer*. Bristol, England: Bristol Baptist College, 1990.

Cochrane, Arthur C. *The Church's Confession under Hitler*. Pittsburgh, Pa.: Pickwick Press, 1976.

Cohen, Hermann, *Religion of Reason: Out of the Sources of Judaism*. Trans. Simon Kaplan. New York: F. Ungar, 1972.

Cone, James H. *Black Theology and Black Power*. Maryknoll, N.Y.: Orbis Books, 1997.

Cox, Harvey G. "Beyond Bonhoeffer: The Future of Religionless Christianity." In *Secular City Debate*, ed. Daniel Callahan, 205–214. New York: Macmillan, 1966.

Dahill, Lisa E. "Jesus for You: A Feminist Reading of Bonhoeffer's Christology." *Currents in Theology and Mission* 34, no. 4 (2007): 250–259.

———. "Probing the Will of God: Bonhoeffer and Discernment." *Dialog* 41, no. 1 (2002): 42–49.

Davidson, Ivor J. "Pondering the Sinlessness of Jesus Christ: Moral Christologies and the Witness of Scripture." *International Journal of Systematic Theology* 10, no. 4 (October 2008): 372–398.

Day, Dorothy. *The Long Loneliness*. New York: HarperCollins, 1997.

De Boer, Martinus C. "Paul, Theologian of God's Apocalypse." *Interpretation* 56, no. 1 (2002): 21–33.

De Gruchy, John W., ed. *Bonhoeffer for a New Day: Theology in a Time of Transition*. Grand Rapids, Mich.: Eerdmans, 1997.

———. *Bonhoeffer and South Africa: Theology in Dialogue*. Grand Rapids, Mich.: Eerdmans, 1984.

———, ed. *The Cambridge Companion to Dietrich Bonhoeffer*. Cambridge: Cambridge University Press, 1999.

———. "A Concrete Ethic of the Cross: Interpreting Bonhoeffer's Ethics in North America's Backyard." *Union Seminary Quarterly Review* 58, no. 1–2 (2004): 33–45.

———. "Confessing Guilt in South Africa Today in Dialogue with Dietrich Bonhoeffer." *Journal of Theology for Southern Africa* 67 (1989): 37–45.

———. *Confessions of a Christian Humanist*. Minneapolis: Fortress Press, 2006.

———. "Re-forming Congregations in a Time of Global Change: Toward a Kenotic Ecclesiology." *Princeton Seminary Bulletin* 27, no. 1 (2006): 51–66.

De Lange, Frits. *Waiting for the Word: Dietrich Bonhoeffer on Speaking about God*. Trans. Martin N. Walton. Grand Rapids, Mich.: Eerdmans, 2000.

Dempsey, Carol J. "'Turn Back, O People': Repentance in the Latter Prophets." In *Repentance in Christian Theology*, ed. Mark J. Boda and Gordon T. Smith, 47–66. Collegeville, Minn.: Liturgical Press, 2006.

D'Costa, Gavin. *Christianity and World Religions*. Oxford: Wiley-Blackwell, 2009.

D'Isanto, Luca. "Bonhoeffer's Hermeneutical Model of Community." *Union Seminary Quarterly Review*: "Theology and the Practice of Responsibility: Essays on Dietrich Bonhoeffer." 46, no. 1–4 (1992): 59–73.

Douglas, Kelly Brown. *Sexuality and the Black Church: A Womanist Perspective*. Maryknoll, N.Y.: Orbis Books, 1999.

Dramm, Sabine. *Dietrich Bonhoeffer and the Resistance*. Trans. Margaret Kohl. Minneapolis: Fortress Press, 2009.

Dumas, André. *Dietrich Bonhoeffer: Theologian of Reality*. Trans. Robert McAfee Brown. New York: Macmillan, 1971.

Ellingsen, Mark. "Bonhoeffer, Race, and a Communal Model for Healing." *Journal of Church and State* 43, no. 2 (2001): 235–249.

Ellul, Jacques. *The Presence of the Kingdom*. Trans. Olive Wyon. Colorado Springs: Helmers & Howard, 1989.

Elshtain, Jean Bethke. "Bonhoeffer and Modernity: *Sic et Non*." *Journal of Religious Ethics* 29, no. 3 (2001): 345–366.

———. "Freedom and Responsibility in a World Come of Age." *Union Seminary Quarterly Review*: "Theology and the Practice of Responsibility: Essays on Dietrich Bonhoeffer." 46, no. 1–4 (1992): 269–281.

———. "Shame and Public Life." *Dialog* 34 (Winter 1995): 18–21.

Feil, Ernst. *Die Theologie Dietrich Bonhoeffer: Hermeneutik, Christologie, Weltverständnis*. Munich, Germany: Chr. Kaiser and Matthias Grünewald, 1971.

———. *The Theology of Dietrich Bonhoeffer*. Trans. Martin Rumscheidt. Philadelphia: Fortress Press, 1985.

Finke, Roger, and Rodney Stark. *The Churching of America, 1776–2005: Winners and Losers in Our Religious Economy*. New Brunswick, N.J.: Rutgers University Press, 2005.

Fiorenza, Elisabeth Schüssler. *Rhetoric and Ethic: The Politics of Biblical Studies*. Minneapolis: Fortress Press, 1999.

Floyd, Wayne Whitson, Jr. "Style and the Critique of Metaphysics: The Letter as Form in Bonhoeffer and Adorno." *Union Seminary Quarterly Review*: "Theology and the Practice of Responsibility: Essays on Dietrich Bonhoeffer." 46, no. 1–4 (1992): 239–251.

———. *Theology and the Dialectics of Otherness: On Reading Bonhoeffer and Adorno*. Lanham, Md.: University Press of America, 1988.

Floyd, Wayne Whitson, Jr., and Charles Marsh, eds. *Theology and the Practice of Responsibility: Essays on Dietrich Bonhoeffer*. Special issue of *Union Seminary Quarterly Review* 46, no. 1–4 (1992): 1–309. Valley Forge, Pa.: Trinity Press, 1994.

Ford, David F. "Bonhoeffer, Holiness and Ethics." In *Holiness: Past and Present*, ed. Stephen C. Barton, 361–380. London: T&T Clark, 2003.

———. "Prayer and Righteous Action: Exploring Bonhoeffer's Suggestion." *New Blackfriars* 66 (1985): 336–347.

———. *Self and Salvation: Being Transformed*. Cambridge: Cambridge University Press, 1999.

Fretheim, Terence E. "Repentance in the Former Prophets." In *Repentance in Christian Theology*, ed. Mark J. Boda and Gordon T. Smith, 25–45. Collegeville, Minn.: Liturgical Press, 2006.

Frick, Peter, ed. *Bonhoeffer's Intellectual Formation: Theology and Philosophy in His Thought*. Tübingen, Germany: Mohr Siebeck, 2008.

———. "Friedrich Nietzsche's Aphorisms and Dietrich Bonhoeffer's Theology." In *Bonhoeffer's Intellectual Formation: Theology and Philosophy in His Thought*, ed. Peter Frick, 175–199. Tübingen, Germany: Mohr Siebeck, 2008.

Fulkerson, Mary McClintock. *Places of Redemption: Theology for a Worldly Church*. New York: Oxford University Press, 2007.

Funamoto, Hiroki. "Penultimate and Ultimate in Dietrich Bonhoeffer's *Ethics.*" In *Being and Truth*, ed. Alistair Kee and Eugene T. Long, 376–392. London: SCM, 1986.

Gasaway, Brantley. "An Alternative Soul of Politics: The Rise of Contemporary Progressive Evangelicals." Ph.D. diss., University of North Carolina, 2007.

Gerrish, B. A. "'To the Unknown God': Luther and Calvin on the Hiddenness of God." *Journal of Religion* 53, no. 3 (1973): 263–292.

Godsey, John D. *The Theology of Dietrich Bonhoeffer*. Philadelphia: Westminster Press, 1960.

Godsey, John D., and Geffrey B. Kelly, eds. *Ethical Responsibility: Bonhoeffer's Legacy to the Churches*. New York: Edwin Mellen Press, 1981.

Gorman, Michael J. *Cruciformity: Paul's Narrative Spirituality of the Cross*. Grand Rapids, Mich.: Eerdmans, 2001.

Gornik, Mark R. *To Live in Peace: Biblical Faith and the Changing Inner City*. Grand Rapids, Mich.: Eerdmans, 2002.

Green, Clifford J. *Bonhoeffer: A Theology of Sociality*. Grand Rapids, Mich.: Eerdmans, 1999.

———. "Trinity and Christology in Bonhoeffer and Barth." *Union Seminary Quarterly Review* 60, no. 1–2 (2006): 1–22.

Green, Garrett, "Introduction: Barth as Theorist of Religion." In *On Religion: The Revelation of God as the Sublimation of Religion*, trans. Garrett Green, 1–29. New York: T&T Clark, 2006.

Grünwaldt, Klaus, Christiane Tietz, and Udo Hahn. *Bonhoeffer und Luther: Zentrale Themen inhrer Theologie*. Hannover, Germany: VELKD, 2007.

Gutiérrez, Gustavo. *A Theology of Liberation: History, Politics, and Salvation*. Ed. and trans. Caridad Inda and John Eagleson. New York: Orbis Books, 1988.

Hall, Douglas John. "*Ecclesia Crucis*: The Disciple Community and the Future of the Church in North America." *Union Seminary Quarterly Review*: "Theology and the Practice of Responsibility: Essays on Dietrich Bonhoeffer" 46, no. 1–4 (1992): 59–73.

Harding, Susan Friend. *The Book of Jerry Falwell: Fundamentalist Language and Politics*. Princeton, N.J.: Princeton University Press, 2000.

Harvey, Barry. "The Body Politic of Christ: Theology, Social Analysis, and Bonhoeffer's Arcane Discipline." *Modern Theology* 13, no. 3 (1997): 319–346.

Hauerwas, Stanley. *Performing the Faith: Bonhoeffer and the Practice of Nonviolence*. Grand Rapids, Mich.: Brazos Press, 2004.

———. *With the Grain of the Universe: The Church's Witness and Natural Theology*. Grand Rapids, Mich.: Brazos Press, 2001.

Hauerwas, Stanley, and Charles Pinches. *Christians among the Virtues: Theological Conversations with Ancient and Modern Ethics*. Notre Dame, Ind.: University of Notre Dame Press, 1997.

Haynes, Stephen R. *The Bonhoeffer Legacy: Post-Holocaust Perspectives*. Minneapolis: Fortress Press, 2006.

———. *The Bonhoeffer Phenomenon: Portraits of a Protestant Saint*. Minneapolis: Fortress Press, 2004.

Haynes, Stephen R., and Lori Brandt Hale, *Bonhoeffer for Armchair Theologians*. Louisville, Ky.: Westminster John Knox, 2009.

Hays, Richard B. *The Faith of Jesus Christ: An Investigation of the Narrative Substructure of Galatians 3:1–4:11*. Chico, Calif.: Scholars Press, 1983.

Hedges, Paul, and Alan Race, eds. *Christian Approaches to Other Faiths*. London: SCM, 2008.

Heidegger, Martin. *Being and Time*. Trans. Joan Stambaugh. Albany: State University of New York Press, 1996.

The Heidelberg Catechism: A New Translation for the Twenty-First Century. Trans. Lee C. Barrett III. Cleveland, Ohio: Pilgrim Press, 2007.

Held, Heinz Joachim. "Schuldübernahme als Ausdruck der Christusnachfolge bei Martin Luther und Dietrich Bonhoeffer." In *Konsequenzen: Dietrich Bonhoeffers Kirchenverständnis heute*, ed. Ernst Feil and Ilse Tödt, 140–168. Munich, Germany: Kaiser, 1980.

Heschel, Abraham Joshua. *The Prophets: An Introduction*. New York: Harper & Row, 1969.

Hilfiker, David. *Not All of Us Are Saints: A Doctor's Journey with the Poor*. New York: Hill and Wang, 1994.

Huber, Wolfgang. "Towards an Ethics of Responsibility." *Journal of Religion* 73, no. 4 (1993): 573–591.

Humphrey, Edith M. "'And I Shall Heal Them': Repentance, Turning, and Penitence in the Johannine Writings." In *Repentance in Christian Theology*, ed. Mark J. Boda and Gordon T. Smith, 105–126. Collegeville, Minn.: Liturgical Press, 2006.

Hunsinger, George. *Disruptive Grace: Studies in the Theology of Karl Barth*. Grand Rapids, Mich.: Eerdmans, 2000.

———. *How to Read Karl Barth: The Shape of His Theology*. New York: Oxford University Press, 1991.

Hunter, James Davidson, and Jennifer L. Geddes. *Hedgehog Review: Critical Reflections on Contemporary Culture*: "After Secularization." 8, no. 1–2 (2006).

Irenaeus. *The Scandal of the Incarnation: Irenaeus against the Heresies*. Trans. John Saward. San Francisco: Ignatius Press, 1990.

Janz, Paul. "Redeeming Modernity: Rationality, Justification, and Penultimacy in the Theology of Dietrich Bonhoeffer." Ph.D. diss., University of Cambridge, 2000.

Jenkins, Willis, and Jennifer M. McBride. *Bonhoeffer and King: Their Legacies and Import for Christian Social Thought*. Minneapolis: Fortress Press, 2010.

Jensen, David H. "Religionless Christianity and Vulnerable Discipleship: The Interfaith Promise of Bonhoeffer's Theology." *Journal of Ecumenical Studies* 38, no. 2–3 (2001): 151–167.

Jenson, Matt. "Real Presence." *Scottish Journal of Theology* 58, no. 2 (2005): 143–160.

Jenson, Robert W. "Luther's Contemporary Theological Significance." In *The Cambridge Companion to Martin Luther*, ed. Donald K. McKim, 272–288. Cambridge: Cambridge University Press, 2003.

Johns, Cheryl Bridges. "Yielding to the Spirit: A Pentecostal Understanding." In *Repentance in Christian Theology*, ed. Mark J. Boda and Gordon T. Smith, 287–306. Collegeville, Minn.: Liturgical Press, 2006.

Johnson, Kristen Deede. *Theology, Political Theory, and Pluralism: Beyond Tolerance and Difference*. Cambridge: Cambridge University Press, 2007.

Jones, L. Gregory. "The Cost of Forgiveness: Grace, Christian Community, and the Politics of Worldly Discipleship." *Union Seminary Quarterly Review*: "Theology and the Practice of Responsibility: Essays on Dietrich Bonhoeffer." 46, no. 1–4 (1992): 59–73.

Jones, Paul D. *The Humanity of Christ: Christology in Karl Barth's* Church Dogmatics. London: Continuum, 2008.

———. "Karl Barth on Gethsemane." *International Journal of Systematic Theology* 9, no. 2 (2007): 148–171.

Kelley, James Patrick. "Prayer and Action for Justice: Bonhoeffer's Spirituality." In *The Cambridge Companion to Dietrich Bonhoeffer*, ed. John W. de Gruchy, 246–268. Cambridge: Cambridge University Press, 1999.

Kelly, Geffrey B. "Kierkegaard as 'Antidote' and as Impact on Dietrich Bonhoeffer's Concept of Christian Discipleship." In *Bonhoeffer's Intellectual Formation: Theology and Philosophy in His Thought*, ed. Peter Frick, 145–165. Tübingen, Germany: Mohr Siebeck, 2008.

———. *Liberating Faith: Bonhoeffer's Message for Today*. Minneapolis: Augsburg Publishing House, 1984.

Kelly, Geffrey B., and C. John Weborg, eds. *Reflections On Bonhoeffer: Essays In Honor of F. Burton Nelson*. Chicago: Covenant Publications, 1999.

Kelly, Geffrey B., and F. Burton Nelson. *The Cost of Moral Leadership: The Spirituality of Dietrich Bonhoeffer*. Grand Rapids, Mich.: Eerdmans, 2003.

———. *A Testament to Freedom: The Essential Writings of Dietrich Bonhoeffer*. New York: HarperCollins, 1995.

Kierkegaard, Søren. *Fear and Trembling*. Trans. Alastair Hannay. London: Penguin, 1985.

———. *Philosophical Fragments*. Trans. Howard V. Hong. Princeton, N.J.: Princeton University Press, 1974.

———. *Training in Christianity and the Edifying Discourse which "Accompanied" It*. Trans. Walter Lowrie. Princeton, N.J.: Princeton University Press, 1944.

———. *Works of Love*. Ed. and trans. Howard V. Hong and Edna H. Hong. Princeton, N.J.: Princeton University Press, 1995.

Kiger, Kristi. "The Southeast White House Guidebook: Companion Guide to an Experiential Learning Journey into the Heart of Southeast D.C." January 2006.

Kittel, Gerhard, ed. *Theological Dictionary of the New Testament*. Vol. 3. Grand Rapids, Mich.: Eerdmans, 1967. 10 vols.

———, ed. *Theological Dictionary of the New Testament*. Vol. 4. Grand Rapids, Mich.: Eerdmans, 1964. 10 vols.

Klassen, A. J. *A Bonhoeffer Legacy: Essays in Understanding*. Grand Rapids, Mich.: Eerdmans, 1981.

Kozol, Jonathan. *Savage Inequalities: Children in America's Schools*. New York: Crown Publishers, 1991.

Krötke, Wolf. "Dietrich Bonhoeffer and Martin Luther." In *Bonhoeffer's Intellectual Formation: Theology and Philosophy in His Thought*, ed. Peter Frick, 53–82. Tübingen, Germany: Mohr Siebeck, 2008.

Liguš, Ján. "Dietrich Bonhoeffer: Ultimate, Penultimate, and their Impact; the Origin and the Essence of *Ethics*." In *Bonhoeffer's* Ethics: *Old Europe and New Frontiers*, ed. Guy Carter et al., 59–72. Kampen, Netherlands: Kok Pharos, 1991.

Lovin, Robin W. "Biographical Context." In *New Studies in Bonhoeffer's Ethics*, ed. William J. Peck, 67–101. Lewiston, N.Y.: Edwin Mellen Press, 1987.

———. *Christian Faith and Public Choices: The Social Ethics of Barth, Brunner, and Bonhoeffer*. Philadelphia: Fortress Press, 1984.

———. *Christian Realism and the New Realities*. New York: Cambridge University Press, 2008.

Lowe, Walter. "Bonhoeffer and Deconstruction: Toward a Theology of the Crucified Logos." *Union Seminary Quarterly Review*: "Theology and the Practice of Responsibility: Essays on Dietrich Bonhoeffer." 46, no. 1–4 (1992): 207–221.

Lull, Timothy F., ed. *Martin Luther's Basic Theological Writings*. Minneapolis: Augsburg Fortress, 2005.

Luther, Martin. *First Lectures on the Psalms*. Vol. 10 of *Luther's Works*, ed. Hilton C. Oswald. Saint Louis: Concordia Publishing House, 1974.

———. *Heidelberg Disputation*. Vol. 31 of *Luther's Works*, ed. Jaroslav Pelikan and Helmut T. Lehman. Philadelphia: Fortress Press, 1955–1986.

———. *The Bondage of the Will*. Vol. 33 of *Luther's Works*, ed. Jaroslav Pelikan and Helmut T. Lehman. Philadelphia: Fortress Press, 1955–1986.

Malesic, Jonathan. *Secret Faith in the Public Square: An Argument for the Concealment of Christian Identity*. Grand Rapids, Mich.: Brazos Press, 2009.

Marsh, Charles. *Beloved Community: How Faith Shapes Social Justice from the Civil Rights Movement to Today*. New York: Basic Books, 2005.

———. *Reclaiming Dietrich Bonhoeffer: The Promise of His Theology*. New York: Oxford University Press, 1994.

———. *Wayward Christian Soldiers*. New York: Oxford University Press, 2007.

Martyn, J. Louis. *Galatians*. New York: Doubleday, 1997. Vol. 33A of *The Anchor Bible*.

———. *Theological Issues in the Letters of Paul*. Nashville: Abingdon Press, 1997.

Mathewes, Charles T. "A Tale of Two Judgments: Bonhoeffer and Arendt on Evil, Understanding, and Limits, and the Limits of Understanding Evil." *Journal of Religion* 80, no. 3 (2000): 375–404.

———. *A Theology of Public Life*. Cambridge: Cambridge University Press, 2007.

Mathewes, Charles, and Christopher McKnight Nichols. *Prophecies of Godlessness: Predictions of America's Imminent Secularization, from the Puritans to Postmodernity*. New York: Oxford University Press, 2008.

Matthews, John W. "Responsible Sharing of the Mystery of Christian Faith: *Disciplina Arcani* in the Life and Theology of Dietrich Bonhoeffer." *Dialog* 25, no. 1 (1986): 19–25.

Matlock, R. Barry. *Unveiling the Apocalyptic Paul: Paul's Interpreters and the Rhetoric of Criticism*. Sheffield, England: Sheffield Academic Press, 1996.

Mayer, Rainer. "Christology: The Genuine Form of Transcendence." In *A Bonhoeffer Legacy: Essays in Understanding*, ed. A. J. Klassen, 179–192. Grand Rapids, Mich.: Eerdmans, 1981.

McBride, Jennifer M. "Bestowing Meaning: A Reflection on Philosophical Theology and Ethnography." *Practical Matters: A Transdisciplinary, Multimedia Journal of Religious Practices and Practical Theology* (Issue 3). Online. Available: http://www.practicalmattersjournal.org.

———. "Christ Episcopal Church amidst Massive Resistance: A Theological Examination of Christian Duty." *The Project on Lived Theology*. January 2003. Online. Available: http://www.livedtheology.org/pdfs/mcbride.pdf.

———. "A Theology of the Southeast White House Hospitable Meal." *The Project on Lived Theology*. December 2001. Online. Available: http://www.livedtheology.org/pdfs/mcbride_hospitable.pdf.

McCormack, Bruce L. *Barth's Critically Realistic Dialectical Theology: Its Genesis and Development 1909–1936*. Oxford: Oxford University Press, 1997.

———. "Karl Barth's Christology as a Resource for a Reformed Version of Kenoticism." *International Journal of Systematic Theology* 8, no. 3 (2006): 243–251.

———. "So That He May Be Merciful to All: Karl Barth and the Problem of Universalism." In *Karl Barth and American Evangelicalism*, ed. Bruce L. McCormack and Clifford B. Anderson. Grand Rapids, Mich.: Eerdmans, 2011.

McFague, Sallie. *Models of God: Theology for an Ecological Nuclear Age*. London: SCM, 1987.

McFarland, Ian A. "Fallen or Unfallen? Christ's Human Nature and the Ontology of Human Sinfulness." *International Journal of Systematic Theology* 10, no. 4 (October 2008): 399–415.

McKim, Donald K. *The Cambridge Companion to Martin Luther*. Cambridge: Cambridge University Press, 2003.

Merton, Thomas. "Apologies to an Unbeliever." *Faith and Violence: Christian Teaching and Christian Practice*. Notre Dame, Ind.: University of Notre Dame Press, 1968.

Moltmann, Jürgen. *Experiences in Theology: Ways and Forms of Christian Theology*. Trans. Margaret Kohl. Minneapolis: Fortress Press, 2000.

———. "The Lordship of Christ and Human Society." In *Two Studies in the Theology of Bonhoeffer*, ed. Jürgen Moltmann and Jürgen Weissbach, trans. Reginald and Ilse Fuller, 21–94. New York: Charles Scribner's Sons, 1967.

———. *The Crucified God: The Cross of Christ as the Foundation and Criticism of Christian Theology*. Minneapolis: Fortress Press, 1993.

———. *Theology of Hope: On the Ground and the Implications of a Christian Eschatology*. Minneapolis: Fortress Press, 1993.

Morone, James A. *Hellfire Nation: The Politics of Sin in American History*. New Haven, Conn.: Yale University Press, 2003.

Morse, Christopher. "The Need for Dogmatic Theology: Bonhoeffer's Challenge to the U.S. in the 1930s and the 1990s." *Ecumenical Review* 47, no. 3 (1995): 263–267.

Muers, Rachel. *Keeping God's Silence: Towards a Theological Ethics of Communication*. Oxford: Blackwell, 2004.

Muller, Denis G. "Bonhoeffer's Ethic of Responsibility and Its Meaning for Today." *Theology* 100, no. 794 (1997): 108–117.

Müller, Hanfried. "The Problem of the Reception and Interpretation of Dietrich Bonhoeffer." In *World Come of Age*, ed. Ronald Gregor Smith, 182–214. Philadelphia: Fortress Press, 1967.

"Myths of a Mega-Church." *Pew Forum on Religion and Public Life* May 23, 2005. Online. Available: http://pewforum.org/events/.

Nave, Guy Dale, Jr. "'Repent, for the Kingdom of God Is at Hand': Repentance in the Synoptic Gospels and Acts." In *Repentance in Christian Theology*, ed. Mark J. Boda and Gordon T. Smith, 87–103. Collegeville, Minn.: Liturgical Press, 2006.

Nelson, F. Burton. "Christian Faith and Public Policy: The View from Below." *Covenant Quarterly* 40 (May 1982): 31–41.

Neumark, Heidi B. *Breathing Space: A Spiritual Journey in the South Bronx*. Boston: Beacon Press, 2003.

Niebuhr, Reinhold. *The Nature and Destiny of Man*. 2 vols. Louisville, Ky.: Westminster Knox Press, 1996.

Nietzsche, Friedrich Wilhelm. *Ecce Homo: How to Become What You Are*. Trans. Duncan Large. Oxford: Oxford University Press, 2007.

———. *Thus Spoke Zarathustra*. In *The Portable Nietzsche*, trans. Walter Kaufmann. New York: Penguin, 1976.

Noll, Mark A., Nathan O. Hatch, and George M. Marsden. *The Search for Christian America.* Westchester, Ill.: Crossway Books, 1983.

Northcott, Michael S. "The Dominion Lie: How Millennial Theology Erodes Creation Care." In *Diversity and Dominion: Dialogues in Ecology, Ethics, and Theology*, ed. Kyle S. Van Houtan and Michael S. Northcott, 89–108. Eugene, Ore.: Cascade Books, 2010.

———. "Soil, Stewardship, and Spirit in the Era of Chemical Agriculture." In *Environmental Stewardship: Critical Perspectives, Past and Present*, ed. R. J. Berry, 213–219. London, T&T Clark, 2006.

———. "The Ecological Spirit: Being Church and Being Creatures." In *Jesus and the Earth: The Gospel and the Future of the Environment.* University of Gloucestershire. February 8, 2003. Online. Available: http://www.jri.org.uk/resource/ecologicalspirit.htm.

Olson, Laura R. "Mainline Protestant Washington Offices and the Political Lives of Clergy." In *The Quiet Hand of God: Faith Based Activism and the Public Role of Mainline Protestantism*, ed. Robert Wuthnow and John H. Evans, 54–79. Berkeley: University of California Press, 2002.

Ott, Heinrich. *Reality and Faith: The Theological Legacy of Dietrich Bonhoeffer*. Trans. Alex A. Morrison. London: Lutterworth Press, 1971.

Pangritz, Andreas. "Dietrich Bonhoeffer: 'Within, Not Outside the Barthian Movement.'" In *Bonhoeffer's Intellectual Formation: Theology and Philosophy in His Thought*, ed. Peter Frick, 245–285. Tübingen, Germany: Mohr Siebeck, 2008.

———. *Karl Barth in the Theology of Dietrich Bonhoeffer*. Trans. Barbara Rumscheidt and Martin Rumscheidt. Grand Rapids, Mich.: Eerdmans, 2000.

———. "Point and Counterpoint: Resistance and Submission." In *Theology in Dialogue: The Impact of the Arts, Humanities, and Science on Contemporary Religious Thought*, ed. Lyn Holness and Ralf K. Wüstenberg, 28–42. Grand Rapids, Mich.: Eerdmans, 2002.

———. "Theological Motives in Dietrich Bonhoeffer's Decision to Participate in Political Resistance." In *Reflections On Bonhoeffer: Essays In Honor of F. Burton Nelson*, ed. Geffrey B. Kelly and C. John Weborg, 32–49. Chicago: Covenant Publications, 1999.

———. "Who Is Jesus Christ, for Us, Today?" In *The Cambridge Companion to Dietrich Bonhoeffer*, ed. John W. de Gruchy, 134–153. Cambridge: Cambridge University Press, 1999.

Park, Andrew Sung. *The Wounded Heart of God: The Asian Concept of Han and the Christian Concept of Sin*. Nashville: Abingdon, 1993.

Peck, William J., ed. *New Studies in Bonhoeffer's Ethics*. Lewiston, N.Y.: Edwin Mellen Press, 1987.

Perkins, John M. *Beyond Charity: The Call to Christian Community Development*. Grand Rapids, Mich.: Baker Books, 1993.

Phillips, John A. *The Form of Christ in the World: A Study of Bonhoeffer's Christology*. London: Collins, 1967.

Plant, Stephen. *Bonhoeffer*. London: Continuum, 2004.

———. "Ethics and Materialist Hermeneutics." *Union Seminary Quarterly Review*: "Theology and the Practice of Responsibility: Essays on Dietrich Bonhoeffer." 46, no. 1–4 (1992): 107–115.

———, ed. *Religion, Religionlessness, and Contemporary Western Culture: Explorations in Dietrich Bonhoeffer's Theology*. Berlin, Germany: Peter Lang, 2008.

Poole, Roger. "Bonhoeffer and the Arcane Discipline." In *Ethical Responsibility: Bonhoeffer's Legacy to the Churches*, ed. John D. Godsey and Geffrey B. Kelly, 271–291. New York: Edwin Mellen Press, 1982.

Porter, Stanley E. "Penitence and Repentance in the Epistles." In *Repentance in Christian Theology*, ed. Mark J. Boda and Gordon T. Smith, 127–150. Collegeville, Minn.: Liturgical Press, 2006.

Prenter, Regin. "Bonhoeffer and the Young Luther." In *World Come of Age*, ed. Ronald Gregor Smith, 161–181. Philadelphia: Fortress Press, 1967.

Pugh, Jeffrey C. *Religionless Christianity: Dietrich Bonhoeffer in Troubled Times.* New York: T&T Clark, 2008.

Purves, Andrew. "A Confessing Faith: Assent and Penitence in the Reformation Traditions of Luther, Calvin, and Bucer." In *Repentance in Christian Theology*, ed. Mark J. Boda and Gordon T. Smith, 251–266. Collegeville, Minn.: Liturgical Press, 2006.

Rasmussen, Larry L. *Dietrich Bonhoeffer: His Significance for North Americans.* Minneapolis: Fortress Press, 1990.

———. *Dietrich Bonhoeffer: Reality and Resistance.* New York: Abingdon Press, 1972.

———. "The Ethics of Responsible Action." In *The Cambridge Companion to Dietrich Bonhoeffer*, ed. John W. de Gruchy, 206–225. Cambridge, Cambridge University Press, 1999.

Rittgers, Ronald K. "Private Confession in the German Reformation." In *Repentance in Christian Theology*, ed. Mark J. Boda and Gordon T. Smith, 189–207. Collegeville, Minn.: Liturgical Press, 2006.

Robertson, Edwin H., ed. *No Rusty Swords: Letters, Lectures, and Notes, 1928–1936, from the Collected Works of Dietrich Bonhoeffer.* Trans. Edwin H. Robertson and John Bowden. New York: Harper & Row, 1965.

Rogers, Eugene F. *Sexuality and the Christian Body: Their Way into the Triune God.* Oxford: Blackwell, 2000.

———. "Supplementing Barth on Jews and Gender: Identifying God by Analogy and the Spirit." *Modern Theology* 14, no. 1 (1998): 43–81.

Rotelle, John E., ed. *The Works of Saint Augustine: A Translation for the 21st Century.* Vol. 17. Trans. Edmund Hill. Brooklyn, N.Y.: New City Press, 1997.

Schellong, Dieter. "Kirchliches Schuldbekenntnis: Gedanken Bonhoeffers und die Wirklichkeit des deutschen Nachkriegsprotestantismus." In *Verspieltes Erbe? Dietrich Bonhoeffer und der deutsche Nachkriegsprotestantismus*, ed. Ernst Feil. Munich, Germany: Chr. Kaiser Verlag, 1979.

Schliesser, Christine. *Everyone Who Acts Responsibly Becomes Guilty. The Concept of Accepting Guilt in Dietrich Bonhoeffer: Reconstruction and Critical Assessment.* Neukirchen-Vluyn, Germany: Neukirchener-Verlag, 2006.

Schnelle, Udo. *Apostle Paul: His Life and Theology.* Trans. M. Eugene Boring. Grand Rapids, Mich.: Baker Academic, 2005.

Scott, Peter. "Christ, Nature, and Sociality: Dietrich Bonhoeffer for an Ecological Age." *Scottish Journal of Theology* 53, no. 4 (2000): 413–430.

Selby, Peter. "Who Is Jesus Christ for Us, Today?" In *Bonhoeffer for a New Day: Theology in a Time of Transition*, ed. John W. de Gruchy, 20–38. Grand Rapids, Mich.: Eerdmans, 1997.

Shipler, David K. *The Working Poor: Invisible in America.* New York: Random House, 2004.

Shultz, Kevin M. "Secularization: A Bibliographic Essay." *Hedgehog Review: Critical Reflections on Contemporary Culture*: "After Secularization." 8, no. 1–2 (2006): 170–177.

Sider, Ronald J. *The Chicago Declaration*. Carol Stream, Ill.: Creation House, 1974.

Slane, Craig J. *Bonhoeffer as Martyr: Social Responsibility and Modern Christian Commitment*. Grand Rapids, Mich.: Brazos Press, 2004.

———. "Existing for God in an Age of Theology's Disestablishment: Bonhoeffer's Penultimate-Ultimate Distinction and Its Prospect for the Christian University." In *Religion, Religionlessness, and Contemporary Western Culture: Explorations in Dietrich Bonhoeffer's Theology*, ed. Stephen Plant and Ralf K. Wüstenberg, 33–57. Berlin, Germany: Peter Lang, 2008.

Smith, Christian. *Christian America? What Evangelicals Really Want*. Berkeley: University of California Press, 2000.

Smith, Gordon T. "The Penitential: An Evangelical Perspective." In *Repentance in Christian Theology*, ed. Mark J. Boda and Gordon T. Smith, 267–286. Collegeville, Minn.: Liturgical Press, 2006.

Smith, Robert O. "Bonhoeffer and Musical Metaphor." *Word and World* 26, no. 2 (2006): 195–206.

Smolik, Josef. "The Church without Privileges." *Ecumenical Review* 28, no. 2 (1976): 174–187.

Stassen, Glen Harold. "The Value of Making an Apology." *Chicago Tribune*, April 19, 2004, 2.9.

Stout, Jeffrey. *Democracy and Tradition*. Princeton, N.J.: Princeton University Press 2004.

Strohl, Jane E. "Luther's Spiritual Journey." In *The Cambridge Companion to Martin Luther*, ed. Donald K. McKim, 149–164. Cambridge: Cambridge University Press, 2003.

"Sudanese Refugees Find New Home in Maine." *Weekend Edition Saturday Transcript, NPR News*, April 29, 2006.

Surin, Kenneth. "Contemptus Mundi and the Disenchanted World: Bonhoeffer's 'Secret Discipline' and Adorno's 'Strategy of Hibernation.'" *Journal of the American Academy of Religion* 53, no. 3 (1985): 383–410.

Taylor, Charles. *A Secular Age*. Cambridge, Mass.: Belknap Press of Harvard University Press, 2007.

"The Spirit of Social Hope: A Collection of Reflections." *The Project on Lived Theology*. April 26–27, 2006. Online. Available: http://www.livedtheology.org/pdfs/silt_2005_reflection_booklet.pdf.

Thiemann, Ronald F. *Religion in Public Life: A Dilemma for Democracy*. Washington, D.C.: Georgetown University Press, 1996.

Tietz, Christiane. "'The Church Is the Limit of Politics:' Bonhoeffer on the Political Task of the Church." *Union Seminary Quarterly Review* 60, no. 1–2 (2006) 23–36.

Tödt, Heinz Eduard. *Authentic Faith: Bonhoeffer's Theological Ethics in Context*. Ed. Ernst-Albert Scharffenorth. Trans. David Stassen and Ilse Tödt. Grand Rapids, Mich.: Eerdmans, 2007.

———, et al., eds. *Dietrich Bonhoeffer Werke* Band 6. *Ethik*. Munich, Germany: Chr. Kaiser Verlag, 1992.

"U.S. Religious Landscape Survey: Summary of Key Findings." *Pew Forum on Religion and Public Life* Online. Available: http://religions.pewforum.org/pdf/report2religious-landscape-study-key-findings.pdf.

Vásquez, Manuel A. *More Than Belief: A Materialist Theory of Religion*. Oxford: Oxford University Press, 2011.

Verter, Bradford. "Furthering the Freedom Struggle." In *The Quiet Hand of God: Faith Based Activism and the Public Role of Mainline Protestantism*, ed. Robert Wuthnow and John H. Evans, 181–212. Berkeley: University of California Press, 2002.

Visser't Hooft, Willem A. "An Act of Penitence." In *I Knew Dietrich Bonhoeffer*, ed. Wolf-Dieter Zimmermann and Ronald Gregor Smith, trans. Käthe Gregor Smith, 193–195. New York: Harper & Row, 1967.

Von Balthasar, Hans Urs. *Dare We Hope: "That All Men Be Saved"?* Trans. David Kipp. San Francisco: Ignatius, 1988.

Vorkink, Peter, ed. *Bonhoeffer in a World Come of Age*. Philadelphia: Fortress Press, 1968.

Wahba, Wafik. "Middle Eastern Perspectives and Expressions of Christian Repentance." In *Repentance in Christian Theology*, ed. Mark J. Boda and Gordon T. Smith, 307–327. Collegeville, Minn.: Liturgical Press, 2006.

Wallis, Jim. *The Great Awakening: Reviving Faith and Politics in a Post–Religious Right America*. New York: HarperOne, 2008.

———. *God's Politics: Why the Right Gets It Wrong and the Left Doesn't Get It*. New York: HarperCollins, 2005.

———. *The Call to Conversion: Why Faith Is Always Personal but Never Private*. New York: HarperCollins, 2005.

Wannenwetsch, Bernd. "Luther's Moral Theology." In *The Cambridge Companion to Martin Luther*, ed. Donald K. McKim, 120–135. Cambridge: Cambridge University Press, 2003.

West, Charles C. "Review of *Dietrich Bonhoeffer: His Significance for North Americans*." *Theology Today* 47, no. 4 (1991): 471–473.

Williams, Rowan. "Christ in Gethsemene." Dietrich Bonhoeffer Centenary Service. St. Matthäus Church, Berlin, Germany. February 5, 2006. *The Archbishop of Canterbury*. Online. Available: http://www.archbishopofcanterbury.org/307?q=Bonhoeffer+2006.

———. "Changing the Myths We Live By." *The Archbishop of Canterbury*. July 5, 2004. Online. Available: http://www.archbishopofcanterbury.org/1064.

———. *Ray of Darkness: Sermons and Reflections*. Cambridge, Mass.: Cowley, 1995.

———. *Resurrection: Interpreting the Easter Gospel*. Cleveland, Ohio: Pilgrim Press, 2004.

Wink, Walter. *Engaging the Powers: Discernment and Resistance in a World of Domination*. Minneapolis: Fortress Press, 1992.

Witten, Marsha G. *All Is Forgiven: The Secular Message in American Protestantism*. Princeton, N.J.: Princeton University Press, 1993.

Woelfel, James W. *Bonhoeffer's Theology: Classical and Revolutionary*. Nashville: Abingdon Press, 1970.

Wolfe, Alan. *The Transformation of American Religion: How We Actually Live Our Faith*. New York: Free Press, 2003.

Wriedt, Markus. "Luther's Theology." In *The Cambridge Companion to Martin Luther*, ed. Donald K. McKim, 86–119. Cambridge: Cambridge University Press, 2003.

Wright, N. T. *Surprised by Hope: Rethinking Heaven, the Resurrection, and the Mission of the Church*. New York: HarperOne, 2008.

Wüstenberg, Ralf K. *Glauben als Leben: Dietrich Bonhoeffer und die nichreligiöse Interpretation biblischer Begriffe*. Frankfurt, Germany: Peter Lang, 1996.

———. *A Theology of Life: Dietrich Bonhoeffer's Religionless Christianity*. Trans. Doug Stott. Grand Rapids, Mich.: Eerdmans, 1996.

Wuthnow, Robert. *America and the Challenges of Religious Diversity*. Princeton, N.J.: Princeton University Press, 2005.

———. "Beyond Quiet Influence? Possibilities for the Protestant Mainline." In *The Quiet Hand of God: Faith Based Activism and the Public Role of Mainline Protestantism*, ed.

Robert Wuthnow and John H. Evans, 381–403. Berkeley: University of California Press, 2002.

Wuthnow, Robert, and John H. Evans, eds. *The Quiet Hand of God: Faith Based Activism and the Public Role of Mainline Protestantism*. Berkeley: University of California Press, 2002.

Yates, Joshua. "11/9/1989 to 9/11/2001 and Beyond: The Return of Jeremiad and the Specter of Secularization." In *Prophesies of Godlessness: Predictions of America's Imminent Secularization from the Puritans to the Present Day*, ed. Charles Mathewes and Christopher McKnight Nichols, 209–231. New York: Oxford University Press, 2008.

Yoder, John Howard. *The Christian Witness to the State*. Scottsdale, Pa.: Herald Press, 2002.

Young, Josiah U. "Dietrich Bonhoeffer and Reinhold Niebuhr: Their Ethics, Views on Karl Barth and Perspectives on African-Americans." In *Bonhoeffer's Intellectual Formation: Theology and Philosophy in His Thought*, ed. Peter Frick, 283–300. Tübingen, Germany: Mohr Siebeck, 2008.

———. *No Difference in Fare: Dietrich Bonhoeffer and the Problem of Racism*. Grand Rapids, Mich.: Eerdmans, 1998.

Ziegler, Philip G. "Dietrich Bonhoeffer: An Ethics of God's Apocalypse?" *Modern Theology* 23, no. 4 (2007): 579–594.

INTERVIEWS

Ayer, Kelly. Portland, Maine. September 6, 2006.

Ayer, Loren. Portland, Maine. September 7, 2006.

Barnett, Hilary (e-mail and telephone). November 29, 2006; October 4, 2007.

Clayton, Cheryl. Portland, Maine. September 10, 2006.

Clayton, Tim. Portland, Maine. September 8–9, 2006; phone interview April 24, 2006.

Dimock, Marilyn. Washington, D.C. October 16, 2006.

Dimock, Scott. Washington, D.C. October 16, 2006.

Dye, Summer. Washington, D.C. November 6, 2001.

Johnson, John. Washington, D.C. October 17, 2006.

Kiger, Kristi. Washington, D.C. October 17, 2006.

Lamberson, Iris. Washington, D.C. October 16, 2006.

Lowery, Jennifer. Washington, D.C. November 6, 2001.

Morrison, Sammie. Washington, D.C. November 6, 2001; August 28, 2006.

Mpelo, Wilma. Washington, D.C. November 6, 2001.

Pillsbury, Evan. Portland, Maine. September 8, 2006.

Pillsbury, Kathryn. Portland, Maine. September 7, 2006.

Robertson, Louis. Washington, D.C. October 18, 2006.

Speed, Denise. Washington, D.C. November 6, 2001; October 17, 2006.

Stankiewicz, Dave. Portland, Maine. September 10, 2006.

Stankiewicz, Sarrah. Portland, Maine. September 9, 2006.

Wingfield, Mike. Washington, D.C. October 17, 2006.

INDEX

GENERAL INDEX

SCRIPTURAL INDEX